D0843031

Reliable Data Communications

Reliable Data Communications

John J. Metzner

The Pennsylvania State University
Department of Computer Science and Engineering
Department of Electrical Engineering
University Park, Pennsylvania

ACADEMIC PRESS

San Diego   London   Boston
New York   Sydney   Tokyo   Toronto

This book is printed on acid free paper. ∞

ACADEMIC PRESS
525 B Street, Suite 1900, San Diego, CA 92101-4495, USA
1300 Boylston Street, Chestnut Hill, MA 02167, USA
http://www.apnet.com

United Kingdom Edition published by
ACADEMIC PRESS LIMITED
24-28 Oval Road, London NW1 7DX
http//www.hbuk.co.uk/ap

Library of Congress Cataloging-in-Publication Data
Metzner, John J.
 Reliable data communications / John J. Metzner.
  p. cm. — (Telecommunications)
 Includes bibliographical references and index.
 ISBN 0-12-491740-2 (alk. paper)
  1. Data transmission systems. I. Title. II. Series:
Telecommunications (Boston, Mass.)
 TK5105.M48 1997
 004.6—dc21   97-35787
                                            CIP

Printed in the United States of America
97 98 99 00 01 IP 9 8 7 6 5 4 3 2 1

Contents

Preface

This book emphasizes a description of techniques to ensure reliable and efficient data transfer. The development of these techniques has both theoretical and practical roots. The theoretical root is Shannon's Mathematical Theory of Communication, which showed that error control codes could be used for reliable data communication without significant sacrifice of data rate. The practical root is the common sense realization that assurance of reliable data transfer needs two-way communication. This is obvious in ordinary conversation, as one expects some acknowledgment that the listener understands or at least has heard what was said. If there is doubt the speaker usually repeats.

The term ARQ has been used as a name for any protocol that uses return channel acknowledgments and transmission of redundant information as needed. Virtually all data transmission protocols designed to ensure reliable communication employ the ARQ concept at some level. It will be explained why both ARQ and error control coding are needed to be both efficient and reliable.

The proliferation of numbers of data network users and amount of data being transferred over multiuser data networks has compounded the problem of ensuring reliable and efficient communication. There are matters of variable traffic, variable channel conditions, network configuration design, variable time delays, feedback link impairments, handling of broadcast communication, multiaccess and interference considerations, and so on. Faced with these varying problems, a wide variety of reliable data communication techniques have evolved. These appear scattered through the literature.

A certain amount of background material is needed in order to understand the many strategies for achieving reliable and efficient data communication. To make the book more self-contained, Chapter 2 covers the basic principles of random signals and noise, and Chapters 3 and 4 cover properties of block and trellis codes. Main results are emphasized, but proofs and detailed discussion are omitted.

After these background chapters, the next four chapters deal with reliable data communication primarily at the link level. Chapters 5 and 6 deal with basic ARQ protocols at the link level. Chapter 7 describes techniques for using memory of past receptions to improve efficiency. Chapter 8 deals with the challenges of communicating reliably and efficiently over time-varying channels.

Four chapters are then devoted to reliable communication in networks and at the (end-to-end) transport level. Chapter 9 deals with multiaccess networks. The emphasis in this chapter is on access protocols rather than noise effects. Chapter 10 deals with general switched data networks, emphasizing ARQ protocols, but again with limited consideration of noise effects. Chapter 11 revisits some of the network structures considered in Chapters 9 and 10, but with emphasis on noisy and varying conditions. Chapter 12 deals with multicast communication—simultaneous transmission to multiple destinations—with acknowledgments.

Each chapter except Chapter 1 includes a summary at the end and a collection of problems. The book could be used as a text for senior or graduate students in Electrical Engineering and in Computer Engineering. It also could be a useful reference for professionals in designing and effectively using new data communication networks.

In general, emphasis in the book is more on ideas and basic principles than on standard practice. Where appropriate, I have tried to include a statement that a particular idea is not part of current standard practice. However, with the growing sophistication of communications, many techniques that were previously considered overly complex to implement are becoming practical.

Reliable Data Communications

Chapter 1

Introduction

With the proliferation of computers and networks, the trend is for most communication and storage of information to be in digital form. Just as the high reliability of computation has been a major factor in broadening its application, so will high reliability in communication be of great importance for many applications.

Consider the possible objectives of a digital communication system. In some applications the main objective is to deliver a message with very *low probability of any error*. Electronic funds transfer and file transfer are examples of such applications. In other applications a specific parcel of information must be delivered within a *specified time limit* in order to be of value to the receiver. Real-time control signals and digitized voice or television signals are examples of such applications. Control signals may be critical and need to be delivered with very low probability of error in addition to the strict time limit; voice and television signals can tolerate occasional errors, although less so if data compression is used. In other cases, there may be no strict time limit, but a short *average time delay* from first transmission to final correct reception is an objective. Another important objective is *efficient utilization of communication resources* in a shared network or link; inefficiency produces congestion and impacts the reliability and delay objectives of all users.

The major emphasis of this book is on applications that require a very high degree of confidence that the data have been received correctly; this is the connotation of the title *Reliable Data Communications*. However, interaction with other applications that do not require as high a degree of reliability cannot be ignored due to the need to share communication resources.

1.1   Feedback and ARQ

The requirement of great confidence in correctness of a communication almost invariably requires some kind of response or feedback from the receiver to the sender. Even if feedback is not used actively during the course of a communication, the sender

1

would at least want some response indicating that the connection to the destination has been made, and probably a final acknowledgment that the complete message has been received.

Consider the employment of feedback in a digital communication system with the principal objective of having a low probability of any error. Simple acknowledgment that something was received is not sufficient, because there must be high confidence that what was received is correct. Thus there must be some checking mechanism. With feedback, this checking could be done at the receiver or at the transmitter, or both. To do the checking at the receiver, redundant data must be added to the transmitted signal so that the receiver can detect errors. The return, or feedback channel then need only be used to report acknowledgment that the reception seems correct or to request repetition or additional information. To do the checking at the sender, enough information needs to be fed back so the sender can determine whether the data have been received correctly and if not, to have perhaps some knowledge of what part or parts were not received correctly.

The process of automatically requesting repeat was introduced in the 1940s [VAND43], and was applied in the RCA overseas teleprinter exchange service during the 1950s [MOOR60]. The procedure was denoted *ARQ*, standing for "automatic request for repeat." RCA's ARQ system employed a simple 7-bit code to represent an alphabet of up to 35 characters. All character codes contained three ones and four zeros, and there are 35 such arrangements. Thus any single error as well as many other error patterns could be detected. When a character did not check, the receiver would not print it, but would instead send back a repeat request. The system was found to be considerably more reliable than an unprotected system. Modern systems using retransmission are much more sophisticated and provide greater reliability for applications requiring it. The name ARQ has stuck, although in some uses the term "automatic request for repeat" is not quite a correct description for the process.

In 1956 Chang [CHAN56] introduced a classification of systems employing feedback as *decision feedback* and *information feedback*. Decision feedback is similar to ARQ, where the receiver reports the decision whether the data need repeating or, more generally, whether some additional redundancy relating to the original data needs to be sent. Information feedback involves reporting information about what was received back to the original sender, and allowing the sender to check for errors and decide what to do to correct the reception. ARQ, or decision feedback, has proved to be by far the more popular of the two classifications. Information feedback does have some applications and value as well. These applications and potential uses will be pointed out at appropriate places. Also, some schemes may be hybrids, having both decision and information feedback aspects.

In decision feedback, there are various options about reporting what needs to be resent. The simplest form, called stop-and-wait, is to send a certain block of information, and then stop and wait for a reply as to whether it has been correctly received or whether to send it over again. Another option is to send a number of blocks of information prior to getting feedback acknowledgment of the first, and have the feedback channel supply information on which blocks have or have not been received correctly, or up to which block has been received correctly. The timeout mechanism also is available to retransmit if no response, to protect against a lost return signal. These protocols permit continuous transmission of blocks without waiting. Chapters 5 and 6 discuss the details of these various options.

1.2 Error Correction with ARQ

Error control coding plays important roles in achieving reliable and efficient communication. One aspect, error detection, fills a basic need for ARQ operation. The other aspect, error correction, can improve system efficiency and delay performance, as well as affect reliability. Efficiency and delay performance are improved because error correction reduces the need for retransmission.

Error correction is a rather complex process that has appeared in much fewer applications than error detection. However, advancing technology is expanding its role. The search for error correction techniques began mostly after Shannon introduced the Mathematical Theory of Communication, or Information Theory [SHAN48]. He showed that, given a quantity called *channel information capacity* —which could be computed based on channel bandwidth, signal power, and noise statistics—it is possible to send as reliably as we wish using error control coding, at any rate less than channel capacity, but it is impossible to communicate reliably at greater than channel capacity. Long codes are needed to approach this capability, and early work suggested that decoding complexity would go up exponentially with code length. Many years of work have produced effective codes with decoding techniques showing only polynomial increases of complexity with code length. Currently, a number of decoding techniques are available for practical use in improving system efficiency, reliability, and delay performance. These techniques mostly rely on doing the error correcting in stages and/or using the structural properties of finite fields.

With ARQ capability, it must be emphasized that we do not need to attempt to correct every possible pattern of errors that the code is capable of correcting. We will see in Chapter 5 that reliable communication is ensured with proper ARQ procedures. The principal role of the error correction part then is to improve efficiency by reducing the need for retransmission. Thus we may have a goal of 10^{-12} block error probability, yet we could be satisfied with probability of 10^{-2} of not being able to correct the errors, since this means simply that one percent of the blocks will be retransmitted. Also, error correction without ARQ could not hope to count on 10^{-12} block error probability for any but the finest of channels, which probably don't need error correction anyway. Channels where error correction is worthwhile encounter frequent errors and tend to have error statistics that are incompletely known and/or varying. A code can be designed to achieve 10^{-12} block error probability based on a statistical model assumed to be always in effect. However, confidence that the statistical behavior really will allow successful error correction falls far short of a 10^{-12} block error probability specification. It is relatively easy to ensure there is enough error detection built in that the probability of undetected block error is less than about 10^{-12}, despite fluctuations in channel condition. Also, if the block of data being checked is in thousands of bits or more, the overhead cost of adding bits just for this error detection capability is at most a few percent of the data size.

When a block of data is not decodable but needs to be retransmitted, there often is a good deal of information in the undecodable block. If the system is such that the receiver often can tell which past undecoded block is being repeated by the current block, a memory of this past reception can be combined with the retransmission reception to enhance the probability of making a correct decision. This technique, called retransmission with memory, is discussed in Chapter 7. A related idea is that the second sending doesn't have to be an exact retransmission of the first, but rather can be some transformed version of the first sending. Combining the original reception with the reception for the transformed version proves to be more effective than straight retransmission with memory.

Some form of feedback also is critical to using a communication channel or network of varying capacity at near maximum efficiency. The characteristics of communication channels are not known exactly, and vary in many ways over a wide range of time scales. Without feedback, the sender would need to take a worst case view and use extra redundancy to improve the chance of success; how much extra redundancy would be enough to be safe is, in fact, unknown. With fairly frequent feedback, it is possible to arrange to send only about the amount of extra redundancy needed for the conditions that evolve on the channels. Even with less frequent feedback, the sender can learn the best rate and redundancy to use, assuming conditions change slowly. Thus the channels can be used very efficiently as well as with high confidence in correct reception. Characteristics of varying channels and the role of error correction and feedback in such channels are discussed in Chapter 8.

1.3   Time-Constrained Communication

In some data communication ARQ is not feasible because of its variable delay. Examples are real-time voice and motion video. In most cases the channel is designed to be adequately reliable without error correction, and anyway some error can be tolerated by the human receiver. If data compression is used, however, errors are less tolerable; this is because data compression removes redundancy. For example, with natural redundancy in voice communication, errors in one or a few samples of sound values are hardly noticeable and rarely affect intelligibility, because the listener automatically interpolates from neighboring samples and context information to mask the defect. However, a similar amount of error in a compressed version will generally affect many samples and may destroy intelligibility.

A general way of combating the problem of reliability under a time constraint is to devote more current resources to the communication, just as a person who needs to be heard right away will shout more loudly and interrupt others. By a priority agreement, an urgent message under a time constraint could be given more bandwidth, more transmitter power, or ability to preempt other messages waiting in a queue. The consequences of such remedies often must be balanced against the cost of the interference with other users. If there is time within the constraint to return some feedback information, ARQ can provide the ability to use these extra resources only to the degree necessary.

1.4 The Basic Communication Process

Preparing data for communication involves several possible steps, as illustrated in Figure 1.1. The figure illustrates a two-way connection between A and B via a communication channel or network. As a possible first stage (box 1), data compression may be used at A to reduce the average amount of bits communicated to convey the desired information. Also, if the information is originally in analog form, an analog-to-digital conversion must be performed first, usually done by sampling and quantization. The net result is a stream of bits, which is the data to be communicated to B. If the information to be sent is already a bit stream needing no compression, box 1 can be skipped. In the other direction, box 1 takes the stream of corrected bits delivered from B and decompresses and/or converts it to meaningful information, as necessary. A possible second stage (box 2) is to add checking data to allow error detection and/or correction. Additional overhead bits are also added for various purposes, such as addressing, data packet delineation, and numbering. The resulting data stream is then used to modulate an electrical or optical waveform (box 3) for propagation over the communication channel. Most commonly, the waveform communication is a time sequence of pulse waveforms, each pulse representing one or more bits of the data stream. In some sophisticated error control schemes the processes of error correction encoding and modulation in boxes 2 and 3 are combined. For the incoming signal, the reversal (demodulation for box 3 and error detection/correction, overhead interpretation for box 2) must be performed. Also shown is a dashed line at box 2, which represents acknowledgment/repeat request feedback bits resulting from error detection.

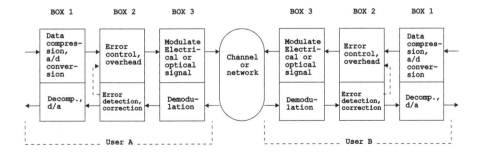

Figure 1.1: Converting information in two-way communication.

1.5   Background

The discussion of reliable and efficient data communication techniques requires some background in digital modulation alternatives, fundamental limits on the rate at which reliable communication is possible, and various coding/decoding strategies. The reader is assumed to have some familiarity with the concepts of probability, random variables, and elementary random process principles. Chapter 2 summarizes some key principles and limitations of communication of data over noisy channels, and Chapters 3 and 4 deal with block and trellis/convolutional error-correcting codes. Readers who already have this background may be able to skip much of Chapters 2 through 4, or just scan them to become familiar with the notation being used. There are, however, a few ideas described in Chapters 3 and 4 that are not widely known.

1.6   Communication Networks

Computer communication networks provide the greatest challenges to the design of effective ARQ coding strategies. The need for many users to share network facilities creates a range of uncertainties that the ARQ techniques must deal with. Different effects require different remedies. Wireless communication tends to have more error occurrences, due to factors of noise, fading, and interference; this may call for error correction in addition to ARQ, and sophisticated receiver and signal design. Wired or optical packet data networks usually have low noise, but congestion leads to lost or excessively delayed packets. Effective strategies are needed to retransmit lost information, yet keep retransmissions from escalating and compounding congestion. With statistical sharing of a channel, the saving in transmission time by eliminating unnecessary redundancy provides additional capacity to others. Local networks operating on a contention basis have potential packet loss or destruction due to collisions.

Networks are beginning to encompass combinations of wired and wireless links and subnetworks. ARQ in wired networks has been trending toward end-to-end acknowledgments rather than link-by-link acknowledgments as transmission rates are increasing. On the other hand, noisy wireless networks and contention-based local subnetworks favor link-by-link acknowledgments. Even in communication over very good channels, sometimes the data file being transferred is so large that an overall check is needed to ensure that the whole transfer has been completed correctly. Problems of reliable transmission in various kinds of networks are dealt with in Chapters 9 through 12.

1.7   Multicasting

A task of growing importance in communications is the dissemination of data to many destinations; this is usually called *broadcasting* if the set of destinations are all network nodes, or *multicasting* if the destinations are a subset of the network nodes.

However, multicasting can be defined to include broadcasting as a special case. In many cases, such as entertainment video, ARQ is not used in multicasting because it is not critical that all destinations receive the data or even are connected. However, it is likely to become increasingly common that files of data will be distributed electronically to many destinations and will need to be correctly received at all destinations. The problem of using ARQ in multicasting to ensure correct reception by all in an efficient manner is the subject of Chapter 12.

Chapter 2

Data Communication Over Noisy Channels

A transmitted electromagnetic signal is subject to many impairments on being received. These can be categorized as noise, attenuation, fading, distortion, and interference.

Random disturbances, referred to as *noise*, usually add a random waveform to the received signal, although there sometimes also are multiplicative effects. Thermal noise due to random motion of electrons is the most fundamental type of noise, and its power per unit bandwidth is directly proportional to the absolute temperature.

Attenuation is a problem when the desired received signal is comparable in strength to or weaker than the noise at the receiver, because amplification after that point will not improve the signal-to-noise intensity ratio.

Fading is a phenomenon in wireless communication whereby the received signal is the sum of electromagnetic waves following several paths from transmitter to receiver. Due to small fluctuations in the path distances, which may correspond to several cycles delay in the high frequency carrier, the receiver sum will at times add destructively and at times constructively. Usually the variations are slow, but in periods when the signal is weak, very little information can be communicated. Also the signal is distorted in shape due to being a sum of signals at different delays. Fading is discussed in more detail in Chapters 8 and 11.

Distortion is either linear or nonlinear. Linear distortion is the most common (at least to a good approximation). Linear distortion is equivalent to a signal going through a linear system. The system function can be written as

$$H(f) = |A(f)|e^{j\theta(f)}. \tag{2.1}$$

Linear distortion can be compensated for by a receiver filter with characteristic $R(f)$, such that $R(f)H(f)$ is approximately constant magnitude, linear phase over the signal band. For this to work effectively, $A(f)$ and $\theta(f)$ must be constant or varying slowly enough for the receiver filter to adapt to changes. Fading is very nearly linear, but is time varying. Nonlinear distortion generally is not compensatable, and is especially a problem when a cable carrying frequency multiplexed signals has a nonlinear response; then products of sinusoids from different frequency bands are created by the nonlinearity, producing sum and difference frequencies that spill over into various bands, creating what is called *intermodulation distortion*.

Interference occurs when several different transmitters' signals are received in the same frequency band. Usually this is not designed to happen, but often occurs unintentionally, particularly in wireless communication. Also, Chapters 9 and 11 discuss multiaccess systems, where intermittently transmitting users intentionally share the same band, and statistically will occasionally interfere.

Digital communication usually is accomplished by sending a sequence of high frequency carrier pulses, each of which carries one or more bits of information by selecting values of the pulse amplitude, carrier frequency, or carrier phase. Intersymbol interference is an interference of successive pulses of one sender, and is most commonly caused by linear distortion of the received pulse shape. This can be compensated for by the technique just described. Actually, exact reconstruction of the pulse shape is not necessary. The pulse is carrying one of a discrete set of values (usually two), and the demodulator's task is to determine that value as reliably as possible, not to reproduce an accurate rendition of the transmitted pulse shape. Actually, for the most common assumption of noise statistics, the optimum demodulator is simply a filter, matched to the overall system response, followed by a sampler that puts out a sequence of numbers used to make the final decisions.

The most fundamental limits to the rate of reliable communication are bandwidth and noise. Information theory provides a means for quantifying these limits given known statistical properties of noise. The limit is known as channel information capacity, measured in bits per second. A brief discussion of these results is given in Section 2.3.

Sending data at rates approaching theoretical capacity requires complex techniques. Often, there is no need to send at rates near capacity. Some data channels employing cable and optical fiber have a great deal of bandwidth and very little noise. Binary transmission normally is used, bit errors are very rare, and transmitted bit rates are more than sufficient to meet demands. However, if the links have so little noise, their information capacity may be many times more than the binary pulse bit rate. Thus if it was necessary to increase data rate further while still confined to the same bandwidth, $n > 1$ bits per pulse could be sent by allowing transmission of one of 2^n levels. The value of n could be increased until the spacing between levels was roughly comparable to little more than the noise standard deviation; then noise would be significant, but in theory we could still send reliably by using coding and ARQ techniques. Processing complexity would increase greatly in order to achieve this result, and at very high transmission rates processing speed itself may become the limitation. In the case of optical fiber a different method of increasing capacity is available. There, only a fraction of the available bandwidth is normally used, due to limitations of electronic processing and spread of transmitted pulse energy with distance traveled. Frequency division multiplexing (referred to as wavelength division multiplexing in optics) can greatly increase the information carrying capacity by making fuller use of the available bandwidth while still sending at electronically processable speeds at each individual wavelength.

In radio communication and some telephone networks on the other hand, bandwidth and noise limitations often provide barely enough capacity to meet rate demand. One example of where the sophisticated multiple-level approach does pay off is in data transmission over telephone channels originally assigned for analog voice. These channels have such a low bandwidth that binary signalling rates are well below desired data transmission rates. Thus, modems are designed for this purpose that use multilevel signalling and coded modulation (to be described in Chapter 4) to increase the transmitted bit rate.

The reader is presumed to have had some exposure to probability, random variable, and random process concepts. The next two sections will review the basic concepts most pertinent to this book, and will introduce the reader to the notation being used.

2.1   Random Variables

Given a set of events with probabilities defined, a random variable is a number associated with each elementary event. Let x be a particular value of a random variable and let X be the general notation for the random variable. The cumulative distribution function of x is defined as

$$F_X(x) = \text{Prob}[X \leq x]. \tag{2.2}$$

The subscript X is needed when there is a discussion of more than one random variable, and x is given some numerical value; then the subscript will distinguish which random variable is being evaluated. When only one random variable is being discussed, or the variable identification is obvious, the subscript can be omitted.

The sample space and associated random variables may consist of discrete points and values or a continuous space and a continuous range of values. $F_X(x)$ is always a nondecreasing function of x. If X has a discrete value x_i with positive probability p_i, $F_X(x)$ versus x exhibits a step of size equal to p_i at x_i.

Figure 2.1 illustrates a case where X has one discrete value, of probability p_i, but is otherwise continuous.

In the continuous case one defines a **probability density** $f_X(x)$ as

$$f_X(x) = \frac{d}{dx} F_X(x) \tag{2.3}$$

Alternately,

$$F_X(x) = \int_{-\infty}^{x} f_X(\lambda)\, d\lambda \tag{2.4}$$

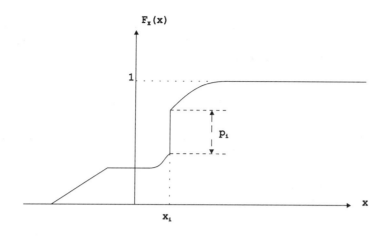

Figure 2.1: Cumulative distribution function with a discrete value at x_i.

If $F_X(x)$ contains a discrete jump of amount p_i at $x = x_i$, as in Figure 2.1, one can still define a probability density by including $p_i \delta(x - x_i)$, an impulse function of strength p_i.

Joint probability density and joint cumulative distribution function are similarly defined.

$$F_{XY}(x, y) = \int_{-\infty}^{x} \int_{-\infty}^{y} f_{XY}(\mu, \lambda) \, d\mu \, d\lambda \tag{2.5}$$

Marginal densities are defined as

$$f_X(x) = \int_{-\infty}^{\infty} f_{XY}(x, y) \, dy \qquad f_Y(y) = \int_{-\infty}^{\infty} f_{XY}(x, y) \, dx \tag{2.6}$$

Conditional probability density:

$$f_{Y/X}(y/x) = \frac{f_{XY}(x, y)}{f_X(x)} \tag{2.7}$$

If X and Y are statistically independent:

$$f_{XY}(x, y) = f_Y(y) f_X(x) \tag{2.8}$$

A time-invariant channel is often modeled in terms of the transmission of a sequence of numbers as values of a random variable X, and, corresponding to each transmitted X, a random variable Y is received, given by

$$Y = X + Z,$$

where Z is a noise random variable. Successive values of Z are usually assumed to be independent, and the random variables X and Z are also assumed independent. This model is called a memoryless additive noise channel.

The density of the sum of two independent random variables is the convolution of the densities of the two random variables being added; this allows use of Fourier transform techniques to find the density of the sum. In probability, the name characteristic function is used corresponding to a Fourier transform operation. It is defined as follows:

$$\phi_X(t) = E[e^{jtx}] = \int_{-\infty}^{\infty} e^{jtx} f_X(x)\,dx \qquad (2.9)$$

Then the characteristic function of the sum of two independent random variables is simply the product of their characteristic functions. Note that (2.9) gives another interpretation, sometimes useful, as the expected value of e^{jtx}. Also note that the characteristic function applies to a more restrictive class of functions than the Fourier transform; namely, it applies only to probability density functions, which must be nonnegative and of unit area.

2.1.1   The Gaussian Random Variable

The one-dimensional Gaussian random variable is defined as follows:

$$f(x) = \frac{1}{\sigma\sqrt{2\pi}} e^{-(x-m)^2/2\sigma^2} \qquad (2.10)$$

where m is the mean and σ is the standard deviation. It can be proven that the sum of Gaussian random variables is also Gaussian.

The two-dimensional joint Gaussian density is the following: If X and Y are zero mean Gaussian random variables with standard deviations σ_x and σ_y, respectively,

$$f_{XY}(x,y) = \frac{1}{2\pi\sigma_x\sigma_y\sqrt{1-\rho^2}} e^{-\frac{\left(\frac{x^2}{\sigma_x^2} - 2\rho\frac{xy}{\sigma_x\sigma_y} + \frac{y^2}{\sigma_y^2}\right)}{2(1-\rho^2)}} \qquad (2.11)$$

where

$$\rho = \frac{E[(x-x_0)(y-y_0)]}{\sigma_x\sigma_y} \qquad (2.12)$$

The joint density of n Gaussian random variables can be written in compact form in terms of a matrix of covariances, but we will omit this representation for brevity. (See pp. 188–197 of [PAPO91].)

Error Probability with Gaussian Noise   Consider binary transmission of $\pm A$ with equal probability and additive Gaussian noise of standard deviation σ. The decision threshold is set at zero at the receiver, and the error probability is the shaded area

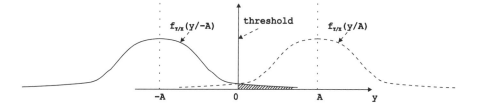

Figure 2.2: Error probability computed as the area under the shaded region.

of the tail of the conditional probability density function $f_{Y/X}(y/ - A)$, as shown in Figure 2.2.

Integrating,

$$P[err] = \int_0^\infty \frac{1}{\sigma\sqrt{2\pi}} e^{-(y+A)^2/2\sigma^2} dy \qquad (2.13)$$

This is most commonly expressed in terms of either the $Q(\ )$ function

$$Q(a) = \frac{1}{2\pi} \int_a^\infty e^{-z^2/2} dz. \qquad (2.14)$$

$$P[err] = Q\left(\frac{A}{\sigma}\right) \qquad (2.15)$$

or the error function $erf(\ )$.

$$erf(x) = \frac{2}{\sqrt{\pi}} \int_0^x e^{-z^2} dz. \qquad (2.16)$$

$$p[err] = \frac{1}{2}\left[1 - erf\left(\frac{A}{\sigma\sqrt{2}}\right)\right] \qquad (2.17)$$

2.2 Random Processes

A continuous time random process associates a time waveform with each elementary event in a probability space. This could be denoted as $x(t, e)$, where t is time and e is the event. Also sometimes considered is a discrete time random process, which associates an infinite sequence with each elementary event.

The collection of possible time waveforms is called the ensemble of waveforms. Often this is an uncountably infinite set, although it can even be a finite set. Figure 2.3 is an example of an ensemble of five possible time waveforms, associated with a set of five elementary events with specified probabilities.

The statistics of a random process are describable in various ways, which may or may not be complete descriptions. A complete description allows computation of

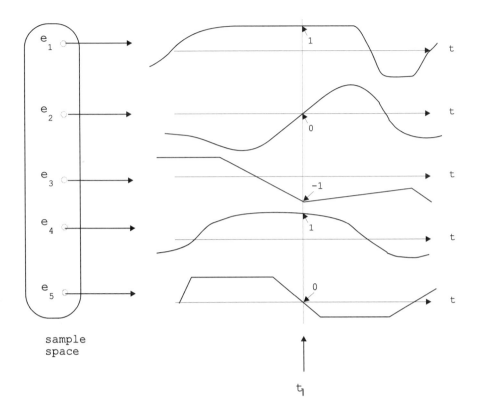

Figure 2.3: An ensemble of five time waveforms.

joint densities of the time function values at any set of n time instants, for any n. Of most importance are the first-order density, at a particular time t,

$$f_{X_t}(x)$$

and the second-order density,

$$f_{X_{t_1} X_{t_2}}(x_1, x_2) \qquad \text{or} \qquad f(x_1, x_2, t_1, t_2).$$

In the example of Figure 2.3 these functions happen to be discrete. At time t_1, x_1 takes on the values 0 with probability $p(e_2 + e_5)$, 1 with probability $p(e_1 + e_4)$, and -1 with probability $p(e_3)$.

2.2.1   The Stationary Random Process

Strict Sense Stationarity   For strict sense stationarity, a time translation must not change any statistical properties. All joint densities are independent of time translation.

$$f(x_1,\ldots,x_k,t_1,\ldots,t_k) = f(x_1,\ldots,x_k,t_1 + T,\ldots,t_k + T) \qquad (2.18)$$

for all T, k, times $t_1,\ldots,t_k$, and values $x_1,\ldots,x_k$.

Wide Sense Stationarity

1. The mean, m_t, averaged over the ensemble at a given time t, is independent of t.
2. The ensemble average autocorrelation,

$$R_x(t_1, t_2) = E[x_{t_1} x_{t_2}] \qquad (2.19)$$

depends only on the time difference $\tau = t_2 - t_1$. In this case, the autocorrelation function is written as $R_x(\tau)$.

As an illustration of a process that is wide sense stationary but not strict sense stationary, suppose the random process consists of four equally likely functions of the form

$$A \cdot \cos[\omega t] + B \cdot \sin[\omega t],$$

where $A = \pm 1$ and $B = \pm 1$.

At any given time, t is fixed, and the ensemble mean m_t is zero because the mean of A is zero and the mean of B is zero. Thus m_t, averaged over the ensemble at a given time t, is independent of t.

The ensemble average at a given time t is

$$E[x_t x_{t+\tau}] = E(A\cos[\omega t] + B\sin[\omega t])(A\cos[\omega(t + \tau)] + B\sin[\omega(t + \tau)]) \quad (2.20)$$

Multiplying terms, the AB terms average to zero because AB averages to zero; A^2 and B^2 are always 1, so

$$E[x_t x_{t+\tau}] = \cos[\omega t]\cos[\omega(t + \tau)] + \sin[\omega t]\sin[\omega(t + \tau)] = \cos[\omega\tau] \qquad (2.21)$$

Thus the ensemble autocorrelation function is also independent of time and the process is wide sense stationary. However, the first-order probability function at $t = 0$ (and also at $t = \pm n\pi$) has only the two values ± 1, while at other points the first-order function has other values. Thus the first-order probability distribution is not time independent, so the process is not strict sense stationary. It can be shown however [PAPO91], that the random process of the form

$$A \cdot \cos[\omega t] + B \cdot \sin[\omega t],$$

where A and B are independent Gaussian random variables, is strict sense stationary.

Spectral Density   For a stationary random process a term called spectral density, $S(f)$, is defined as the Fourier transform of $R_x(\tau)$. $S(f)$ describes the distribution of power over frequency. It is an even function of f and is nonnegative. Some useful relationships are the following:

1.
$$R_x(0) = \int_{-\infty}^{\infty} S(f) \, df. \qquad (2.22)$$

This indicates that the average power of the random waveform is the total area under the $S(f)$ curve, since $R_x(0) = E[x^2]$.

2.
$$S_y(f) = |H(f)|^2 S_x(f) \qquad (2.23)$$

where x and y are the input and output, respectively, of a linear system with transfer function $H(f)$. Thus, the notion of spectral density is useful to analyze the effect of passing a random waveform through a linear system. The output autocorrelation function also can be determined from the input autocorrelation, either directly through a double integral convolution (not shown) or indirectly through the Fourier transform and (2.23).

Ergodic Random Process   This is a stationary random process for which all time averages are equal to all ensemble averages. Thus every time waveform is typical and exhibits the same long-term statistics; this is usually the characteristic of random noise.

Gaussian Random Process (GRP)   This is a random process where the joint density of any N sample values at N different times is an N-dimensional joint Gaussian density. All the joint densities can be computed, and thus a complete statistical description obtained, through knowledge of just the mean m_t and the autocorrelation function $R_X(t_1, t_2)$.

It can be proven that if the input to a linear time invariant system is a stationary Gaussian random process, the output is also.

White Gaussian Noise (WGN)   The spectral density of white Gaussian noise is

$$S(f) = \frac{N_0}{2} \qquad (2.24)$$

The autocorrelation function is

$$R_X(\tau) = \frac{N_0 \delta(\tau)}{2} \qquad (2.25)$$

White Gaussian noise is a mathematical idealization; either (2.24) or (2.25) would imply infinite power, which is impossible. However, thermal noise has a spectral density that is very nearly flat out to frequencies beyond the range of communication signals, and in any practical communication channel the noise output will be almost exactly the same for the idealized model as for a model where the noise spectral density is flat in the passband range, but falls rapidly somewhere beyond the passband range. It also can be seen from (2.23) that even if $S_x(f)$ is a constant, indicating infinite power in x, the output process y will have finite power if the system function $H(f)$ goes to zero fast enough beyond some frequency.

For any function $f(t)$, if $n(t)$ is a sample function of a GRP,

$$n_T = \int_0^T n(t)f(t)\,dt \tag{2.26}$$

is always a Gaussian random variable.

For zero mean WGN,

$$y_T = \frac{1}{T} \int_0^T n(t)\,dt; \qquad E[y_T^2] = \frac{N_0}{2T}. \tag{2.27}$$

This is a time average of white Gaussian noise, and its variance is inversely proportional to the averaging time T.

2.2.2 White Noise Related to Representation by a Complete Set of Orthonormal Waveforms

Express the noise waveform $n(t)$ as

$$n(t) = \sum_{k=1}^{\infty} z_k \phi_k(t), \qquad T_1 < t < T_2 \tag{2.28}$$

where

$$\int_{T_1}^{T_2} \phi_k(t)\phi_l(t)\,dt = 0, \qquad k \neq l \tag{2.29}$$
$$= 1, \qquad k = l.$$

Suppose $n(t)$ is WGN.

$$z_k = \int_{T_1}^{T_2} n(t)\phi_k(t)\,dt \tag{2.30}$$

z_k is Gaussian.

$$E[z_k z_l] = E\left[\int_{T_1}^{T_2} n(t)\phi_k(t)\,dt \int_{T_1}^{T_2} n(\lambda)\phi_l(\lambda)\,d\lambda\right]$$
$$= \int_{T_1}^{T_2} \int_{T_1}^{T_2} E[n(t)n(\lambda)]\phi_k(t)\phi_l(\lambda)\,dt\,d\lambda \tag{2.31}$$

By (2.25),

$$E[n(t)n(\lambda)] = \frac{N_0}{2}\delta(t - \lambda),$$

integrating the right side of (2.31) with respect to t, the only contribution occurs at $t = \lambda$, where the δ-function has unit area. Thus

$$E[z_k z_l] = \int_{T_1}^{T_2} \frac{N_0}{2} \phi_k(\lambda)\phi_l(\lambda)d\lambda = \frac{N_0}{2} \qquad k = l,$$

$$= 0 \qquad k \neq l. \tag{2.32}$$

The $\{z_k\}$ are independent Gaussian random variables with mean zero and identical variance $N_0/2$; this is true in any orthonormal set expansion.

Data signals can be expressed also as a combination of orthonormal waveforms.

$$s(t) = \sum_{k=1}^{\infty} s_k \phi_k(t), \qquad T_1 < t < T_2. \tag{2.33}$$

One example is

$$\phi_k(t) = \sqrt{2F} \frac{\sin[2\pi F(t - \frac{k}{2F})]}{[2\pi F(t - \frac{k}{2F})]}, \tag{2.34}$$

which can be shown to be orthonormal functions, and are bandlimited to highest frequency F.

As an example, suppose we wish to make a presence-absence decision regarding a signal $x(t)$ of known shape in the time interval 0 to T, with additive white Gaussian noise. There is a theorem that we can form a complete orthonormal set of waveforms by starting with any arbitrary finite set of orthonormal waveforms. Thus we can express the first orthonormal waveform $\phi_1(t)$ as the same shape as $x(t)$: $x(t) = (\sqrt{E})\phi_1(t)$, where E is the signal energy. If we use this as the first orthonormal function in the expansion for white noise $n(t)$ and received signal $y(t) = x(t) + n(t)$ (signal present) or $y(t) = n(t)$ (signal absent), then $y_1 = \sqrt{E} + n_1$, signal present, or $y_1 = n_1$, signal absent. $y_i = n_i$, $i > 1$, either case. Since the $\{n_i\}$ are statistically independent in any orthonormal expansion of white noise, only y_1 is relevant to the decision, and this is a random variable with mean $\sqrt{E}$ (signal present) or 0 (signal absent), and conditional variance $N_0/2$. The optimum receiver needs only to compute the value

$$y_1 = \int_0^T y(t)\phi_1(t)\, dt, \tag{2.35}$$

which can be obtained by sampling the output at time T of a filter matched to the signal waveform, and comparing to the threshold $\sqrt{E}/2$. Note that for a given white noise spectral density, the error probability depends only on the signal energy, not on its shape.

If the noise were not exactly white, we could still choose to use this decision method, even though it would be suboptimum. Thus the waveform decision is reduced to a number decision.

The orthonormal function concept is closely related to the concept of signals as vectors. If we have any M signals, the signals are of some dimension $d \leq M$, which is the smallest number of orthonormal waveforms needed to represent the set. In that case the signals can be represented as M points in d-dimensional space, and with white noise the computation of the d components of the received signal captures all the information relevant to making an optimum decision. We will not go into the details of showing how to find the dimensionality of a set of waveforms, which involves a process called Gram-Schmidt orthogonalization. We will use the concept mostly in two ways: to justify the use of discrete time channel representation and to work with two-dimensional signal point representations of combined amplitude and phase modulation.

2.2.3 The Time–Discrete Markov Process

It is often useful to model some statistical phenomena in terms of a sequence of states. Let there be a set of L states, $s_0, s_1, \ldots, s_L$. Consider a sequence of states:

$$\ldots Z_0, Z_1, Z_2, \ldots,$$

where each Z_i is one of the L states.

In a Markov chain, the *current state sums up the whole past history*. Thus the conditional probability

$$P[Z_i/Z_0, Z_1, \ldots, Z_{i-1}] = P[Z_i/Z_{i-1}] \tag{2.36}$$

for all possible values of the states in the sequence.

Figure 2.4 illustrates possible types of states in a Markov chain. Arrows indicate those transitions whose probabilities are greater than zero.

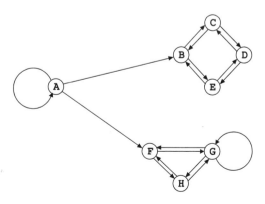

Figure 2.4: A Markov chain illustrating types of states.

A is a *transient* state. Other states are *persistent*. A state is persistent if the probability of an eventual return to that state after leaving it is unity. Otherwise it is transient.

A *closed* set of states is such that a one-step transition from any state in the set can lead only to a state of the set.

Closed sets: 1. A, B, C, D, E, F, G, H.   2. B, C, D, E.   3. F, G, H.

A Markov chain is *irreducible* if only the set of all sets is closed. Otherwise it is *decomposable*.

There are two types of persistent states:

1. *Periodic* (B, C, D, E)

2. *Aperiodic* (F, G, H)

A state is periodic with period $T > 1$ if a return to the state is possible only in an integer multiple of T steps. For the set (B, C, D, E), $T = 2$.

An irreducible Markov chain contains either all periodic states with the same period or all aperiodic states. In the latter case it is called an *ergodic* Markov chain.

In an ergodic Markov chain a sequence of states tends to statistical equilibrium independent of the starting state. Usually this type of Markov chain is assumed, and statistical equilibrium is assumed to have been reached.

In some models, the states are a Markov chain, but the events of primary interest are not the states themselves but probabilistic functions of the states; this is sometimes called a hidden Markov model. Applications of this latter type will be seen in time-varying channel models in Chapter 8. For example, a channel can be in a "good" state where the probability of error is low, or in a "bad" state where the probability of error is high. The events, error or no error, probabilistically depend on the state, but the good/bad state transitions occur due to some other physical phenomena not caused by the prior occurrence of error or no error. The Markov chain is hidden because the past error events do not uniquely define the state, although a good estimate of the current state can usually be made based on a combination of these events and observations of physical characteristics of the received signals.

2.2.4   The Poisson Process

The Poisson random process describes the statistics of the times of occurrence of a sequence of events. It is a common statistical assumption for arrivals and departures in queueing analysis. A key property is that it is memoryless, meaning that the probability density of the time to next arrival relative to the present is independent of how long it has been since the last arrival. This corresponds to an exponential distribution of the arrival times. If t is the time to next arrival and T the general time random variable, we have the relationships:

$$\text{Prob}[T > t] = e^{-\lambda t} \tag{2.37}$$

Cumulative distribution function:

$$F_T(t) = 1 - e^{-\lambda t} \tag{2.38}$$

Probability density function:

$$f_T(t) = \lambda e^{-\lambda t} \tag{2.39}$$

Expected value: $1/\lambda$.

Another quantity of interest is the probability function of the number of arrivals in some time interval τ. This is

$$P[n \text{ arrivals, time } \tau] = \frac{(\lambda\tau)^n}{n!} e^{-\lambda\tau} \tag{2.40}$$

2.3 Fundamental Information Theory Limits

Information theory provides fundamental limitations on the rate at which data can be communicated reliably over a communication channel and on the amount that information source data can be compressed.

2.3.1 Source Entropy and Lossless Data Compression

The concept of entropy plays a key role in information theory. Given a set of k mutually exclusive and exhaustive events, such as selecting one of k symbols with probability p_i of selecting event i, the entropy, denoted $H(X)$, associated with selecting an event is

$$H(X) = -\sum_i^k p_k \log_2 p_i \tag{2.41}$$

Entropy can be interpreted as the average initial uncertainty regarding the selection. With a base-2 logarithm, the units are called bits.

A source of information generates a sequence of symbols, each symbol chosen from an alphabet of K symbols. Some statistical laws are assumed to govern the generation of the source sequence. If the successive symbols have probabilities independent of past and future symbols, the source is called a *zero memory source*. More commonly, successive symbols are not statistically independent. For a zero memory source, the entropy per generated symbol is simply given by (2.41), where the $\{p_i\}$ are the symbol probabilities. In the general case of a stationary source, the entropy can be defined if all joint probabilities are specified. If all the joint probabilities $\{p(s_1, s_2, \ldots, s_n)\}$ are known for a sequence of n successive source symbols, the nth order entropy

$$H(X_1, X_2, \ldots, X_n) = H_n(X)$$

is

$$H_n(X) = -\sum p(s_1, s_2, \ldots, s_n) \log_2[p(s_1, s_2, \ldots, s_n)], \tag{2.42}$$

where the sum is over all k^n sequences of length n. The source entropy is then

$$H(X) = \lim_{n\to\infty}\{H_n(X)/n\}. \tag{2.43}$$

If the source is encoded by a uniquely decodable binary code, $H(X)$ is the limit, in bits per source symbol, on the smallest average number of binary code digits per source symbol. This data compression limit can be approached as closely as desired by sufficiently long codes.

The detailed techniques of data compression will not be discussed because it is an extended topic that would justify its own textbook. The relevance to the study of reliable communication is that, because efficient data compression coding removes most of the redundancy present in the message, it tends to make the encoded message more seriously affected by errors than an uncompressed version. Thus it makes error-free communication more important. An illustration of this is a technique known as run length coding. In run length coding, if the same symbol appears a large number n times in a row, instead of sending the same number n times, it is sent once followed by a count of how many times it appears in succession. Without compression, an error in one or a few of the n successive identical values would not be serious in some applications, whereas an error in the count of the number of consecutive copies could be catastrophic.

In video compression it is possible to do the compression in parts: low frequency components separated from high frequency components, detail separated from general background information, still frames from motion information, such that more critical parts can be better protected for reliability. Also, loss of other parts can be compensated for by techniques such as interpolation to fill in a missing frame. Again, the details will not concern us here; only the general principle that a portion of the overall data may be more important to protect than another portion.

2.3.2 Entropy and Large Number Laws

Consider a long sequence of N symbols generated by a source whose per-symbol entropy is $H(X)$. A remarkable property of large numbers is that, as N increases, the set of all sequence outcomes divides rather neatly into two subsets: a set called the likely set whose total probability is $1 - \epsilon$, where ϵ can be made as small as we wish for sufficiently large N, and the rest with total probability ϵ. The number of members in the likely set is $2^{N(H(X)+\delta)}$, where δ can be as small as we wish for sufficiently large N, and each member of the set has probability approximately $2^{-NH(X)}$. The word "approximately" is in the exponential sense, meaning if written in the form 2^{-Nb}, then $H(X)$ is close to b, percentagewise. Thus, if we only had to code the likely set, $NH(X)$ bits would be sufficient, or $H(X)$ bits/symbol. This likely set concept is also a key concept in understanding the noisy channel capacity theorem and the limiting capabilities of crror control coding.

The derivation of this property, called the *asymptotic equipartition property*, is contained in most information theory textbooks. A less elegant, but revealing approach to seeing the behavior can be to make use of the Stirling approximation for factorials. Stirling's approximation is as follows:

$$n! \simeq n^{n+\frac{1}{2}} e^{-n} \sqrt{2\pi}. \tag{2.44}$$

Stirling's approximation is quite accurate; it is within 1 percent for n as small as 10 and the error percentage goes down inversely with n.

Consider the statistics of a sequence of N independent choices of one of two events: 1 with probability p and 0 with probability $q = 1 - p$. A "typical" sequence has about Np ones. Assuming Np is an integer, the probability of one such sequence of Np ones is

$$p^{Np} q^{Nq}$$

and

$$\frac{1}{N} \log_2[p^{Np} q^{Nq}] = -h(p) \tag{2.45}$$

where

$$h(x) = -x \log_2 x - (1 - x) \log_2(1 - x).$$

Thus this typical sequence has probability $2^{-Nh(p)}$. Again assuming Np is an integer, the number of sequences with Np errors is

$$\binom{N}{Np}.$$

The typical set should be somewhat greater, since it should include a range of sequences with number of ones close to Np, but suppose we get an approximation to just the number with exactly Np errors. Stirling's approximation is:

$$\binom{N}{i} \simeq 2^{Nh(i/N)} \sqrt{\frac{N}{2\pi i(N-i)}}; \qquad \binom{N}{Np} \simeq 2^{Nh(p)} \sqrt{\frac{1}{2\pi Npq}}. \tag{2.46}$$

Exponentially, the approximate number of sequences in the set follows $2^{Nh(p)}$. Since the probability of each sequence with Np ones is $2^{-Nh(p)}$ and the total probability cannot exceed 1, the number of sequences with Np ones can't exceed $2^{Nh(p)}$, which is consistent with (2.46). The likely set should also include sequences with close to, but not exactly, Np errors. If these were included it would account for the discrepancy. An exact accounting for the whole likely set gets a bit messy, but the correct exponential behavior can already be seen. It might be worth noting that the standard deviation of the number of ones is

$$\sqrt{Npq}$$

As a rough estimate of the number of members of the likely set, we could multiply
the number the result of (2.46) for $i = Np$ by twice the standard deviation, yielding

$$2^{Nh(p)}\sqrt{\frac{2}{\pi}}.$$

2.3.3   The Communication Channel Model

In digital communication, it is useful to model the communication channel as follows:

1. Each unit of time, the sender selects for transmission one symbol from an alphabet
    of K channel "symbols." Physically, this may mean generating one of K pulse
    waveforms, $\{p_i(t - jT)\}$, $i = 1, 2, \ldots, K$, once each T seconds. The transmitted
    symbol may be denoted as the random variable X, which takes on one of the
    values $1, 2, \ldots, K$.

2. As in the zero memory channel model mentioned previously, for each channel
    symbol sent, the receiver records a number that is denoted as the random vari-
    able Y. For a completely discrete channel model, the number is one of a discrete
    set of J values. Normally, $J \geq K$, and when $J = K$ it corresponds to deciding
    which of the K symbols was sent. Alternatively, the number Y can be one of a
    continuous range of values. (The continuous and $J > K$ cases are pertinent when
    a receiver symbol decision is based not just on the current reception, but also on
    past and future receptions, as might be done in an error-correcting code.)

3. The channel is specified by the conditional probabilities $\{p_{Y/X}(y/x)\}$ in the discrete
    case, or the corresponding conditional probability densities if Y is continuous. This
    implies the zero memory assumption that the output Y depends statistically only
    on the corresponding transmitted value X according to the assumed conditional
    probability. The possibility of intersymbol interference is ignored in this model.

Figure 2.5 illustrates the input/output per-symbol model for the cases of continuous and discrete output.

2.3.4   Information in Discrete Input/Output Alphabet Channels

The joint event of sending a symbol x from a K-symbol alphabet and receiving a
symbol y from a J-symbol alphabet is of paramount importance in measuring the
information carried over a communication channel. If the symbols are given numerical
values, such as $0, 1, \ldots, K - 1$ for x and $0, 1, \ldots, J - 1$ for y, they can be considered
random variables. Representation of symbols as random variables is convenient but
not necessary in the discrete input-output case, since a symbol doesn't have to have
numerical significance. However, numerical representation is necessary for the case
of continuous-valued inputs and outputs.

Communication over the channel is considered to be the sending of a sequence
of symbols from the input alphabet. Corresponding to each transmission of an input
symbol, a symbol from the output alphabet is received. Most commonly, a time-

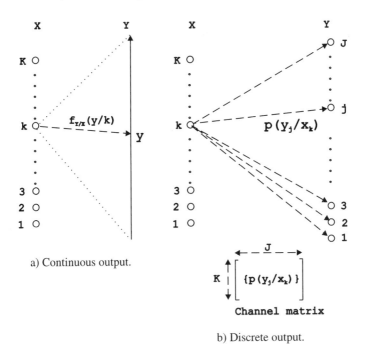

a) Continuous output.

Channel matrix

b) Discrete output.

Figure 2.5: Channel input output events per transmitted symbol.

invariant zero memory channel is assumed, which means that if a symbol x_k is transmitted at some point in the sequence, the probability of receiving y_j at that point is the fixed $p(y_j/x_k)$ in a $K \times J$ matrix of channel input-output transition probabilities; this is called the *channel matrix*. The channel model and matrix are illustrated in Figure 2.5b.

Suppose $\{p(x_k)\}$ are known. Given a received value y, the probabilities $\{p(x_k/y)\}$ can readily be calculated from the given channel probabilities $\{p(y_j/x_k)\}$. Conditional entropy given a particular y can then be computed as

$$H(X/y) = -\sum_{k=1}^{K} p(x_k/y) \log_2[p(x_k/y)]. \tag{2.47}$$

Averaging over y, conditional entropy is

$$H(X/Y) = \sum_{j=1}^{J} p(y_j)H(X/y_j). \tag{2.48}$$

Mutual information between X and Y is defined, in bits per symbol, as

$$I(X;Y) = H(X) - H(X/Y) = H(Y) - H(Y/X). \tag{2.49}$$

An alternative form is

$$I(X; Y) = \sum_{k=1}^{K} \sum_{j=1}^{J} p(x_k, y_j) \log \left[\frac{p(x_k, y_j)}{p(x_k) p(y_j)} \right]. \tag{2.50}$$

The term mutual information is used because of the interchangeability of X and Y in the relation. It can be shown that $I(X; Y) \geq 0$; this is equivalent to $H(X) \geq H(X/Y)$. An intuitive interpretation of these inequalities is the following: The average uncertainty about X on learning of an event Y is never greater than the average uncertainty about X without knowing Y. The average reduction in uncertainty about X provided by Y is the average information gained by the receiver.

Channel capacity C is defined as the maximum of $I(X; Y)$ over all choices of the input symbol probabilities.

A common example of a channel is the binary symmetric channel, where the receiver decides for each reception which of the two symbols was sent ($K = J = 2$), and the probability is p that the receiver decision symbol is wrong, given either transmitted symbol. Capacity in this case is when both input symbol values are equally likely, and is given by

$$C = 1 + p \log_2 p + (1 - p) \log_2 (1 - p). \tag{2.51}$$

2.3.5   The Noisy Channel Coding Theorem

The significance of C is expressed in terms of the following theorem:

1. Given a channel of capacity C bits/symbol, an arbitrarily small $\epsilon > 0$ and $\delta > 0$, and sufficiently large $N(\epsilon, \delta)$, it is possible to encode for communication in blocks of N symbols at any rate $R < C - \epsilon$ with average symbol probability of error $< \delta$.

2. It is not possible to communicate reliably at any rate $R > C$.

Rate R is achieved by selecting 2^{NR} sequences of length N, called *code words*, out of the K^N possibilities, using them with equal probability, and having the receiver make a decision, for each received block of N, which code word was received. Since the number of code words goes up exponentially with N, there is the potential that complexity of decoding might increase exponentially with N. However, techniques for coding/decoding have been devised that have only a polynomial increase in complexity with N. The rate of decrease obtainable in error probability with N has been shown to be exponential for fixed $R < C$, but the exponential coefficient of N becomes smaller as R comes closer to C.

Aside from the complexity problem, it is worth noting that one version of the proof of the theorem involves selecting the code words at random and showing that the average error probability over all code choices satisfies the theorem. There must be a code as good as the average. In fact, most random code choices will satisfy the theorem. However, the complexity/storage problem makes it impractical to choose them at random. Fortunately, it has been shown that the theorem result can be achieved using the important class of codes known as linear, or parity check codes. Error-correcting codes will be discussed in Chapters 3 and 4.

2.3.6 Information in Time-Discrete, Amplitude Continuous Channels

The discrete sequence model of a communication channel is readily extended to the case of time-discrete, amplitude continuous channels, where the input x, visualized as a random variable, can have a continuum of values, as can the corresponding output y. By dividing the real line of values of x into intervals Δx and similarly for y into intervals Δy, the input and output sets of intervals correspond to a discrete input-output channel where equation (2.50) applies. In the limit as $\Delta x \to 0$ and $\Delta y \to 0$, sums become integrals, probabilities become probability densities, and the relation (2.50) for mutual information becomes

$$I(X;Y) = \int_{-\infty}^{\infty} \int_{-\infty}^{\infty} f_{XY}(x, y) \log \left[\frac{f_{XY}(x, y)}{f_X(x) f_Y(y)} \right] dx \, dy \qquad (2.52)$$

The channel matrix is replaced by the conditional probability density function $f_{Y/X}(y/x)$. Capacity is the maximum of $I(X;Y)$ over all choices of $f_X(x)$, subject to some constraint on x, usually a peak or mean square value constraint.

Since mutual information for the continuous case for a given $f_X(x)$ can be approached arbitrarily closely by a discrete input-output with sufficiently small Δx and Δy, Shannon's noisy channel coding theorem applies also to capacity in the continuous case. Although the number of possible input sequences of length N is infinite in the continuous case, one still can choose a finite set of 2^{NR} code words of length N to send at some rate R less than C, and achieve the promise of Shannon's theorem.

The continuous analogy for entropy of a random variable is called *differential entropy*. It is defined as

$$H(X) = -\int_{-\infty}^{\infty} f_X(x) \log(f_X(x)) \, dx. \qquad (2.53)$$

Unlike entropy of a discrete source, differential entropy can be either positive or negative, and is changed by a scale factor change in x. However, differential entropy under a peak or variance constraint is a quantity of importance. It can be proved that, for a fixed variance, a Gaussian random variable has the maximum differential entropy.

$$H_G(X) = \log_2[\sigma \sqrt{2\pi e}] \qquad (2.54)$$

where e is the natural logarithm base and σ is the noise standard deviation. This property is used to derive the important capacity equation (2.55) that follows.

For additive Gaussian noise with variance σ^2 and signal variance constraint E, capacity is achieved when x has a zero mean Gaussian density, and is

$$C = \frac{1}{2} \log \left(1 + \frac{E}{\sigma^2} \right) \text{ bits/symbol.} \qquad (2.55)$$

2.3.7   Waveform Channels

In communication, even if the data being sent are discrete, the transmitted signal, noise, and received waveforms are continuous. In this case information capacity can be computed with the aid of the orthonormal series representations described in Section 2.2.2. If transmitted waveform, noise waveform, and received waveform are all represented by the same set of orthonormal waveforms, it is equivalent to sending a discrete sequence of numbers (the coefficients) and receiving a discrete set of numbers, each the sum of the transmitted number and a noise number. In the case of white Gaussian noise, the different noise numbers are independent, identically distributed Gaussian random variables, so the problem reduces to the zero memory discrete sequence additive Gaussian noise channel.

In the time continuous case, rates and capacities should be expressed in bits per second. These will be denoted R_t and C_t, respectively. For sufficiently large time T, and $R_t = C_t - \epsilon$, one can send one of

$$M(T) = 2^{TR_t} \qquad (2.56)$$

waveforms, such that the decision will be correct with probability $> 1 - \delta$. As a practical matter, the set of waveforms in time T is derived from a sequence of N coefficient numbers, similar to the time-discrete continuous channel case.

For the case where a channel is bandlimited from 0 to a highest frequency F, the orthonormal sinc functions in (2.34) can be used. The data transmitted can be the coefficient numbers of these functions, which occur at the rate $2F$ numbers per second. Per number, the capacity is given by (2.55). The signal power $P = 2FE$, and σ^2 is $N_0/2$. Multiplying by $2F$ samples per second, the capacity for a bandlimited channel with white Gaussian noise becomes

$$C_t = F * \log \left(1 + \frac{P}{N_0 F} \right) \text{ bits/second.} \qquad (2.57)$$

An additional justification for the importance of this expression is that it is a worst case in the sense that the capacity with white Gaussian noise can be shown to be lower than the capacity with any other noise having the same power $N_0 F$ in the band F. The intuitive reason for this is that if the noise spectral density is not flat over the band, the transmitter could take advantage by putting more of its power into the part of the band where the noise power density is lower.

Although at first glance (2.57) suggests a linear increase of capacity with bandwidth, as F increases to where $P/N_0 F \ll 1$, C approaches asymptotically the limit

$$C_t \rightarrow \frac{P}{N_0} \log_2 e \text{ bits/second.} \qquad (2.58)$$

Thus if there is no bandwidth constraint, the capacity is determined just by the ratio of signal power to noise power density.

2.4 Transmitted Waveform Selection

The object is to convey a discrete sequence of symbols, which we can take to be binary in virtually any practical application. The bit stream to be conveyed may already have been processed for data compression and may have had redundant bits added for error detection and correction. We will look now at the modulation/demodulation problem: to convert this bit stream into electrical or optical waveforms for transmission over a noisy communication channel, and then reconstruct the bit stream at the receiver.

2.4.1 Modulation Methods

One method is for the modulator to convert each bit independently into a waveform and transmit the sum of these successive waveforms for successive bits. The alternatives in this case are the following:

Binary Phase Shift Keying (BPSK) In BPSK, the two alternatives are communicated by selecting one of two phases for a carrier during a T-second interval. Almost invariably the two phases are chosen 180 degrees apart, since this makes the two alternatives as different as possible, which is optimum for decision in the presence of random noise. Thus, for the ith bit, the choice is $A\cos(\omega_c t)$ if the bit is a 1, and $A\cos(\omega_c t + \pi) = -A\cos(\omega_c t)$ if the bit is a 0, for $(i-1)T < t < iT$.

A variation of PSK is **differential PSK (DPSK)**, where the phase difference in two successive intervals is 0 or 180 degrees according to whether the bit is a 0 or a 1.

Bipolar Amplitude Shift Keying ($\pm$ASK) A basic pulse shape $p(t)$ is chosen, and a sequence of 0's and 1's is sent as

$$x(t) = \sum A_i p(t - iT) \cos(\omega_c t). \qquad (2.59)$$

Basically, $\pm$ASK is related to PSK in that each A_i is $+A$ if the bit is a 1, and $-A$ if the bit is a 0. The pulse shape is chosen so it goes through 0 at all integer multiples of T except $t = 0$. In this way sampling at integer multiples of T extracts $+A$ or $-A$ according to whether the corresponding bit is a 1 or a 0, respectively. The minimum bandwidth $p(t)$ that has this property is the sampling waveform

$$p(t) = \frac{\sin\left(\frac{\pi t}{T}\right)}{\frac{\pi t}{T}}. \tag{2.60}$$

This shape is difficult and critical to approximate in practice, so waveforms having about 1.5–2 times this bandwidth are ordinarily used.

Unipolar Amplitude Shift Keying   The transmitted $x(t)$ in this case also can be represented as in (2.60), but the two different A_i values are nonnegative. For maximum difference between the two alternatives, one of them is made zero, and the scheme is called **On-Off Keying (OOK)**. This method is useful in cases where the receiver cannot make effective use of phase information, and thus uses envelope detection.

Binary Frequency Shift Keying (BFSK)   In each T-second interval, the carrier is at one of two frequencies according to whether the bit is a 1 or a 0: $A\cos(\omega_1 t + \theta_i)$ if the bit is a 1, and $A\cos(\omega_0 t + \alpha_i)$ if the bit is a 0, for $(i-1)T < t < iT$. The θ_i and α_i can be chosen to maintain phase continuity for successive T-second intervals; if instead there is a switching between two independent oscillators, the θ_i and α_i may be constant.

The techniques just described are readily extended to carry more than one bit per pulse by using multiple amplitudes, phases, frequencies, or some combination. The most popular choice is a two-dimensional set (constellation) of points corresponding to combined amplitude and phase modulation or just phase modulation. Two examples are given in Figure 2.6.

These two-dimensional diagrams can be related directly to the previously-mentioned concept of signals as vectors. If $p(t)$ is considered as a rectangular pulse

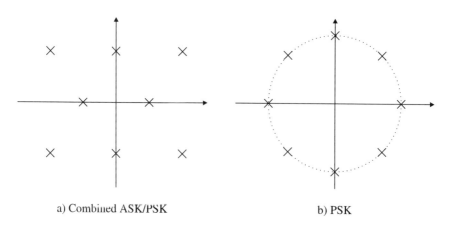

a) Combined ASK/PSK   b) PSK

Figure 2.6: Examples of two-dimensional signal constellations.

of duration T, the two orthonormal waveforms are

$$\phi_1(t) = \sqrt{\frac{2}{T}} \cos[\omega_c t] \quad \text{and} \quad \phi_2(t) = \sqrt{\frac{2}{T}} \sin[\omega_c t]. \quad (2.61)$$

If a signal is plotted as a point with coefficients (a_1, a_2) corresponding to

$$a_1 \phi_1(t) + a_2 \phi_2(t),$$

then the distance from the point to the origin is the square root of the signal energy, and the distance between any two points is the square root of the energy of the difference between the signals. Thus the minimum distance between any two signals in this two-dimensional space is a key parameter in estimating the probability of erroneous decision.

As an example, suppose a decision is to be made between two equally likely signals in white Gaussian noise with spectral density $N_0/2$. If the two signals are a distance d apart, the error probability is

$$P(error) = Q\left(\frac{d}{\sqrt{2n_0}}\right) \quad (2.62)$$

where $Q(\ )$ is the Q-function defined in (2.14).

If there are $n > 2$ signals, two-dimensional space can be divided into decision regions as illustrated in Figure 2.7 for 8-phase PSK and equiprobable signals. The probability of correct decision is obtained by integrating the conditional two-dimensional joint Gaussian density over the decision region. In general this can be rather complex. An upper bound on error probability can be obtained from the union bound: add the probabilities of error from the reference signal to each of the other signals as if a binary decision were being made between only two signals. Sometimes not all cases need to be added. For the Figure 2.6 example only two components need to be included (see Problem 2.3). The union bound approaches the true value as the signal-to-noise ratio increases.

2.4.2 Decisions with Codes

If block codes are being used, the demodulator and decoder ideally would be one unit, and would look at the whole received waveform to decide the most likely code word. Techniques for designing block codes will be described in Chapter 3. As a practical matter, the number of alternative code words is usually too large to make the decision directly from the exact received waveform. Thus, as a first step, the demodulator will in those cases make decisions about each component symbol value, and pass these decisions on to the decoder. Most commonly these are *hard* decisions, which means the demodulator decides exactly which of the symbol values has been sent.

Sometimes it is feasible for the demodulator to make *soft* decisions for each symbol. A *soft* decision means that the demodulator will provide a greater number of

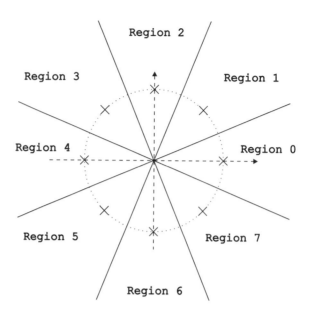

Figure 2.7: Decision regions for 8-phase PSK.

levels of decision than there are possible symbol values. These decisions are a measure
of the likelihood that the symbol has each possible value. This likelihood information
would be discretized as finely as justified by cost/benefit tradeoffs. Actually, if the
pulse shapes are ideally spaced sampling waveforms (which are orthogonal) and the
noise is white Gaussian, exact likelihood information recorded for each transmitted
symbol is as optimum as looking at the whole waveform.

It generally is too complex to make use of soft decision information in decoding long block codes. However, *convolutional codes* can make effective use of
soft-decision information. Convolutional codes will be discussed in Chapter 4. Also,
there is a class called *modulation codes*, which can combine the modulation waveform selection with convolutional or short block codes such as to use soft decision
information effectively. Modulation codes will also be discussed in Chapter 4.

2.5   Summary

This chapter reviews basic probability and statistical concepts useful for the analysis
of data communication over noisy channels.

A **random variable** is a number associated with an event with probabilities
defined. Its statistics are described by the cumulative distribution and probability
density functions as defined in (2.2)–(2.4). Statistics of **joint random variables** are
described in (2.5)–(2.8). The **characteristic function** (2.9) of a random variable is like

a Fourier transform. The **Gaussian** and **joint Gaussian random variables** (2.10)–(2.12) are often used in analysis. **Error probability** expressions with a Gaussian noise random variable are given in (2.13)–(2.17).

A **random process** is a time waveform associated with each event in a probability space. **Ensemble** statistics involve joint statistics of values at specific times over the set or "ensemble" of all time waveforms. These statistics include averages (ensemble mean, ensemble autocorrelation function) and joint probability densities. A **strict sense stationary random process**, defined in (2.18), is one where a time translation does not change statistical properties. A **wide sense stationary random process** requires only that the ensemble mean and ensemble autocorrelation function be unaffected by a time translation (2.19)–(2.21). **Spectral density** (2.22)–(2.23) is an important tool in stationary random process analysis. An **ergodic random process** is one where almost every waveform is typical and exhibits the same long-term statistics. A **Gaussian random process** is one where the joint density of any N sample values is a joint Gaussian density. It is a natural process for thermal noise, which is the sum of many independent effects of random particle motion. It also has many useful mathematical properties. **White Gaussian noise** (2.24)–(2.25) is a special stationary Gaussian random process where the spectral density is a constant over all frequencies. Thermal noise has a property of essentially constant spectral density over most ranges of signalling frequencies employed. Although white noise is a mathematical idealization that implies infinite power, it has the same wide usefulness as the common delta function assumption in linear system analysis. White noise represented by a set of **orthonormal waveforms** has some very simple properties (2.28)–(2.32) when representing time-continuous waveforms by sequences of numbers, as we commonly do with the Fourier series. It allows reduction of the problem of processing received **data signal waveforms plus additive noise** to one of processing a sequence of data numbers disturbed by independent Gaussian noise random variables (2.33)–(2.35). The **Markov chain** is a useful tool for modelling statistics such as channel condition changes or information sources with memory. Basically, there are a set of states, and the current state sums up the whole past history, independent of how one arrived at the state. The **Poisson process** (2.37)–(2.40) is a fundamental statistic of times of event occurrence where the time statistic to the next occurrence is independent of how long it has been since the last occurrence. The Poisson process is a natural process like the Gaussian random process as a limit of many independent effects, but it often is used even where it is not valid because of its nice mathematical properties related to its exponential distribution.

Information theory specifies the fundamental limits to the rate of reliable communication and the amount of data compression. It also shows that these limits can be approached, though at a high cost in complexity, assuming given statistical laws. **Entropy**, defined in (2.41)–(2.43), sets the limit to data compression, and also relates to channel information capacity. **Laws of large numbers** are the key to the reason these results can be achieved. The asymptotic equipartition property shows that the set of long sequences of events divide into a likely set, which has about 2^{NH} members of about equal probability, where N is the sequence length and H is the entropy, and a usually much larger set that has a very small probability, approaching zero as N increases. This is illustrated for a special case in (2.44)–(2.46). A **discrete-time channel model** is often used to model a communication channel and compute **channel capacity** (2.47)–(2.55). The **noisy channel coding theorem** shows that with coding it is possible to communicate with arbitrarily high reliability at any rate R less than the channel capacity C. The choice of practical codes to achieve this is a difficult problem. Coding techniques will be discussed in Chapters 3 and 4. Capacity of continuous waveform channels can be determined with the aid of the orthonormal signal concept previously described that converts continuous waveforms into sequences of numbers. White Gaussian noise capacity is shown in (2.57)–(2.58).

Data to be communicated are normally in binary form but must be sent with continuously varying waveforms. For **binary signalling** the alternatives are **Phase Shift Keying, Frequency Shift Keying,** and **Amplitude Shift Keying**. However, to save bandwidth or send at a higher rate, more than one bit can be sent with each pulse waveform. Most commonly, signalling for sending k bits is done by selecting 2^k points in a **two-dimensional signal constellation**. The orthonormal signal concept can be used to represent these points as components of orthonormal cosine and sine functions (2.61). With white Gaussian noise assumed, the error probability between different signal points is related to the distance between them (2.62). With error-correction encoded transmissions, normally, **hard decisions** are made on each symbol point and these decisions are then used by the error-correcting code. However, it would be better (except for the complexity) to retain the actual received points (**soft decisions**) for use in deciding the whole code block. This alternative will be considered in some detail in Chapter 4.

2.6   Problems

2.1.   A random variable Y is a function of a random variable X defined as follows:

$$y = 0, \ x \leq 0 \quad \text{and} \quad x \geq 6.$$

$$y = x, \ 0 \leq x \leq 4.$$

$$y = 4, \ 4 \leq x \leq 5.$$

$$y = 24 - 4x, \ 5 \leq x \leq 6.$$

X has a density,

$$f_X(x) = 1/10, \ -2 \leq x \leq 8$$

$$f_X(x) = 0, \ \text{elsewhere.}$$

a.   Find and sketch the cumulative distribution function, $F_Y(y)$.
b.   Find and sketch the probability density, $f_Y(y)$.

2.2. Let x_1 and x_2 be independent zero mean Gaussian random variables each of unit variance. Find the probability that (x_1, x_2) lies in the region defined by $x_1/2 + x_2 > 1$. Express the answer in terms of the Q function, which is defined by Equation (2.14).

2.3. An observed two-dimensional random variable **y** is given by $\mathbf{y} = \mathbf{S}_i + \mathbf{n}$, where $\mathbf{S}_i$ is the vector represented by one of six equally likely signal points shown in Figure P2.1, and n is an additive noise vector whose two components are independent equal variance zero mean Gaussian random variables. Suppose Prob$[n_1 > d/2] = p$.

    a. For an optimum decision rule, find the average probability of decision error in terms of p.

    b. In what way could you generalize the assumption about the noise statistic and still get the same answer in terms of p?

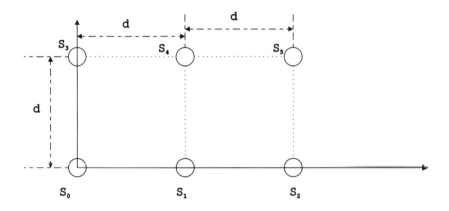

Figure P2.1: Six-point signal constellation.

2.4. Prove that the random process consisting of waveforms of the form $A\cos[\omega t] + B\sin[\omega t]$, where ω is fixed and A and B are independent Gaussian random variables, is strict sense stationary.

2.5. Derive the result stated in Equation (2.27).

2.6. Justify the statement that n_T defined in (2.26) is always a Gaussian random variable, based on the concept of an integral being the limit of a sum.

2.7. Prove that the $\phi_k(t)$ given by (2.34) are orthonormal. Hint: Use the Parseval relation between integration of time products and Fourier transform products.

2.8. Derive (2.51) from (2.50).

2.9. A pair of random variables X and Y have a joint probability density that is constant over the interior of a circle of unit radius and zero elsewhere.

    a. Find the marginal densities of X and Y.

    b. Write an integral expression for $I(X; Y)$. Evaluation of the integral is not required, but show the limits of integration properly and include in the integrand any appropriate marginal density from (a).

    c. Assuming Y is the received signal, if the receiver lost the sign of the output but retained the magnitude, would any information be lost? Explain.

    d. What would be the effect of making the circle radius 2 instead of 1, with other assumptions the same?

2.10. **a.** Prove that, for a continuous random variable of fixed variance, the Gaussian random variable has the maximum differential entropy.

    b. Prove that, given a continuous random variable is constrained to lie between the values 0 and A, the maximum differential entropy is attained by a uniform probability density.

2.11. Derive (2.55) from (2.54).

2.12. Refer to the 8-PSK example of Figure 2.7. Let the noise be white Gaussian with spectral density $N_0/2$, and let the signals be sinusoids:

$$S_i(t) = A\cos[\omega_c t + \Phi_i], \qquad i = 1, 2, \dots, 8, \qquad 0 \le t \le T.$$

Assume the coordinates represent the coefficients in the two-dimensional orthonormal expansion of the signals.

    a. Write a union upper bound for the probability of error in terms of just two other signal points. Express the answer in terms of the Q function of the given parameters A, T, and N_0.

    b. Write an integral expression for the actual probability of error.

Chapter 3

Block Error Control Codes

In data communication, it is common for data symbol errors to occur more frequently than can be tolerated by an application. This is especially true if channel data transmission rates are pushed close to channel capacity. Errors can be reduced to acceptable levels by a combination of error detection, error correction, and ARQ techniques.

Error-detecting codes are usually organized in fixed-length blocks of symbols, referred to as a *block code*. Error detection is performed separately on each block, to determine whether that block does or does not contain any error(s). The symbols are selected from an allowed alphabet of q values. Most commonly $q = 2$. Second most commonly is $q = 2^r$, with r an integer greater than one. Other values of q are generally impractical.

Block codes also can be used for error correction. Error-correction techniques are the means of approaching the promise of Shannon's noisy channel coding theorem in a practical manner, and that theorem provided the impetus for most of the work on error correcting codes. The practicality of using coding techniques to achieve this goal has been very much open to question in the past, however. The inherent difficulty is that, although error probability can be reduced exponentially with N, the number of code words to decide among increases exponentially with N. If decoding complexity also went up exponentially with N, it would not be practical to use long codes to achieve reliable communication at rates close to capacity. Fortunately, coding/decoding techniques have been found that do not require exponential growth of complexity with code length.

A class of error-correcting codes that does not require segregation into blocks is called *trellis* or *convolutional*. A convolutional code is a special kind of trellis code where the coding process is a linear operation. Trellis and convolutional codes have some properties that lend themselves to simpler decoding. These classes of codes will be described in Chapter 4.

Another code construction that helps simplify decoding is called *concatenated coding*. Concatenated codes have codes within codes. For example, an inner block code with r data symbols can have its code words serve as individual symbols for an outer block code; the outer code's symbols are thus from an alphabet of size $q = 2^r$. Concatenated codes simplify decoding by breaking the task into two stages. In general, the inner and outer codes could be individually either block or convolutional. Additional stages of concatenation are also possible, but rarely considered for use.

Perhaps the most important simplifications of the decoding problem stem from the use of a linear encoding process and the structures of finite groups, rings, and fields. The class of codes called cyclic codes, and particularly a subclass called BCH codes, allow for considerable simplification of the error correction task.

3.1   The General Block Code

A block of n symbols from the alphabet has q^n possible values. q is an integer, most commonly equal to 2. A block code of length n has a set of allowable sequences that is a subset of these possible values. The members of the allowed subset are called *code words*. The number of code words is normally far smaller than q^n. Thus when symbol errors occur in transmission, the presence of errors is usually detected because the received sequence rarely will be a code word.

Without any special structure, error detection would require comparison of the received sequence with every code word to see that no match is found, and error correction would require comparison with as many code words as needed until a code word was found that was sufficiently like what was received (on average half the set of code words would have to be tried). For most useful codes this is entirely impractical because the code word set grows exponentially with block length, and for most useful codes this is far too large. Parity check codes provide a structure that makes the tasks of encoding and error detection simple without sacrificing the effectiveness of the code. The parity check structure alone, however, does not suffice to make error correction simple, except for single-error correction and a few other special cases. For practical error correction it is necessary in most cases to build additional structure into the code.

3.2   Parity Check Block Codes

Let the q members of the symbol alphabet be represented as the q elements of a finite field, denoted as $GF(q)$. In Section 3.3 we will look into some properties of finite fields that are required to understand certain codes. Mostly, we will assume $q = 2$. Operations in $GF(2)$ obey ordinary modulo-two arithmetic: $1 + 1 = 0$, and so on.

3.2.1   Matrix Representation

An (n, k) parity check code is a linear one-to-one mapping of the q^k arrangements of a sequence of k data symbols into q^k code words of block length n. The mapping can be expressed in matrix form as follows, where $[c_0, c_1, \ldots, c_{n-1}] = \mathbf{c}$ represents a code word and $[d_0, d_1, \ldots, d_{k-1}] = \mathbf{d}$ represents the data symbols.

$$[c_0, c_1, \ldots, c_{n-1}] = [d_0, d_1, \ldots, d_{k-1}]G \tag{3.1}$$

In abbreviated notation,

$$\mathbf{c} = \mathbf{d}G.$$

The $k \times n$ matrix G must be of rank k. It is called the generator matrix of the code.

If $q = 2$, the g_{ij} entries of G are each 0 or 1. It is usually desirable for the first k consecutive symbols of the code word to be identical to the data, because then the data are easily extracted after decoding. The code is then called systematic. Notation varies as to whether to place the data on the left or the right. In a systematic parity check, G can be written in the partitioned form:

$$G = [\, I_k \quad P \,] \tag{3.2a}$$

or

$$G = [\, P \quad I_k \,], \tag{3.2b}$$

depending on which convention is used. For this section, we will use the (3.2a) convention. For the important case of cyclic codes, the form (3.2b) is more common, so we will switch to that format in describing cyclic codes.

Error detection is also accomplished easily with a matrix multiplication. (Later we will see that the class of codes called cyclic codes permit an even simpler computation). To see how matrix multiplication can accomplish error detection, note that for a systematic code the last $n - k$ columns of G describe how the $n - k$ check symbols depend on the data symbols. If we write the code word as

$$[c_0, c_1, \ldots, c_{n-1}] = [d_0, d_1, \ldots, d_{k-1}, p_0, \ldots, p_{n-k-1}],$$

multiplication of the data vector by column $k + i$ in (3.1) yields a parity check equation:

$$p_i = \sum_{j=0}^{j=k-1} d_j g_{j,k-1+i}$$

or

$$\sum_{j=0}^{j=k-1} d_j g_{j,k-1+i} - p_i = 0 \qquad i = 0, 1, \ldots, n - k - 1. \tag{3.3}$$

In matrix form, the $n - k$ equations (3.3) can be written as

$$[P^T - I_{n-k}]\mathbf{c}^T = \mathbf{0}^T = [H]\mathbf{c}^T, \tag{3.4}$$

where P is the submatrix in (3.2), P^T is its transpose, and $\mathbf{0}^T$ is a column vector of $n - k$ zeros. H is called the parity check matrix. If q is a power of 2, which almost always is the case, the minus sign in (3.3) and (3.4) can be ignored because $-1 = 1$ in modulo-2 arithmetic.

To check for errors when an n-symbol block $\mathbf{y}$ is received, compute

$$\mathbf{s}^T = H\mathbf{y}^T. \tag{3.5}$$

$\mathbf{s}$ is called the syndrome. If $\mathbf{s}$ is not zero, errors are detected, because if $\mathbf{y}$ were a code word $\mathbf{s}$ would be zero. If $\mathbf{s}$ is zero, the reception is assumed to be error-free, although there is a small chance that the errors have transformed the transmission into some wrong code word. The received sequence is related to the transmitted code word $\mathbf{c}$ by

$$\mathbf{y} = \mathbf{c} + \mathbf{e},$$

where $\mathbf{e}$ is called the error vector, and has nonzero components in all the positions that are in error. Applying (3.5),

$$\mathbf{s}^T = H\mathbf{y}^T = H(\mathbf{c} + \mathbf{e})^T = H\mathbf{e}^T. \tag{3.6}$$

Thus the syndrome of the received sequence is identical to the syndrome of the error vector.

A parity check code does not have to be systematic. One way to view the set of code words is as the vector space generated by taking all q^k combinations over $GF(q)$ of the row vectors of the generator matrix G. A generator matrix G could be derived by taking any set of k linearly independent vectors of that row space, and the set of code words would be the same. Thus, there are many G matrices that describe the same set of code words, though only one of these is systematic with the first k positions as the data digits. Also, any $k \times n$ matrix over $GF(q)$ whose k rows are linearly independent can be converted into a systematic code without changing the set of code words except for a possible reordering of the symbols. The reordering may be necessary if the first k columns of the original matrix happen not to be linearly independent. Reordering symbols does not change the set of distances between code words, and distances between code words is a key factor in error-correcting capability.

The parity check matrix also doesn't have to have a $(n - k) * (n - k)$ diagonal submatrix. Since $\mathbf{0}^T = [H]\mathbf{c}^T$, and each row of H multiplied by $\mathbf{c}^T$ is like a vector dot product, any code word is orthogonal to all rows of H, and any member of the row space of H is orthogonal to any member of the row space of G. In this case, the row space of H is what is called the null space of the row space of G. The null space is of dimension $n - k$, which is consistent with the number of check symbols. Thus, any $n - k$ linearly independent vectors in the null space of the row space of G can be selected as the rows of H, and can serve as the parity check matrix for a given code. Choosing a different H changes the syndrome pattern different errors produce. Sometimes this property is useful in finding an error pattern most likely to have caused a given syndrome. For example, if H is in the form (3.4) and all the errors are in the last $n - k$ positions, the syndrome will be identical to the error pattern in those $n - k$ positions. If the H matrix could be transformed so that a different set of $n - k$ positions formed an identity, then any error confined to those $n - k$ positions would be revealed. Such techniques are useful for correcting errors in the common case that errors are clustered in one part of the code word.

3.2.2 Error Correction and Hamming Distance

The Hamming distance between two code words is the number of symbols by which two code words differ. Of special interest is the minimum Hamming distance between any two code words. Denote this as d_{min}. Suppose there are e errors. If $d_{min} > 2e$, then the received sequence will always differ in fewer symbols from the correct code word than from any other code word. Thus, if the decoder chooses the code word that has the smallest Hamming distance from the received sequence, the decoder will be correct. To correct all patterns of t or fewer errors, d_{min} must be at least $2t + 1$. However, a correct decision often can be made even when $2t + 1 > d_{min}$, because the t errors are not necessarily all in positions where two code words differing by d_{min} disagree. Correction of numbers of errors beyond the d_{min} bound is especially worthwhile considering when q is large; in this case, an error in a symbol where two code words differ will have only about a $1/(q - 1)$ chance of creating an agreement with the symbol of the wrong code word, whereas with $q = 2$ it always would agree with the wrong code word.

3.2.3 Group Structure of Parity Check Codes

We have seen that the set of code words can be considered as a subspace of the space of n-tuples. Another useful structural description of the set of code words is as a q^k-element subgroup of the group of q^n n-tuples. Again assume $q = 2$, but much of the statements extend readily to general q.

Group Properties   A group is a set G of elements and an operation (*) satisfying the following rules:

1. If $a \in G$ and $b \in G$, then $a * b \in G$ (closure property).
2. There is a unique identity element $e \in G$ such that $a * e = e * a = a$.
3. For each $a \in G$ there is a unique inverse element $a^{-1} \in G$ such that $a * a^{-1} = e = a^{-1} * a$.
4. The associative law holds: if a, b, c are three elements of G, $a * (b * c) = (a * b) * c$.

Consider the example of binary parity check codes, and let S be the set of code words of an (n, k) code. Let the operation be vector modulo-2 addition of two code words written as n-component binary vectors. It then is more descriptive to denote the operation by "+" instead of "*". We can show S forms a group.

Property 1. If $H\mathbf{a}^T = \mathbf{0}^T$ and $H\mathbf{b}^T = \mathbf{0}^T$, then $H(\mathbf{a} + \mathbf{b})^T = \mathbf{0}^T$, so we have closure.

Property 2. The identity is a vector of n zeros. It is in S by (3.4) since $H\mathbf{0}^T = \mathbf{0}^T$.

Property 3. If $\mathbf{c}$ is a code word, $\mathbf{c} + \mathbf{c} = \mathbf{0}$, due to modulo-2 addition. Thus each element is its own inverse, and it is unique.

Property 4. The associative law follows from the associativity of modulo-2 addition.

Additional Properties and Definitions   A subset of a group that itself is a group is called a *subgroup*. The number of elements in a subgroup of a finite group is a factor of the number of elements in the group. This follows from the generation of the whole group by cosets of the subgroup as explained in the example that follows.

If $a * b = b * a$ for every $a, b \in G$, the commutative property holds and the group is called an *Abelian* group. The groups we consider here are all Abelian.

Cosets   It is particularly useful to consider the organization of the Group V of 2^n n-tuples into the 2^{n-k} cosets of the subgroup C of 2^k code words. One coset is considered as C itself. Each additional coset is formed by taking a member $\mathbf{v}$ of V that is not in C or in any of the cosets thus far formed and operating (adding) it in turn to each member of C. This creates a coset, denoted $\mathbf{v}C$, whose members are all different from each other and different from all the members of the cosets formed thus far. Continuing in this way, 2^{n-k} cosets are formed, which contain all q^n n-tuples, exactly once each. The element used to generate a coset is called the *coset leader*. Actually, any element of the coset can be chosen as coset leader, and the same coset will result. The process is illustrated for a $(5, 2)$ binary code with the following generator and check matrices:

$$G = \begin{bmatrix} 1 & 0 & 1 & 1 & 0 \\ 0 & 1 & 0 & 1 & 1 \end{bmatrix} \qquad H = \begin{bmatrix} 1 & 0 & 1 & 0 & 0 \\ 1 & 1 & 0 & 1 & 0 \\ 0 & 1 & 0 & 0 & 1 \end{bmatrix}$$

Sequences					Syndrome
00000	10110	01011	11101	← subgroup C	000
00001	10111	01010	11100	coset 2	001
00010	10100	01001	11111	coset 3	010
00100	10010	01111	11001	coset 4	100
01000	11110	00011	10101	coset 5	011
10000	00110	11011	01101	coset 6	110
11000	01110	10011	00101	coset 7	101
01100	11010	00111	10001	coset 8	111

It is useful to view the elements of this array either as the set of possible received sequences or as the set of possible error patterns. Note that, either as received sequences or as error patterns (see (3.6)), all members of a coset have the same syndrome. This is because, if **v** is the coset leader, all members of **v**C are of the form **v** + **c**, where **c** is a code word.

$$\mathbf{s}^T = H(\mathbf{v} + \mathbf{c})^T = H\mathbf{v}^T. \tag{3.7}$$

Also, the 2^{n-k} different syndromes map 1:1 into the 2^{n-k} different cosets. Thus, the coset members consist of all the received sequences that have the syndrome associated with that coset, and they also consist of all the error vectors that have the same associated syndrome.

　　If a syndrome is computed and a decision must be made as to what was sent, the most likely transmitted code word should be sought. Usually, it is assumed that the added error vector is statistically independent of which code word was transmitted and all code words are assumed equally likely a priori; then the decision can be based on the most likely error vector without regard to the associated code word. Where hybrid error detection and correction is permissible, the error detection option can be applied if the confidence in a proposed correction does not exceed some threshold; in pure error detection, detection without correction occurs whenever the computed syndrome is nonzero.

　　In the $(5, 2)$ code illustrated, if the syndrome corresponds to one of cosets 2 through 6, each of these cosets contains exactly one single-error pattern. A single error normally is substantially more likely than the other error vectors in the coset, so a single-error correction might be attempted. If the syndrome corresponds to one of cosets 7 or 8, there are in each case two double errors with the same syndrome, and if these two double-error patterns are equally likely, there would be somewhat less than a 50/50 chance that a correction decision would be correct, so double-error correction might not be attempted.

　　Syndrome computation and pure error detection are rather easily implemented operations. Error correction can be quite complex, however. Mapping of syndrome into most likely error pattern is the main problem. A tabulation of syndromes versus associated most likely error pattern is a practical solution only for very short codes, because the list of syndromes grows exponentially with $n - k$. Also, there is no direct mapping of syndromes into most likely error vectors, except for some limited subsets. To get practical error-correcting algorithms it usually is necessary to select parity check codes with specialized structure. The structure of cyclic codes has proved to be the most successful in developing practical decoding algorithms. The basic properties of cyclic codes are discussed in the next section.

3.3　Cyclic Block Codes

We saw that general block parity check codes are conveniently described in terms of vectors and linear algebra operations. Each symbol of the code is usually binary, but occasionally may be a binary r-tuple, which can be thought of as members of $GF(2^r)$. Usually, only the simple modulo-2 operations of $GF(2)$ are involved. Cyclic codes, however, depend heavily on the properties of finite fields and polynomial algebra. Thus, some properties of finite fields need to be discussed first.

3.3.1   Fields (and Rings)

A field is a special kind of ring. A ring R is a set of elements and two operations, satisfying the following axioms. The operations are denoted as addition $(+)$ and multiplication $(*)$ for convenience, but they could have other meanings. The elements a, b, and c referred to in the statements are not necessarily distinct.

1. The set R is an Abelian group under addition.
2. For any $a, b \in R$, $a * b \in R$.
3. For any $a, b, c \in R$, $a * (b + c) = a * b + a * c$ and $(b + c) * a = b * a + c * a$ (the distributive law).

A ring is called commutative if, for any $a, b \in R$, $a * b = b * a$.

A ring always has an additive identity, called 0, based on property 1. The single element 0, actually, is a trivial example of a ring with only one element. A ring may or may not contain a multiplicative identity and an element of a ring does not necessarily have a multiplicative inverse.

Having a multiplicative inverse is very important for many applications, particularly when there is a need to solve equations. A field has this desirable property.

A **finite field** $GF(q)$ is a commutative ring of q elements that contains a multiplicative identity and contains a multiplicative inverse of every nonzero element. The smallest value of q is 2, in which case the field is ordinary modulo-2 arithmetic with the two elements 0 and 1. Following are some properties of finite fields. Additional properties will be presented during the cyclic code discussion.

1. A $GF(q)$ exists iff q is a power of a prime.
2. the $q - 1$ nonzero elements form an Abelian group under multiplication.
3. If q is a prime, the field structure is isomorphic to the arithmetic of integers modulo q.
4. If q is a power of a prime p, $q = p^r$, then the field structure is isomorphic to the operations modulo an irreducible polynomial over $GF(p)$ of degree r. "Polynomial over $GF(p)$" means the coefficients must be in $GF(p)$.
5. A primitive element a of a field is an element such that by successive multiplications of a by itself (powers of a) all the nonzero elements of the field are generated. It can be proved that every field contains at least one primitive element.
6. The order of a nonzero field element is the smallest number of times it can be multiplied by itself to yield 1. A primitive element is of order $q - 1$. The order of a nonzero element in general must be a factor of $q - 1$. This latter property follows from the fact that an element and its powers form a subgroup of the multiplicative group of $q - 1$ elements.

As an example of a field with a prime number of elements, consider integers modulo 5. The elements are $0, 1, 2, 3, 4$. The reader can verify that these operations satisfy the necessary conditions for a field by observing the following addition and multiplication tables:

+	0	1	2	3	4		*	0	1	2	3	4
0	0	1	2	3	4		0	0	0	0	0	0
1	1	2	3	4	0		1	0	1	2	3	4
2	2	3	4	0	1		2	0	2	4	1	3
3	3	4	0	1	2		3	0	3	1	4	2
4	4	0	1	2	3		4	0	4	3	2	1

By considering the subset of nonzero elements in the multiplication table, it is readily seen that they form an Abelian group under multiplication. The element 3 is a primitive element, because $3 * 3 = 3^2 = 4, 3^3 = 2, 3^4 = 1$. Also, 2 is primitive. The element 4 is of order 2, since $4^2 = 3^4 = 1$.

As an illustration of a field with a non-prime number of elements, consider $q = 4$. In this case $p = 2, r = 2$. The irreducible polynomial used in describing the field operations must be of degree $r = 2$, and its coefficients must be the binary elements of $GF(p) = GF(2)$. The only such polynomial is $1 + X + X^2$. The four elements, written as polynomials, are: $0, 1, X, 1 + X$. To reduce $f(X)$ modulo $p(X)$, one divides $f(X)$ by $p(X)$ and takes the remainder. Thus $X * (X + 1) = 1 * (1 + X + X^2) + 1$, and the remainder is 1. Another example is $X * X = 1 * (1 + X + X^2) + X + 1$, and the remainder is $X + 1$.

In the example, both X and $X + 1$ are primitive elements. Whenever $q - 1$ is prime, all nonzero elements except 1 are primitive, since the order of a nonzero element must be a factor of $q - 1$. For doing multiplication, it is convenient to write elements as powers of a primitive element, whereas for doing addition the polynomial representation is more convenient. For this reason a tabulation often lists the elements both ways, as shown next for this example.

Polynomial Element	Power of X
0	not applicable
1	0 or 3
X	1
$1 + X$	2

3.3.2   Finite Field Operations with Feedback Shift Registers

Feedback shift registers are a useful aid in understanding field operations. Multiplying by X can be represented by a single shift; this is illustrated in Figure 3.1 for $GF(4)$. Basically, whenever we have an X^2, it needs to get replaced by $X + 1$ based on the modulo $X^2 + X + 1$ rule. This is what the circuit does.

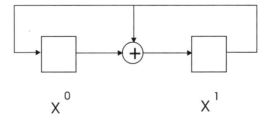

Figure 3.1: Multiplying by X in $GF(4)$.

The general format for multiplying by X in $GF(2^r)$ with $p(X) = 1 + p_1X + \cdots + p_{r-1}X^{r-1} + X^r$ is as shown in Figure 3.2.

When X is a primitive element, shifting the feedback shift register with an initial entry of X generates all the nonzero field elements. It can be shown that for any field it is possible to find an irreducible polynomial that makes X the primitive element. Such a polynomial is known as a primitive polynomial.

3.3.3 Definition and Basic Properties of Cyclic Codes

In general, a sequence of n code symbols can be represented either by an n-dimensional vector or by a polynomial of degree $< n$. That is, the n-tuple or n-dimensional vector $(c_0, c_1, \ldots, c_{n-1})$ can be represented as the polynomial:

$$c(X) = c_0 + c_1X + \cdots + c_{n-1}X^{n-1}. \tag{3.8}$$

A cyclic code is a parity check code for which every cyclic shift of a code word is a code word. A one-step right cyclic shift of $c(X)$ can be written as $Xc(X)$ modulo $X^n - 1$. The effect of modulo $X^n - 1$ is to replace X^n by 1 in $Xc(X)$; thus the former leading (rightmost) X^{n-1} term that would become X^n is replaced by X^0, which brings it to the leftmost position.

It can be shown that a (n, k) cyclic code with symbols in $GF(q)$ has a unique lowest degree polynomial code word $g(X)$, called the *generator polynomial*, with the following properties:

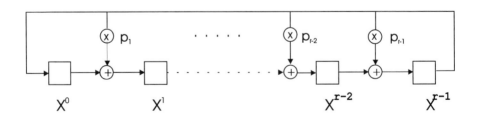

Figure 3.2: Multiplying by X in $GF(2^r)$.

1. the degree of $g(X)$ is $n - k$.
2. Every code word has $g(X)$ as a factor, and any polynomial over $GF(q)$ in the form $a(X)g(X)$, where the degree of $a(X) < k$, is a code word.
3. $g(X)$ is a factor of $X^n - 1$.
4. The code words $g(X), Xg(X), X^2g(X), \ldots, X^{k-1}g(X)$ form a linearly independent set of k code words that as vectors span the space of code words. These code words as n-tuples could be used as the rows of a (generally nonsystematic) generator matrix for the code.

Also, any $g(X)$ over $GF(q)$ that satisfies properties 1 and 3 generates a (n, k) cyclic code.

The use of a generator polynomial rather than a generator matrix greatly simplifies encoding and decoding operations.

3.3.4 Cyclic Codes for Pure Error Detection

Although encoding and error detection are simple even for general parity check codes, high-speed communication sometimes demands even simpler operations. With cyclic codes, encoding and error detection can be realized by very simple feedback shift register techniques.

Consider first the encoding operation. Usually systematic coding is preferred. The basic idea is to let the data symbols be the coefficients of the high degree part of the code polynomial, and then pick the check part so that the resulting polynomial has $g(X)$ as a factor. Let

$$d(X) = d_0 + d_1X + \cdots + d_{k-1}X^{k-1} \tag{3.9}$$

be the data written in polynomial form and take $X^{n-k}d(X)$ to shift it into the highest degree positions. Compute a check part $r(X)$ as follows:

$$r(X) = \text{remainder}\{X^{n-k}d(X)/g(X)\}. \tag{3.10}$$

This remainder has degree $< n - k$. Then we can form the code word

$$c(X) = X^{n-k}d(X) + r(X). \tag{3.11}$$

$c(X)$ contains $g(X)$ as a factor because the remainder on dividing by $g(X)$ would be zero. Computation of $r(X)$ is accomplished simply by feeding the data into a feedback shift register whose feedback connections are according to the coefficients of $g(X)$. Consider for example $n = 15$, $k = 11$, and $g(X) = 1 + X + X^4$. Then the division to form $p(X)$ can be accomplished by the circuit shown in Figure 3.3.

The 11 data bits are shifted into the register, and at the same time they are transmitted. As soon as all 11 data bits have been shifted in, the register will contain $r(X)$. Then, the feedback connection should be broken, and the check bits are sent out for transmission.

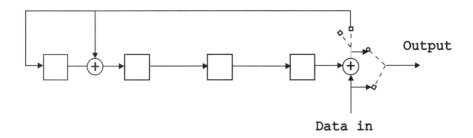

Figure 3.3: Circuit for systematic encoding of a (15, 11) cyclic code.

It should be noted that the same division process can be used with this $g(X)$ for any n and k for which $n - k = 4$. If $k < 11$, the effect would be as if the first $11 - k$ data symbols were always zero by convention; thus these first $11 - k$ symbols need not be transmitted or used for encoding. The division also can be done for $k > 11$, correspondingly $n > 15$. However, it usually is not desirable to have n greater than the length of the shortest length cyclic code having $g(X)$ as generator polynomial, because then some double-error patterns would not be detected: namely those of the form $X^i(X^n + 1)$, since $g(X)$ is a factor of $X^n + 1$.

Standard generator polynomials called "cyclic redundancy check" polynomials have been adapted for the purpose of checking data frames of variable size. Most commonly they are chosen of degrees 16 or 32.

There is one caution to be noted in using cyclic codes for error detection. A time shift error can easily result in an undetected error. Let $c(X)$ be a code word. If the decoder judged the code block to be timed one unit later, what appears to be the power positions $n - 1, \ldots, 0$, would actually be the positions $n - 2, \ldots, 0, (-1)$. Thus $g(X)$ would divide into $Xc(X) - X^n c_{n-1} + a_{-1}$, where a_{-1} represents a sample one unit later that is outside the code block. If it happens that $c_{n-1} = a_{-1}$, the reception will check, but actually the data are displaced and also the leading data position c_{n-1} is lost. Timing errors are not unusual, so this source of undetected error would be of concern.

A solution is to add a pseudorandom but known pattern $m(X)$ to all or part of the code word prior to transmission. This pattern should be designed so as not to correlate well with its shifts. Then the receiver can subtract $m(X)$ prior to decoding. With the previous shift error, the apparent reception is $Xc(X) + Xm(X) - X^n(c_{n-1} + m_{n-1}) + a_{-1}$. Even if $c_{n-1} = a_{-1}$, subtracting $m(X)$ will leave a term, added to the falsely cyclically shifted code word, of $(X - 1)m(X) - X^n m_{n-1}$, which can be designed by choice of $m(X)$ not to be divisible by $g(X)$. Thus the result will be very unlikely an undetected error.

3.3.5 Cyclic Code Systematic Generator Matrix

Because the code generation makes it convenient to transmit the data digits first (while the checks are being computed) and the data digits are the highest-degree terms in the polynomial, the convention is that the transmission order proceeds from highest-degree to lowest-degree term in the code polynomial. Since the generator matrix columns are being numbered from 0 to $n - 1$, the data positions should appear on the right in systematic form. Thus the systematic generator matrix form (3.2b) will be used for cyclic codes. Incidentally, because cyclic shifts of code words are code words, any $n - k$ consecutive positions could serve as the data positions; this property is not true for parity check codes in general.

It is useful to observe that the encoding circuit is a linear system. Thus the response to a sequence of input data is the sum of its responses to each 1 in the input data sequence. We can use this idea to build up a systematic form generator matrix for this code. Consider for the (15, 11) code example the system response to ten zeros followed by a single data 1 in the last, eleventh, position. The data sequence is written 10000000000, because the high degree right terms are sent first. This 1 will create the response 1100 in the register (refer to Figure 3.3), because this is where the feedback links place the 1. Thus 110010000000000 is a code word (high degree on the right), and it can be also used as the first row of the generator matrix. Suppose the data were 01000000000. Then the single 1 would come in next-to-last and there would be a shift of the register, yielding 0110 as final output. To get the response to a 1 in the ninth time position (X^2 polynomial position), shift one more time, and get output 0011. For a 1 in the eighth position, shift another time; this time there is a feedback, and the result 1101. Thus, the successive check position patterns are gotten by multiplying by X modulo $1 + X + X^4$. Using these results to write in rows of a generator matrix, from top row to bottom, we obtain:

$$G = \begin{bmatrix} 1100 & 10000000000 \\ 0110 & 01000000000 \\ 0011 & 00100000000 \\ 1101 & 00010000000 \\ 1010 & 00001000000 \\ 0101 & 00000100000 \\ 1110 & 00000010000 \\ 0111 & 00000001000 \\ 1111 & 00000000100 \\ 1011 & 00000000010 \\ 1001 & 00000000001 \end{bmatrix} \qquad (3.12)$$

3.3.6   Some Simple–Error Correction Circuits

In general, error correction is rather complex. However, single-error correction and burst-error correction are two cases where error correction is simple, especially with cyclic codes.

Single-Error Correction   Consider a (7, 4) single-error-correcting cyclic code with $g(X) = 1 + X + X^3$. Consider the response of the syndrome computing circuit in

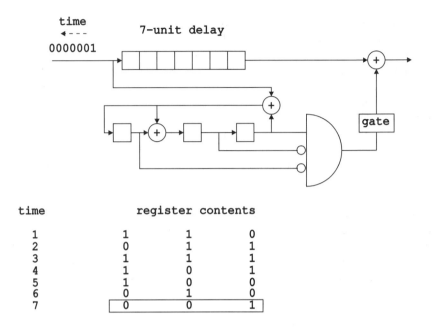

Figure 3.4: A simple single-error-correcting circuit.

Figure 3.4 to a single error in the X^6 position, which is the first position arriving in time. Note that in the 7th shift, which is when all 7 bits have entered the buffer, the response 001 appears in the feedback circuit. The response to any other single error among the 7 would give one of the other six nonzero patterns listed. If these outputs were fed to the three-input and gate with two inverters as shown, an output 1 from the and gate could automatically correct this error in the X^6 position, while a single error in one of the other positions would not have this effect. Note that the code word itself would give zero response at this point. If the error were instead in the X^5 position, the response would be delayed one unit of time, so 001 would appear one unit of time later, just in time to correct that error. Similarly, any single error would produce 001 response exactly at the time it was departing from the delay buffer. Thus this simple circuit would correct any single error.

This technique would work on any cyclic code that has single-error correction ability. This particular code does not have any error-detecting ability when used as a single-error-correcting code, but if the cyclic code was one with additional error detection capability, error detection would occur on finding a nonzero syndrome that never produced a 1 at the and gate output.

3.3.7 Burst Error Correction and Error Trapping

Another type of decoding that is simple is when errors are clustered in a "burst." A burst in a block code can be defined as the number of positions from the first error position, inclusive through the last error position. Because of the nature of cyclic codes, the term "cyclic burst" is also defined. If the n positions are arranged in a circle, as shown in Figure 3.5, a cyclic burst of length b is a pattern of errors where the shortest arc including all the errors covers b positions. This includes patterns that are partly at the beginning and partly at the end of the block, which are less likely physically but are easily corrected along with the ordinary bursts, due to the cyclic symmetry of the codes.

The number of bursts of length b or less for a binary code can be shown to be $(n - b + 2)2^{b-1}$. A code can correct all bursts of length b or less if all such bursts lie in different cosets, which is equivalent to saying that no two such bursts add to a code word. A key bound on the burst error correcting capability is $b \le (n - k)/2$.

The error correction procedure is referred to as *error trapping* or *burst trapping*. It was mentioned in Section 3.2 that if the parity check matrix has an identity submatrix and the errors are in the $n - k$ positions correponding to the identity submatrix position, the syndrome will look like the error pattern. Analogously, for cyclic codes, it can be shown that, if the errors are all in a span of $n - k$ consecutive positions, the error pattern can be revealed by one of n shifts of a syndrome in the feedback shift register.

Consider the circuit shown in Figure 3.6. After n symbols n bits have been shifted in, it can be shown that the feedback shift register contains $\mathrm{rem}\{X^{n-k}e(X)/g(X)\}$.

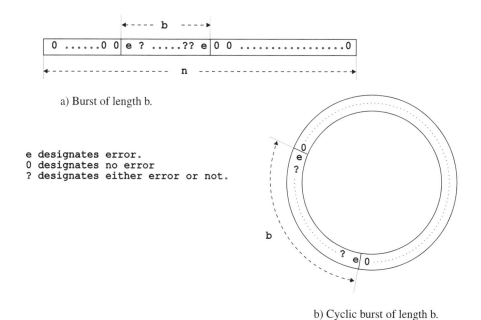

a) Burst of length b.

e designates error.
0 designates no error
? designates either error or not.

b) Cyclic burst of length b.

Figure 3.5: Distinction between a burst and a cyclic burst.

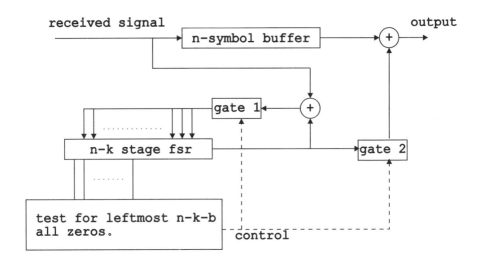

Figure 3.6: A burst-error-correcting circuit.

Suppose

$$e(X) = e_{n-1}X^{n-1} + \cdots + e_kX^k. \tag{3.13}$$

$$\text{rem}\{X^{n-k}(e_{n-1}X^{n-1} + \cdots + e_kX^k)/g(X)\}$$
$$= \text{rem}\{X^n(e_{n-1}X^{n-k-1} + \cdots + e_kX^0)/g(X)\}$$
$$= \text{rem}\{(e_{n-1}X^{n-k-1} + \cdots + e_kX^0)/g(X)\}$$
$$= e_{n-1}X^{n-k-1} + \cdots + e_kX^0. \tag{3.14}$$

The last two steps in (3.14) follow because $\text{rem}\{X^n/g(X)\} = 1$ and $g(X)$ is of degree $n - k$. Thus the register content is the same as the error pattern. If this pattern is a burst of length b or less and the code was designed to correct all bursts of length b or less, an error pattern of the correctible class has been found. If there is a burst of length b or less in a different range, the syndrome at this point will be nonzero but will not look like a burst of length b or less (this can be proved). Recall that the feedback register contents at that point depend only on the response to the error pattern. If the error pattern started i positions later, then if we shift the feedback shift register i positions, its response value will be as if there was a similar error pattern i positions earlier. Thus, the method is to continue shifting with no further input until a burst of length b or less is found or all possible burst positions are covered. To remove the complexity of counting the burst length at each shift, we take advantage of the fact that if the burst is of length b or less, it will eventually appear solely in the rightmost b positions. Thus we need only to test for zero in all the $n - k - b$ leftmost positions.

When a burst in the correctible set is found, the feedback gate 1 is blocked, and the previously blocked error correction gate 2 is opened, so that the discovered pattern is added to the delayed reception, which corrects all the errors. The buffer can be shortened to k bits if it is only required to correct errors in the data positions. There is an additional complication if it is desired to correct cyclic bursts that are not regular bursts, but we will not go into this case.

The error trapping principle is not restricted just to burst error correction. Any error pattern whose shortest cyclic span from first error through last error can be trapped by the shifting and testing process. As long as the set of error patterns we are permitted to correct has no two in the same coset (i.e. same syndrome), any error pattern in the set that gets trapped can be corrected with the assurance no other error pattern in the correctible set could have occurred. For example, if the code is capable of correcting all single and double errors and is of rate less than $1/2$ ($n - k > k$), any single or double error that occurs will be trapped and correctly identified in one of the shifts. This is because for $n - k > k$ a cyclic span of length $n - k$ always can be found that encompasses any two specified positions.

3.4   BCH Cyclic Codes

Cyclic codes provide very simple correction of single errors or error patterns that can be trapped. General cyclic codes do not provide simple error correction of all patterns of numbers of errors up to the guaranteed capability t_G for $t_G > 1$, where t_G is the largest integer for which $2t_G < d_{min}$. The class of BCH cyclic codes has the property of simplifying the decoding up to t_G or fewer errors, $t_G > 1$.

Since all code polynomials of a cyclic code have $g(X)$ as a factor, they also must have all roots of $g(X)$. Thus, another way of checking for errors is to see if a received polynomial has the roots of $g(X)$. Furthermore, it is shown that t_G can be designed into the code simply by specifying which roots of a certain field must be contained in $g(X)$.

Primitive BCH codes have block length $q^m - 1$. They are constructed in terms of roots chosen from $GF(q^m)$. Select a primitive element α from that field. Then a code is derived that has minimum distance at least $2t + 1$, and thus can correct all patterns of t or fewer errors, by constructing a $g(X)$ that is the lowest-degree polynomial over $GF(q)$ that has as roots: $\alpha, \alpha^2, \alpha^3, \ldots, \alpha^{2t}$. The constraint $2t < q^m - 1$ is necessary. Sometimes the minimum distance is greater than $2t + 1$; $2t + 1$ is called the designed distance.

The generator polynomial $g(X)$ is constructed from the minimal polynomials for each of the specified roots by taking the least common multiple. The minimal polynomial of a field element of $GF(q^m)$ is the lowest-degree polynomial over $GF(q)$ that has the element as a root.

Following is a list of some of the BCH codes. A more complete list as well as a more detailed explanation of how to find $g(X)$ is given, for example, in [LIN83].

n	k	t
15	11	1
	7	2
	5	3
31	21	2
	16	3
63	45	3
	39	4
	36	5
127	106	3
	99	4
	85	6
	78	7
	71	9

3.4.1 Decoding Complexity of BCH Codes

Decoding of BCH codes is rather complicated to explain. Details will not be given here. Basically, the following steps are involved:

1. Find the syndrome components by evaluating the received polynomial at the $2t$ powers of α that are supposed to be roots of $g(X)$.
2. Find what is called an error-locating polynomial.
3. Find the roots of the error-locating polynomial, which allows the error locations to be identified.
4. If the code is binary, the errors have been found, but if the code is not binary an additional step is needed to find the error values.

Although complex to describe, implementation is feasible. The most time-consuming part would be the equivalent of a matrix inversion, which normally takes an order of t^3 operations. However, algorithms using symmetries in the matrix reduce the number to order of t^2. Special purpose chips with parallel and pipelined computation allow for fast real-time decoding.

3.4.2 Error-Correcting Limitations of BCH Codes

For binary codes, it is found that correction of all patterns of up to t errors requires at most mt check bits, though for large t it often requires close to this bound. If the objective is to correct at least a fixed fraction of the errors for longer and longer codes, $t/n \cong f$, we note the following: $n = 2^m - 1 \cong 2^m$

$$R \cong (n - mt)/n \cong 1 - mf \cong 1 - f * \log_2 n. \tag{3.15}$$

Thus the bound suggests that R goes down as n increases. Actual calculation of number of check symbols has shown that R does decrease toward zero as n increases, but it starts going down at values of n normally beyond the range of practical interest.

3.5 Reed-Solomon Codes

BCH codes of length $q^m - 1$ normally have symbols over $GF(q)$, and most commonly $q = 2$. Reed-Solomon codes are a special kind of BCH code where the symbols and thus the code polynomials are over $GF(q^m)$, the same as the field of roots. Then, specifying that the zeros of $g(X)$ be the lowest-degree polynomial with roots $\alpha, \alpha^2, \alpha^3, \ldots, \alpha^{2t}$ means that one can write directly that

$$g(X) = (X - \alpha)(X - \alpha^2)(X - \alpha^3) \cdots (X - \alpha^{2t}), \qquad (3.16)$$

which is of degree $n - k = 2t$. Thus the code minimum distance is $2t + 1 = n - k + 1$, which is the greatest minimum distance that any (n, k) code can have. A code with minimum distance $n - k + 1$ is called a maximum distance code. Thus the codes are powerful and also can be decoded in the same way BCH codes are decoded. Reed-Solomon codes are used in a variety of applications, and Reed-Solomon decoder chips are available.

As an example, consider $q = 2$, $m = 4$, $t = 1$. The code can correct any single-erroneous 4-bit block.

$$g(X) = (X - \alpha)(X - \alpha^2) = X^2 + (\alpha + \alpha^2)X + \alpha^3. \qquad (3.17)$$

Thus it is a $(15, 13)$ cyclic code with 16-ary symbols. In terms of binary symbols it would be a $(60, 52)$ code. However, the individual symbols to be corrected or not are in 4-bit units. A symbol is counted as one symbol error independent of whether 1, 2, 3, or all 4 of its bits are in error.

To see what $(\alpha + \alpha^2)$ is we need to write the elements of $GF(16)$ as polynomials modulo $D^4 + D + 1$. We use a different letter than X to prevent confusion.

Power of α	Polynomial
1	D
2	D^2
3	D^3
4	$D + 1$
5	$D^2 + D$
6	$D^3 + D^2$
7	$D^3 + D + 1$
8	$D^2 + 1$
9	$D^3 + D$
10	$D^2 + D + 1$
12	$D^3 + D^2 + D + 1$
13	$D^3 + D^2 + 1$
14	$D^3 + 1$
15	1

From the table, we see that $(\alpha + \alpha^2) = \alpha^5$. As a binary sequence with high powers to the **right** (both for X and D), the code word $g(X)$ is

$$0001, 0110, 1000, 0000, 0000, 0000, 0000, 0000,$$
$$0000, 0000, 0000, 0000, 0000, 0000, 0000.$$

The code word $Dg(X)$ is

$$1100, 0011, 0100, 0000, 0000, 0000, 0000, 0000,$$
$$0000, 0000, 0000, 0000, 0000, 0000, 0000.$$

The code word $XDg(X)$ is

$$0000, 1100, 0011, 0100, 0000, 0000, 0000, 0000,$$
$$0000, 0000, 0000, 0000, 0000, 0000, 0000.$$

3.6   Concatenated Codes

One of the most important tools for correcting large numbers of errors in a long block length is to use two stages of coding/decoding. The first stage uses short block codes; alternatively, it could use simple convolutional codes, as will be described in Chapter 4. The short codes should be designed to correct successfully most of the time, but when they fail a cluster of errors is left for the second stage to correct. The first-stage codes are called the *inner codes*, and the second-stage codes are called *outer codes*. This two-stage structure is sometimes referred to as *concatenated codes*, or sometimes as *nested codes*.

Reed-Solomon codes are ideal as outer codes in concatenated coding. With a block inner binary code, the data bits of an inner code block can constitute one symbol of the outer code. Then, if an inner code decodes incorrectly, there usually are many bit errors, but this appears as only one symbol error to the outer Reed-Solomon code.

Erasures can arise if the inner code is used for error detection instead of or in addition to error correction. With error detection, the inner code could report an erasure to the outer code. With error correction, it could attempt to correct the symbol, and report the symbol decision, possibly erroneous, to the outer code. Erasures could occur in other ways. For example, recognition of a strong noise burst could lead the decoder to decide to consider a symbol received during the burst as an erasure; as another example, if a numbered packet of data constituted a symbol and such a packet were lost, it could be considered an erasure.

Reed-Solomon codes can be used to fill in erasures. Since the minimum distance is $2t + 1$, up to $2t$ erasures can be filled in if the unerased symbols are all error-free. Thus all the data can be derived from any $n - 2t$ of the symbols. Since $2t$ also is the number of check symbols and $n - 2t$ is the number of data symbols, it is impossible for any decoder to uniquely derive the data given less than $n - 2t$ symbols. In this respect also, the Reed-Solomon code is the best possible. In terms of the packet transmission example cited above, if p redundant packets were sent, derived by a Reed-Solomon code, the destination could tolerate up to any p lost packets and still reconstruct the data correctly.

The condition that the code length be $q^m - 1$ is not as restrictive as it sounds. Any number of data symbols can be deleted from the code (i.e., defined to be always 0) without destroying the maximum distance property, which depends only on the number of check symbols. Also, if i check symbols are deleted, called puncturing of the code, the mimimum distance is reduced by i, but the resulting punctured code remains a maximum minimum distance code.

3.7 Majority Logic Decoding

Majority logic decoding is a scheme where one is able to decode one data bit at a time. The simplest version applies to codes that are said to be one-step majority logic decodable. For these codes a set of J parity equations are found in which the bit position being decided appears in all J parity equations, while all other bit positions appear in at most one of the J equations. Then the bit will be decided correctly if $\lfloor J/2 \rfloor$ or fewer errors are present. If J is even, such as $J = 4$, let the rule be to change the bit only if a clear majority of the equations disagree. For $J = 4$ this will always work if there are two or fewer errors, because if the bit is wrong there will be only one other error; then three of the four equations will disagree with the bit and the erroneous bit will be changed. If the bit is correct, at worst two of the four equations will disagree, and the bit will not be changed. If J is odd, it is obvious that correct decisions will be made if $\lfloor J/2 \rfloor$ or fewer errors are present. Sometimes cases of greater numbers of errors can be corrected, but this cannot be guaranteed.

The maximum value of J is $d_{min} - 1$, since the guaranteed error-correcting capability of a block code cannot exceed $\lfloor (d_{min} - 1)/2 \rfloor$. However, only a limited class of codes permit $J = d_{min} - 1$.

If the code is cyclic, majority logic decoding is very easy to implement, because basically the same equations, shifted, can be used for each bit in turn. As an illustration, consider a $(21, 11)$ cyclic code whose generator polynomial is

$$g(X) = 1 + X^2 + X^4 + X^6 + X^7 + X^{10}.$$

For this code, it is found that $J = 5$, and five equations, which are five members of the row space of H, are:

$$\begin{bmatrix} 0 \\ 0 \\ 0 \\ 0 \\ 0 \end{bmatrix} = \begin{bmatrix} 000000000100110000101 \\ 010000000001001100001 \\ 000010100000000010011 \\ 100001010000000001001 \\ 001100001010000000001 \end{bmatrix} \begin{bmatrix} r_0 & r_1 & \cdots & r_{20} \end{bmatrix}^T. \quad (3.18)$$

The rightmost position, 20, which is under test, appears in all five equations, whereas the other positions appear in just one equation each.

Figure 3.7 shows what is called a type II one-step majority logic circuit for this code. The received bits enter in the time order $r_{20} \cdots r_0$, as gate 1 passes and feedback

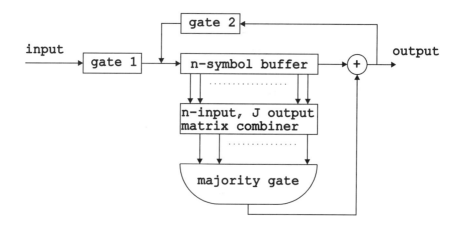

Figure 3.7: A type II one-step majority logic decoder.

gate 2 is blocked. Then the tests begin with gate 1 blocked and gate 2 passing. The first bit tested is r_{20}. If a majority of the outputs yield a 1, r_{20} is changed and the correction fed back to help in the remaining tests. Due to the cyclic code structure, cyclically shifting one step provides a majority rule testing of r_{19}, and further shifting tests and corrects errors provided there are no more than two errors. If there are more than two errors the decoding may or may not succeed.

One problem with majority length decoding is that codes suitable for the technique generally have poor minimum distance characteristics, which limits the number of errors the code can correct compared to the ideal. However, we will see in Section 3.11 that, as an outer code of a concatenated coding scheme, a code with a majority logic structure can have powerful error-correcting capability as well as simplicity.

3.8 Product Codes

Another useful code structure is that of two-dimensional, or *product*, codes. These are constructed as a two-dimensional array of $n_1 \times n_2$ symbols, usually binary symbols. There are $k_1 \times k_2$ data symbols, which can be thought of as a rectangular subset within the $n_1 \times n_2$ symbol array, as shown in Figure 3.8. Each column is a code word in the same (n_1, k_1) parity check code, and each row is a code word in the same (n_2, k_2) parity check code. It can readily be shown that the lower-right check positions that check both rows and columns are consistent with both codes.

The minimum distance of this resulting $(n_1 n_2, k_1 k_2)$ code is the product of the minimum distances of the row code and the column code. This usually is much lower than the minimum distance of most $(n_1 n_2, k_1 k_2)$ parity check codes that are not restricted to being of the product form. However, these codes have the capability of correcting many error patterns beyond the guaranteed error-correcting capability.

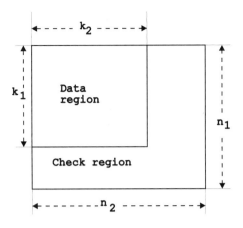

Figure 3.8: Product code array.

Also, as with concatenated codes, the decoding is simpler because it is broken up into stages with shorter component codes.

As an illustration, consider a case where the row and column codes are both single-error-correcting, with minimum distance of 3. The product code has a minimum distance of 9, and thus is guaranteed to be able to correct all cases of up to four errors. A popular way of decoding is to first correct all possible rows, and then all possible columns; sometimes additional stages of row and column correction can yield further correction. Consider the case of eight errors, as in Figure 3.9. In this case six of the errors are in one column. If the time order of transmission is column by column, this is like the phenomenon of an error burst. Single-error correction by rows, if done first, will correct six of the errors, which appear one per row. The row containing two errors may result in a third error being added if the syndrome for that

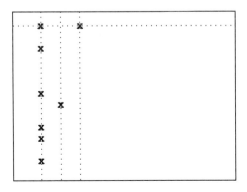

Figure 3.9: Example of eight correctible errors.

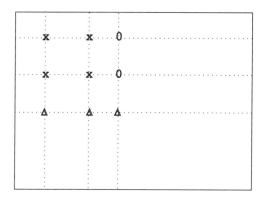

Figure 3.10: An example of false correction with four initial errors.

error pattern is the same as for some other single error, or may be left unchanged if it doesn't correspond to any single-error pattern. In either case, the columns will have at most one error each, and all two or three remaining errors will be corrected, resulting in correction of all eight errors.

Attempts to correct more than the guaranteed amount of errors can also lead to false apparent correction. With the row followed by column decoding procedure, this can even occur with only four errors, which is within the guaranteed correction capability; this is illustrated by the four-error pattern in Figure 3.10. The four errors, indicated by x, are on the corners of a rectangle, and say the positions happen to be where the two errors in a row happen to be two of the three nonzero positions of a weight-three row code word, and a similar event occurs for the two error positions in the column code. Then a row correction will add an error in each of two rows, indicated by a O. Then the column correction will add an error, indicated by a Δ, in each of the three now-erroneous columns. Now there are nine errors, but everything checks. More complex processing could remember the five places that errors were added, and compute that the other four positions could also have been changed to give the same result. Some methods have been developed that ensure success for any correction of errors up to the guaranteed bound [BLAH83]. They make use of erasures and memory of numbers of errors corrected during the row-column correction process.

3.8.1 Burst Correction for Product Codes

Suppose the symbols are transmitted column by column. Suppose the row codes are single-error correcting. Then any burst of length n_1 or less can be corrected. This is because n_1 consecutive positions must all be in different rows. In addition, if the row codes can correct all bursts of length b or less, then physical bursts of length up to $b * n_1$ can be corrected, since these would appear as a burst of length at most b in each row.

Product codes where $n_1 = k_1$ (no column coding) and column-by-column transmission are referred to as interleaved codes. They have the objective of spreading out a burst of errors so that each row sees only one or a few errors. This can be a useful technique when it is known that errors are bursty but otherwise very rare.

Concatenated codes have a related, but somewhat different approach to handling bursts. A burst of errors causes only one or a few symbol errors to the outer code. A symbol error then is just one error to the symbol correcting code, no matter how many bit errors are in the symbol. The components of the symbol are not then ordinarily looked at individually in the outer correction stage, unlike in product codes. However, we will see in Section 3.9 that there is a hybrid nested/product code technique called vector symbol decoding, which can have simple and powerful correcting capability in some applications.

3.9 The Role of Error-Correcting Codes in Reliable Communication

It is useful at this point to take a look at the basic objectives and capabilities of error correction. Shannon's theory of communication provided the principal incentive in the search for practical error-correcting codes. Given the statistical laws on the random behavior of "noise" disturbances when sending symbols over a communication channel, one can compute a channel information capacity, and it would be possible to communicate with any degree of reliability at a rate less than channel capacity by use of a properly designed error-correcting code and an associated decoding rule. For example, given a binary symmetric channel with a bit error probability of 0.1, the channel capacity is .531 bits/symbol, and an error-correcting code at a rate somewhat less than this could be found that could reduce the bit error probability after decoding to, for example, 10^{-12}. The fallacy in relying on this in a real situation is in assuming the bit error probability always can be counted on as being 0.1. Maybe the channel really does behave as if the error probability is $\leq .1$ for 99.99% of the time, but if it is extra noisy over a code block length as often as 10^{-4} of the time (and it doesn't take much physical change to alter an error probability from .1 to, say .15), this destroys the hope of achieving 10^{-12} error probability for the designed code. One might try to use interleaving to spread the code out over a very long period so as to smooth the statistics, but the long-term statistics may even be less reliable. A past history of duration T has about T/τ intervals of duration τ. As τ increases, fewer past samples are available.

The conclusion is that coding alone cannot be depended on to achieve extremely high reliability over a noisy channel in an efficient manner; this is because of the uncertainty of underlying statistics. It is only with the help of error detection and retransmission that the extremely high reliability promised by Shannon's theorems can be achieved. Error detection is more robust than error correction; with say 30 or more parity bits added exclusively for error detection, the chance of undetected error can be made negligible regardless of the level of noise. However, pure error detection with retransmission is very inefficient over a noisy channel for which most received blocks have errors. Thus error correction also is needed to improve efficiency so that, combined with error detection/retransmission, error rates like 10^{-12} can be achieved efficiently over realistic noisy channels.

Error correction and error detection can be designed somewhat independently. About 30–40 check bits provide almost foolproof error detection, essentially independent of how many data bits they are checking. These check bits do not necessarily have to be devoted to a single code block of the error correcting code. They could provide error detection over many blocks; the amount of data needing retransmission on error detection is whatever amount of data is being checked. The error correction task is to do as much error correction as possible; the error detection stage will then follow to see if the correction was done right.

Sometimes there is a situation where a return channel is not available. This is not a good situation if highly reliable communication is desired. It is intuitively obvious that some form of return acknowledgment is necessary to have a high confidence that the data were received correctly. Confidence in correct reception cannot exceed confidence that the transmitted rate was less than the channel capacity that was prevalent during transmission. This confidence will not be high if the channel is noisy; this is in addition to uncertainties about things like whether the receiver was turned on or functioning properly.

Attempts to have high confidence of success without a return signal require an inefficient worst-case strategy. Suppose it is desired to send data in a time interval of approximately T seconds, and a history of one million most recent T-second intervals of channel intervals is available. Ignoring the additional uncertainty as to whether the channel will behave in the future as it did in the past, if we desired a failure rate of less than 10^{-6}, we would choose a rate of transmission that was lower than any rate that would have failed in any of the one million past history intervals; this is likely to be a rate far below the average.

3.10   Decoding Beyond Guaranteed Error Correction Bounds

The argument of Section 3.9 indicates that error correction should strive to correct as much as possible within the limits of computational complexity. Separate error detection bits will check to see if the correction is done right. A code whose minimum Hamming distance is d_H is guaranteed capable of correcting any arrangement of up to $\lfloor (d_H - 1)/2 \rfloor = t$ errors. Much emphasis in coding has been on the guaranteed ability to correct all cases of up to t errors, and to seek codes with the largest possible d_H, subject to complexity constraints. However, it often is worthwhile to decode with errors substantially exceeding the guaranteed bound. Also, it is found that, once it is decided to do corrections beyond the guaranteed correction limit, it becomes less important for a code to have the largest possible d_H. This is especially true when the symbols of the code are nonbinary.

A clue to the usefulness of decoding beyond the guaranteed bound is the fact used to prove Shannon's noisy channel coding theorem that codes chosen at random can be used to achieve low error probability at any rate below channel capacity. Let us look at the minimum Hamming distance for a randomly-chosen binary parity check code. Let $N(w)$ be the average number of code words of weight w over all choices of parity check codes. It is shown in [METZ60] using simple combinational arguments and Stirling's approximation that

$$N(w) = 2^{n[R-(1-h(\frac{w}{n}))]} \tag{3.19}$$

where n is the code length, R is the code rate in bits/symbol, and $h(x) = -x\log_2 x - (1-x)\log_2(1-x)$.

Consider $w = np$. Then (3.19) becomes

$$N(np) = 2^{n[R-C]} \tag{3.20}$$

where C is the binary channel capacity. Since $R < C$, $N(np) < 1$, so very few codes have a minimum distance $t_H \geq np$. But the guaranteed error probability is $< t_H/2$, which for most codes is thus less than *half* of np, the average number of errors! Yet, for $R < C$ and large enough n, most codes can correct most cases of np errors. Thus most binary codes can correct most errors up to more than twice their guaranteed error-correcting capability.

3.10.1 Hamming Distance in Nonbinary Codes

In binary codes, if two code words, A and B, differ in a particular symbol, an error in that symbol when word A is sent will cause that received symbol to agree with B rather than A. If A and B differ in d positions, errors in a majority of these d positions will bring the received signal closer to B than to A, which is likely to lead to an erroneous decoding. If the symbols are members of a large alphabet, an error in one of the positions where A and B differ rarely will result in the symbol agreeing with B. The probability that a majority of the d positions will be changed due to errors from agreeing with A to agreeing with B is much rarer still. Thus, the chance of an error into a particular other word is very small even if it is fairly close in Hamming distance; this encourages consideration of correcting beyond the bound. Actually, Hamming distance between code words is much larger for codes with nonbinary symbols, since two code words chosen at random will differ in most of their symbol values, rather than about one-half in the binary case.

3.10.2 Decoding Beyond the Guaranteed Bound
for Concatenated Codes

We have seen that concatenated codes are very useful. For the outer code of a concatenated code, the basic symbol often consists of a large number, say r, of bits.

These basic symbols can be thought of either as r-bit vectors or $GF(2^r)$ field elements. Reed-Solomon codes are popular as outer codes because they are maximum distance codes. However, we will see that high minimum distance is not really very important for nonbinary codes. What is important is a not too complex method of finding the likely errors. The error detection stage will detect any false decoding.

Nonbinary symbol concatenated codes involve rather large amounts of data. The trend is toward communication and processing of larger amounts of data than in the past, and ability to buffer and store large amounts of data has increased rapidly. Also, it is in large bulk data transfer that efficiency is most important. If one has only a few bits to send, being efficient is not very important in terms of system loading, while transmission of many bits is important to system efficiency. Thus the trend should be to use longer codes than in the past, as long as the decoding can be done in a sufficiently simple manner.

If minimum distance doesn't set the limit on error correction for nonbinary codes, then we may ask what does set the limit. This can readily be answered, asymptotically, by some simple random coding arguments. Suppose there are t actual symbol errors. Can we estimate the probability that the received sequence is closer to some wrong word than to the correct word?

Suppose we have an (n, k) block code, and Q is the size of the symbol alphabet. Suppose for now that the Q^k code words are selected at random without regard to whether we have a linear code. Let V_t be the number of points in a "sphere" of radius t. Then the probability that any of the other $Q^k - 1$ other randomly chosen code words are within t of the received sequence is upper bounded by

$$P = V_t * \frac{Q^k}{Q^n} = V_t * Q^{-(n-k)} \tag{3.21}$$

Now, for Q large,

$$V_t = \sum_{i=0}^{t} \binom{n}{i}(Q-1)^i \cong \binom{n}{t}Q^t \tag{3.22}$$

Equation (3.22) is a very good approximation because the t term is more than $Q - 1$ times as large as the $t - 1$ term, for $t < n/2$.

Substituting the (3.22) approximation in (3.21),

$$P = \binom{n}{t}Q^{-(n-k-t)}. \tag{3.23}$$

Stirling's approximation yields:

$$\binom{n}{t} \cong \sqrt{\frac{n}{2\pi t(n-t)}} * Q^{nh(t/n)\log 2(Q)}. \tag{3.24}$$

Substituting (3.24) in (3.23),

$$P \cong \sqrt{\frac{n}{2\pi t(n-t)}} * Q^{-n\left(1-k/n-t/n-\frac{h(t/n)}{\log_2 Q}\right)}. \tag{3.25}$$

For very large Q, the exponent in (3.25) is negative if t/n is slightly less than $1 - k/n$, the proportion of check symbols. For example, if $k/n = .7$, the exponent will be negative if t is as large as 90% of the number of check symbols, provided there are at least 28 bits in the nonbinary symbol. With concatenated codes, it would not be unusual for the symbols presented to the outer code to contain 28 or more bits. It is even possible the basic symbols could be whole data packets, which are 53 bytes or 424 bits each in ATM systems.

It is clearly futile to try to correct more errors than the number of check symbols, or up to any number d that makes the exponent in (3.25) positive, but the previous argument indicates that, even for codes chosen at random, it may be worthwhile attempting to correct a number of nonbinary symbol errors up to something close to the number of check symbols, which is close to twice the maximum minimum distance. Decoding beyond the guaranteed bound seems to be especially effective when errors tend to be clustered in bursts, which is a common phenomenon. Simple schemes exist for correcting most bursts of errors up to burst lengths well beyond the guaranteed correctibility. Product codes and majority logic codes often can correct numbers of errors well beyond the guaranteed bound, though this is partly because their minimum distance is low. In concatenated codes, the outer code sees errors in clusters, where a cluster represents an inner code block that has failed to be corrected by the inner code, and appears as an erroneous symbol to the outer code. An interesting recent technique called vector symbol decoding can enhance the ability of concatenated codes to correct errors well beyond the guaranteed bound.

3.11 Vector Symbol Decoding

In the prior section we saw the value of trying to correct beyond the guaranteed correctible bound. The question remains as to how this can be done in a relatively simple manner, since decoding complexity tends to increase rapidly with the amount of attempted error correction. Vector symbol decoding [METZ90] is an example of such a technique, and can work with a broad class of randomly chosen nonbinary symbol linear codes. Many of these codes have poor minimum distance, and thus very low guaranteed error-correcting capability, and yet, perhaps surprisingly, have a probability of decoding success that usually exceeds that of maximum distance codes restricted to decoding only up to the guaranteed number of vector symbol errors.

In a (n, k) code designed for vector symbol decoding, the symbols are r-dimensional (usually binary) component vectors, but the parity check matrix is usually binary. The code structure basically is the same as for r-fold interleaved (n, k) codes. If there is an inner (n_1, r) code for each r-bit vector component, the structure is just like a (nn_1, kr) product code, where the column code is (n, k) and the row code is (n_1, r). Any (n, k) parity check code can be chosen for the column code, also called the outer code. However, the $n_1 - r$ columns are discarded prior to outer code decoding. There is a general decoding technique that will work about equally simply for any allowable choice, although some code structures can allow further simplification in decoding.

3.11.1   The Outer Code Structure

Let H be a $(n - k) \times n$ parity check matrix of a binary parity check block code, and consider a (n, k) code of n r-bit code symbols consisting of all code words that satisfy the parity equations:

$$
\begin{bmatrix} 0 \end{bmatrix} = \begin{bmatrix} H \end{bmatrix} \begin{bmatrix} \dots \mathbf{v}_1 \dots \\ \dots \mathbf{v}_2 \dots \\ \vdots \\ \dots \mathbf{v}_n \dots \end{bmatrix} \tag{3.26}
$$

$$(n - k) \times r \qquad (n - k) \times n \qquad n \times r$$

where $\dots \mathbf{v}_i \dots$ is an r-bit row vector.

If a sequence of n symbols $\{\mathbf{y}_1, \mathbf{y}_2, \dots, \mathbf{y}_n\}$ is received, a syndrome matrix is calculated:

$$
\begin{bmatrix} S \end{bmatrix} = \begin{bmatrix} H \end{bmatrix} \begin{bmatrix} \dots \mathbf{y}_1 \dots \\ \dots \mathbf{y}_2 \dots \\ \vdots \\ \dots \mathbf{y}_n \dots \end{bmatrix} = \begin{bmatrix} H \end{bmatrix} \begin{bmatrix} \dots \mathbf{e}_1 \dots \\ \dots \mathbf{e}_2 \dots \\ \vdots \\ \dots \mathbf{e}_n \dots \end{bmatrix} \tag{3.27}
$$

where $\mathbf{e}_i = \mathbf{y}_i - \mathbf{v}_i$ is the error vector in position i.

3.11.2   Linear Independence of Error Vectors

A key assumption that the decoder makes in vector symbol decoding is that the error patterns as vectors are linearly independent. Before proceeding with the decoding technique, it is worth considering when and why this assumption is reasonable.

Consider first where the error patterns are randomly-chosen sequences of 0's and 1's, statistically independent of each other. If we look at a sequence of t error vectors one at a time, for independence to hold, the ith error vector must not be in the space generated by the first $i - 1$, for all $0 < i \leq t$. Then the probability that the t vectors will be linearly independent is

$$
\prod_{i=0}^{t-1} \frac{2^r - 2^i}{2^r} \cong 1 - 2^{-(r-t)}. \tag{3.28}
$$

If r is significantly greater than t the probability of linear dependence will be negligible, especially if error correction is in its efficiency role, with separate error detection/retransmission.

In reality, error patterns are not usually random patterns of zeros and ones. There is a processing technique described in [METZ90] that can make this a good approximation, however. The technique is to transform each symbol prior to transmission and inner code encoding (if used), using a different transformation for each symbol; then the corresponding inverse transforms are applied to each symbol prior to vector symbol decoding. Any error patterns on reception or remaining after false inner code correction will be transformed into pseudorandom patterns after the inverse transform. The transformations can be fairly simple to implement. One possibility is to multiply each symbol by a different power of a primitive element in $GF(2^r)$, and then multiply by the inverse power at the receiver; this can be done with feedback register circuitry similar to what is employed in standard CRC checking.

The transform technique may not be necessary in some circumstances. If there is an inner coder, possibly one code for each symbol, the inner code will correct small numbers of bit errors, so symbols that remain wrong will usually have a large number of errors. These will have a smaller probability of being linearly dependent than patterns with just one or two errors. If modulation codes or convolutional codes are used (both to be described in Chapter 4), residual errors after decoding tend to be clustered, so blocks of r bits would usually contain either no errors or many errors. Also, errors on many channels tend naturally to occur in bursts.

As previously mentioned, if extremely high reliability is desired, error correction is most important in an efficiency role. Because of the uncertainty of error statistics, only error detection with subsequent corrective transmission can be counted on for extremely low error probability on noisy channels. It is perhaps remarkable that vector symbol decoding, using codes with very poor minimum distance, can actually have a greater probability of successful decoding over a wide range of r-bit symbol error probabilities than equal-rate Reed-Solomon codes, which have the greatest possible minimum distance, but are confined to correcting only up to the guaranteed correction limit.

3.11.3 Description of the Technique

Every member of the row space of H defines a parity equation on the vector symbols that must be satisfied by a code word. If we can find a member of the row space of H that checks, then every position where that n-bit row space vector is a one is error-free, assuming that the r-bit error vectors are linearly independent. Such a vector in the row space of H is referred to as a *null combination*. Sometimes a syndrome row vector will be zero; this means the corresponding row of the H matrix is a null combination. A zero syndrome vector will be denoted a null indicator [OH94].

The task of finding null combinations can be delegated to manipulations of the rows of S. If a combination of rows of S add to zero, the corresponding combinations of rows of H will be a null combination. Elementary column operations on a matrix do not change which combinations of rows of S add to zero. Elementary column operations can perform the equivalent of a Gauss-Jordan reduction, which, after a possible interchange of rows, transforms S as:

$$S' = \begin{bmatrix} I & \vdots & 0 \\ \cdots & \cdots & \cdots \\ M & \vdots & 0 \end{bmatrix} \tag{3.29}$$

If the t errors are linearly independent, the I submatrix will be of rank t. The combinations of rows of S' that add to zero are readily revealed in this form, which is the same as the combinations of S that add to zero except for any row interchanges. (Actually, the row interchanges don't have to be done to reveal the combinations, but they are done here for simplicity of representation.) There will be $n - k - t$ such null indicators, and by forming the vector modulo-2 sums of corresponding rows of H, $n - k - t$ null combinations are found. (If the code is cyclic, the null combinations can be found by multiplying the check polynomial by a polynomial defined by the null indicator). The union of these null combinations is defined as the vector logical or of the $n - k - t$ null combination vectors. The union of null combinations will, under conditions to be described, have 0's in all t positions where there are errors, and 1's wherever there is no error. If there is any linear dependence, the rank of S will be less than t, and it is shown [METZ90], [OH94] that in most cases the rank of S will not agree with the number of 0's in the union of null combinations. Once the error locations are found, a $t * t$ submatrix can be extracted from the t columns of H corresponding to error locations, and the exact error values found by multiplying an inversion of this submatrix by a corresponding t rows of S.

3.11.4   Conditions for Successful Decoding

The following uses the notation of [OH94]. Let H_t be a submatrix of H consisting of the t columns corresponding to the t error locations. Let H_t^i denote the event that H_t is of rank t. Let H_{n-t}^i denote the event that none of the other $n - t$ columns of H are in the column space of H_t. Let E_t^i denote the event that the t error vectors are linearly independent vectors. Then, it is shown in [OH94] that decoding is successful whenever all three of the events, H_t^i, H_{n-t}^i, and E_t^i, are true. For codes chosen at random, the probability of successful decoding is very high even up to numbers of errors exceeding the maximum distance code guaranteed correctible bound [OH94]. One example in [OH94] is a $(1000, 950)$ code with $r = 50$ bit symbols, where the maximum guaranteed correctibility for any code is 25 symbol errors, corresponding to a maximum distance of 51, yet the average randomly chosen code can correct 99.9% of the cases of $t \leq 30$ symbol errors, even though the average minimum Hamming distance of the codes in the class is only 6.

Reed-Solomon codes and vector symbol codes treat the r-bit symbol as a single entity; either it is wrong or not, independent of the number of errors in the symbol. If erroneous symbols usually have only a small number of erroneous bits, then the interleaved code may be more effective, even though it is less powerful, because the number of errors per component is usually considerably smaller than the number of multibit symbol errors. Because vector symbol codes already have the interleaved code structure, the possibility exists of combining the techniques. There are many patterns of errors that vector symbol decoding can correct but interleaved codes cannot correct, and there also are many patterns of errors that interleaved codes can correct but vector symbol decoding cannot correct. Thus two parallel decoders could perform the two different decoding modes, and built-in error detection would discover whether or not either was successful.

3.11.5 Example of Vector Symbol Decoding

The following is a $(10, 3)$ $r = 5$ interleaved binary code, with a minimum Hamming distance $d = 5$. Assume there are three linearly independent errors in positions $1, 2, 4$, as shown.

$$
S = \begin{bmatrix} 00100 \\ 01101 \\ 11010 \\ 11010 \\ 10111 \\ 01101 \\ 01101 \end{bmatrix} = \begin{bmatrix} 0011000000 \\ 1110100000 \\ 1010010000 \\ 1010001000 \\ 0110000100 \\ 1100000010 \\ 1100000001 \end{bmatrix}
\begin{bmatrix} 11010 \\ 10111 \\ 00000 \\ 00100 \\ 00000 \\ 00000 \\ 00000 \\ 00000 \\ 00000 \\ 00000 \end{bmatrix}
\begin{matrix} \leftarrow \\ \leftarrow \text{ Three} \\ \text{independent} \\ \leftarrow \text{ errors} \\ \\ \\ \\ \\ \\ \end{matrix}
$$

Column operations on S yield:

$$
S' = \begin{matrix} 10000 \\ 01000 \\ 00100 \\ 00100 \\ 01100 \\ 01000 \\ 01000 \end{matrix}
\begin{matrix} \\ \\ \text{Null indicators} \\ \leftarrow \text{row 3 + row 4} \\ \leftarrow \text{row 2 + row 3 + row 5} \\ \leftarrow \text{row 2 + row 6} \\ \leftarrow \text{row 2 + row 7} \\ \text{Union of null combinations } \rightarrow \end{matrix}
\begin{matrix} \text{Corresponding null} \\ \text{combinations} \\ \\ 0000011000 \\ 0010110100 \\ 0010100010 \\ \underline{0010100001} \\ \overline{0010111111} \end{matrix}
$$

The three errors are revealed as the only positions where there is a zero in all four discovered null combinations of H.

To find the exact error patterns, take rows $1, 2, 3$ (corresponding to I_3 of S') and columns $1, 2, 4$ (corresponding to error positions) of H

$$
\begin{matrix} 001 \\ 110 \\ 100 \end{matrix}
$$

Invert this matrix and multiply rows $1, 2, 3$ of S:

$$\begin{bmatrix} 001 \\ 011 \\ 100 \end{bmatrix} \begin{bmatrix} 00100 \\ 01101 \\ 11010 \end{bmatrix} = \begin{bmatrix} 11010 \\ 10111 \\ 00100 \end{bmatrix} .$$

The rows of the result are the error pattern.

3.12   Majority-Logic-Like Decoding of Vector Symbols

We have seen that codes with poor minimum distance can be good decoders when used as the outer code of a concatenated code. Also, a simpler decoding technique is desirable. This leads naturally to the investigation of using majority logic codes, since these codes have the possibility of simple decoding, yet have poor minimum distance.

3.12.1   Example of Vector Decoding with a (21, 11) Majority Logic Block Code

J equations are chosen from the row space of H exactly as in a binary majority-logic code. Consider a (21, 11) difference set majority logic code listed in Table 7.2 of [LIN83]. $J = 5$, and the five equations written as rows of a matrix M are:

$$M = \begin{bmatrix} 000000000100110000101 \\ 010000000001001100001 \\ 000010100000000010011 \\ 100001010000000001001 \\ 001100001010000000001 \end{bmatrix} \tag{3.30}$$

If we number the positions 0 through 20, left to right, position 20 is the test position, appearing in all five equations, and the other positions appear in one equation each. As an ordinary binary majority logic code, it is only possible to guarantee correction of all cases of two or fewer errors.

As a vector code, in a syndrome calculation each syndrome vector will be a vector sum of the errors in the five positions checked by its row Equation in (3.29). There are five syndrome vectors corresponding to the five equations. Suppose the test position, 20, is in error. If there are no more than three other errors, the error value will appear as the syndrome in at least two syndrome vectors.

This suggests a very simple decoding rule: When testing a vector symbol, form the J r-bit vector sums and compare them. If none of the sums are zero and two of the sums have the same value, declare this to be the error, and correct the test symbol. Otherwise make no correction.

Continue at least until every symbol has been tested; perform two or more passes through the symbols as allowed or warranted.

After the corrections, error detection can be used, either based on the remaining failure of some parity equations, or by including additional parity somewhere in the data, to ensure the correction was done right.

To see why the technique works, assume first that all error vectors are linearly independent. The appropriateness of this assumption has already been discussed in Section 3.10. Under the assumption, two syndrome sums s_a and s_b are identical nonzero results if and only if there are no errors in the two test equation positions except for an error in the test symbol equal to the value of the duplication. This is because $s_a + s_b = 0$, and $s_a + s_b$ is the vector sum of all the error patterns in the positions other than the test positions that appear in the two equations. Due to the linear independence this sum cannot be zero unless they are all zero. Thus, instead of needing a majority of equations with no other errors, we need just two equations with no other errors.

Note that even if there is some linear dependence among the error vectors, it still is rather unlikely that errors in the particular set of other positions will happen to add to zero. For one thing, the errors in a particular sum or pair of sums may only be a subset of all the errors. Moreover, even if, for example, four error vectors are a linearly dependent set, this doesn't imply that the sum of the four is zero.

The decoder circuit block diagram is shown in Figure 3.11. The test symbol is denoted F, while the letters A, B, C, D, E denote which adder a particular symbol goes to. Since F would appear in every sum, it is not included to save wiring, since its effect would cancel in the comparisons. A difference from the prior explanation is that if a duplication is found it represents the true value F^* rather than the correction to be added to F. Thus, rather than adding a correction $F^* + F$ to F, just replace F

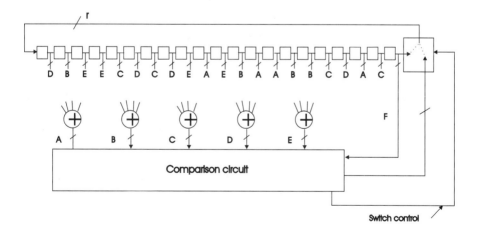

Figure 3.11: Decoding circuit for the $(21, 11)$ code.

by F^*. If $F^* = F$, then no correction is needed, but one may want to include logic to record error-correction events. Twenty-one shifts of the circular vector shift register counts as one pass.

Additional refinements to the test rule can be made to cover multiple duplicate events, or an event where a sum (including the F) adds to zero, yet two nonzero sums (including F) are identical. These events can occur only when there is linear dependence. Simulation shows only a small benefit to using these refinements except for extremely small vector sizes or small average number of bits in error per erroneous vector. The bulk of the benefit appears to be achieved simply by adding the feature of doing no correction when one of the sums is zero, even if there is a nonzero duplication.

Following is a simulation [METZ96] for the (21, 11) code previously defined. First, error symbol positions were selected randomly with symbol error probability p. Then, a vector size was selected and the exact bit error pattern generated for each random error, selecting bit errors randomly according to a chosen bit error probability p_b. If it happened that the random selection yielded no errors, the selection was redone. Thus the actual bit error probability for the vectors was slightly higher, namely,

$$\frac{p_b}{1 - (1 - p_b)^r},$$

due to the conditioning.

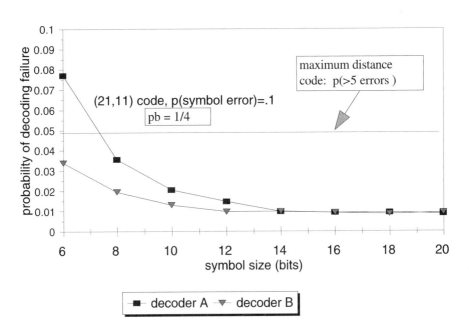

Figure 3.12: Decoder failure probability versus vector symbol size.

As the basis of comparison, consider a $(21, 11)$ maximum distance code that has a minimum distance of 11 and corrects all cases of up to five errors, but no cases of more than 5 errors. Such a code can be derived from a shortened Reed-Solomon code. The probability of decoding failure for random errors is readily computable as

$$P[fail] = \sum_{i=6}^{21} \binom{21}{i} p^i (1 - p)^{21-i} \tag{3.31}$$

where p is the symbol error probability.

Figure 3.12 shows the probability of decoding failure with $p = .1$, and $p_b = 1/4$ and decoders A and B as a function of vector symbol size r. Decoder B is a refinement of the basic decoder A previously described. The deterioration at small vector size is the effect of the occurrence of linear dependence events. Note for this example there is no significant deterioration if the vector size is 16 bits or more, and even at as small as 6 bits the failure probability of decoder B is lower than for a maximum distance code.

3.13 Summary

This chapter reviews some basic concepts of block error control codes. The next chapter will consider nonblock (trellis) codes. Almost all practical uses of block codes have been linear codes because of their relative simplicity. Their properties are conveniently described and understood based on matrix, vector space, and group theory representations. Error detection involves computing a vector called a syndrome to see if it is zero. If it is not zero, error correction seeks to find the most likely error pattern, if any, in a correctible set, that would have caused the syndrome. Single error correction and burst error correction are rather simple for general linear codes.

Correcting larger numbers of randomly positioned errors in a simple manner requires that codes have additional mathematical structure. This additional structure comes from the theory of finite fields, and the class of codes using this structure are the cyclic codes. A cyclic code can be described by a generator polynomial, which is simpler than the general linear code matrix description. Field operations, cyclic code encoding, error detection, and some kinds of error correction can be performed by simple feedback shift register circuits; this is simpler than matrix multiplications required by a general linear code. Also, the useful concept of error trapping is practical for cyclic codes because of their cyclic nature. A special class of cyclic codes called BCH codes provide even simpler decoding. They are designed by specifying roots that the generator polynomial must have. The number of specified roots is exactly twice the designed guaranteed error probability. The more roots specified, the higher is the degree of $g(X)$. The degree of $g(X)$ equals the number of check symbols.

Reed-Solomon codes are a special class of BCH codes where the symbols are in the same field as the specified roots. They have the property of having the maximum possible minimum distance: one more than the number of check symbols. Thus they can correct a number of errors up to one-half of the number of check symbols, or fill in a number of erased symbols up to the number of check symbols. Check symbols can be punctured to create codes with the same maximum minimum distance property but a higher rate. Concatenated codes are two levels of codes, where the code words of an inner code serve as the symbols of an outer code. Reed-Solomon codes are ideal as an outer code. Concatenated codes break the decoding problem into two stages, which allows for simpler decoding for an overall total code length.

Majority logic decoding is designed to decode one data bit at a time by a majority rule. The codes are cyclic, and rely on having a set of check equations that all check the test bit, but no other bit appears in more than one of the equations. Although simple, the minimum distance of such codes usually is far inferior to BCH codes, which reduces their usefulness.

For nonbinary codes, minimum distance is not really that important because many error patterns beyond the guaranteed correction capability can be corrected while retaining for long codes, a great deal of protection against undetected error. Also, extra check bits can be added to the data, if necessary, to see if the correction was done right, at little cost in efficiency if the code length is long. For this reason, general linear codes called vector symbol codes, can do as much as or more correction than Reed-Solomon codes restricted to correcting up to their guaranteed error-correcting capability, even though the guaranteed error correction of a vector symbol is generally far inferior. A simpler version of vector symbol decoding known as majority-logic-like decoding uses cyclic majority logic code structure to obtain a probability of decoding failure that is in many instances lower than a Reed-Solomon code.

The two roles of coding are error correction and error detection. The effectiveness of error correction is highly dependent on the channel statistics. Error detection is more robust and fairly insensitive to channel statistics.

3.14   Problems

3.1.   A $(5, 2)$ binary code has the generator matrix

$$G = \begin{bmatrix} 1 & 1 & 0 & 1 & 1 \\ 1 & 1 & 1 & 0 & 0 \end{bmatrix}$$

Note this code is not systematic.

a.   Find an H matrix for this code. The required properties for H are that its three rows must be orthogonal to all rows of G. Also the rows of H must be linearly independent. Note that the H matrix is not unique, but the vector space formed by the rows of H is unique, and is the space (denoted "null space") of all vectors orthogonal to the vector space of code words.

b.   Show by example for this code that a nonzero vector can be in a vector space and also in the null space of that vector space.

c.   Find the cosets of the group of code words as a subgroup of the group of binary 5-tuples. Identify the syndrome that associates with each row.

d.   What is the sum of two members of the same coset?

    e. What is a common property of the sum of any member of a coset aH with any member of a coset bH, $a \neq b$?

    f. Why is it not possible to use the first two positions (or the last two positions) as the data symbols for this code?

3.2.   **a.** Find the order of each nonzero element of $GF(7)$.

      b. What is the order of each of the following elements: α^3, α^5, α^2, α^{102}?

3.3. Prove the statement in Section 3.2 that adding an element **v** to each of the 2^k members of the subgroup C of code words creates 2^k all different sequences, none of which are members of C.

3.4. Consider the field $GF(2^4)$ expressed as polynomials modulo $1 + X + X^4$.

    a. Draw a feedback shift register circuit that generates all the nonzero elements of $GF(2^4)$.

    b. Show the successive outputs of the shift register circuit with initial contents 1000.

    c. What kind of polynomial is $1 + X + X^4$?

    d. Repeat a.–c. for $GF(2^4)$ expressed as polynomials modulo $1 + X^3 + X^4$.

    e. $1 + X + X^2 + X^3 + X^4$ is also irreducible and can be used as the modulo polynomial to describe $GF(2^4)$. See if a feedback shift register circuit using this polynomial for the feedback connections generates all the nonzero elements. Can you explain why or why not?

3.5. A $(7,4)$ cyclic code has generator polynomial $X^4 + X + 1$. Suppose a 7-bit received sequence is fed into a $g(X)$ feedback shift register shown in Figure P3.1. Suppose there is a single error in the X^3 position of the received sequence.

    Find the syndrome response after all 7 bits have been shifted in. Find it in two ways:

    a. By showing the error response at successive shifts of the circuit.

    b. By computing a remainder on division of the appropriate polynomial by $g(X)$.

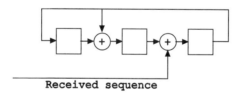

Received sequence

Figure P3.1: Circuit for Problem 3.5.

3.6. Consider a $(15,7)$ binary cyclic code with $g(X) = 1 + X^4 + X^6 + X^7 + X^8$. A code word is:

$$v(X) = v_0 + v_1 X + \cdots + v_{14} X^{14}.$$

    a. Suppose the receiver learns v_{12}, v_{13}, v_{14}, v_0, v_1, v_2, v_3, but the other digits are "erased," and thus unknown to the receiver. Show how the other digits of the code word can be found by polynomial operations and by equivalent shift register operations.

b. Could the decoder always find the erased code word for this code if the eight erased digits were not cyclically consecutive? Explain your answer.

3.7. **a.** Prove that for a cyclic code the code word can be specified uniquely given any k cyclically consecutive symbol values. This means that, if any $n - k$ cyclically consecutive symbols were "erased" and there were no other errors, the decoder could solve for the missing symbol values.

    b. Prove that if $n - k$ arbitrary symbols were erased, it is not true that any cyclic code decoder could solve for the missing symbols. There is, however, one class of cyclic codes that could do this. What class is it?

3.8. Find the condition on n and k for a (n, k) code capable of correcting all cases of three or fewer errors to be able to trap all error patterns of three or fewer errors.

3.9. **a.** Derive the formula that the number of bursts (not including end-around cyclic bursts) is $(n - b + 2)2^{b-1}$.

    b. Generalize the result for symbols in $GF(Q)$.

3.10. Prove the assertion following Eq. (3.14) that, given the ability to correct all bursts of length b or less, a burst of length b or less will at no point in the test look like a false burst of length b or less.

3.11. Explain what operations on $A_0 + A_1X + A_2X^2$ in $GF(8)$ modulo $X^3 + X + 1$ are being performed by the circuits in Figure P3.2. Demonstrate that your answer is correct.

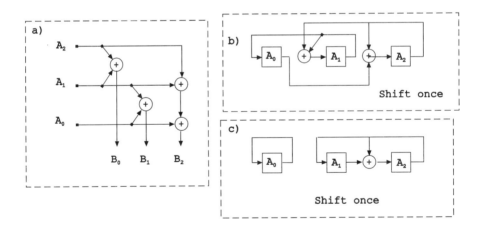

Figure P3.2: Circuits for Problem 3.11.

3.12. A cyclic binary code is defined by the generator polynomial $g(X) = X^4 + X^3 + X^2 + 1$.

    a. Find the shortest code length and the code rate.

    b. Find the minimum distance of the code.

    c. Show the code can correct all bursts of length 2 or less.

    d. Draw an error-trapping decoder that will correct bursts of length 2 or less.

3.13. **a.** Find the generator polynomial for a double-error-correcting length 31 Reed-Solomon code over $GF(32)$.

    b. How many code words are in this code?

    c. How many syndromes are there? How many of the syndromes correspond to patterns of 0, 1, or 2 errors?

    d. Suppose this code were used and e symbols of the 31 were "erased," but the other $31 - e$ were received without error. What is the largest value of e such that the missing symbols could be found, no matter where the e erasures were?

3.14. In the product code, prove that the positions that check both rows and columns have consistent values.

3.15. A $(49, 25)$ product code with $GF(8)$ symbols is constructed so each row is a single-error-correcting $(7, 5)$ Reed-Solomon code with $g(X) = \alpha^3 + \alpha^4 X + X^2$, where α is a primitive element of $GF(8)$. Also, each column is a code word of the same $(7, 5)$ Reed-Solomon code.

    The decoder first acts to correct any apparent single error in each row. If the row does not appear to have a single error it does nothing. The decoder then acts to correct any apparent single error in each column. If the column does not appear to have a single error it does nothing. No further error correction is attempted.

    Suppose the error pattern is the following four errors:

$$\begin{bmatrix} 0 & 0 & 0 & 0 & 0 & 0 & 0 \\ 0 & \alpha^6 & 1 & 0 & 0 & 0 & 0 \\ 0 & 1 & \alpha & 0 & 0 & 0 & 0 \\ 0 & 0 & 0 & 0 & 0 & 0 & 0 \\ 0 & 0 & 0 & 0 & 0 & 0 & 0 \\ 0 & 0 & 0 & 0 & 0 & 0 & 0 \\ 0 & 0 & 0 & 0 & 0 & 0 & 0 \end{bmatrix}$$

Powers increase toward the right or the row code.

Powers increase downward for the column code.

    a. Show that, even though the minimum distance of this code is 9, the decoder will fail to correct the errors.

    b. Show the resulting pattern of remaining errors after the decoder is finished.

3.16. Consider the $(10, 3)$ code in the Section 3.11.5 example. Suppose $r = 5$ and the following syndrome is computed:

$$\begin{bmatrix} 0 & 0 & 0 & 1 & 1 \\ 0 & 0 & 1 & 1 & 0 \\ 1 & 1 & 0 & 0 & 1 \\ 1 & 1 & 1 & 1 & 0 \\ 0 & 0 & 0 & 0 & 0 \\ 1 & 1 & 1 & 1 & 0 \\ 1 & 1 & 1 & 1 & 0 \end{bmatrix}.$$

There are four linearly independent errors. (Although only all cases of up to $d - 2$ linearly independent errrors are guaranteed correctible, cases like this meeting the conditions for successful decoding stated in Section 3.11.4 are also correctible.) Find the four error locations and their values.

3.17. **a.** For the binary $(21, 11)$ majority logic code with equations given by (3.18), suppose that there are three errors in the positions 14, 15, 19. Demonstrate whether or not all errors get corrected after testing each of the 21 positions once.

  b. For the vector symbol $(21, 11)$ majority logic-like code, suppose there are five error vectors in positions 0, 2, 13, 18, 20, and suppose they are linearly independent vectors. Demonstrate whether or not all errors get corrected after testing each of the 21 positions once.

3.18. The class of cyclic codes of parameters $(2^m - 1, m)$, in which the check polynomial is an m-degree primitive polynomial, has minimum distance 2^{m-1} and is called the class of maximal length codes. They are known to be majority-logic one-step decodable. Consider such a code: $(15, 4)$. The $J = 7$ parity equations for majority logic decoding of e_{14} are:

$$\begin{bmatrix} 0 & 0 & 0 & 0 & 0 & 0 & 0 & 0 & 0 & 0 & 1 & 0 & 0 & 1 & 1 \\ 0 & 0 & 0 & 0 & 0 & 0 & 1 & 0 & 0 & 0 & 0 & 0 & 1 & 0 & 1 \\ 1 & 0 & 0 & 0 & 0 & 0 & 0 & 0 & 0 & 0 & 0 & 1 & 0 & 0 & 1 \\ 0 & 0 & 0 & 0 & 1 & 0 & 0 & 0 & 0 & 1 & 0 & 0 & 0 & 0 & 1 \\ 0 & 1 & 0 & 0 & 0 & 0 & 0 & 0 & 1 & 0 & 0 & 0 & 0 & 0 & 1 \\ 0 & 0 & 0 & 0 & 0 & 1 & 0 & 1 & 0 & 0 & 0 & 0 & 0 & 0 & 1 \\ 0 & 0 & 1 & 1 & 0 & 0 & 0 & 0 & 0 & 0 & 0 & 0 & 0 & 0 & 1 \end{bmatrix}.$$

  a. As a binary code, show that this code can correct all patterns of 3 or fewer errors by majority logic decoding in one pass through the symbols.

  b. Suppose the symbols instead are 16-bit vectors. Suppose there are t symbol error vectors. Given the condition that the t errors are a linearly independent set of vectors, show what is the greatest value of t such that majority-logic-like decoding is guaranteed to correct all t errors in one pass.

Chapter 4

Trellis Codes, Modulation Codes, and Soft Decision Decoding

Most decoder/demodulators begin by extracting a number, or sample, corresponding to each transmitted symbol. If the sample number is converted directly into a decision as to the symbol value, either as a final decision or as a first step of decoding, this is referred to as a *hard* decision. If instead more information about the received sample value is retained to combine with the information about other samples, it is referred to as a *soft* decision. The capacity of a communication link is reduced as a result of making hard decisions instead of soft decisions, because some information is lost in the decision conversion.

Trellis codes differ from block codes in that there is no prescribed segregation into blocks. Convolutional codes are linear codes, which form a special class of trellis codes. Trellis and convolutional codes have some advantages over block codes in terms of reduced decoding complexity and simpler ability to make use of soft decision information. Historically, most studies dealt with the convolutional code form until modulation codes were introduced. Modulation codes combine the processes of coding and carrier modulation. This involves nonlinear operations, which makes the trellis code concept more appropriate.

4.1 General Principles of Convolutional Encoding

In a trellis code encoding, at each unit of time k data symbols are fed into the system, and $n > k$ symbols come out, which are a function of both the k current input bits and the m previous sets of input bits, as shown in Figure 4.1. If the trellis code is a

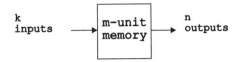

Figure 4.1: A trellis or convolutional code encoder.

convolutional code, the box in Figure 4.1 represents a discrete linear finite memory system. Usually k and n are small, such as 1, 2, or 3. The rate is k/n. The code is denoted as (n, k, m). We will assume in the examples of this section that the symbols are binary, although it is easy to generalize to $GF(q)$ field element symbols.

Figures 4.2 and 4.3 illustrate two simple convolutional encoders. The circled adders are performing addition modulo-2.

Convolutional codes can be described in many ways. In addition to the block diagram descriptions in Figures 4.1 through 4.3, they can be described by: a matrix of unit pulse responses or corresponding generator polynomials; a semi-infinite generator matrix; a state diagram; or a trellis diagram.

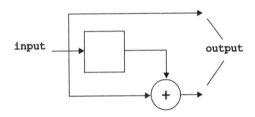

Figure 4.2: A $(2, 1, 1)$ convolutional encoder.

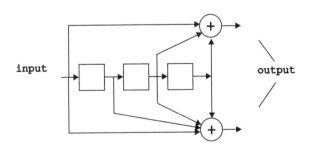

Figure 4.3: A $(2, 1, 3)$ convolutional encoder.

4.1.1 Matrix of Unit Pulse Responses

This is a $k \times n$ matrix, where the (i, j) entry is the unit pulse response of the jth output to the ith input. Because the system is linear, response to any input sequence is obtainable from this data by superposition. For the $(2, 1, 3)$ code of Figure 4.3, this matrix is the following:

$$\begin{bmatrix} 1011 & | & 1111 \end{bmatrix}.$$

The entries also can be written as polynomials in powers of D. The polynomial representing the unit pulse response of the jth output to the ith input is written as $g_i^{(j)}(D)$. Then the matrix of unit pulse responses is

$$\begin{bmatrix} g_1^{(1)}(D) & g_1^{(2)}(D) & \cdots & g_1^{(n)}(D) \\ \cdots & \cdots & \cdots & \cdots \\ \cdots & \cdots & \cdots & \cdots \\ g_k^{(1)}(D) & & \cdots & g_k^{(n)}(D) \end{bmatrix}.$$

4.1.2 Semi-Infinite Matrix Representation

This matrix representation is a direct analogy to the generator matrix of block codes. A set of $m + 1$ submatrices, each $k \times n$, is defined as $G_0, G_1, \ldots, G_m$, where G_i describes the effect on the current n output bits of the k input bits that occurred i input block times earlier. The general form of the matrix is

$$G = \begin{bmatrix} G_0 & G_1 & G_2 & \cdots & G_m & 0 & 0 & \cdots & \cdots & \cdots \\ 0 & G_0 & G_1 & G_2 & \cdots & G_m & 0 & \cdots & \cdots & \cdots \\ 0 & 0 & G_0 & G_1 & G_2 & \cdots & G_m & 0 & \cdots & \cdots \\ 0 & 0 & 0 & G_0 & \cdots & \cdots & \cdots & \cdots & G_m & 0 \\ & & & & \cdots & \cdots & \cdots & \cdots & \cdots & \cdots \end{bmatrix}. \tag{4.1}$$

For the same $(2, 1, 3)$ of Figure 4.3,

$$G = \begin{bmatrix} 11 & 01 & 11 & 11 & 00 & 00 & 00 & \cdots & & \\ 00 & 11 & 01 & 11 & 11 & 00 & 00 & 00 & \cdots & \\ 00 & 00 & 11 & 01 & 11 & 11 & 00 & 00 & 00 & \cdots \\ 00 & 00 & 00 & 11 & 01 & 11 & 11 & 00 & 00 & \cdots \\ 00 & 00 & 00 & 00 & 11 & 01 & 11 & 11 & 00 & \cdots \\ & & & & \cdots & & & & & \end{bmatrix}. \tag{4.2}$$

4.1.3 State Diagram Representation

A convolutional encoder with a memory dependent on m previous k-bit input symbols may have as many as 2^{km} states. If this number is not too large, it is convenient to describe the decoder by a diagram showing the states and the state transitions and outputs resulting from the 2^k possible inputs. For example, Figure 4.4 shows the state diagram for the $(2, 1, 2)$ encoder whose circuit is also shown.

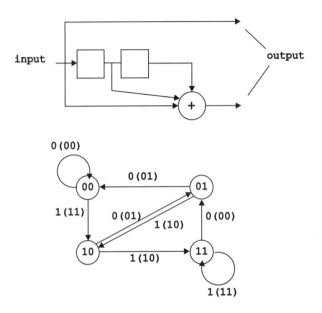

Figure 4.4: Circuit and state diagram for a $(2, 1, 2)$ code.

4.1.4   Trellis Diagram Representation

A trellis diagram expands the state diagram to show how the states change with time. Figure 4.5 shows the trellis diagram for the same $(2, 1, 2)$ code encoder circuit of Figure 4.4. The input for each transition is shown, and outputs are shown in

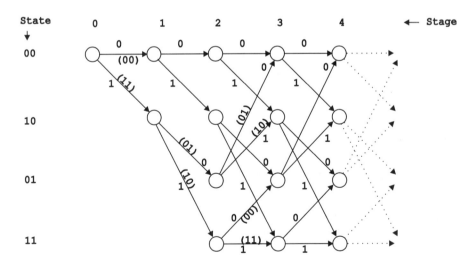

Figure 4.5: Trellis diagram for the encoder of Figure 4.4.

parentheses. Any two of the same state-to-state transitions have the same outputs and inputs. Thus, not all outputs are shown to reduce clutter.

4.1.5 Constraint Length

The memory constraint length m (or km in terms of input data symbols, nm in terms of code output symbols) of a convolutional code plays a role somewhat like block length for a block code. The constraint length of convolutional codes generally can be much shorter than the block length of block codes for equivalent decoding power. In many cases convolutional codes allow for simpler decoding of a large number of errors than do block codes.

4.1.6 Minimum Distance

As with block codes, a large minimum distance between code sequences is desirable. Also as with block codes, the distances between code words can be determined by using the all-zero sequence as the reference code word without loss of generality. There are several distance measures, but probably the most important is the free distance d_{free}. This is defined as the smallest weight of any path in the trellis diagram that starts from the zero state, transitions to a nonzero state, and ends in the zero state.

For the code of Figure 4.2, $d_{free} = 3$. For the code of Figure 4.3, $d_{free} = 6$. The response to a unit pulse for the Figure 4.3 code is 11 01 11 11, which is weight 7, but the response to input 1 1 is:

$$
\begin{array}{r}
11 \ \ 01 \ \ 11 \ \ 11 \\
+ \quad 11 \ \ 01 \ \ 11 \ \ 11 \\
\hline
= \ 11 \ \ 10 \ \ 10 \ \ 00 \ \ 11
\end{array}
$$

which has the minimum weight 6. The code of Figure 4.4 has $d_{free} = 4$.

With the aid of the state diagram and application of Mason's gain formula [MASO60], it is possible to compute the distribution of weights and durations of the various code word responses to data inputs, although the complexity of this computation goes up rapidly with the number of states. These weight distributions are also helpful in estimating the probability of decoding error.

The trellis diagram is also useful to visually count the path weights from zero state and back.

4.1.7 Catastrophic Error Propagation

Nonsystematic codes require an inverse to recover the data, because the data are not segregated in the code word. Nonsystematic codes are noncatastrophic or catastrophic according to whether they do or do not have a feed-forward inverse, respectively. In a catastrophic code the effect of certain decision errors propagates and can cause an infinite number of decision errors afterward. For $k = 1$, a code is noncatastrophic if and only if the greatest common divisor of its n generator polynomials is D^i, where $i \geq 1$. For $k > 1$, there is a more complex condition on the matrix of transfer functions [MASS68]. It is not difficult to find good codes that are not catastrophic.

4.1.8 Convolutional Codes with Feedback Circuits

It is desirable that a code have a high free distance. For a fixed amount of memory, nonsystematic convolutional codes often have a higher free distance than systematic codes. For example, with $m = 2$, the nonsystematic code shown in Figure 4.6 has $d_{free} = 5$, whereas the systematic code in Figure 4.4 has $d_{free} = 4$. However, the code of Figure 4.6 can be converted into a systematic code with the same amount of memory and $d_{free} = 5$ by including a feedback connection in the circuit. As a first step in seeing how this could be, note that the upper output sequence labelled Y is a 1:1 mapping of the input sequence. Thus if we made y the true data sequence, we could uniquely derive the input X, and from that the other output Z. The Y, Z sequence pair would be a possible output of the circuit with the proper X input, and thus have the same sequence weight distribution, but now it would be systematic. Let's see what kind of circuit derives Z from X directly.

In terms of transfer functions:

$$Y = (1 + D^2)X; \tag{4.3}$$

$$Z = (1 + D + D^2)X. \tag{4.4}$$

Solving for X in (4.3) and substituting in (4.4),

$$Z = (1 + D + D^2)Y/(1 + D^2). \tag{4.5}$$

This is generated by the feedback circuit shown in Figure 4.7. Note that the circuit is now systematic, has $d_{free} = 5$, and only 2 memory positions (although the unit pulse response now has infinite duration). To terminate after a preagreed length, the last two bit values of Y are not actual data, but are entered such as to return to the state 00.

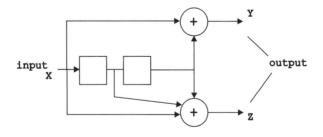

Figure 4.6: A nonsystematic $(2, 1, 2)$ code.

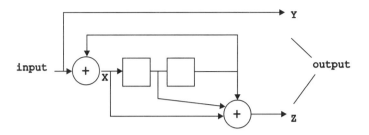

Figure 4.7: Conversion of Figure 4.6 into a systematic code by use of feedback.

4.1.9 Punctured Convolutional Codes

Single-input codes are the simplest, but have a rate that must be $1/n$, where n is an integer greater than one. Often it is desirable to have codes of rate considerably greater than $1/2$. With 2 inputs per unit time the rate can be $2/3$, and with 3 inputs it can be $3/4$. However, more inputs means more memory states and is a less desirable condition from complexity considerations. A way of getting a wide range of higher rates without losing the benefit of single input circuits is to puncture (not send) a preagreed portion of redundant symbols that appear at the encoder output [CAIN79, HAGE88]. The Viterbi and sequential decoding techniques to be described are able to operate almost the same way with a punctured code as with a nonpunctured code, so little complexity is added. Also, the same code circuit can be used with many different rates. How to best select the symbols for puncturing is an important consideration. Selection of good high-rate punctured codes is described in [HACC89].

4.1.10 Terminating a Convolutional Code

A convolutional code can always be terminated into a block code by bringing the state back to the zero state after a preagreed length. In the non-feedback-circuit method of code generation, this can be done after L k-bit inputs simply by inputting mk zeros to return to the zero state. In the feedback mode, mk bits can be input so as to return the state to zero, but these are not necessarily all zero. A total of $n[L + m]$ bits are actually transmitted, of which kL are data bits, so the resulting code is a $(n[L + m], kL)$ block code with a convolutional code inner structure. The code rate,

$$\frac{kL}{n[L + m]},$$

is only slightly less than k/n when $L \gg m$.

4.2 Convolutional Code Decoding Techniques

Three main decoding techniques are available for convolutional codes: sequential decoding, Viterbi decoding, and majority logic decoding. Sequential decoding, invented by Wozencraft [WOZE59], involves making trial hypotheses about the data and performing a tree search, abandoning a branch when its hypothesis disagrees too much from what is received. It is an effective technique for use with long constraint length codes. Viterbi decoding is a technique that has gained broad application. Majority logic decoding for convolutional codes is a direct extension of the technique for cyclic block codes.

4.2.1   Soft Decisions and Their Use in Decoding

The usual steps in demodulation/decoding of a received signal conveying data by a sequence of binary pulses are:

1. Sample so that for each pulse a number is obtained that, in the absence of intersymbol interference, is a combination (usually assumed to be the sum) of the transmitted value and noise

2. For each number, compare against a threshold to decide if the bit is zero or one

3. Use the binary block or convolutional code to correct and/or detect errors in the binary decisions.

Step 2 is a hard binary decision. However, it is more effective to make a soft decision, which ideally would be a record of the likelihood ratio of the two alternatives. The soft decision can be a quantization of the likelihood ratio; a few bits of quantization retain most of the information in the received sample value that would be lost by a hard decision.

To illustrate the soft decision operations mathematically, suppose a sequence of symbols $c_0, c_1, \ldots, c_{n-1}$ is transmitted, and received numbers $r_0, r_1, \ldots, r_{n-1}$ are recorded. In a memoryless, stationary channel, as is often assumed, the probability density of r_i given the input sequence $c_0, c_1, \ldots, c_{n-1}$ depends only on c_i. Thus, the conditional density of receiving $r_0, r_1, \ldots, r_{n-1}$ is

$$f(r_0, r_1, \ldots, r_{n-1}/c_0, c_1, \ldots, c_{n-1}) = \prod_i f(r_i/c_i). \tag{4.6}$$

Taking logarithms,

$$\log\{f(r_0, r_1, \ldots, r_{n-1}/c_0, c_1, \ldots, c_{n-1})\} = \sum_i \log\{f(r_i/c_i)\}. \tag{4.7}$$

Thus, only a summation of log-likelihood numbers needs to be done to calculate a sequence likelihood, assuming symbols are independently disturbed by noise. For the frequently assumed case of Gaussian noise, if transmission is binary and is one of two levels $\pm A$,

$$\frac{f(r/A)}{f(r/-A)} = \frac{\dfrac{1}{\sigma\sqrt{2\pi}}e^{-\frac{(r-A)^2}{2\sigma^2}}}{\dfrac{1}{\sigma\sqrt{2\pi}}e^{-\frac{(r+A)^2}{2\sigma^2}}} = e^{\frac{2Ar}{\sigma^2}} \tag{4.8}$$

Taking logarithms,

$$\log[f(r/A)] - \log[f(r/-A)] = \frac{2Ar}{\sigma^2}. \qquad (4.9)$$

The difference is thus directly proportional to r. The log likelihood for a sequence of n binary symbols $c_0, c_1, \ldots, c_{n-1}$ is then directly computed by the sign-weighted sum

$$\sum_{i=0}^{n-1} \text{signum}[c_i] * r_i.$$

A simple example of the advantage of using soft decisions on binary digits prior to a final code word decision is a code with two code words, $(0, 0)$ and $(1, 1)$, where 0 is sent as $-A$ and 1 as $+A$. Figure 4.8 shows the decision regions for the case where individual binary decisions are made and the case where likelihood information is saved for each component prior to making a decision. It is assumed the correct code word is $(0, 0)$. With likelihood values saved, the correct decision region is the union of regions R, S, and T. With hard binary decisions, only R is a correct decision region; regions S and T correspond respectively to $(0, 1)$ and $(1, 0)$ decisions, in which case the decoder can only guess whether the code word is $(0, 0)$ or $(1, 1)$.

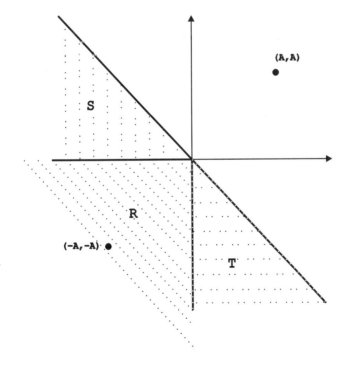

Figure 4.8: Decision between two length-2 code words using hard or soft per-symbol decisions.

Useful block codes almost always have a large number of code words, so the hard binary decision approach almost always is taken because there are too many code words to make it feasible to use soft decision information. One notable exception is the ability to record erasures for individual symbols when the block code is capable of combined error-erasure decoding. Block decoders that work on the principle of decoding one bit at a time [BATT79, GALL63] could make use of soft decision information. A possible application of soft decisions could be if the hard decision decoder was able to narrow the decision down to a small number of probable words; then a memory of soft decisions could help to select the most reliable candidate and/or evaluate the confidence in the decoder decision.

Convolutional codes inherently can make use of soft decision information more easily. This will become clear with the discussion on Viterbi and sequential decoding.

The soft decision concept is also applicable to nonbinary symbol transmission. This application is discussed in Section 4.4 on modulation codes.

4.2.2   Viterbi Decoding

Refer to the trellis diagram of Figure 4.5. After stage 1 there are four states at each stage. At stage 3 there are two paths leading from the start to each state. The decoder computes the likelihood of each path based on what is received. This could be based on either hard or soft decisions about the component bits. In the hard decision case the likelihood is reflected just by the number of disagreements between the received sequence and the hypothesized path. In the soft decision case the appropriate measure, assuming independent disturbances of different symbols, is the sum of the log likelihoods as in Equation (4.7). This likelihood measure can be quantized to just a few bits with little loss of performance.

Going into each state, one of the two paths will be more likely than the other (except if a tie). The decoder selects the more likely one as the "*survivor*," and remembers it as well as its likelihood. The others are rejected, because, assuming future noise events are independent of past noise events, a nonsurvivor will never be as likely a prefix to the future string as the chosen survivor. Thus at each stage the decoder has to remember only four survivors and their likelihood numbers, or in general as many survivors as there are states. Again, at stage 4 and subsequently, it selects one of the alternatives as the survivor. At each stage, the survivors are the only prefixes of the whole path to the end of the code that could be the maximum likelihood path (or a tie with it). For a code terminated after L input blocks, the final stage $L + m - 1$ will have only one state and thus one final survivor. However, decisions normally can be made on symbols with delays more comparable to m time units than the whole code length of $L + m$ time units, because in most cases all the survivors will agree up to a point a moderate length back from the current reception.

As long as the number of states, which is 2^m for $k = 1$, is not too large, the Viterbi algorithm is a very practical decoding method, and can work on all the information in the received waveform, not just the binary decisions.

4.2.3 Sequential Decoding

This technique, which predates Viterbi decoding, was discovered by Wozencraft [WOZE60]. Starting from a known state of the transmitted sequence, which could be the start of transmission, one envisions a tree showing the possible paths that could be taken depending on the input data. There are 2^k branches from each node. The decoder starts following these paths as hypotheses about what the actual data might be. For each branch the decoder compares n received numbers with the n bits that should have been generated. Paths are followed or eliminated based on the comparison result. There are two main approaches: one is based on a threshold criterion and the other on a stack algorithm. Both approaches use a metric of the likelihood of the hypothesized path given the received signal.

Wozencraft showed that the average number of computations grows only as a small power of the constraint length of the code. Although Viterbi decoding is simpler than sequential decoding for small values of m, sequential decoding is simpler on average for large m, because the number of states grows exponentially with m, and Viterbi decoding needs a memory proportional to the number of states.

One problem with sequential decoding complexity is that, although the average number of computations is reasonable, there is a wide variation about the average. Thus, despite the good average, the fraction of cases where the computation required exceeds the decoder's capability can easily exceed the desired probability of error.

Decoding Metric   An important goal in sequential decoding is to eliminate unlikely paths without eliminating the correct path, so as to keep to a minimum the number of paths that need to be searched while maximizing the probability of a correct decision. In Viterbi decoding, the path alternatives to determine a survivor are of the same length. Thus the maximum likelihood choice of path could be made based on (4.7). In sequential decoding, however, paths being compared often are of different length. Length needs to be taken into account, because a long path with a given amount of disagreement with the reception should be given more weight than a shorter path with the same amount of disagreement. An intuitive metric that reflects this property was postulated in [FANO63], and later given justification as a minimum error probability strategy in [MASS72]. For the case of binary symbol transmission, the metric for a sequence ℓ units long should be

$$M[\bar{r}, \bar{c}, \ell] = \sum_{i=0}^{n\ell-1} \log[p(r_i/c_i)] + (n - k)\ell. \qquad (4.10)$$

The second term on the right of (4.10) is a bias term that increases linearly with ℓ.

Threshold Methods   In these schemes, if the metric falls below some specified threshold, the hypothesized path and all paths for which it is a prefix are eliminated from consideration, at least for that assigned threshold (some schemes allow the threshold to be changed). The decoder backtracks to try other path(s), or searches

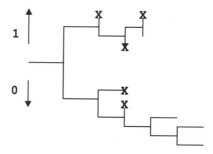

Figure 4.9: Sequential tree search with a threshold elimination criterion.

can be performed in parallel. Figure 4.9 illustrates a possible stage in the search. The convolutional code is assumed to have $k = 1$, but other parameters are unspecified in the illustration. For each input, if the decoder hypothesizes a 1 it takes the upper branch, and if it hypothesizes a 0 it takes the lower branch. Using the coder rules, the decoder knows the state at the beginning of the branch and what bits should have been transmitted for each hypothesized branch, and can compute the new metric after adding the branch. Where an X is marked, that path and all paths for which it is a subpath are eliminated from further consideration, unless the threshold is changed. At this point, four paths and their subpaths remain in contention.

The Stack Algorithm This is a clever algorithm that does not rely on an exact threshold, but keeps a stack-organized memory of candidate paths. Starting from the known initial zero state, the decoder computes the metrics of the 2^k possible first branches and orders them in a stack, with the best match on the top. The top path is then split into the 2^k successor paths, a metric is computed for each, and the stack is reordered, again with increasing metric from bottom to top. For $k = 1$, the size of the stack increases by 1 for each step, but in general it increases by $2^k - 1$ per step. If the decoder memory is exhausted, the paths with the worst scores can be dropped. If the convolutional code is terminated and the top path is at the end of the tree, the decoder is finished and outputs that path.

As an example, consider the $(2, 1, 2)$ code of Figure 4.4. Sequential decoding is applied mostly for large m codes, but this example is chosen for simplicity of explanation. Suppose the input is terminated after only 4 input digits. The total transmitted length is $(4 + m)n = 12$ to complete the termination. The state diagram of Figure 4.4 can be used to keep track of the responses to hypothesized inputs. Also assume for simplicity that hard binary decisions are being made. If the bit error probability is estimated to be p, then $\log[f(r/c)]$ is $\log[1 - p]$ if they agree and $\log[p]$ if they disagree. If $p = 1/8$ these numbers are $-.1926$ and -3. Also, increasing ℓ by 1 adds 1, or .5 per output bit since there are two output bits at a time. Thus, bit agreement should add a score of $.5 - .1926 = .3074$, and disagreement should add -2.5. Because the numbers can be scaled by the same factor, and also p is just an estimate, we could scale and then pick convenient integer-approximation scores such as 1 for agreement and -8 for disagreement.

data in	1	0	1 1	(0)	(0)	
code sent	1 1	0 1	1 0	1 0	0 0	0 1
	x			x		
received	1 0	0 1	1 0	1 1	0 0	0 1

There are two errors, indicated by an x above. The zeros in parentheses are preagreed terminating bits. The first hypothesis are 0 and 1, whose responses would be 00 and 11, respectively; both have 1 disagreement, so both get a score of -7.

0(−7)	1(−7)	10(−5)	101(−3)	101100(−4)
1(−7)	00(−14)	00(−14)	00(−14)	00(−14)
	01(−14)	01(−14)	01(−14)	01(−14)
		11(−23)	100(−21)	100(−21)
				101000(−24)

If 0 is chosen arbitrarily as the top and split, the second column results after ordering. Then path 1 is split into 10 and 11. When the last of the four inputs is hypothesized, the last two known zeros can be included. The final decision is then arrived at: 1011, which happens to be correct.

This particular example was simple, and not many steps were needed. However, the number of steps can vary widely with the nature of the error or noise event history. In this example, if after the 101 split one of the two new sequences did not appear at the top of the stack, 00 would have to be split, and several additional splits might be needed. With large values of L and m, much more dramatic differences in amount of computation for different error histories could be demonstrated. As a general rule, when the number of errors are small the computations are very fast, but they rise rapidly on average as the number of errors approach some critical value. In addition to the rise in the average number of errors, there is a wide variation depending on the positions of the errors.

4.2.4 Majority Logic Decoding

The majority logic decoding technique described in Section 3.7 for cyclic block codes also is applicable to convolutional codes; this is because both types of codes can employ the sliding check rules that allow testing of each symbol by the same set of equations. Because this is a syndrome decoding technique, reference needs to be made to a parity check matrix for a systematic convolutional code. For simplicity we will confine the discussion to systematic codes with $k = 1$ and $n = 2$. In this case $g_1^{(1)}(D) = 1$, and the only other response polynomial is

$$g_i^{(2)}(D) = g_0 + g_1 D + \cdots + g_m D^m.$$

The generator matrix is

$$
G = \begin{bmatrix}
1 & g_0 & 0 & g_1 & 0 & g_2 & \cdots & 0 & g_m \\
 & & 1 & g_0 & 0 & g_1 & 0 & g_2 & \cdots & 0 & g_m \\
 & & & & 1 & g_0 & 0 & g_1 & 0 & g_2 & \cdots & 0 & g_m \\
 & & & & & & \cdots
\end{bmatrix} \tag{4.11}
$$

A corresponding parity-check matrix is

$$
H = \begin{bmatrix}
g_0 & 1 \\
g_1 & 0 & g_0 & 1 \\
g_2 & 0 & g_1 & 0 & g_0 & 1 \\
\cdot & \cdot & \cdot & \cdot & \cdot & \cdot & \cdot & \cdot \\
\cdot & \cdot & \cdot & \cdot & \cdot & \cdot & \cdot & \cdot \\
g_m & 0 & g_{m-1} & 0 & \cdot & \cdot & \cdot & \cdot & \cdot & \cdot & g_0 & 1 \\
 & & g_m & 0 & g_{m-1} & 0 & \cdot & \cdot & \cdot & \cdot & \cdot & g_0 & 1
\end{bmatrix} \tag{4.12}
$$

The syndrome computation is

$$
S^T = H\mathbf{y}^T = H\mathbf{e}^T
$$

where $\mathbf{e}^T$ is the pattern of errors written as a column vector. Noting that data and check symbols alternate, we can write the error sequence as

$$
e_{d0}, e_{c0}, e_{d1}, e_{c1}, \ldots e_{di}, e_{ci}, \ldots
$$

Noting that the even columns form an identity, the syndrome equation can be written in two parts:

$$
S^T = \begin{bmatrix}
g_0 \\
g_1 & g_0 \\
g_2 & g_1 & g_0 \\
\vdots & \vdots & \vdots \\
g_m & \cdot & \cdot & \cdot & g_0
\end{bmatrix}
\begin{bmatrix}
e_{d0} \\
e_{d1} \\
e_{d2} \\
\vdots \\
e_{dm}
\end{bmatrix}
+
\begin{bmatrix}
e_{c0} \\
e_{c1} \\
e_{c2} \\
\vdots \\
e_{cm}
\end{bmatrix} \tag{4.13}
$$

To test e_{d0}, we need to find combinations of rows that have a 1 in the first position such that no other position appears twice. This can be found easily if we use a difference set principle [ROBI67] in selecting $g^{(2)}(D)$. The appropriate polynomials are listed in [LIN83]. In this case we just need to pick the equations where the first column term (g_i) is a 1.

As an example, for $m = 17$, g_i is a 1 for $i = 0, 2, 7, 13, 16, 17$. This leads to $J = 6$ equations to test a particular data symbol. If, for example, e_{d0} is in error, it will be corrected if there are at most 2 other errors among the 33 following symbols. In some cases it might even be corrected with more errors if some errors were in the same equation. If all data errors have been corrected up to a certain point, correction of the next data symbol is just like correction of e_{d0}. If not, past as well as future data symbol errors can affect the result. For correction at some point p, the check equations look as follows:

$$
S = \begin{bmatrix}
1100100000100000101 \\
0011001000010000101 \\
0000000110010000010000101 \\
0000000000000110010000010000101 \\
00000000000000001100100000100000101 \\
000000000000000011001000001000000101
\end{bmatrix}
\begin{bmatrix}
e_{d,p-17} \\
e_{d,p-16} \\
\vdots \\
e_{d,p} \\
\vdots \\
e_{d,p+17}
\end{bmatrix}
+
\begin{bmatrix}
e_{c,p} \\
e_{c,p+2} \\
e_{c,p+7} \\
e_{c,p+13} \\
e_{c,p+16} \\
e_{c,p+17}
\end{bmatrix}
\quad (4.14)
$$

For $p < 17$, the components with negative subscripts are zero; this corresponds to the memory of the convolutional code starting at seventeen 0's when the code begins.

The majority-logic-like decoding described in Section 3.12 can also be applied when there are vector symbols. In this case there are six equations checking symbol p, and if two of the rows of S_6 are identical, this duplicate will in most cases be the error value $e_{d,p}$.

4.3 ARQ with Convolutional Codes

Because convolutional codes eventually are terminated into a block code, one possible ARQ procedure could be to wait until the whole block was transmitted and then retransmit if it was not acknowledged. Because the block may be quite long, this may be inefficient if either (a) the decoder had been successful until just near the end, and thus does not need everything repeated or (b) the decoder had trouble near the beginning and needed retransmission earlier. The late-trouble problem could be improved if the decoder could include with the negative acknowledgment a specification of where to go back to in the retransmission. The early-trouble problem could be improved by earlier negative acknowledgments. What is meant by "trouble" is somewhat different for different kinds of decoders. This will be discussed next for each decoding technique.

4.3.1 ARQ with Sequential Decoding

In sequential decoding there is a wide deviation in computation dependent on the error events, so that too frequently an error event history can occur that is beyond the maximum computational capability. Usually this is due to an above-average cluster of errors. This was noted by Wozencraft in [WOZE60] and led naturally to the thought of using ARQ to retransmit recent portions of the code sequence starting back from just before the point where excessive computation was encountered [WOZE61]. Thus, as soon as computation limits are reached, the decoder should send a retransmission request, specifying how far back to repeat, or perhaps by convention to always go back some amount that depends on the code constraint length.

4.3.2 ARQ with Viterbi Decoding

ARQ has also been proposed for use with Viterbi decoding [YAMA80]. It is suggested that the receiver request retransmission whenever all survivors become overly uncertain. It was shown in the reference that the technique allows a significant reduction in the constraint length needed to attain a specified post-decoding error rate. In the event that feedback delay is large, a form of selective repeat could be employed: new receptions could continue to be recorded, so when the retransmission is received the decoder can replace the repeated block and hopefully continue successfully with the Viterbi decoding. The technique is rather dependent on having a good feedback channel, so the right bits are retransmitted when requested and the decoder can confidently distinguish the retransmitted bits from the new bits.

Another thought is that whenever a particular survivor wins by a close vote, say 60/40, that survivor could be marked "tainted," along with a record of the stage at which it became tainted. If the survivor loses out later, this tainted mark is no longer significant. However, if a tainted survivor wins in the end, then there is a 40 percent chance that the prefix of the survivor that was discarded at the tainted point was the true path. By just getting retransmission of the disagreeing portion of the tainted path, this problem could be resolved; that is, the decoder could adjust the likelihoods for the retransmitted symbols, and redo the decoding, assuming the symbol likelihoods in the uncertain section had all been saved. The use of retransmissions combined with prior transmissions touches on the idea of *memory ARQ*, which will be discussed in Chapter 7.

4.3.3 ARQ with Majority Logic Decoding

A paper [WICK90] suggests using ARQ with majority logic decoding of convolutional codes. When making a bit decision, instead of strictly using a majority vote rule, it is suggested that a repeat be requested when the vote is closer than some threshold. This technique also gives improved results but relies heavily on the feedback channel reliability; to send back a repeat request on a bit-by-bit basis requires a great deal of feedback capacity, which also needs to be reliable. It would seem that less information capacity would be required if a repeat was made a full constraint length at a time. This can be fairly efficient because a close vote means a cluster of errors in the constraint length, and it might be more cost effective, considering feedback capacity constraints, to repeat the whole group rather than specify exactly which bits.

4.4   Modulation Codes

Traditionally, error control coding has been applied at the binary symbol stream level, producing a new binary sequence with redundancy added. This new encoded binary stream is then applied to the modulator. The modulator might use binary or some form of nonbinary transmission, but this would be done independently of the binary code. Because binary or nonbinary pulses are normally sent at as high a rate as practical for the given bandwidth, the extra redundancy of the error control code increases required bandwidth for the same transmitted information rate.

More recently, there has been great interest in combining coding and modulation in a way that improves both bandwidth utilization and reliability. Coded modulation can also be used as the first stage of a concatenated code, with the second stage being a traditional symbol error-correcting code, such as a Reed-Solomon code.

A key measure of the code effectiveness is called the *coding gain*. Coding gain, measured in dB, is the amount of reduced signal power using coding to attain the same bit error probability as sending at the same data rate without coding. For a long time it was believed that coding gain came at the cost of increased bandwidth. Thus, it came as a surprise to many when Ungerboeck [UNGE82] showed a way of simultaneously reducing bandwidth and improving reliability.

When bandwidth is constrained, simple error-correcting codes using hard binary decisions can be ineffective for a random noise channel. Consider, for example, a rate $1/2$ code. A fairly simple rate $1/2$ code might seem to be effective because, for the same binary pulse transmission rate the bit error probability after decoding usually is significantly lower than the raw bit error probability of the individual binary decisions. This is not a fair comparison, however, because the data rate is reduced to one-half, so with uncoded transmission the bits could be twice as long for the same reduced rate, and the raw bit error rate also would be reduced. Often, the resulting improvement in bit error probability by just doubling the bit duration can be better than what is achieved by the rate $1/2$ code, and besides the coded system bandwidth is twice as great. This would be a case of a negative coding gain despite increased bandwidth. A sufficiently long rate $1/2$ code will produce a positive coding gain if the information rate is below channel capacity, but still at the cost of occupying twice the bandwidth.

The difficulty in obtaining a positive gain over a system that just sends each bit twice might seem strange, since repeating each bit is a rather trivial special case of a rate $1/2$ code. The advantage of two successive identical transmissions is the ability to combine the two sendings by likelihood or soft decisions. This combination occurs automatically when the pulse length is doubled and an optimum binary decision is made. Doubling the pulse length doubles the signal energy, and we have seen in Section 2.2 that in white Gaussian noise, error probability depends just on the ratio of signal energy to noise power spectral density. Another viewpoint is, for the same signal power, halving the pulse rate halves the bandwidth, which halves the noise power (assuming noise spectral density is flat in the region), and thus doubles the power signal-to-noise ratio.

Modulation codes create savings in both bandwidth and reliability by using nonbinary pulse modulation and combining coding with modulation. Also, relatively simple codes achieve good coding gains. Ordinarily, as we go from binary to multilevel or multiphase transmission, bandwidth occupancy for a given bit rate improves at the expense of higher symbol error probability due to closer signal spacing. Modulation codes have the ability to use soft decision information to produce better coding gain.

An important parameter in determining the correcting power of binary codes is the minimum distance between code words. The distance between code words, called the *Hamming distance*, is the number of bits in which two code words differ. With multilevel/multiphase modulation codes, the minimum energy difference between code word sequences is more important than the Hamming distance. The square root of this energy difference is called the *Euclidian distance*, since it is the distance between points representing the signals in n-dimensional vector space. Thus it is more important that good codes have large minimum Euclidean distance than large Hamming distance. For binary and 4-phase modulation, maximizing minimum Hamming distance also maximizes minimum Euclidean distance. However, for cases of greater than 2 bits per pulse there is not a close relationship between minimum Hamming distance and minimum Euclidian distance.

Suppose we try to use coding to improve reliability without a bandwidth increase, but by doing nonbinary modulation/demodulation separately from the coding. The following example is from [UNGE87]. Say we are trying to improve reliability sending 2 bits per pulse. Without coding, 4-phase modulation could be used. With coding separate from modulation, we could use 8-phase modulation and a binary rate $2/3$ code at the same pulse rate and bandwidth as uncoded 4-phase modulation. Each phase transmitted is assumed treated as three bits in a binary code. The bit error probability with 8-phase modulation decisions is higher than with 4-phase modulation decisions. For the example given, the bit error probability is 10^{-5} with 4-phase modulation, but is 10^{-2} with 8-phase modulation. According to Ungerboeck, if a hard decision is made for each 3-bit symbol prior to binary code decoding, a rather complex code is required just to bring the bit error probability back to 10^{-5}, which would be a coding gain of zero. Specifically, a convolutional code with 64 states and Hamming free distance of 7 is needed to do this.

Now consider combining the modulation and coding processes. Trellis codes that permit Viterbi coding appear to be the most suitable. For the trellis code implementation a $(k + r)$-bit signal constellation, consisting of 2^{k+r} points in two dimensions, is used for the basic pulse transmission. The information rate is k bits per pulse. The way the code uses each set of k bits to select one of the 2^{k+r} constellation points is shown in Figure 4.10. At each unit of time, k bits are input. k' of these bits are sent into a $(k' + r, k', m)$ convolutional encoder, and the remaining $k - k'$ bits do not go into the encoder. In most practical implementations $r = 1$ is chosen. Note that the mapping into binary representation of the signal points is linear. However, the linearity is lost when the binary representation is mapped into modulated signals. Thus the more general trellis code concept is more appropriate to the combined coding-modulation process.

The following example from [UNGE87] uses a trellis code for 8-PSK modulation, with $k = 2, r = 1, k' = 1$, to send 2 bits/pulse with a coding gain. The convolutional code has 2 bits of memory and thus 4 states. Figure 4.11 shows the 4-state trellis diagram and 8-PSK signal set. The comparable uncoded system would be four-phase, with a normalized Euclidean distance of $\sqrt{2}$ between nearest signal points.

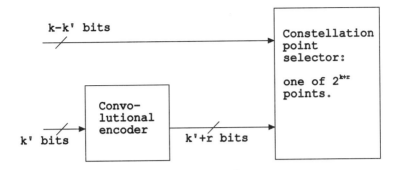

Figure 4.10: Convolutional code selection of coded modulation constellation points.

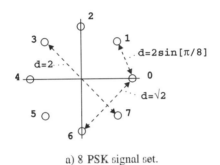

a) 8 PSK signal set.

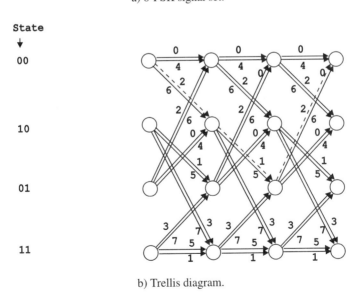

b) Trellis diagram.

Figure 4.11: A modulation code example using 8-PSK. Source: (b) Adapted from "Trellis-coded modulation with redundant signal sets—Part I: Introduction," *IEEE Commun. Mag.*, vol. 25, pp. 5–11, February 1987. ©1988, IEEE

Several different convolutional code circuits (not shown) could result in the trellis diagram shown. Signal constellation points are paired up $(0, 4)$, $(1, 5)$, $(2, 6)$, $(3, 7)$ so that the two in the same pair are $180°$ apart, the farthest possible, Euclidean distance 2. The uncoded bit is used to specify which one of the pair to use. The coded bit determines the state transition, which is of course one of two possibilities. The two in one pair differ by $90°$ from each of the two in the alternative. The free Euclidean distance is the nonzero path that has the smallest Euclidean distance from the all 0's path. One such smallest distance path is a single phase 4, all other 0's, with Euclidean distance 2. Another possible candidate is the dashed path indicated. This has Euclidean distance

$$\left(\sqrt{2}^2 + \sqrt{2}^2 + \left[2 * \sin\left(\frac{\pi}{8}\right) \right]^2 \right)^{1/2} > 2.$$

Thus 2 is the minimum Euclidean distance, which is the primary determinant of error probability. This compares to $\sqrt{2}$ for the uncoded 4-phase, and a coding gain of 3 dB is achieved.

According to [UNGE87]: "Roughly speaking, it is possible to gain 3 dB with 4 states, 4 dB with 8 states, nearly 5 dB with 16 states, and up to 6 dB with 128 or more states." This compares to the theoretical limit of achievable gains, which is about 7–8 dB.

4.5 Iterative Soft Decision Decoding

We have seen that soft decision information is practical to use in convolutional code decoding. It could be used in very short block codes, where the number of code words is small enough to make a comparison of each with the received sequence. In longer block codes, another application is per-symbol decoding techniques where the information in all the parity equations on a particular symbol are taken into account to compute the symbol likelihood [GALL63, MASS63, BATT79]. We have also seen in Section 3.8 an iterative decoding method for product codes, where shorter component codes are used in rows and columns of a two-dimensional array. The iteration consists of first doing row correction, then column correction, and possibly further iterations of row and column corrections. Only hard decision decoding was considered in that section.

Recently, great interest has been shown in techniques that use soft decision in an iterative exchange between two codes, somewhat like product code iterative decoding. The component codes can be short-constraint-length convolutional codes or short block codes. The possibility of reliable transmission at rates within a dB or so of the theoretical limit with moderate complexity has been demonstrated. The codes have been denoted as *turbo codes* or *parallel concatenated codes* [BERR93, BENE96, HAGE96].

One difference between turbo codes and product codes is that the checks on checks in the lower right corner of the rectangular array (Figure 3.8) are not transmitted or used. Another difference is that the interleaving can be more randomized than the row/column code structure. Often it is better to visualize the data area as a single stream of k bits rather than as an array of $k_1 k_2$ bits. Coder 1 accepts the k bits in a certain prescribed order. Coder 2 accepts the same k bits except in a permuted order. The permutation could be a direct interleaving much as in a product code; coder 1 sees the data row by row from a $k_1 k_2$-bit array, while coder 2 sees the data column by column, and the actual transmission order can be either row by row or column by column. However, turbo codes are more general, and any permutation of the k bits is allowed. Some permutations may be better than others, and because of the difficulty of exact analysis, an average performance over all permutations has been used as a measure [BENE96].

4.6 Summary

Trellis codes have the property that there is no prescribed segregation into blocks. They can, however, be terminated into a block code after a certain number of symbol transmissions. Trellis codes are desirable for their ability to work relatively simply with soft decisions, providing more decoder information and higher channel capacity.

Convolutional codes are linear trellis codes. Except for modulation codes, most trellis codes that have been studied are convolutional. An (n, k, m) convolutional encoder accepts k input symbols at a time, and outputs n symbols, based on the k input symbols and mk past input symbols. Convolutional codes can be described by a generator polynomial matrix, a semi-infinite generator matrix, a state diagram, or a trellis diagram. There are several distance measures between code sequences; the free distance probably is the most important. Nonsystematic codes often have a greater free distance than systematic codes of the same memory m. However, nonsystematic codes have systematic feedback equivalents of the same memory. Puncturing of check symbols can be used to create higher rate codes without increasing decoder complexity.

The decoding techniques for convolutional codes are sequential decoding, Viterbi decoding, and majority logic decoding. Sequential decoding is good for long constraint length codes, which are very powerful. Sequential decoding also works with soft decisions; its disadvantage is that some decoding events require excessive computation, even though average decoding complexity is reasonable. Viterbi decoding has the advantage that decoding complexity is deterministic. It also works with soft decisions, and is optimum in some sense for the code. Its disadvantage is that it is limited to short constraint length codes because memory goes up exponentially with constraint length. Majority logic codes are very simple, but are generally designed to work only after hard symbol decisions. Vector symbol majority-logic-like decoding is a possibly attractive decoding method as the outer code of a concatenated coding scheme.

Modulation codes combine modulation with coding to achieve a positive coding gain while also saving bandwidth. Most schemes use the structure of trellis codes and make use of soft decision to achieve reliability at higher data rates than can be had otherwise. Recently developed turbo codes, mostly using component trellis or convolutional codes, have been shown capable of achieving reliable communication rates very close to channel capacity.

4.7 Problems

4.1. The circuit diagram of a $(3, 1, 2)$ convolutional code is shown in Figure P4.1.
  a. Write the matrix of generator polynomials.
  b. Write the first three rows of the infinite generator matrix.
  c. Draw the trellis diagram for this code for three successive stages, starting from state 00. Do not assume the input is terminating. Show for each transition the decoder output.
  d. State whether or not this code is catastrophic, and give a reason.
  e. What is the free distance of this code?

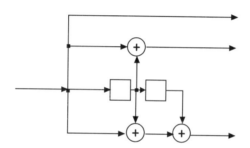

Figure P4.1: Circuit diagram for Problem 4.1.

4.2. The transfer function matrix of a $(3, 2, 1)$ convolutional code is

$$\begin{bmatrix} 1 & D & 0 \\ 0 & 1 & 1+D \end{bmatrix}$$

  a. Draw the encoder block diagram.
  b. Write the semi-infinite generator matrix.
  c. Find the code word sequence corresponding to the information sequence: (11 01). (All zeros input before and after.)

4.3. For the feedback circuit of Figure 4.7, suppose the input data is 10110011. Suppose that after these eight input values we wish to terminate the code by bringing the state back to 00.
  a. What two additional bits need to be appended to the Y sequence?
  b. Find the output Z sequence.

4.4. Show a convolutional code circuit that has a trellis diagram matching that of Figure 4.11.

4.5. A $(3, 1, 2)$ convolutional code has generator sequences

$$g^{(1)} = 100, \qquad g^{(2)} = 101, \qquad g^{(3)} = 111.$$

   a. Starting in state 00, how many paths lead to state 11 after exactly three steps? (There are 1 input, 3 outputs per step). After exactly four steps?

   b. Although not optimum, assume for simplicity that hard binary decisions are made prior to Viterbi decoding. Starting in known state 00, the following twelve digits are received: 101 101 011 000. In Viterbi decoding, what would be the survivor for state 11 after 3 steps? Note there is a possibility of a tie, in which case either could be chosen as survivor. What are the other three survivors after 3 steps?

4.6. A $(3, 1, 2)$ code has generator sequences

$$g^{(1)} = 1 + D; \qquad g^{(2)} = 1 + D^2; \qquad g^{(3)} = 1 + D + D^2.$$

   a. What is the free distance?
   b. Draw the state diagram.
   c. For a 3-bit terminated input $(L = 3)$, draw the complete trellis diagram.
   d. Although not optimum, assume for simplicity that hard binary decisions are made prior to Viterbi decoding. Suppose the data input is 100, and the error sequence is 010 100 000 000 000. Show the final decision path in the trellis.
   e. With Viterbi decoding, show each surviving path to each state at each stage.

4.7. Suppose you were trying to find the survivor between the two sequences 0001 and 1010. Given the two sequences are equally likely a priori and noise affects different bits independently, suppose you want to base the decision on the the actual received sequence $\mathbf{r} = (r_1, r_2, r_3, r_4)$. The following probabilities are computed:

Bit i	$p(1/r_i)$	$p(0/r_i)$
1	.9	.1
2	.8	.2
3	.1	.9
4	.6	.4

   a. Find the ratio $p(0001/\mathbf{r})/p(1010/\mathbf{r})$, and decide the survivor.
   b. Check the similarity of forming bit metrics as follows:
   1. For each bit, compute the larger of

$$\log[p(1/r_i)/p(0/r_i)]$$

   or

$$\log[p(0/r_i)/p(1/r_i)],$$

   assign that value as metric for the more likely bit, and assign 0 as metric for the less likely bit.
   2. Add the metrics for 0001 and for 1010, and pick the larger.
   3. As a further check, take the antilog of the difference of the metrics for 0001 and for 1010. This should equal $p(0001/\mathbf{r})/p(1010/\mathbf{r})$.

4.8. The circuit for a rate $1/3$ convolutional code is shown in Figure P4.2.

  a. What is the minimum weight of any nonzero output sequence?

  b. Draw the state diagram for this code.

  c. Starting in known old state 00, the following twelve digits are received: 001 110 110 010. Find the state path and input data that agree to within two or less digits with the received sequence.

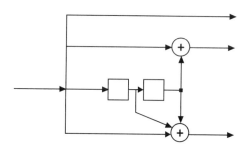

Figure P4.2: Circuit diagram for Problem 4.8.

4.9. Consider the 4-state 8-PSK trellis code of Figure 4.11.

  a. Two nearest neighbor paths from state 00 to state 00 are $0°, 0°, 0°$ and $90°, 45°, 90°$. Assume additive, constant strength white Gaussian noise. Suppose the starting state is known to be 00, and the observed received points are:

$$(3/4, 1/4), \qquad (\cos[25°], \sin[25°]), \qquad (1/4, 3/4).$$

Which of the two paths are more likely correct?

  b. In comparing two PSK signal points, does the amplitude of the received point have any affect on the relative likelihood of the two signal points? Explain your answer.

4.10. Given the $(2, 1, 2)$ systematic convolutional code with $g^{(2)}(D) = 1 + D + D^2$, fill in the data values given the following output sequences containing erasures (indicated by X) but no errors.

| Output 1 | 0 | 0 | 0 | X | 0 | X | 1 | 0 | X | X | X | 1 |
| Output 2 | 0 | 0 | 0 | 1 | X | X | 0 | 0 | X | 0 | 1 | 0 |

Chapter 5

Reliable Block-Coded ARQ

We have seen in Chapter 3 that a (n, k) parity check block code can be designed for error correction and detection. According to Shannon's Noisy Channel Coding Theorem it is theoretically possible, given assumed channel statistics, to construct a coding and decoding procedure so that the probability of not being able to correct the errors can be made as small as we wish, for large enough n, provided that k/n is less than a quantity called *channel capacity*, which is computed based on the channel statistics. Even if it were practical to do this, however, there is a problem with relying on this technique for ensuring reliable communication. The problem is that in reality channel statistics are not known exactly, and even if they are carefully measured over a long period, it cannot be assured with great confidence that the underlying statistics will remain invariable for any future duration more than a tiny fraction of the measuring period.

A key to the solution to this problem is to provide for error detection to cover cases where the channel behavior produces more errors than the decoder is capable of correcting. When uncorrectable errors are detected, then retransmission or transmission of additional redundant information is called for.

The need for error detection and retransmission was recognized as early as the 1940s when the term ARQ was introduced. Since the 1960s various error control protocols employing ARQ have been introduced for data links and data networks. This text concentrates more on basic principles than details of standards. Some discussion of link control standards is given in Section 5.10, and various network standards in Chapters 9 and 10.

5.1 Error Detection Properties

Provision of error detection beyond what is needed for error correction costs something in efficiency. In this section we give a quantitative measure of that cost.

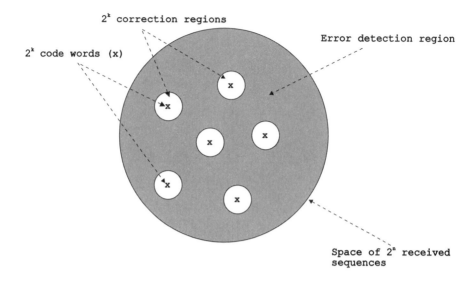

Figure 5.1: Decision space with hard binary decisions.

Consider an (n, k) binary block code. Suppose the decoder makes preliminary binary decisions for each binary digit. Figure 5.1 is an abstract picture of decision space over the 2^n possible received binary sequences. There are 2^k regions corresponding to the 2^k code words, and the rest of the space is the error detection region.

Define P_c as the probability a correct decision is made on a code word, P_d as the probability of error detection without correction, and P_e as the probability of erroneous decision. P_d is the probability of a reception outside all of the code word regions, P_c is the probability of a reception in the correct code word region, and P_e is the probability of a reception in one of the incorrect code word regions. Thus,

$$P_c + P_d + P_e = 1. \tag{5.1}$$

For parity check codes, an alternative visualization is in terms of the group of n-tuples written as cosets of the subgroup of code words, as shown in Figure 5.2. Decoding decisions are made based on the syndrome, and all members of the same coset have the same syndrome. The n-tuples in the figure can be interpreted in either of two ways, depending on one's objectives:

1. The n-tuples are the received sequences.
2. The n-tuples are the error patterns.

Each nonzero syndrome leads either to error detection with no correction attempted, or attempted error correction. A zero syndrome is of course interpreted as no errors present (although an error pattern identical to some nonzero code word may have occurred).

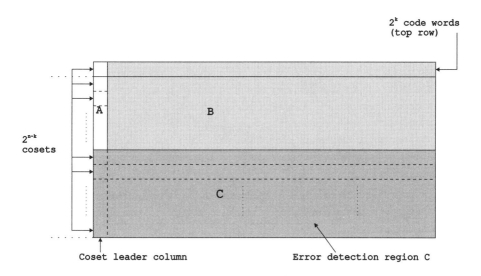

Figure 5.2: Decision regions related to code word subgroup.

Interpreted as *error patterns*, region *A* (coset leaders) corresponds to error patterns that are correctly decoded, region *B* corresponds to error patterns that are incorrectly decoded, and region *C* corresponds to error patterns that are detected without correction. (In region *C* the coset leader is irrelevant.) It is most common to assume that the binary channel is symmetric; then the probability of an error pattern is independent of the code word transmitted.

Interpreted as *received sequences*, all received sequences in region *C* are in the error detection region. With the correctable error patterns as coset leaders, the array interpreted as *received sequences* becomes a *decoding table*, and each received sequence in regions *A* or *B* is decoded as the code word above it in the table.

5.1.1 The Cost of "Fail-Safe" Protection

With an empty error detection region, each code word decision region would contain 2^{n-k} points. The code rate is k/n. We wish to see the cost and effect of adding an error detection region. One way of modifying the code to permit error detection is to use only $2^{k'}$ of the code words, where $k' < k$, but keep the *same number* 2^{n-k} of points per region. (It is easier here to use the Figure 5.1 visualization, because in Figure 5.2 the subgroup would change.) Thus P_c will remain approximately the same, P_d will increase and P_e will decrease. The fraction of points that lie in error correction decision regions is then

$$f = 2^{-(k-k')}. \tag{5.2}$$

The rate is reduced by a factor k'/k.

If a sequence is received that is complete noise, we would have $P_e = f$. This has been called the *"fail-safe"* probability, since it is the probability of an undetected error if the channel temporarily fails. It is not necessarily the minimum P_e under any channel condition, but it often approximates a worst-case situation.

The cost in rate to get good protection against undetected error is modest if the number of bits per code block is fairly large. For example, if $k = 500$ and $k' = 460$, the rate is reduced by only 8 percent and $f = 10^{-12}$. With the trend to communicate and process data in increasingly large amounts, the rate cost of nearly perfect error detection is often much less than a 1 percent reduction.

5.1.2   Error Detection with Soft Decision Decoding of Binary Codes

Suppose an (n, k) binary code is used for transmission, but the decoder records a number for each bit as a soft decision. This number may have a continuous range of values. Then the reception can be thought of as a point in n-dimensional real space. The code words correspond to a set of 2^k points in that space. Under many statistical environments the optimum decision is to pick the closest code word point to the received signal point; this is the minimum Euclidean distance to any code word point. Without error detection, the entire n-dimensional region of possible receptions is divided into 2^k regions, one for each code point. (As a practical matter this region is of finite extent, because there is a limit to how large a signal can be produced at the receiver output. Actually, with high probability a received point will be near the surface of a sphere of radius $\sqrt{(S + N)}$, where S and N are the average signal and noise power, respectively.) Suppose we assume for simplicity that all these regions have the same amount of n-dimensional volume V. Then we can use the same trick as in the hard decision case: use only $2^{k'}$ of the 2^k code words, but associate the same volume V with each code word as if all were used. Then the ratio of volume in all decision regions to total volume will be the same as f in (5.2) with the same k'/k rate reduction factor. Thus the same fail-safe protection is attained as in the hard decision case, but higher rates are possible because the capacity is higher with soft decisions than with hard decisions. With binary transmission the gain is most significant for low signal-to-noise ratios, because at high signal-to-noise ratios the capacity is close to 1 bit/symbol in either case.

5.2   Fundamental ARQ Protocol Principles

Error detection by itself or combined with error correction is not the complete answer to the problem of ensuring very low probability of error. Provision for errors or lost information on the return retransmission request channel must also be considered. Return channel imperfection could lead to frames not being retransmitted when requested, or retransmitted when not requested. Means must be provided for the receiver to confidently assemble the various transmitted pieces into the correct message.

Because request for retransmission of a block basically involves only one bit of information returned for each block of many bits sent forward, the return signal should be easier to send reliably than the forward signal. Thus, some investigators have assumed an error-free return channel. This is not a very good thing to rely on in general, however. Designs of protocols to ensure reliable communication despite errors on both the forward and return channels emerged in about 1960 [METZ60], [REIF61], [WOZE60]. Basically, three fundamental principles are involved:

1. Use sufficient error detection that P_e is negligible.

2. Provide a bias in the return channel acknowledgment interpretation such that, if there is any significant doubt, the data are retransmitted.

3. Provide sequence numbering of successive frames, so that an unrequested repeat can be distinguished from a new frame.

The next sections will show how these principles are applied. The protocols to be described all assume there is sufficient error detection built into a frame that the occurrence of an undetected error can be neglected. The fail-safe region arguments have demonstrated that the probability of such an undetected error event can be reduced exponentially with added check bits to any desired level, at a rate cost that is negligible for large frame blocks.

5.3 Protocols for Reliable Stop-and-Wait Communication

Consider a two-way communication channel where station X sends a coded frame of data to station Y, and waits for a return signal from Y before sending the next frame. This process, called *stop-and-wait*, is the simplest for explaining how ARQ protocols work.

Suppose further that Y as no data to send to X. Thus the signal from Y to X will just relate to acknowledgment or retransmission request. Also, assume that communication proceeds on a fixed timing schedule, so that Y will receive a frame in a certain interval, and sends back a response at a fixed time after the end of its frame reception interval, whether or not Y is able to successfully decode the frame. Later in this chapter we will introduce the complication of variable delay.

It was previously stated that sequence numbering of successive frames was necessary to prevent ambiguity. In the simple stop-and-wait case where one frame is sent at a time, the sequence number can be as small as one bit, in which case it will be referred to as an alternating bit.

There are two possible ways of generating the return acknowledgment signal.

Method 1. Send ACK (acknowledge) or NAK (negative acknowledge, or retransmit) related to whether the last received frame had any uncorrectable detected errors.

Method 2. Send an identification of the sequence number of the next expected frame (or in some protocols the sequence number of the most recently decoded frame).

The ACK/NAK method was used in [METZ60]. The sequence number return method is described in [METZ63], [BART69], and [METZ72]. We will see that method 2 is to be preferred for several reasons.

One way of providing bias in the return decision is to use a fairly large number c of bits to carry a one-bit ACK/NAK or alternating bit identifying the expected next frame. Then, of the 2^c possible received sequences on the Y-to-X channel, interpret only one of them as ACK or new alternating bit, and the other $2^c - 1$ as NAK or old alternating bit. Alternately, one could use any multidimensional waveform to represent the ACK or new alternating bit, and any reception that did not correlate extremely closely with the ACK signal would be interpreted as a NAK or old alternating bit.

Another decision bias commonly used in practice, and particularly useful when delay is variable, is to provide for a "timeout" duration. If no reply is received by the time the timeout period expires, NAK or old alternating bit is assumed, and the prior frame is retransmitted by X. However, the variable delay/timeout strategy creates problems with method 1 (see Section 5.3.1).

Figure 5.3 shows space-time diagrams for the ACK/NAK method. Figure 5.3a shows how a return channel error is handled. The upper case letters A, B, and so on designate successive different frames, and the number in parentheses is the sequence number, which is a single alternating bit in this case. The second returned ACK is misinterpreted as a NAK, an event that is not uncommon due to the decision bias. Y will receive $B(1)$ twice in succession, and will recognize the second frame as an unrequested repeat, which it will discard. Although the occurrence of an unrequested repeat could in this case also be recognized by the fact the frame has identical data to the last one, we do not want to rely on this characteristic; the sender may in fact wish to send the same frame twice as part of its message. This is a context question that should be recognized only at a higher level.

Figure 5.3b shows the sending of a NAK due to error detection. Clearly no problem arises in this case. If the NAK was turned into an ACK on the return channel, this would be a serious problem, since X would skip resending $B(1)$ and move on to sending $C(0)$. Then Y would never get a copy of $B(1)$ under the conditions provided in the protocol. The use of the biased ACK/NAK decision is intended to ensure this almost never happens.

The ideal timing assumption is a realistic one if X and Y are connected by a direct dedicated two-way link. With statistically shared links and networks this model is not valid. First, delays are variable due to the variability of shared user traffic, so it is not certain when to expect the next frame or response. Also, a frame or response can be lost completely.

5.3.1   Variable Delay and Ordering

A still more serious problem occurs when frames arrive out of order. If all frames are sent on the same link in the order received, the order is retained even with statistical sharing, as long as each individual user's frames are served in the same order received.

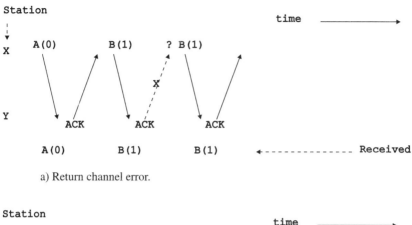

a) Return channel error.

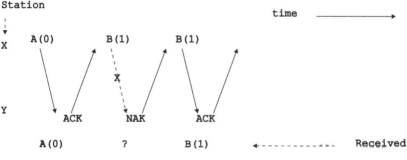

b) Forward channel error.

Figure 5.3: Effect of errors, ACK/NAK stop-and-wait protocol.

However, we will see that in the case of a datagram network, successive frames may travel on different paths, and thus may arrive out of order.

Consider the effect of variable delay and loss of frames and/or acknowledgment signals, but retain the assumption of ordered arrival. A loss of a frame or acknowledgment could result in waiting forever in the stop-and-wait protocol (since the round trip time is variable) unless a timeout mechanism is used. However, even if the timeout is used, method 1 suffers from a critical failure [BERT92]. Figure 5.4 illustrates the problem. The sender transmits a frame $A(0)$, which is correctly received, but the return acknowledgment gets delayed past the timeout. $A(0)$ is sent again and ACK returned again. Then the first ACK finally arrives at the sender, and $B(1)$ is sent. $B(1)$ is not received correctly and a NAK is sent back. But the second ACK for $A(0)$ finally comes back and is incorrectly interpreted as ACK for $B(1)$. The sender then discards $B(1)$ from its memory as having been confirmed, and transmits $C(0)$. $B(1)$ will never be transmitted again, so the protocol has failed.

Method 2 avoids this failure because the acknowledgment signal gives some identification of what is being acknowledged. Method 2 requires the ordering assumption, but allows lost signals and variable delays (see Problem 5.5).

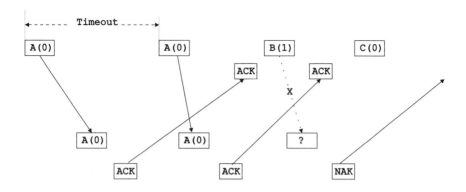

Figure 5.4: Effect of variable delay on method 1.

5.3.2 Efficiency Comparison

Method 2 is also more efficient than method 1. The difference is most pronounced when errors are frequent. Figure 5.5 illustrates why it is more efficient. For method 1 (Figure 5.5a) to advance to sending a new frame, both forward and return channels must be successful on the same round trip. For the return sequence number procedure

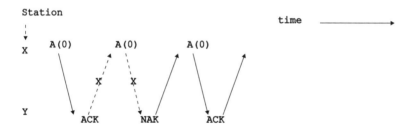

a) Method 1: ACK/NAK transmissions.

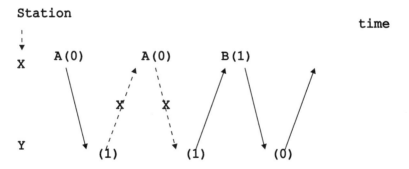

b) Method 2: Transmissions with next expected sequence number.

Figure 5.5: Efficiency comparison of ACK/NAK with next expected.

(Figure 5.5b) to advance, there needs to be a forward success, followed by a return success at any future time.

The two acknowledgment procedures can readily be compared analytically, assuming independent errors. Let p_1 be the probability that the X-to-Y sending fails, and let p_2 be the probability the Y-to-X sending fails. Let T_a be the ratio of total frame sendings to new frame sendings in the ACK/NAK case, and let T_b be the corresponding ratio in the other case. In the ACK/NAK case the fraction of successes is just $(1 - p_1)(1 - p_2)$, so

$$T_a = 1/[(1 - p_1)(1 - p_2)] \tag{5.3}$$

In the other case suppose it takes i tries to get the frame successfully from X to Y, and following that it takes j tries to get the next expected sequence number from Y to X. Then simple enumeration shows that the number of frames sent from X to Y to advance to sending the next block is $i + j - 1$. Thus

$$T_b = E[i + j - 1]$$

$$E[i] = 1 - (1 - p_1) + 2p_1(1 - p_1) + 3p_1^2(1 - p_1) + \cdots = 1/(1 - p_1);$$

$$E[j] = 1/(1 - p_2).$$

Thus,

$$T_b = [1 - p_1p_2]/[(1 - p_1)(1 - p_2)] \tag{5.4}$$

It can easily be seen that $T_b \leq T_a$, although the difference is slight if either p_1 or p_2 is small.

5.3.3 Stop-and-Wait with Two-Way Communication

Continuing the assumption of stop-and-wait communication with X sending one frame at a time to Y, suppose Y also has frames of data to send to X. Then, instead of sending back just an acknowledgment signal for each block, Y could also send back a frame containing data destined for X. Acknowledgment signals can also be sent "piggyback" in this same frame. The parity bits necessary to provide error detection for the data can serve the additional purpose of providing the bias protection for the acknowledgment signal. If the acknowledgment signal forms part of the frame data, whenever errors are detected in the Y to X signal, the ACK signal is ignored and X retransmits the prior frame; if errors are not detected, all data, including the acknowledgment signal, are almost surely correct, so X can read the acknowledgment signal and act accordingly. Similarly, X can incorporate acknowledgment of the Y to X data into the X to Y frames.

Consider now the sequence number acknowledgment method. Each transmitted frame that contains data will have two sequence numbers; one, called the *send sequence number*, is the number of the data unit in the frame; the other, called the *receive sequence number*, is the piggybacked acknowledgment. If a station has no data to send, it would still send a frame containing the receive sequence number.

5.3.4   A One-Sequence-Number Policy

A technique has also been proposed [METZ63, METZ72] that uses only a single sequence number to cover both purposes. This technique is applicable only to the case where frames are sent one-to-one on an alternating basis, which is the case now under consideration. On the other hand, the two-sequence-number policy is more versatile.

The one-sequence-number technique has been called the "new-word (meaning new frame) policy," because each station sends a new frame to the other if and only if it receives a new frame from the other station; otherwise it repeats the previously sent frame. Figure 5.6 illustrates the operation of this protocol using a one-bit sequence number. Note that all frames are sequence numbered, regardless of whether they contain data. By convention, one station (X) changes the alternating bit on sending a new frame, while the other (Y) sends the alternating bit of the received new frame. In the figure station Y sends the data units M and N, but in its third transmitted frame sends only the alternating bit because it has no data to send. In the next cycle Y detects errors in the received frame, and thus must repeat the prior (0). Note that even if Y now had data to send it would not be permitted to put it into this next frame, because it must send exactly what it sent last time.

This one-sequence-number protocol has an interesting extension to the case of a ring of stations, as we shall see in Chapter 9. Historically, the idea for employing the one-sequence-number new word policy originated from a study of ARQ with memory [METZ63]. With the new word policy a retransmitted frame always has the same piggybacked acknowledgment, and is bitwise identical; thus it is more easily combined with a memory of its past reception. Memory ARQ will be discussed in Chapter 7.

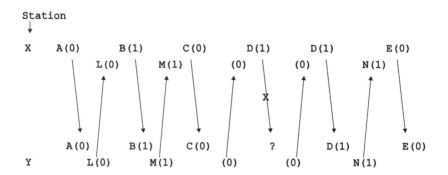

Figure 5.6: Illustration of the new word policy.

5.4 Stop-and-Wait with Multiple Frames Outstanding

In this section we relax the condition that only one frame is sent before stopping and waiting for acknowledgment. To do this, the sequence number size must be expanded beyond one bit. A multibit sequence number also will be needed to handle the problem of out-of-order receptions (to be considered in Chapter 10 on data networks). Suppose the sequence number has b bits. Then frames are numbered in cycles of 2^b. Also, in order to be able to acknowledge several frames at a time, and to be able to acknowledge some but not all of a set of frames, the use of the sequence number method of acknowledgment, with separate send and receive sequence numbers, becomes imperative. It has been become standard to acknowledge all frames up to a certain point by stating the sequence number of the next expected new frame. An alternative is to request retransmission of a specific frame by specifying its sequence number.

The number of frames that can be sent out before getting acknowledgment is constrained by the sequence number cycle. The maximum number of consecutive unacknowledged frames in the stop-and-wait procedure is $2^b - 1$. One might think at first that it should be 2^b, but the following example shows that this can lead to ambiguity. Suppose $b = 3$ and the eight frames numbered 0, 1, 2, 3, 4, 5, 6, 7 were sent out prior to acknowledgment; the next frame, not yet sent, would have the sequence number 0. If Y received all eight frames it would send back "expecting frame 0"; but if it received none of the eight it would send back the same thing, since it would be expecting the older frame 0 next. A one-unit reduction in the range will prevent this ambiguity from arising.

Figure 5.7 is an example where X sends more than one frame at a time to Y. For simplicity, this example does not have Y sending any data to X, although this could easily be done also, and the acknowledgment signal from Y could be piggybacked on a data frame going to X. Sequence number size $b = 3$ is assumed. X begins by sending five frames to Y, sequence numbered 0, 1, 2, 3, 4. Y acknowledges all five together by sending expected sequence number 5. Then X sends four more frames,

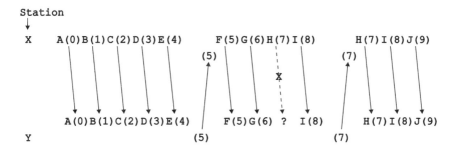

Figure 5.7: Stop-and-wait with multiple frames outstanding.

but the third of these, $H(7)$, is not decodable. Y sends back expecting (7), which implies acknowledgment of $F(5)$ and $G(6)$. Note that $I(0)$ has already been correctly decoded by Y, but the most common procedure is to keep things in order by ignoring this reception. Then X will go back and repeat both $H(7)$ and $I(0)$. In a more complex procedure, Y could send back that it received $F(5)$, $G(6)$, and $I(0)$, but did not receive $H(7)$, so that X need only retransmit $H(7)$.

Note that the option to accept part of a set of successive frame transmissions is also useful as a flow control mechanism to prevent the sender from overwhelming the receiver with data. For example, in Figure 5.7, if in the second sending group station Y only had room to absorb $F(5)$, it could refuse to look at $G(6)$, and send back (6) to force X to go back and repeat $G(6)$, and also eventually $H(7)$ and $I(0)$.

5.5   Full Duplex ARQ Protocols

In reading Section 5.4, where varying numbers of frames may be sent prior to ac-knowledgment, the reader may notice that the stop-and-wait rule does not really have to be obeyed if the channel is full duplex, meaning that signals can be sent in both directions at the same time. The important thing is that a sender does not allow a greater range of unacknowledged frames to be outstanding than permitted by ambi-guity avoidance constraints. In fact, a continuous flow of frames in both directions, with no waiting, is possible if the sequence number alphabet is large enough to ensure not running out of permitted frame numbers before an acknowledgment is returned.

Consider now the retransmission strategy. There are three different ways a sender can perceive a need for retransmission:

1. A decoded return signal can contain a specific instruction to retransmit; this was previously met in the case of the NAK signal. Extended to the case of multibit sequence numbers, this could combine the NAK signal (actually called REJ in this application) with the sequence number of the frame that was not correctly received.

2. In a synchronized system, a nondecodable return signal at the time when ac-knowledgment of a past frame or set of frames was scheduled to be received would indicate the need to retransmit.

3. In a variable delay system, no decodable acknowledgment has been returned, and a timeout period has expired since the transmission of a particular frame.

Given the sender discovers the need to transmit, there are alternatives as to just what to transmit. The simplest and most common strategy is called the *go-back* strategy; in this strategy the sender goes back and resends the frame needing retrans-mission and all subsequent transmitted frames. A more efficient but more complex strategy is called *selective repeat* or *selective reject*. In the selective repeat strategy, the sender selectively repeats only the frame or frames that are negatively acknowl-edged or have their timeout expired, and does not retransmit the later outstanding ones unless necessary. Selective repeat will be discussed in Chapter 6.

5.6 The Go-Back Protocol with Continuous Two-Way Transmission

With the go-back protocol the limit on number of consecutive unacknowledged frames that the sender can transmit is $2^b - 1$, just as with multiple-frame-outstanding stop-and-wait. Figure 5.8 explains this limit more rigorously. Go-back does not permit the receiver to accept frames out of order. In the following, frame i refers to its true integer numerical order, not its sequence number, which would be (i) modulo 2^b. At any given time the receiver has already decoded and accepted all frames up to the ith frame, as indicated in the figure, and the only new frame the receiver is allowed to accept is frame number $i + 1$. Since the sender has sent frame i it could not *afterward* send any frame that was number $i - 2^b + 1$ or earlier because the sender window limit would not have allowed it to send the frame i if $i - 2^b + 1$ were still in its window. The only frame it could then send with sequence number $(i + 1)$ modulo 2^b is then the frame $i + 1$. The receiver thus will not next accept any possible new transmitted frame except frame $i + 1$, and only the true frame $i + 1$ can be transmitted with sequence number $(i + 1)$ modulo 2^b. This argument assumes that frames are received, if received at all, in the same time order as they were transmitted. Note the previous emphasis on the word "afterward." If time order was not preserved, a frame sent earlier than frame i that had a sequence number $(i + 1)$ modulo 2^b could arrive later than frame i and cause an error. If all frames traverse the same path and are sent out first come, first served at any relay point, time order will be preserved. If frames follow different paths through a network, time order would not be preserved in general.

Figure 5.9 illustrates operation of the go-back strategy for a case of continuous transmission in both directions. We will assume here the case where the frame

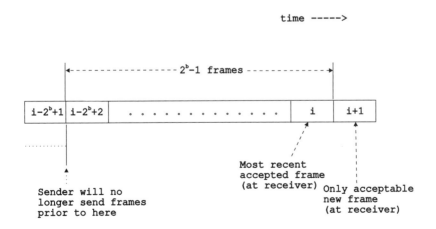

Figure 5.8: Demonstration of the go-back ambiguity prevention limit.

Notation: (Asr), A=frame content identifier,   s=send seq. no.,
r=receive next expected.

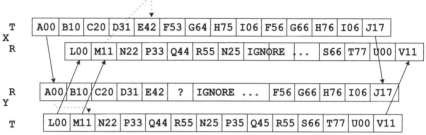

Figure 5.9: Continuous transmission with the go-back rule.

duration is the same in both directions, and each frame should be individually acknowledged. Later we will look at more complicated cases for which the frame and acknowledgment rates are different in the two directions. In the illustration, three-bit sequence numbers are used.

For the round-trip time in this example, a station sends out four frames before it gets back acknowledgment of the first. For example, station X sends out $(A, 0)$, $(B, 1)$, $(C, 2)$, and $(D, 3)$ before $(M11)$ is decoded, acknowledging $(A, 0)$. Actually the acknowledgment of $(A, 0)$ is decoded while $(D, 3)$ is being sent out, but this is too late to make a change. The acknowledgment of $M1$ is placed in the $E4$ frame, as indicated by the dotted directed line. We assume that the four-frame round trip count remains stable, and both stations are aware of this count.

In the example, frame $(F53)$ is not decoded by Y. Y indicates this by not advancing its received sequence number. Also, since it could not decode the frame, Y is not sure whether X has received $(N, 2)$, so it retransmits $(N, 2)$ with the received sequence number 5 piggybacked on the frame. Since it knows that X will send 3 more new frames that will be repeated when X learns of the nonreception, Y ignores the next three receptions. Also, Y must retransmit $(P, 3)$, $(Q, 4)$, and $(R, 5)$ by the go-back rule.

A discerning reader may notice that the procedure above could be modified to improve efficiency while still retaining the go-back feature with its protection against ambiguity. For example, when Y fails to decode $(F53)$, the undecodable frame very likely contained an acknowledgment of $(N, 2)$. Because Y has not run out of sequence numbers for the ambiguity constraint, it could try going ahead and sending $(S65)$. In this case it would be rewarded, because the subsequent reception of $(G64)$, $(H75)$, and $(I06)$ would acknowledge $(N, 2)$ as well as $(P, 3)$, $(Q, 4)$, and $(R, 5)$. On the other hand, if it later discovered that $(N, 2)$ had not been acknowledged, Y would have to go back and resend a greater number of frames. Station X should not use this trick in this case, however, because reception of $(**5)$ immediately after receiving $(R55)$ means, under the assumed one-for-one acknowledgments and stable round-trip time, that Y definitely did not receive $(F53)$.

5.7 Efficiency of the Continuous Go-Back Strategy

Consider for simplicity the case where errors occur only on the X to Y link, with probability of an uncorrectable frame being P, independent for successive frames. Also, we will look only at the efficiency of sending data on the X to Y link. A key parameter is the number K of frames that must be sent out consecutively before the return acknowledgment can be decoded. ($K = 4$ in Figure 5.9.) We ask how many frames must be sent, on average, for every new frame accepted by Y. If a frame is sent successfully the first try, it will never have to be retransmitted, so it will require only one frame sending. If a frame is not successfully decoded, K frames will be wasted, and the frame will then have to try again. From this argument, the expected number of sendings to advance to the next frame is

$$T_{GB} = 1 \cdot (1 - P) + (K + 1) \cdot P \cdot (1 - P) + (2K + 1) \cdot P^2 \cdot (1 - P)$$

$$+ (3K + 1) \cdot P^3 \cdot (1 - P) \ldots$$

$$T_{GB} = [1 + (K - 1)P]/(1 - P). \tag{5.5}$$

For an ideal selective repeat system, a fraction $1 - P$ of the sendings would be successful new frames, and only unsuccessful frames need be repeated, so

$$T_{SR} = 1/(1 - P). \tag{5.6}$$

Comparing Equations (5.5) and (5.6), for small values of KP there is little to gain from using the selective repeat procedure. However, for very noisy channels (large P) or long distance channels such as satellite channels (large K), the difference can be quite large.

5.8 Continuous Transmission with Unequal Frame Durations

If frame sizes vary or if the frame rates in the two directions are unequal, acknowledgments will not always be on a one-for-one basis. Figure 5.10 illustrates a case where the frames from Y to X are twice as long as the frames from X to Y. The frame lengths remain constant in this example. Assume both sequence numbers are 3-bits long. The propagation time is taken as half an X-frame in each direction, and decoding time is assumed negligible.

Figure 5.10a is a case with no errors, while Figure 5.10b shows an error in the X to Y direction. In Figure 5.10a, note that X sends out up to six frames before the first is acknowledged. At first, X sends out five frames $(A, 0)$ through $(E, 4)$ before acknowledgment of $(A, 0)$ comes back, but gets acknowledgment of $(A, 0)$ before it needs to send $(F, 5)$. X then sends $(F, 5)$ and $(G, 6)$, resulting in six frames outstanding, before receiving a frame from Y that acknowledges both frames $(B, 1)$ and $(C, 2)$. In this case the limit of at most seven outstanding frames is never reached. However, if

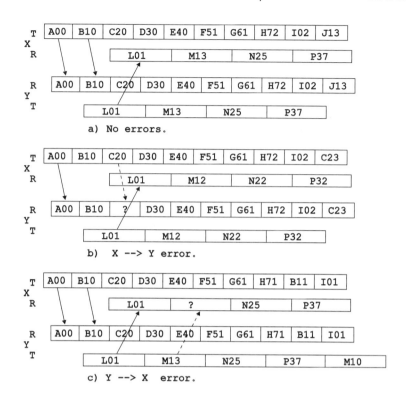

Figure 5.10: Examples of go-back with unequal frame lengths in the two directions.

the propagation times were longer or Y's frames were longer, X might have to stop due to reaching the limit of outstanding frames. If the delay was still longer X would reach a timeout and have to go back to resending the oldest unacknowledged frame.

In Figure 5.10b, frame ($C20$) cannot be decoded by Y. Since Y has only one outstanding unacknowledged frame, it can use the improved procedure described in Section 5.7 and send a frame with the new data unit ($M, 1$), and at the same time acknowledge ($B, 1$) by inserting received next expected number 2. Y continues to look at the next five frames for acknowledgment information, although the data in these frames will be repeated and thus could be ignored. In this case new acknowledgments do come, starting at ($F51$), so the flow of data from Y to X does not get interrupted. When X decodes ($N22$), it recognizes that the acknowledgment number has not been advanced even though by this time it should have, and in addition X has run out of unambiguous sequence numbers. Thus X invokes the go-back procedure and resends ($C, 2$), but with the new receive sequence number 3, acknowledging ($N, 2$).

In Figure 5.10c, frame ($M13$) cannot be decoded by X. At this point X has six outstanding unacknowledged frames (B, C, D, E, F, G), so can send one more. However, the additional frame ($H71$) is sent before the next frame is fully received from Y. Thus X has the option of waiting until the next frame from Y is decoded or until a timeout is reached, or going back immediately to $(B, 1)$; the illustration shows the latter option. When $(N25)$ gets decoded, this acknowledges B, C, D, E, so X could go ahead to the new frame $(I, 0)$. Thus the X to Y flow is held up only briefly by the error, and would not have been held up at all if $(N25)$ had arrived a little earlier. The go-back rule requires that the data $(N, 2)$ be discarded, since it is not the next expected new frame. Since X is still waiting for $(M, 1)$ it does not advance its receive sequence number. When Y decodes $(H71)$ and $(B11)$ it sees that X's acknowledgment sequence number has not been advanced for four consecutive frames. Also, $(B11)$ represents a go-back or in any case is not the frame Y is allowed to accept as the next new one. Thus Y invokes go-back and resends $(M, 1)$ as well as $(N, 2)$ and $(P, 3)$.

5.9 Condition for Continuous Transmission

In this section we derive a condition for the minimum size sequence number to permit continuous transmission, assuming fixed size frames in each direction. In Figure 5.11, the transmission delay is assumed to be T_p in each direction, and the minimum decoding time T_d for each station. The frame durations for X and Y are T_X and T_Y, respectively. For the go-back procedure we can have at most $2^b - 1$ outstanding frames, so to allow continuous transmission by X we must have

$$2^b - 1 \geq 1 + \frac{2T_p + T_Y}{T_X}. \tag{5.7}$$

The minimum condition for Y can be found by just interchanging T_X and T_Y. We can see by this observation that the constraint is more severe for the sender that has the smaller frames. It may not be possible to achieve both minima simultaneously, because in minimizing for X we have conveniently spaced Y's frame to begin right after a frame from X has been decoded. If Y also wants to send continuously and at a different frame rate, this cannot always be possible. In the worst case, the decoding might be completed just after Y has started sending a frame, which could cause an additional round-trip delay of T_Y.

In general, frames of both senders can vary in length and data is not necessarily generated continuously. If one of the stations has no data frames to send, an ACK

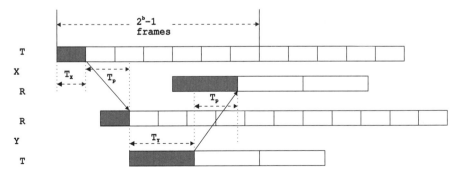

Figure 5.11: Constraint for continuous transmission.

frame without data could be sent when needed. For a worst-case design, if there is a known T_{pmax}, T_{Ymax} and T_{Xmin}, b could be the smallest integer satisfying:

$$2^b - 1 \geq 1 + \frac{2T_{pmax} + 2T_{Ymax}}{T_{Xmin}}. \tag{5.8}$$

where the $2T_{Ymax}$ term allows for just missing the start of the Y frame. However, it is not always necessary to have continuous transmission. When channels are statistically shared, pauses do not necessarily represent wasted time, since other users' packets can be sent. Another factor with statistical sharing is that time delay from sender to receiver can vary widely because of queuing that varies with traffic intensities.

It is not always necessary to acknowledge each frame individually. Several frames can be acknowledged simultaneously, even without preventing continuous transmission if there is sufficient leeway in inequality (5.7). Less frequent acknowledgments can reduce congestion in a shared-channel situation.

With variable delays the use of a timeout rule is important. When a frame from the opposite direction is not decodable, none of the information in the frame is trusted; it is not necessarily even known to which user of a shared channel the frame belongs. Thus this may have contained a negative or positive acknowledgment, or maybe is not at all a response to the sender in question. If it is a positive acknowledgment, with the next expected sequence number approach, the acknowledgment will get included in a future return frame. The sender could go back immediately on receiving an undecodable frame without destroying the error-protecting feature of the process, but on average it would in many cases be more efficient to wait some additional time for future return receptions before going back. Eventually a time is reached where it likely would be more efficient to go back; this would be ideally at the timeout point relative to the frame that has not yet been positively acknowledged. In most cases this timeout value would be set at a time longer than the time to send the permitted $2^b - 1$ frames at a continuous transmission rate.

A different factor that could affect the minimization more favorably is the possibility that an acknowledgment number could be inserted into a frame after transmission of the frame has already begun. The piggybacked acknowledgment is encoded just like data and could be the last part of data encoded. The only part that would necessarily follow this would be the parity check sequence. For example, in Figure 5.10a, Y could send possibly $(L03)$ instead of $(L01)$ and $(M15)$ instead of $(M13)$. Thus round-trip acknowledgment time could be reduced considerably in this way if frame formats allowed it. Almost a full frame length delay is saved in the round-trip.

Clearly Equation (5.7) would have to be modified according to the considerations mentioned in the previous three paragraphs.

5.10   Data Link Control Standards

In the 1960s IBM introduced the Binary Synchronous Control (BSC) protocol. It is a half-duplex stop-and-wait protocol and uses the alternating bit acknowledgment protocol. Error detection is performed with a block check count at the end of a frame.

This is not very protective against undetected errors, because a pair of opposite errors can go undetected in the count. It is a character-oriented protocol, whereas later protocols are mostly bit-oriented.

The principal bit-oriented data link control standard is HDLC (High level Data Link Control). It is listed as ISO 3309 and ISO 4335 of the International Standards Organization. It was derived from IBM's Synchronous Data Link Control protocol (SDLC). A good tutorial explanation of bit-oriented protocols is given in [CARL80]. The protocols are designed to permit full duplex communication, which can be continuous in both directions.

5.10.1   The Place of Link Error Control in a Network

Although detailed consideration of network communication protocols will be reserved for later chapters, it is important at this point to see how link error control fits into the operation of a data communication network. There is a seven-layer hierarchical framework called the open systems interconnection (OSI) model for handling the whole process of transferring information from one user of the network to another. Going from top to bottom, the highest layers are the *application, presentation,* and *session* layers. These need not concern us at this point, except to say that different sessions involve different user to user connections. Next is the *transport* layer, which deals with end-to-end communication through the network, possibly multiplexing several sessions into a single network connection. The transport layer takes messages from the sessions, breaks the messages into packets at the sending end, and reassembles the packets into messages for delivery to the connected session on the other end. Information to identify the packet session and order must of course be included in the packets. The transport layer also can perform end-to-end error control and ARQ. Transport layer ARQ protocols will be discussed in Chapter 10. Next lower is the *network* layer, whose principal task is proper routing of the data and setting up virtual circuits. The network layer takes transport packets and incorporates them into a network data unit by adding a routing information header. As this network unit visits nodes in the network, the node will examine this routing header, make modifications as needed, and send it on the next hop to its destination. Next lowest is the *link* layer, which is currently the layer of interest. The link layer is given a stream of network data units. The link layer just treats these as a stream of packetized data. It does not look at any routing or transport information in the packets, and has no knowledge of which session each is. Its task is simply to make sure they all get delivered over the link correctly and in the same order as the link received them. It adds its own error control header to help accomplish this task. At the link receiving end, frames considered correct are stripped of their link control overhead, and the network data units are delivered to the network layer for further processing and routing. The lowest layer is the *physical* layer, which is concerned with the waveforms, voltages, and modulation methods to communicate the basic signal elements (usually binary-valued).

Flag	Address	Control	Information	CRC	Flag

Figure 5.12: Fields of an HDLC frame.

5.10.2   The HDLC Standard

Below is a brief description of HDLC, with emphasis on properties relating to reliability and efficiency of communication.

The HDLC frame is of variable length and comprises several different types. The components of an HDLC frame are shown in Figure 5.12.

Flag   This consists of the 8-bit pattern: 01111110 to identify the beginning and the end of the frame. Provision is made to ensure this pattern does not appear anywhere else by stuffing a 0 after any run of five consecutive 1's in the data. The stuffed 0 appearing after five 1's is automatically deleted by the receiver logic.

Address   This field is normally 8 bits, but can be extended to multiples of 8 bits. This field exists mostly because the standard was developed to include the mode of having a primary station communicating to many secondaries; thus an address is needed to specify which secondary is being polled or which secondary is responding. In the mode as a link of a network, this field is not really needed, but is included anyway. Any addressing information about sessions using the link is contained in the network data unit that is encapsulated in the HDLC information field. The data link layer does not make use of this information.

Control   This field is normally 8 bits but can be extended to 16 bits. One of its tasks is to distinguish one of three frame formats. These three formats are shown in Figure 5.13.

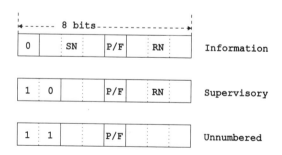

Figure 5.13: Control field for the three HDLC frame formats.

The *information frame* is distinguished by the leading frame being a zero. It contains a 3-bit send sequence number, which serves the purpose described above. There is also a piggybacked acknowledgment—the received sequence (next expected) number. In the extended 16-bit control field mode the sequence numbers are 7 bits each. The poll-final bit was intended for the primary-secondary mode, but also serves various purposes in command and response.

The *supervisory frame* is for sending acknowledgment without sending data. It is distinguished by a 10 start. Since no data are being sent it doesn't need a send sequence number. It does need a received sequence number, which again is normally 3 bits, extendable to 7 bits in the extended control field mode. In addition to the poll-final bit there are 2 bits left, which are used to identify four acknowledgment types. These are as follows:

RR (Receive ready). This is an ordinary acknowledgment. The RN is the next expected frame number.

RNR (Receive Not Ready). The RN again acknowledges all frames prior to the number, but indicates the receiver is not ready to accept any more frames.

REJ (Reject). This requests the sender to go back and retransmit the specified RN as well as any following.

SREJ (Selective Reject). This requests the sender to retransmit the specified RN but not necessarily retransmit more recently sent frames. Only one outstanding frame is allowed to be selectively rejected at any given time.

The *unnumbered frame* is for sending various mode changing, control, connection, disconnection, and various other commands. A starting 11 pattern identifies this type. Since there are 5 bits available, 32 different commands are possible. For example, one command is to use the extended control field, in case 7-bit sequence numbers are desired. Others include setting one of three modes: normal response mode (NRM), asynchronous response mode (ARM) and asynchronous balanced mode (ABM). NRM and ARM are concerned with primary/secondary operations, where the primary is in complete control. ABM is the mode of interest for point-to-point network link communication, where both ends have equal control status.

Information Field   This is a variable-length field of length that must be a multiple of 8 bits. Its maximum length is not specified in the standard but will have some maximum set by a particular implementation. This field is treated as pure data by HDLC, although it contains network routing information and other header information that will be used of at higher layer levels.

CRC or Frame Check Sequence   This field is 16 or 32 bits long and is used for error detection. It is formed by dividing all the bits in the rest of the frame except for the flags by a generator polynomial $g(X)$ and taking the remainder, as defined by Equation (3.10) in Section 3.3. If the frame does not check, its contents are discarded and it will eventually get retransmitted. There are some standard 16- and 32-degree CRC polynomials, as seen here.

Degree 16: $1 + X^2 + X^{15} + X^{16}$
$1 + X^5 + X^{12} + X^{16}$.

Degree 32: $1 + X + X^2 + X^4 + X^5 + X^7 + X^8 + X^{10} + X^{11} + X^{12} + X^{16}$
$+ X^{22} + X^{23} + X^{26} + X^{32}$.

The polynomials just given are designed to detect any double error, and the 16-degree polynomials also will detect any odd number of errors because they have $X = 1$ as a zero. The choice of a small number of nonzero terms in the 16-degree case also simplifies the circuitry because there are few feedback connections. The fail-safe probability is $1/65636$ for the 16-degree polynomials, and about $2 * 10^{-10}$ for the 32-degree polynomials. Actually, complete double-error-detecting capability limits the frame length to 65535 bits in the 16-bit case, because $g(X)$ is a factor of $X^{65535} - 1$. However, the chance of two errors being exactly 65536 bits apart with no other errors still is quite small for random error occurrences.

In designing to avoid common occurrences that may cause undetected errors, provision is made to avoid all zeros being a valid code word, since some failures could result in a train of all zeros. The following standard method is used to accomplish this:

In computing the check sequence, first invert the leading $n - k$ data bits. This computes

$$r(X) = rem \left(\frac{X^{n-k} d(X) + X^k i(X)}{g(X)} \right) \tag{5.9}$$

where $i(X) = X^{n-k-1} + \cdots + X + 1$, $(n - k$ consecutive ones). The transmission is

$$X^{n-k} d(X) + r_{inv}(X),$$

where $r_{inv}(X)$ is $r(X)$ with all bits inverted.

The receiver puts back the inversion $X^k i(X)$ and reinverts $r_{inv}(X)$ back to $r(X)$ before computing

$$rem \left(\frac{X^{n-k} d(X) + X^k i(X) + r(X)}{g(X)} \right)$$

which will be zero if there are no errors. If some channel fault causes a sequence of all zeros to be received, the decoder, as a result of the two inversions, computes (noting $r_{inv}(X) + i(X) = r(X)$)

$$rem \left(\frac{[X^k + 1] i(X)}{g(X)} \right)$$

which is not zero if $k < 2^{n-k}$.

The above inversion provides only partial protection against a one-bit synchronization error, as discussed in Section 3.3. This is because a one-bit shift in $i(X)$ is not different enough from $i(X)$. However, there is protection for the following reasons: if the flags are correctly detected there is no synchronization error, while if there is a false or lost flag there is a large displacement and usually a length change, so the chance of undetected error is almost as if for a random pattern, which is the fail-safe probability f.

HDLC frames clearly are designed for links on which errors are quite rare. If there were an average of even one bit error per frame the retransmission rate would be excessive, especially for go-back with a large value of K. Also, it takes only a single bit error to lose a flag or create a false flag. As just noted, the chance of this leading to an undetected error is about f. Even if it does check, some other inconsistency might cause it to be discarded. Nevertheless, operation with the 16-bit version with $f = 1/65536$ might not be protective enough for some applications. Just another 16 bits reduces f to 10^{-9}. Also, if bit errors are really as rare as they should be when HDLC is employed, it might be better to just do the ARQ at the transport layer instead. Maybe a simple error correction scheme might be done at the link layer to eliminate some of the common error occurrences such as single errors or small bursts. ARQ at the transport layer could provide high reliability as needed. Really noisy links, such as some wireless links or wired links with excessive attenuation, could use ARQ and error correction, but not likely in the HDLC format, with its excessive reliance on flags that could be easily faulted in an error-prone environment. As data communication rates have increased, the need for greater processing speed tends to discourage the use of HDLC over each individual link, especially when network bit errors are rare and the transport level is also handling error control.

5.11 Summary

ARQ protocols for ensuring reliable data communication are based on the three foundations of near-perfect error detection, sequence numbering, and a policy of resending whenever in doubt. The "fail-safe" probability f of an undetected error for a random reception decreases exponentially with the number of check symbols added for this purpose. For transfer of large amounts of data, where efficiency is most important, these extra check bits are a negligible contribution to data traffic. However, if errors are frequent, error detection alone would mean excessive retransmission; error correction would be a way to keep communication efficient in that case, while still keeping a good fail-safe probability at little cost. This is true even if soft decisions are used to aid in correction power.

Stop-and-wait protocols are the simplest. They may be inefficient, but not necessarily if the channel is being shared statistically. Alternating bit protocols are preferable to sending NAK/ACK because of greater efficiency and, more importantly, because variable delay will create uncertainty as to what is being ACKed or NAKed.

For continuous transmission or transmission with multiple frames outstanding, multibit sequence numbering is necessary. The go-back protocol, which does not allow the decoder to leave gaps in its accepted frame sequence, is the most popular for continuous transmission due to its simplicity. With b bits in the sequence number, the sender cannot send more than $2^b - 1$ new frames without getting acknowledgment of the first of the frame set. Acknowledgments can be cumulative, as indicated by the next expected frame. Selective repeat is more efficient than go-back if frame errors are frequent or if the round-trip time encompasses many frames. Chapter 6 will study selective repeat strategies in greater detail.

Acknowledgments have to be protected by error detection so that an acknowledgment is not believed unless almost certain to be correct. If doubt exists, the acknowledgment signal is ignored, as if lost. Acknowledgments are well suited for piggybacking into frames going in the same direction, since these frames already carry error detection protection. Such frames normally would contain two independent sequence numbers: one (send sequence number) to identify the frame-carrying data, and the other (received sequence number, usually next expected number) to provide acknowledgment. A one-sequence number policy number has also been devised, but is generally less efficient and less flexible. We will later see a possible application for slotted ring networks, however.

HDLC is a standard data link protocol that incorporates most of these concepts. It was intended for ensuring reliability on each hop of a network before passing the data on. With the trend to higher speed data communication and use for the most part of very low error rate channels, HDLC is losing favor compared to end-to-end error control protocols. We will see that most of the ARQ and HDLC principles are applicable end-to-end. There will be some additional complications, however, due to out-of-order arrival possibilities and extremely variable delays.

5.12   Problems

5.1.   What is the "fail-safe" probability of a parity check $(500, 400)$ binary parity check code that corrects all burst errors of duration 40 or less?

5.2.   Consider the stop-and-wait "new word" policy where X needs to send to Y the sequence of data frames $A, B, C, D, E \ldots$, and Y needs to send to X the sequence of data frames $M, N, P, Q, R \ldots$. Assume X starts first with alternating bit 0, and Y acknowledges by including the bit the same as the one in the X-frame last successfully decoded. The following sequence of events occurs on successive transmissions (S = successful, F = failure).

$$X \rightarrow Y: \quad S, S, F, F, S, S$$
$$Y \rightarrow X: \quad S, F, S, F, F, S$$

Show the transmissions by X and Y for this sequence of events.

5.3.   Consider the two-way stop-and-wait process where the two senders take turns sending a frame to each other. On a link employing ARQ, it is common practice for a frame carrying data to have two sequence numbers, one to number its own data and one to serve as an acknowledgment by giving the next expected number. There is also the single-sequence-number policy described in Section 5.3.

a. Show why Equation (5.4) applies whether the two-sequence-number or the one-sequence-number policy is used.

b. The one-sequence-number policy obviously is not suitable when it is desired to be able to acknowledge a variable number of past frames by the expected number. However, even in the case where one-for-one stop-and-wait is used, show why the two-sequence-number method may be preferable even though Equation (5.4) seems to indicate that their efficiencies are equal.

5.4. Fixed sized packets arrive for transmission at a node at an average arrival rate of λ packets per second. Each packet requires a basic transmission time of one second. The transmitter is using a one packet at a time stop-and-wait communication method, so a new packet is not sent until an acknowledgment of the previous one is received. The node is assumed to have unlimited buffer capacity.

Assume the acknowledgment process always obeys the following statistical rules. Packets sometimes get lost but otherwise there are no errors. If transmission starts at time t with probability $1/3$, a return acknowledgment is decoded at time $t + 3$. With probability $1/3$, a return acknowledgment is decoded at time $t + 5$. With probability $1/3$ the packet is lost, so the node times-out and starts to retransmit at time $t + 6$.

Find the maximum average rate λ that the node can handle.

5.5. Prove that method 2 for the stop-and-wait protocol works with lost frames and variable delays, as long as order is preserved.

5.6. A is sending a steady stream of *one-second duration* frames to B, and B is sending a steady stream of *two-second duration* frames to A. The *propagation time is 0.1 second in each duration* and the decoding/processing time is assumed negligible. B includes in each frame a piggybacked acknowledgment of all frames decoded *before* the start of the frame transmission. The two streams are synchronized in time so that B's frame starts just after a frame from A has been received and decoded.

a. Show a diagram of the communication timing.

b. What is A's smallest window size of unacknowledged frames such that A does not have to stop before sending new frames assuming no errors or lost information? An analytic justification of the answer is required.

5.7. For the case of Figure 5.10c, suppose that after X has sent $(H71)$ it stops and waits until the $N25$ frame is completely received. Show the timing and transmissions for several more X and Y transmissions after that, assuming no more errors.

5.8. Suppose the go-back protocol is used for continuous transmission of a long stream of sequence numbered 5000-bit packets at a 100 megabits/second rate. Suppose the round trip acknowledgment time is .3 seconds, and each packet is individually acknowledged. Any packet containing error is not accepted (error detection but no error correction). Suppose the forward channel bit error probability is 10^{-8} with independent errors, and the acknowledgment channel is error-free.

a. Find the average efficiency and compare with ideal selective repeat.

b. Suppose the packet size is increased to 50000 bits, again with individual packet acknowledgment and the same assumed error statistics. Would this improve efficiency? What packet size would maximize efficiency?

5.9. Suppose A is broadcasting simultaneously the same data frames to B and to C using a stop-and-wait protocol. The probability that a frame will be received erroneously at B is p, and, independently, the probability also is p that it will be received erroneously at C. Assume error detection is perfect, and both B and C respond with an alternating bit (next expected) acknowledgment over an error-free return channel. A will retransmit the frame until it receives correct next expected acknowledgment from both B and C.

Find the expected number of times that A will have to send a frame.

Chapter 6

Selective Repeat Strategies

We have seen that selective repeat allows substantial efficiency gains if a channel is noisy or if the round trip acknowledgment time is many frame durations in length. Earlier networks hardly ever used selective repeat because the go-back procedure was simpler and adequate. However, interest in and use of selective repeat are growing due to several factors, which are listed below.

1. Storage capacities have grown rapidly. Thus there is no significant storage problem in buffering frames with spaces for missing frames that will get retransmitted.

2. In file transfer of data via satellite, the round-trip time is so large that hundreds or thousands of frames may be sent before an acknowledgment of even the first frame sent can get back. Thus it would be very wasteful if a whole round-trip's worth of frames had to be repeated just because one frame was received in error.

3. A similar effect arises in long distance wire lines. Although the propagation delay is much less than with a satellite, the increasingly high data rates result in more outstanding frames per round-trip. Even if the noise level is low, the very large number of frames makes it likely that one or a few will have errors in a round-trip time. Also, as the data are relayed through a network, some frames may be lost due to buffer overflow or misdirection at some node.

4. The amounts of data being transferred in a session are rapidly growing. For the very fact that networks normally introduce very few errors, it makes sense to send back only occasional acknowledgments, maybe even just one at the end of a long file transfer. Then, if just one or a few frames are lost or erroneous, the receiver could send back a list of the frames that need repeating.

5. There is increasing interest in multicasting the same data to many destinations in a network. The need to get through successfully to all these destinations roughly multiplies the number of failures by almost the number of destinations (a little less because of dependent errors). At the same time we don't want to make

acknowledgments too often because the acknowledgment traffic is multiplied by the number of destinations.

6. Wireless data communication is coming into wider use. These channels are noisier than wire or optical networks. Thus go-back schemes would suffer in efficiency. By sending no more than necessary, selective repeat schemes reduce interference for other senders and increase the number of allowed simultaneous users.

7. If a channel is relatively noise-free with binary transmission, and there is a need to send at rates higher than the symbol rate allowed by the bandwidth, multilevel transmission could be used up until where continuous signal level capacity was being approached. However, then the channel would be noisy, as with the wireless channel.

There are a significant number of selective repeat strategies. Some of these will be described in the sections that follow. These selective repeat strategies are mostly for a single data link. Since networks are to be described in later chapters, descriptions of some of the network schemes will be more appropriate in those chapters. Similarly, the discussion of acknowledgments in multicasting will be reserved for Chapter 12.

6.1   Selective Repeat Strategies with Frame-By-Frame Acknowledgments

The earliest selective repeat strategies for continuous data transmission were described by Metzner and Morgan in [METZ60], although the term "selective repeat" arose much later. Two strategies were described, entitled "circulating memory" and "interlacing." The strategies were designed for frame-by-frame acknowledgment of continuous two-way streams of equal-sized frames over a single data link, although the ideas have a somewhat broader application. To handle the case where data actually is sent more sporadically, the frames could be thought of as slots that are always there, as in a time division multiplexing (TDM) system. Thus if there were no data to send the slot would contain an idle frame, which would need to be so identified. It is assumed that an acknowledgment always returns before J consecutive frames (including the frame being acknowledged) have finished being sent out. Maintaining the slot structure aids in synchronization and eliminates the need for frame flags. Frame synchronization could be accomplished as is done for TDM voice channel PCM frames. Also, the error-detecting nature of the frame contents can in itself be used to protect against synchronization error, since any slippage would result almost always in error detection,[1] whereas the correct synchronization point would usually result in successful decoding of a frame.

---

[1] It was mentioned in Section 3.3 that cyclic codes are potentially vulnerable to synchronization error, but this can be averted by adding a pseudo-random known pattern prior to transmission.

6.1.1 The Circulating Memory Technique

The scheme to be described is not one in use anywhere. However, it serves as an illustration of how selective repeat could be accomplished in a conceptually simple fashion. Historically, it was described in [METZ60] using the ACK/NAK bit method, and in [METZ65] using the new word policy described in Section 5.3 for stop-and-wait.

Imagine a synchronized two-way communication of streams of equal duration frames. Each sender retains a circulating ring memory of up to *J* previously transmitted frames, as illustrated in Figure 6.1. The circulating memory shifts clockwise once per frame transmission. When the switch is at position *A*, the next or idle frame is given the next sequence number and copied into position 1 of the circulating memory; at the same time, it is encoded with a piggybacked acknowledgment included and is transmitted. Thus frames are given sequence numbers, including any idle frames, in the order they are first sent out. If the switch is placed at position *B*, the frame sent *J* positions back is retransmitted (even if it is an idle frame) and returned to position 1 of the circulating memory. The new frame not yet transmitted remains in the box attached to point *A*. Position *B* is set in one of two cases: (1) if acknowledgment of the frame sent out *J* units back is not obtained, or (2) if a new frame is not allowed to be sent out because some frame in the circulating memory is too old, as will be specified later. If perfect synchronization is assumed, the piggybacked acknowledgment can be either an ACK/NAK bit or a single alternating bit, but for greater safety should also include identifying to which of the *J* time slots in the cycle it belongs.

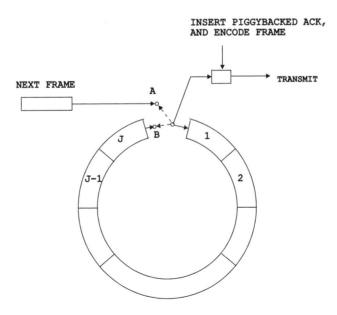

Figure 6.1: Transmission with the circulating memory technique, synchronous case.

The reason for not advancing when one frame is too old is to prevent ambiguity due to the reuse of the finite set of sequence numbers. The constraint rule will now be described. Suppose we have a b-bit sequence number. To prevent ambiguity, each of the 2^b values of the sequence number must have a unique interpretation. We assume sufficient error detection power that we can neglect any possibility that an accepted frame is wrong or that the sender thinks something is accepted when it has not been.

The concept of a window is useful at this point. Refer to Figure 6.2. The sender and receiver each have a window. The sender's window represents the range of frames from the oldest unacknowledged frame through the most advanced frame the sender is permitted to send. Let W be the size of this transmitter window. In addition, by the nature of the circulating memory technique there can be at most J unacknowledged frames in this window.

For the receiver, two key points of reference are the oldest frame not yet correctly received (OX) and the newest frame so far correctly received (NC). Because the circulating memory is of size J, the furthest extent to which the sender could be sending new frames is J undecoded frame positions starting with OX (see Figure 6.2a). If OX is the one just after NC (see case (b) of Figure 6.2), this extends exactly J positions beyond NC. Since the receiver knows the sender's window is W, it can mark off W frames back, including NC, with the assurance the sender will not try to send anything older than that, because otherwise it would not have been allowed to send NC. Note that we are relying here on the assumption that if a frame A is sent before frame B, frame A will never arrive after frame B. We allow, however, that frame A or frame B or both may never arrive.

The receiver has a window of at most $W + J$ frames that the sender might possibly be sending. If all $W + J$ successive frames have different sequence numbers, the receiver will always be able to properly interpret them. Thus, if the sequence number has b bits, we require:

$$W + J \leq 2^b, \quad \text{or} \quad W \leq 2^b - J. \tag{6.1}$$

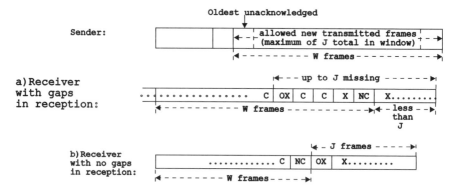

Figure 6.2: Condition for no ambiguity in the circulating memory technique. (X = still missing; C = correctly received; O = oldest; N = newest).

6.1.2 Generalization and Modification of the Circulating Memory Technique

Although the circulating memory technique was originally proposed on the presumption that all frames were the same size and were individually acknowledged with a fixed delay, it has much more general application. Assuming perfect error detection, there really are only the following constraints on ensuring correct operation:

1. The sender can allow no more than J transmitted frames to be left unacknowledged (not necessarily consecutive).
2. The sender must obey the window constraint (6.1).
3. The first transmissions of new frames must be in order.
4. The channel must preserve the order of transmission, as was also required for proper go-back protocol operation, unless the sequence number range is so large that ambiguity due to reuse is not a problem.

Following are some generalizations that can be made.

1. The memory does not have to be circulating; it could just consist of up to J transmitted but unacknowledged frames. A new frame could be sent out and entered into memory any time a memory position was available and the $W \leq 2^b - J$ constraint would not be violated. Once frames are entered into the memory they can be retransmitted in any order.
2. There would be no need to number or send idle frames, other than to carry acknowledgments.
3. Frames would not have to be individually acknowledged; an acknowledgment signal could acknowledge several frames at a time.
4. The frame sizes do not have to be the same and the delay does not have to be fixed. However, the value of J should be chosen large enough so that in most cases an acknowledgment is received before $J - 1$ following frames have been sent; if not, transmission could simply wait, or some old frame in the memory that has not been acknowledged in a while could be retransmitted while waiting.

Returning to the synchronized slotted format, Easton [EAST81] suggested a modification of the circulating memory technique whereby, upon not being able to go ahead because of an old unacknowledged frame, the sender should continue to send the old frame when the limit was reached, rather than retransmit something J frames back that already was acknowledged. This would clearly improve efficiency in cases where the limit of what could be sent is often reached. However, simulations [Metz66, 67, 77B] have indicated that the event could be quite rare for normal values of J and a reasonable number of bits in the sequence number. In the generalized version, old frames could be sent out at any time.

Note that each added bit doubles the allowed range. In high bit-rate satellite data communication, where selective repeat is very beneficial, J is normally quite large. Certainly the range needs to be at least J if there is to be any hope of continuous transmission, if we make it $2J$, adding one sequence number bit, we would only suffer problems of hitting the limit if the same frame were not received twice in a row. If frame failure rates are low this would be a rare event.

6.1.3   The Interlaced Memory Technique

The circulating memory procedure began with the use of fixed-size time slots, although this structure proved not to be essential. The interlaced memory procedure is a little more closely tied to a slot structure. The idea is to interlace J independent stop-and-wait processes in J slots, so that communication could be continuous, assuming an acknowledgment always returns within the time duration of J slots. Each slot ideally could operate with a one-bit sequence number, assuming one could always tell which slot was which. If not, $\lceil \log_2 J \rceil$ additional bits could be provided to identify the slot.

If one has J separate message streams, the interlaced approach is very appropriate. A more troublesome case is where there is just one message stream, which needs to be distributed, probably in round-robin order, into the different slots. If J separate slot sets proceed independently in a noisy environment, it is a basic statistical property that the difference between the number of successes in the luckiest slot and the number of successes in the unluckiest slot grows without bound, even if all slots have the same statistics. This creates a potential buffering problem if all the slots have the same message as their source; the difference in original message position between the most advanced and least advanced frame continues to grow, until buffer limitations require the receiver not to accept any more frames in the most advanced slot. This is reminiscent of the window limit for the circulating memory technique, but the reason for it is different. Nevertheless, we also studied in [METZ66, 67] the effect of such a limit on efficiency. Generally, the interlaced memory procedure was more affected by a difference limitation of a given size, as would be suggested by the potentially unbounded statistics. Since one effect depends on sequence number size while the other depends on buffer capacity, the two results are not really comparable. One place where the interlaced model is quite appropriate is in a slotted ring, about which more will be said in Chapter 9.

Another possible concern about distributing a single message into J slots or parallel channels is the order of reception and how that would reflect on the ambiguity problem. Note that the gap between oldest and newest accepted frame can become quite large, and yet only $1 + \lceil \log_2 J \rceil$ bits per frame are used for numbering. However, if the frames are always distributed in a known round-robin order this does not create an ambiguity problem. To see this, it is helpful to visualize the set of transmitted frames as organized in a two-dimensional array of J rows and a number of columns that depends on the total message length, as illustrated in Figure 6.3.

The correct order is indicated by the numbering in the frame boxes. In each slot, frames are accepted in order due to the stop-and-wait protocol for that slot. Since the receiver knows which slot a frame comes in on (the row) and its order in the slot (the

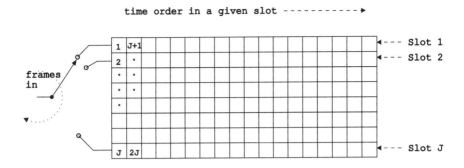

Figure 6.3: Distribution of frames of one message over *J* slots. Boxes are numbered in true frame order of message.

column), the receiver can properly place each frame in the array and, by reading out column-by-column, have the proper order after message reception is complete.

6.2 Another Window Approach to Selective Repeat

A more common window rule for selective repeat is to let the window size *W* be the constraint on sending new messages, without regard to how many unacknowledged frames among the *W* are outstanding. This leads to a somewhat more severe restriction on *W*. To see this restriction, refer to Figure 6.4.

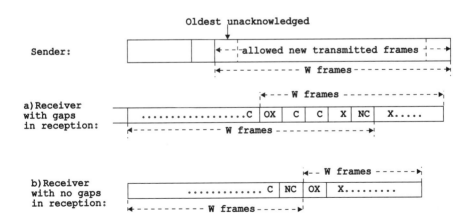

Figure 6.4: Condition for no ambiguity in general *W* constraint (X = still missing; C = correctly received; O = oldest; N = newest).

The range of possible receptions is now $2W$, so the requirement for no ambiguity becomes:

$$2^b \geq 2W, \quad \text{or} \quad 2^{b-1} \geq W. \tag{6.2}$$

The number of frames sent before acknowledgment of the first is returned cannot be greater than 2^{b-1}, since otherwise continuous transmission would not be possible under either this or the circulating memory procedure. Thus, if $J \leq 2^{b-1}$,

$$2^b - J \geq 2^{b-1}, \tag{6.3}$$

and the allowed transmitter window size is always at least as great with the circulating memory as with other selective repeat strategies.

6.3 Selective Repeat with Cumulative Acknowledgments

The cumulative acknowledgment scheme of indicating the next expected frame is a valuable tool for improving the usefulness of the acknowledgment channel. If acknowledgments are made frame-by-frame, a missing acknowledgment need not automatically trigger an unnecessary retransmission because the next return frame will include an acknowledgment of that frame as well. Alternatively, acknowledgments may be returned less often than frame-by-frame, thus saving on return channel traffic and increasing the flexibility in piggybacking acknowledgments on return channel frames. It is important, though, that acknowledgments relating to a frame return before the timeout period for that frame occurs.

However, the cumulative acknowledgment by itself lacks important information for a selective repeat strategy. It can only acknowledge everything up to some frame, plus the fact that the next expected frame has not yet been decoded; it cannot indicate if some subsequent frames have already been accepted. Thus if timeout expires on the next expected frame, the sender will retransmit it. This may be the only frame missing in a longer string, but the sender does not know this and after retransmitting the frame may have to retransmit additional unnecessary frames until an acknowledgment of the frame in question comes back. The other alternative is for the sender to retransmit the expired frame and then go into a stop-and-wait mode until the acknowledgment for this returns, which wastes potential transmission time.[2] Improved performance may be possible by supplying supplemental selective reject information. Considerations are slightly different depending on whether frames that are not lost always arrive in the order sent, or whether they can arrive out of order.

---

[2]In a statistically shared communication medium waiting to transmit is not always a waste. We will see many examples of this in later chapters.

6.3.1   In-Order Arrival

If there is a direct link or if all frames follow the same path, frames ordinarily arrive in order if they arrive at all. The direct link error control protocol HDLC uses the SREJ command, specifying that a particular frame needs to be repeated. Only one frame can be mentioned in this command. The fact that it is SREJ rather than REJ does imply that at least one later frame has been accepted. If the convention were that SREJ is used only if there is exactly one missing, followed by an accepted frame, the sender would know on receiving the feedback information that at least the frame after the reject frame does not have to be retransmitted. This would extend the timeout by one frame interval, which might allow the sender to go slightly further while waiting acknowledgment of the retransmitted SREJ frame. If this convention were augmented by a second piece of information as to the next expected assuming the SREJ frame were received, the sender on retransmitting the frame could extend its timeout considerably further, subject to not exceeding the ambiguity limit window. If the SREJ comes back well before the timeout occurs, the frame can be retransmitted and additional new frames sent following as long as the timeout has not run out on later not-yet-acknowledged frames.

It is not obvious whether these modifications of the HDLC SREJ method would allow significant improvement. As an example, suppose frames are all of unit length and frames of data are being sent continuously. There are three time parameters to consider. One is the ambiguity window size, W, which would be 2^{h-1} or 2^h J. Another is the timeout, N_{out}, in integer number of frames counted, for this example, to include the frame in question, up through the frame just sent. The third is the variable round-trip time, t_R, measured in number of frames including the frame being transmitted when the acknowledgment is decoded.

The time duration to reach the ambiguity limit will vary because it only counts new transmissions, but its minimum duration will be W. Even N_{out} doesn't have to be fixed. Mostly it is based on waiting long enough that it appears likely that the desired acknowledgment has been lost, so it is better to go back and retransmit.

One case is if the number of bits in the sequence number is very large, and thus W is so large it need not be considered as a limitation. Suppose a SREJ returns at t_R with the information that i frames after the SREJ are accepted. One viewpoint is to advance the start of the timeout period by $i + 1$ frames, to measure N'_{out} frames from the start of the point where no report information has yet been received; this is indicated in Figure 6.5. Another approach, also indicated in Figure 6.5, is to advance the start by t_R frames, to measure N''_{out} frames from the start of the second transmission of the SREJ frame.

The main objective is to get a successful transmission of the SREJ frame, which suggests application of an idea presented in [WELD82]. The idea is that, if a frame needs to be repeated, then greater than one copy can be sent the second time. More generally, more redundancy or signal energy could be put into the second transmission. This could be applied to the case of SREJ frames, whereas frames repeated due to timeouts could be repeated by just one copy as usual.

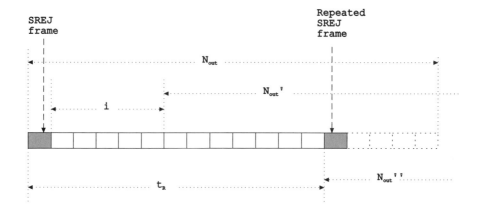

Figure 6.5: A selective reject example.

6.3.2 Out-of-Order Arrival

We will see that for some networks frames or packets arrive out of order. In the ordered case the receiver discovers a missing frame when it receives one with a skipped sequence number. In the out-of-order case a skipped sequence number may simply mean a particular packet has taken a longer delayed route. As the receiver accumulates packets, it is not sure whether a certain packet needs repeating until a certain time has elapsed relative to other received packets. Cumulative acknowledgments still are an important tool, but there are other considerations that are better discussed in Chapter 10, when networks are covered. Some additional comments relating to large file transfer are discussed in the following section.

6.4   Selective Repeat in Large File Transfer

A trend in modern data communication is toward reliable communication of larger files of data and greatly increased storage capability. Also, many network communications are at very low bit error rate, although we have seen there are important exceptions. Still, loss of data and unrequested retransmissions due to timeouts occasionally are serious problems. It often makes sense to send a large amount of data before attempting any retransmissions, and then fix it up after the first transfer. The large amount of available storage capacity on both ends of the transmission makes this relatively easy to do. Cases where significant reception problems were encountered could be handled with a special return negative acknowledgment, and occasional checkpoints can be used to confirm satisfactory progress.

It may seem strange to speak of sending back occasional negative acknowledgments, since we have said the NAK to ACK error should be avoided, and yet the absence (maybe the loss) of a negative acknowledgment implies a sort of positive acknowledgment that things are going well. The saving property is that we are going to require positive acknowledgment before being satisfied that the whole file or some large portion of it has been transmitted correctly, so any failure of the negative acknowledgments will get corrected at that later time.

Clearly selective repeat would be advantageous if a large amount of data were sent before acknowledgment. With go-back, one small error could be enough to cause an average of half the data to be resent, although the negative acknowledgment technique could help prevent some of this waste. A sensible procedure with selective repeat is to send back a list of the missing or uncorrectable blocks of data, and have these retransmitted. This has been proposed as part of the protocol known as XTP (eXpress Transfer Protocol) [CHES88, COHN88]. A good description of XTP can be found in Chapter 12 of [STAL94].

Error correction also has an important role to play in transfer of large amounts of data prior to acknowledgment. We have already seen in Chapter 3 that in concatenated codes symbols can be large blocks of data, and each such block can have its own built-in error detection and correction. When sending a large file of data, a few redundant frames can be added, determined perhaps by a Reed-Solomon code. Then, a number of missing or detected erroneous frames could be filled in by the outer code as long as the number of missing frames did not exceed the number of check frames. Alternatively, the redundant check frames could be sent only as needed, as indicated by a return acknowledgment specifying the number of missing frames. Also, because of the large amount of data being processed, enough checking redundancy can be added at negligible cost in efficiency to allow undetected error rates of less than one in a million years (neglecting computer errors or natural disasters).

Processing speed, which is an important consideration in many real-time tasks due to the inherent complexity of error correction, might not be that much of a problem in large file transfer, since the error correction computation need be completed only at the end of the transfer. Although computation time may be rather large, computation time *per bit transferred* may be very small compared to "simpler" decoding of short blocks. Thus computation time can easily be a very small fraction of the total data transfer time.

6.4.1 Buffer Storage Limitations

In the past, one of the major concerns that limited application of selective repeat was the fact that the receiver needed a good deal of buffer storage to hold data while waiting to fill in gaps. This is less of a concern now, due to the large storage capacities available compared to the past. However, delay in delivering the corrected data is still an important concern in some applications. The buffer size needs to be at least J frames (one round-trip time) if continuous transmission is desired with selective repeat. It should be at least twice as great to reduce the likelihood of reaching the limit on sending new data, in case of an error. If the buffer limitation is more severe than the ambiguity limitation, and lies somewhere between J and $2J$, then an idea presented in [WELD82] can be used. The idea is that, if a frame needs to be repeated, then greater than one copy can be sent the second time, thus reducing the chance that the receiver fails to accept it a second time, and thus cannot accept some new frames due to lack of buffer space.

6.5 Memory and Incremental Redundancy Techniques

A generalization of the [WELD82] idea is to devote more transmitted signal energy to the second frame transmission, which is related to using more redundancy. Another way of improving the chance of acceptance on the second sending is to use memory techniques. If the first frame sending is not decodable due to error detection, yet contains some useful information, a memory of this information could be retained for combination with its retransmission, thus increasing the likelihood of acceptance on the second sending. A major reason that the new word policy was introduced in [METZ63] was that, with the new word policy, a retransmission would always be identical (including its piggybacked acknowledgment), which facilitates using memory combinations. However, using memory of past receptions is subject to uncertainty about which past reception is currently being repeated. Memory techniques will be discussed in some detail in Chapter 7.

Rather than "repeat" or "retransmission," a more general approach is to send additional redundancy that is not necessarily restricted to a repeat of what was previously sent. For example, a subsequent sending can be like additional check symbols of an extended block code. For example, instead of sending a repeat of a block transmission, the first block can be treated as the data symbols of a rate one-half block code, and the second block can be the associated check symbols. Another example is to send the additional check symbols in small incremental blocks until the receiver is able to decode. The idea previously mentioned of sending additional frames related to prior frames by a Reed Solomon code to fill in missing frames is an example of this. What we are considering here is not really "selective repeat," but it has a similar aim of sending only the minimum necessary additional redundancy so as to be as efficient as possible.

The incremental redundancy concept will appear frequently in subsequent chapters.

6.6 Summary

Interest in selective repeat is growing as a result of the need for greater efficiency to handle increased data transfer demands, coupled with large increases in storage capacity and processing capability. Also, wireless communication needs more efficient use of transmitted signal energy to be able to accommodate large numbers of simultaneous data communicators.

The circulating memory and interlacing scheme are examples showing that implementation of selective repeat is not basically difficult. These were designed initially for frame-by-frame acknowledgment over a single link, although the general ideas can be applied over networks with some modifications.

Cumulative acknowledgment is a powerful technique not considered in the circulating memory and interlacing schemes. HDLC combines cumulative acknowledgment with a SREJ command that allows selective retransmission of single missing or erroneous frames. This is an effective technique for links or paths with ordered arrival. Sending multiple copies or in general more signal energy for retransmission of selectively rejected frames can be useful for clearing a lagging old frame.

In large file transfer, it may be advantageous to transmit the whole file first, and then send back selective information about small pieces that need to be repeated or the amount of additional redundancy that needs to be supplied. An alternative is to send additional redundant frames with the original file, in which case error correction could reduce the need for further transmission.

Selective reject in networks and selective reject combined with memory will be discussed in more detail in later chapters.

6.7 Problems

6.1. Consider the circulating memory selective repeat protocol with $J = 5$ and a 4-bit sequence number. The circulating memory currently holds the frame numbers in the clockwise order 14, 13, 10, 5, 8. Frames are individually acknowledged in synchronism, and suppose the next four acknowledgments for the next four frames are accept, reject, accept, accept. What four frames should be sent out after these responses in the following two cases? (1) The protocol as described originally; (2) The modification suggested in [EAST81] and described in Section 6.1.

6.2. Consider a selective repeat scheme using $b = 6$-bit sequence numbers. Assume the common selective repeat rule limiting the sender's window to 2^{b-1} successive packets starting with the oldest unacknowledged. Suppose the receiver has decoded successfully all packets up through number 5, has also decoded the following 9, 10, 11, 12, but is missing packets 6, 7, 8. While the receiver is in this state, what is the most advanced packet number that the sender would be allowed to send without violating the condition to prevent ambiguity?

6.3. Answer the question in Problem 6.2 if instead the circulating memory technique is being used with $J = 14$ and a $W \leq 2^b - J$ window constraint.

6.4. The method of interlacing J channels has the problem that the difference between progress on the different channels grows without limit. An obvious solution is to stop sending new frames on any channel if it is more than K frames ahead of the channel that is most lagging. Find a more efficient solution. Assume each frame has a channel identifier of $\lceil \log_2 J \rceil$ bits.

6.5. Consider a "stop-and-wait" selective repeat scheme where n frames are sent, and then a return signal is sent specifying which of the n frames need to be resent.

a. Consider two different ways that the feedback information could be sent:

   i. An n-bit number, where bit i indicates acknowledgment for frame i;

  ii. A list of the numbers of the positions of frames that need to be repeated. If $n = 128$, how many frames would need repeating for method 2 to require more return bits to specify the missing frames? (Method 2 needs to include a count indicator.)

b. Suppose in this scheme frames continue to be sent n at a time. Assume an acknowledgment signal regarding the n frames either arrives by a certain timeout or never arrives. If the feedback instruction is to repeat j frames, the next round the j old frames and $n - j$ new frames are sent. If a return acknowledgment is erroneous or lost, all n frames are repeated. Let p be the probability a frame is received in error, independently for each frame. Let p' be the probability the return acknowledgment is in error or lost. Find the average number of new frames delivered per cycle.

c. Do you see a problem with schemes 1 or 2 or both if an acknowledgment is delayed well beyond the timeout and turns up after a retransmission of the n frames? Explain or recommend a solution to any such problem.

6.6. Suppose a combination is used of negative per-frame REJ and final positive acknowledgment at the end of transmission of a long string of frames. (Occasional positive responses might be needed to ensure the connection is active.) On receiving a REJ, the sender repeats the specified frame but then goes on to send new frames until it receives another REJ. Assume the sequence number is large enough that all frames can be uniquely identified.

a. This may serve the need for selective repeat. Why?

b. To adapt to a noisy but imperfectly known forward channel, it is suggested that whenever a retransmission is sent because of a REJ, the retransmission will be sent at half the data rate, such as by sending two copies, using a rate $1/2$ code, or stretching the pulses to be twice as long. This will reduce the probability of a frame error from p to some lower value p'. Assume the return channel is error-free. For what values of p and p' will this produce a net saving in transmission time?

Chapter 7

ARQ with Memory

When a reception corresponding to a transmitted block cannot be decoded, the record of this reception is ordinarily discarded. Actually this discarded record often contains a considerable amount of information about which message was transmitted. In memory ARQ, some of the information in this nondecodable signal is retained and combined with future reception(s) about this same information to enhance decoding possibilities. The future transmitted blocks can be retransmissions of the first transmitted block or, more generally, can provide additional incremental redundancy equivalent to adding more check symbols to the original code block.

A system without memory is subject to a sharp threshold in system efficiency. For example, if error detection only is used and some channel deterioration causes random errors of somewhat greater frequency than one error per block, efficiency falls off drastically due to excessive retransmission. Even if error correction is included to correct up to e errors, if the channel should deteriorate to an average error frequency somewhat greater than e per block, the same drastic reduction in efficiency occurs. With memory, the sharp deterioration threshold is avoided, and the system effective rate automatically adapts to something close to the evolved channel capacity.

Memory of past undecodable past receptions is also valuable in multiaccess networks, where one sender's signal is another sender's interference. Memory can reduce the amount of transmission, and thus the amount of interference to others. More will be said about this in later chapters.

Some discussion of terminology is needed at this point. The term **hybrid ARQ** [ROCH70] has been used to denote ARQ schemes that use a combination of error correction and error detection, rather than just error detection. This does not seem to be too important a distinction to this author, since the latter is just a special case of the former, but the term has prevailed for a long time. Also, one needs to distinguish whether memory of past receptions is used or not, and whether the additional information supplied is an exact retransmission or redundancy in a different form. The first memory case could be called **memory ARQ**, which emphasizes the two characteristics that there is *memory* of past receptions and the exact original data are being *retransmitted* (the original meaning of ARQ was "Automatic Repeat Request"). For the incremental redundancy case, which employs memory and error correction as well as error detection, the traditional term is **Type II hybrid ARQ** [LIN82]. (Another possible terminology [Metz85] is to call it **modified memory ARQ**).

One problem with the prevalent nomenclature is that **Type I hybrid ARQ** is used to denote a memoryless system using combined error correction and error detection. This leaves **memory ARQ** out in the cold. Also, **Type II hybrid ARQ** does not have the word memory in it.

Table 7.1 indicates the terminology we will follow here, with the objective of making the necessary distinctions without causing too much additional confusion. Type II continues to refer to the same system as currently, and the memory usage is made explicit. Sufficient protection against undetected error is assumed, because this is essential for reliable communication.

Although Type II memory ARQ includes Type I memory ARQ as a special case and is superior in theory, the choice is not always clear cut due to some practical considerations. The first is that, since retransmissions are exactly the same, Type I can more simply apply soft decisions (e.g., likelihood information about individual symbols) in making combined decisions (however there are ways of using soft decisions in some Type II schemes). Another advantage of Type I is that each transmission contains all the information in the correct form, which is useful in case earlier transmissions are completely garbled or lost (Type II could provide all the information in each sending, but rearranged for different transmissions). Finally, Type I memory ARQ is completely compatible with ARQ without memory. It is entirely the option of the receiver as to whether memory is employed. The transmitting station does not even need to be aware of whether the receiver is using memory, which is not true for Type II.

In this chapter we will look at both methods separately and then in comparison.

Table 7.1: Some ARQ terminology.

Characteristics				
Error Correction?	Memory?	Retransmission or Incremental?	Current Terminology	Terminology in This Chapter
no	no	retransmission	ARQ	ARQ
yes	no	retransmission	Type I hybrid ARQ	ARQ
no	yes	retransmission	?	Type I memory ARQ
yes	yes	retransmission	?	Type I memory ARQ
yes	yes	incremental	Type II hybrid ARQ	Type II memory ARQ

7.1 Type I Memory ARQ

In this method data are transmitted as a code word of an (n, k) block code. This code is used for error detection, and possibly error correction as well. If uncorrectable errors are detected, the same code word is repeated. The receiver retains some memory about each reception that cannot be decoded, and combines that information with future receptions corresponding to that code word.

Ideally, the memory of past receptions should retain all the information, but compromises are necessary. Because of the enormous number of code words in a long block code, practical considerations usually dictate that the combinations be made on a per-symbol basis. (However, once a tentative decision on a code word has been made, the reliability of that decision could be checked by comparison with all receptions.) The symbol set would usually be small—the binary symbol case being by far the most common. The accumulation of information in successive retransmissions would gradually reduce the per-symbol error probability and enhance the chances of accepting the block. In the case where the channel disturbance affects successive symbols independently and there is no intersymbol interference, recording the probability of each of the symbol values for a given reception is ideal in the sense that no information is lost. The information in successive sendings of that symbol could then be combined ideally by multiplying these probabilities (or better, by adding their logarithms).

Case of Binary Symbols   If the noise is independent Gaussian of constant strength, the optimum combining procedure would reduce to simple addition or averaging of successive reception levels for a given bit. For binary transmission in the presence of independent non-Gaussian noise, each received level should undergo a nonlinear transformation, which outputs a value approximating the log likelihood ratio; these outputs are then added to produce the cumulated record. In the case of varying signal-to-noise ratio, a weighted sum of receptions should be used with weightings based on running signal-to-noise ratio estimates (or this could be accounted for in the log likelihood computation).

Case of Nonbinary Symbols   Transmission can be represented as sending a point in signal space. In the case of white Gaussian noise the optimum combining rule reduces to an averaging in each dimension in signal space to yield a resultant average vector. For a one-dimensional symbol set, a simple level averaging is optimum.

7.1.1   Memory Storage Considerations

The storage of analog values presents practical problems, particularly in view of the fact that the retransmission of a particular symbol may occur thousands of symbol intervals after its first transmission. However, the analog case serves as a convenient benchmark of comparison against more practical schemes.

Consider now the prospect of quantizing the reception for a single symbol. Quantization destroys some information in the received signal, but the practical advantages may outweigh this loss. The amount of information loss often is slight for a rather coarse quantization. For example, for binary symbol transmission, it has been noted by Bloom et al. [BLOO57] that quantization into as few as three or four levels of decision retains a great proportion of the information in the signal. They showed that, whereas a binary decision causes a loss in information equivalent to the effect of a 3 dB reduction in signal-to-noise ratio, a ternary decision with optimal threshold settings results in a loss equivalent to only a 1.5 dB reduction on signal-to-noise ratio, and a four-level decision results in a loss equivalent to only a 1.1 dB reduction. The three- or four-level decisions with binary symbol transmission probably represent the most practical ways of retaining received level information for combined decision purposes.

Three levels of decision are called 0, 1, and "null" or "erasure." The use of the erasure symbol is particularly useful with burst-type noise, where any digit received during a recognized burst can be recorded as an erasure. It also arises naturally in combined binary decision rules where the counts of 0 and 1 decisions for past receptions of a binary digit are equal.

The use of four levels of quantization has been referred to [BLOO57] as "double-null-zone reception." The decision regions are illustrated in Figure 7.1. Four levels of quantization provide only slightly more information than three levels, but they possess some practical advantages. For some purposes the a_1 and a_0 regions can be combined into a single null zone or erasure symbol, while for other purposes, b_1 and a_1 (and similarly, b_0 and a_0) can be combined for a binary decision, as normally would be needed for the (n, k) code decoding. Also, in storage it usually is as convenient to store a four-level decision as a three-level one.

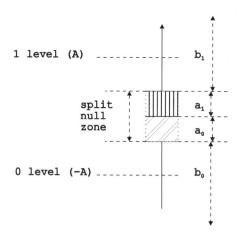

Figure 7.1: Double-null-zone decision regions.

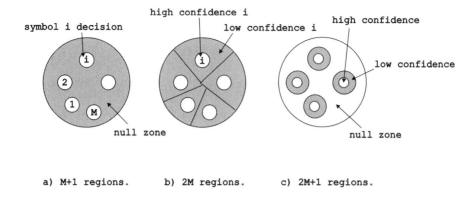

a) M+1 regions.   b) 2M regions.   c) 2M+1 regions.

Figure 7.2: Different decision regions for M symbols.

The concepts of single- and double-null zone reception can be extended to nonbinary symbol alphabets. Let M be the number of different symbol values. Then single-null-zone reception would involve division of received signal space into $M + 1$ regions (see Figure 7.2a). M of these regions would correspond one-to-one to high confidence regions that each of the M symbols were sent. The remaining region would be a null zone or region of erasure decision. The analogy to double-null-zone reception would be $2M$ decision regions; each of the M symbols would have two decision regions—a high confidence region and a low confidence region favoring that symbol value (see Figure 7.2b). Another possibility is to add an erasure region for a total of $2M + 1$ regions (see Figure 7.2c).

7.2 Combining Rules for Type I Memory ARQ

We will now look more closely into the methods of combining the recorded information in successive binary symbol retransmissions. It has already been noted that adding logarithms of probabilities for each symbol value often is an optimum procedure, and for the case of additive, independent, equal variance Gaussian noise a simple adding of received levels for successive retransmissions is equivalent to this. However, a practical system would almost certainly need to work with quantized individual decisions.

Memory limitations will set a maximum of some number, say b, of bits that can be devoted to storage of the cumulative information about a particular bit decision. This provides the combiner with at most 2^b states. A goal would be to make most effective use of this number of states.

One possible approach would be to quantize the log likelihood ratio into 2^b levels; this would suffice for storing the log likelihood ratio approximation for the first sending. Then the log likelihood ratio for the second reception could be computed exactly, added to the first quantized log likelihood ratio, and requantized into 2^b levels. This would make effective use of the constrained number of states, but it makes heavy demands on the ability to compute multiple threshold comparisons. Also, statistics are not known that exactly in practice, nor is the Gaussian assumption an exact model. Thus it would be more realistic to use only a number of decision regions for individual bit receptions that is considerably smaller than the number of allowed states. If it is found that performance is close to what can be achieved by an ideal analog cumulative technique, then there would be little incentive to further complicate the decision rule.

7.2.1   Combining Rules with Single- and Double-Null-Zone Reception

Keeping the above considerations in mind, let us now restrict individual reception decisions either to four-level (double null zone) or three-level (single null zone). The combined (cumulative) record for each binary digit will, however, be limited by a larger number of allowed states [METZ63, METZ85A].

Storage of the history of all past decisions after k receptions would require 4^k or 3^k states for the two cases, which obviously would quickly run into the state limitation with increasing k. Also, it is more detail than can be put to practical use. To save just the number of decisions of each type would require

$$\binom{k+3}{3}$$

states in the double-null-zone case and

$$\binom{k+2}{2}$$

states in the single-null-zone case. This still increases rather rapidly with k.

A more reasonable combining rule is to have a linear chain of states. Number the states

$$S_{-x}, \ldots S_{-1}, S_1, S_2, \ldots S_x,$$

where $x = 2^{b-1}$.

A positive subscript corresponds to more likely a 1, and a negative subscript corresponds to more likely a 0. Increasing magnitude subscripts correspond to increasing likelihood magnitude. In the double-null-zone case, one possible rule is that a B-type decision results in a two-step move, while an A-type decision results in a one-step move. One could suggest that the B-level decision should result in more than a two-step move, but this would tend to be a more extravagant use of states, might reach boundaries more quickly, and as a result not perform as well under the state constraint.

In the single-null-zone case, a logical rule is to move by one step or remain in the same state, depending on the three regions [METZ63]. In order to make the number of states even and to avoid erasure combined decisions, the first decision should be double null zone; then all subsequent individual decisions can be single null zone.

In the double-null-zone case, the number of states needed if unconstrained would be $4k$, whereas in the single-null-zone case the number would be $2k + 2$. When either of these quantities reach 2^b, the state boundary may be reached. When the boundary state is reached, the rule chosen will be to remain in that boundary state if the new individual decision reinforces the combined decision or is an erasure, and to go down the appropriate number of steps (one or two) if it is opposite.

Figure 7.3 illustrates state transitions for the case of double-null-zone decisions with 8 states in the combiner. To reduce clutter, not all transitions are shown. If state S_4 is reached, a b_1 or a_1 individual decision results in staying in state S_4, an a_0 results in transition to S_3, and a b_0 results in transition to S_2.

Figure 7.4 illustrates state transitions for single-null-zone decisions (with an initial double-null-zone decision).

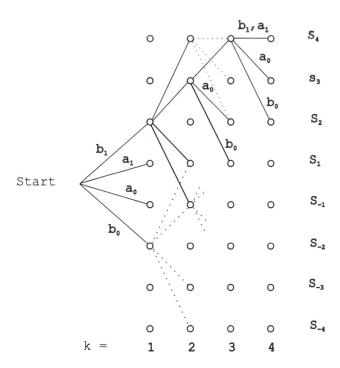

Figure 7.3: Eight-state combiner with double-null-zone transitions.

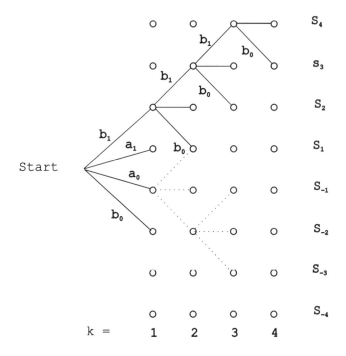

Figure 7.4: Eight state combiner with single-null-zone transitions.

7.3   Performance of a Finite State Combiner

In this section we will study finite state combiners of single- and double-null-zone decisions. Their performance will be compared with the ideal but impractical analog combiner for the case of transmissions independently disturbed by constant variance Gaussian noise. The limit on the maximum number of states will be assumed to be a power of two, consistent with use of binary storage elements.

There are two key performance goals. One is the initial rate of reduction of error probability with number of combinations, which should be close to ideal analog communication. The other is the asymptotic minimum achievable error probability, which should be low enough to give a good chance of accepting the block. For a fixed threshold, these goals are conflicting. We will find that a narrower null zone favors a more rapid initial reduction in error probability, while a wider null zone favors a lower asymptotic error probability, because nonnull decisions have greater reliability. The conflict can be resolved by allowing a null zone that is small initially, and then widens.

Increasing the number of states increases memory storage requirements. However, the access is not random. Information is always accessed and modified in the same order when a new reception arrives. With each state access/modification a cur-

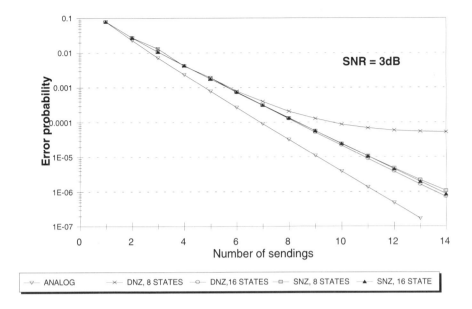

Figure 7.5: Probability of error versus number of sendings for single- and double-null-zone combining compared to analog combinations.

rent binary decision is supplied to the block decoder. Thus, memory costs should not be high and decoder speed should not be significantly affected.

The derivation of the optimum threshold formulas is rather specialized, and is given in Appendix 7A.

Figure 7.5 shows the comparative reduction of error probability for analog combinations and for 8- and 16-state double-null-zone and single-null-zone combinations, at a signal-to-noise ratio of 3 dB. The thresholds have been selected optimally according to Equations (7A.13) and (7A.15). Figure 7.6 shows the corresponding values of optimum threshold with number of sendings.

Departure from ideal analog combinations is not too bad for the first few transmissions. These are the most important cases, since we would not like to operate in a channel so bad as to require many retransmissions. If the channel is that bad, it would be better to send future transmissions and retransmissions at a lower rate or with greater signal energy, if feasible.

With 8 states, the single-null-zone combination rule is always at least as good as the double, and the double-null-zone combination deteriorates markedly after about 7 or 8 transmissions. The latter case is actually levelling off asymptotically. The reason for this is explained in the last paragraph of Appendix 7A. With 16 states the single-null-zone case improves just slightly, but double-null-zone reception improves substantially and becomes a shade better than single-null-zone reception in the 8–14 transmission range.

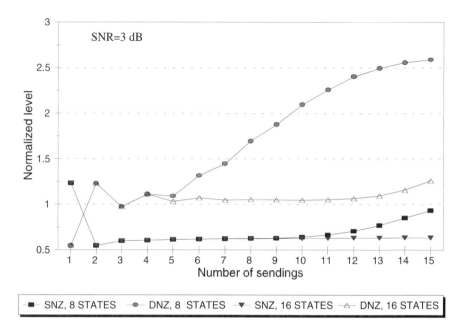

Figure 7.6: Variation of optimum threshold with number of sendings.

7.3.1   Performance Summary

A double-null-zone decision is desirable initially because it eliminates erasure or tie decisions. However, double-null-zone combinations are more costly in number of memory states and are inferior asymptotically for any finite number of states. Eight-state single null combination with double null reception on the first sending seems a good compromise between performance and memory cost. Compared to ideal analog, the performance cost is equivalent to only a 0.9 dB loss in signal-to-noise ratio after 14 transmissions, and only 0.7 dB loss up to 5 transmissions. Note that this deterioration is actually less than the 1.1 to 1.5 dB loss in amount of information received due to single- or double-null-zone reception that was cited in Section 7.1. The reason we can get closer is the restriction to Type I memory ARQ in this section. Restriction to retransmission does not make optimum use of the received information; ideal Type II memory ARQ does.

7.4   Type II Memory ARQ: The Incremental Redundancy Concept

When a code block cannot be decoded, more information is needed. Exact retransmission of the block is the normal procedure, but if the receiver has the capability of retaining memory of the prior block reception, more information can be supplied in other ways. One way is to provide additional incremental redundancy in the form of additional check symbols. The additional number of bits on the second and further sendings does not have to be the same as on the first sending. Following are some options:

Send smaller increments. This would have the advantage of coming closer to supplying just the amount of redundancy needed to be able to decode. It has the disadvantage of requiring more frequent acknowledgments and more total exchange cycles.

Send increments the same size as the original. This has the advantage of uniform size blocks and the possibility of containing all the information in the second sending. This latter feature is valuable in case the first sending is hit by a strong noise burst while the second sending is relatively error free. The second sending is then not the same as the first, or it would be the same as Type I, but it is best designed to be derivable from the first by an invertible transform.

Send larger size increments than the first sending. This normally is not desirable, because it drops the effective data rate more drastically. It might be used through additional feedback information indicating a much noisier channel than expected. A reduction to a lower initial data rate might be called for in such a situation.

7.4.1 The Small Increments Approach

If there are k data symbols and the first sending is an (n_1, k) code, while the second sending is n_2 symbols, the combined sending can be treated as a $(n_1 + n_2, k)$ code. This is like sending n_2 additional check symbols, and further sendings could be like sending additional check symbols. It is desirable to have some common structure for the original code and its increments. One way to do this is to start with a low rate code with k data symbols, puncture it (delete some check digits) to make it a (n_1, k) code for the first sending, and supply the missing check bits with further sendings as needed. A good method of doing this was presented by Mandelbaum [MAND74] using punctured Reed-Solomon codes. Reed-Solomon codes are ideal for this purpose because of their maximum distance property, which is retained when the code is punctured. Also, the decoding technique for the punctured code is very similar to the technique for the unpunctured code.

For example, suppose we take as the basic structure a $(255, 60)$ Reed-Solomon code, which has 8-bit symbols, or one byte. The first block sending could be a $(70, 60)$ code obtained by puncturing 185 check symbols. The minimum distance of this $(70, 60)$ code would be 11, so it could correct all patterns of up to 5 error bytes out of 70, although a lesser amount of correction might be used to preserve more error detection capability. The second sending could be 20 of the previously punctured check symbols, creating a $(90, 60)$ code with minimum distance 31, and ability to correct 15 errors out of 90. Additional punctured check symbols could be transmitted incrementally if needed, continuing to use the same Reed-Solomon code structure, up to where a total of 255 symbols are sent, for which up to 97 octal errors out of 255 could be corrected. If this still were not sufficient, which is highly unlikely, retransmission of the original $(70, 60)$ block code (or even the $(255, 60)$ unpunctured code) might be resorted to. There is then the option of discarding the prior reception, or possibly using Type I with memory on the retransmitted block.

Reed-Solomon codes are also effective for erasure decoding. An (n, k) punctured Reed-Solomon code has the property that the code word can be uniquely derived from any k symbols. Thus, if any $n - k$ or fewer symbols are erased and the rest are correct, the data can be correctly extracted. Alternatively, if $n' > k$ are unerased and there are errors, the error-correcting capability of an (n', k) code with minimum distance $n' - k + 1$ is still available. It is even possible to use double-null-zone memory for the symbol decisions, and convert null zone decisions (the less confident symbol decisions) into erasures in a further attempt at decoding. This is particularly useful in burst noise or varying channel conditions, since symbols received under burst or high noise conditions could be recorded as lower confidence decisions and discarded as erasures when appropriate. In particular, if retransmission were necessary because of exhausting the whole 255 symbols, all the less-confident, first-transmitted symbols could be replaced by the new receptions, while the more-confident, first-transmitted symbols could be retained and possibly combined with the repeats using symbol memory combining rules.

One drawback of the incremental redundancy approach using long block codes is that the decoding schemes usually require hard binary decisions prior to decoding. These binary decisions destroy some of the information in the received signals. This information was used in the combining rules of the Type I memory ARQ schemes. One way of making use of soft decisions is to use a convolutional code structure relating the first block symbols to the second. Decoding of convolutional codes can make convenient use of soft decision information. The punctured code idea mentioned in Section 4.1 also can be used for incremental redundancy in the convolutional code case. This will be discussed further in Section 7.9. Another way is to do the departure from retransmission at the symbol or small subblock level. This will be described in the next section.

7.5   Type II Memory ARQ with Equal Size Increments

Positive features of Type I memory ARQ are the equal size increments, the fact that each transmission contains all the data, and soft decision combining possibilities. However, even with soft decision combining, the second transmission under constant SNR achieves at most a 3 dB equivalent SNR improvement. This is because sending each symbol twice is equivalent to doubling the transmitted energy per bit. If the signal had been sent with twice the energy the first time, performance equivalent to sending twice would be achieved without having the trouble of forming combinations. Type II memory ARQ with equal size increments also can be designed to have all the information in each sending at little or no cost in decoding capability. The successive sendings are, however, scrambled versions of the first sending.

It is possible to use soft decisions in a Type II system with equal size increments to obtain more than a 3 dB equivalent signal-to-noise ratio improvement at a nonbinary symbol or subblock level. To see this, consider the basic reason why Type II systems are more effective. If two code words are minimum distance d apart and are repeated, the two code words as a combination still are minimum distance $2d$ apart. However, if the second sending is a transformed version of the first, the difference of the two transformed code words is almost surely greater than $2d$; that is, code words close in the original sending usually are not close on the second sending. For long code blocks the exact transformation is not too critical, since the property is valid for the overwhelming proportion of random transformations.

Soft decisions may be difficult to make use of in long block codes. The greater than 3 dB improvement can be achieved more simply at the level of a small subblock or a nonbinary symbol level; that is, data-to-nonbinary symbol relationships can be scrambled on the second sendings so that signal points close on the first sending are further apart on the second. Another practical approach is to use convolutional codes. We will look first at the small subblock/nonbinary symbol level.

7.5.1 Improved Sequential Signaling for Nonbinary Signals

Let the first encoded block sequence sent be $(a_1, a_2, \ldots a_n)$, where a_i is a nonbinary symbol. Let the second sending be $(b_1, b_2, \ldots b_n)$. In Type I ARQ, $b_i = a_i$, but in improved sequential signaling $b_i \neq a_i$. Both b_i and a_i are chosen from the same set of signal points, but b_i is derived from a_i such that two signal points for a_i that are close are mapped into two points for b_i that are far apart. See [METZ77A].

Multilevel Amplitude Modulation Consider first equispaced bipolar 4-level PAM as shown in Figure 7.7a. For convenience assume that a is the separation between levels normalized to the noise standard deviation, as the quantity d in [VANT68, p. 99]. Straight retransmission would multiply the effective minimum level separation by a factor of $\sqrt{2}$, which is a 3 dB improvement in signal-to-noise ratio. However, by simply repeating the 4-level signal we are not taking full advantage of the added dimension or degree of freedom. For improved sequential signaling we change the level order for the second sending (Figure 7.7b), producing the two-dimensional decision region (Figure 7.7c). Assuming identical Gaussian noise on both sendings, the nearest neighbor distance now is $a\sqrt{5}$, which represents roughly a 7 dB improvement in effective signal-to-noise ratio compared to one sending. This makes it equivalent in effectiveness to binary transmission, as is shown for comparison. This estimate assumes that error probability depends primarily on nearest neighbor distance, which is asymptotically true with increasing SNR.

Further Sendings In the event the receiver still cannot decode after two sendings, a possibly effective third sending is the binary signal shown in Figure 7.8a, creating the

a) first sending   b) second sending

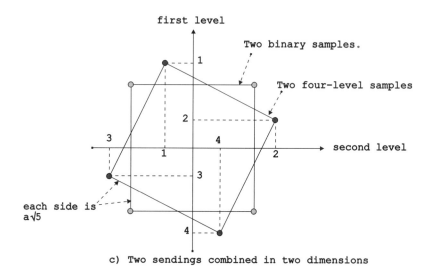

c) Two sendings combined in two dimensions

Figure 7.7: Transformed 4-level samples compared with two independent binary samples. *Source:* Adapted from J. J. Metzner, "Improved sequential signaling and decision techniques for nonbinary block codes," *IEEE Trans. Commun.*, vol. COM-25 pp. 561–563, May 1977. © 1998 IEEE.

three-dimensional configuration shown in Figure 7.8b. The effective signal-to-noise ratio for three sendings under identical noise conditions is then about 10 dB above that of the first sending, compared to a 4.77 dB gain that simple repetition would yield. Note that this choice has the disadvantage that not all the information is in the third sending. If the first two sendings were lost or completely noisy, the third sending could not allow decoding even if the channel cleared up. Thus this choice probably would not be a good one for the third sending.

It is interesting to note that the three-dimensional configuration after 3 sendings in Figure 7.8b is equivalent to the simplex set [WOZE65] of 4 signals, which is also equivalent to the three-sample binary code set 000, 011, 101, 110. This set is optimum for sending 2 bits in time T with no bandwidth limitation.

Providing additional dimensions is basically equivalent to having more bandwidth. Why is this so? Consider the i sendings as if they were sent simultaneously over i parallel channels with equal noise and signal powers. In symbol time T we are sending i samples over the i channels, so effectively are using i times the single

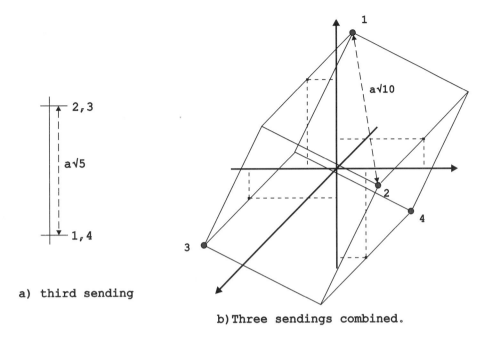

a) third sending

b) Three sendings combined.

Figure 7.8: Possible third sending, with initial 4-level PAM. *Source:* Adapted from J. J. Metzner, "Improved sequential signaling and decision techniques for nonbinary block codes," *IEEE Trans. Commun.*, vol. COM-25 pp. 561–563, May 1977. © 1998 IEEE.

channel bandwidth. The total transmitted power is multiplied by i as well. With identical sendings the power signal-to-noise ratio is multiplied by i; this is the reason for the simple repetition gain of 3 dB for 2 sendings, 4.77 dB $= 10\log_{10} 3$ for 3 sendings, used in the comparison. Since we cannot improve on the simplex set for any number of additional dimensions, no additional benefits would arise from the scrambling technique in this case, so it would be just as well to resort to repetition if any further sendings were required.

If the number of levels is greater, however, the benefits of scrambling extend over a greater number of sendings, and the benefits are greater because the signals are so close initially. For the case of 2^k levels, the simplex set of signals has $2^k - 1$ dimensions, so potentially improvements over simple repetition may extend out to about $2^k - 1$ sendings. Figure 7.9 illustrates the optimum scrambling and dB improvement with 8-level transmission.

Multiphase PM Phase modulation starts with two dimensions, which gives the signals larger initial separation. However, scrambling still gives improvement over repetition, even in the 4-phase case. Figure 7.10 shows some good scrambling choices for the cases of 4, 8, and 16 phases (denoted P4, P8, P16). The second and third choices

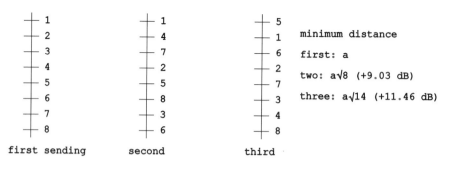

Figure 7.9: An effective sequence of sendings for 8-level PAM. *Source:* Adapted from J. J. Metzner, "Improved sequential signaling and decision techniques for nonbinary block codes," *IEEE Trans. Commun.*, vol. COM-25 pp. 561–563, May 1977. © 1998 IEEE.

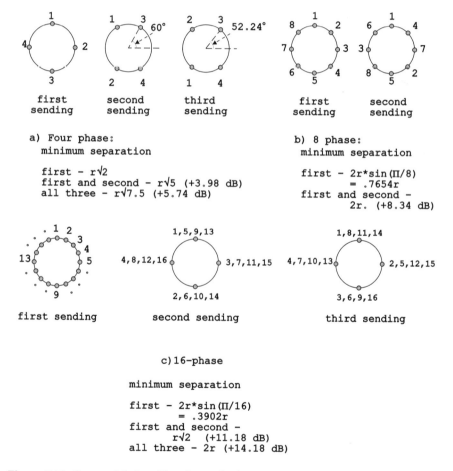

Figure 7.10: Sequential signalling for multiphase modulation. *Source:* Adapted from J. J. Metzner, "Improved sequential signaling and decision techniques for nonbinary block codes," *IEEE Trans. Commun.*, vol. COM-25 pp. 561–563, May 1977. © 1998 IEEE.

are designed assuming the same signal-to-noise ratio on all sendings. The P16 choices are poor ones if channel conditions vary, because only the first sending carries all the information. Different 16-phase arrangements could be used on the second and third sending, as done in P8. The improvements still would be good, but not as high as shown.

The previous analysis assumes exact analog values can be saved. Because in actual practice the received values would have to be quantized, some deterioration in performance would result.

Relation to Modulation Codes The improved sequential signaling techniques are somewhat related to modulation codes. In modulation codes, signal points are selected from a two-dimensional signal constellation. Data-related points are in time-consecutive samples, whereas in improved sequential signaling the related points are further apart in time, corresponding to successive sendings relating to a symbol. This places much more severe requirements on receiver memory than with modulation codes. Other differences are that modulation codes are designed for bandwidth compression, and consecutive samples relate to new data as well as old, in a convolutional fashion. In improved sequential signaling, no new data are introduced in the successive transmissions. Also, bandwidth saving is not a direct consideration in improved sequential signaling, although the reduction of required sendings compared to repetition is in a sense equivalent to a bandwidth saving.

If the 8-PSK case of Figure 7.10b was used to send 2 copies of the symbol initially in succession, this would correspond to a $(2,1)$ octal block modulation code. The data rate would be 1.5 bits per symbol, and the Euclidean distance would be equal to that of a binary PSK. After adjusting for equal transmission rates, this corresponds to a 1.76 dB gain, which is rather slight, plus a reduction to $2/3$ of the binary transmission bandwidth. However, in the ARQ application the second pulse is sent only as needed, which improves efficiency compared to always sending two pulses.

7.5.2 Subblock Mapping Improvements

Likelihood or soft decision information is more easily used when the number of alternatives is rather small. Such was the case for the nonbinary sequential signaling just described. It is entirely impractical in general for long block codes, because the number of alternatives is enormous. However, soft decisions are feasible if a code has a small number of data bits. Take the n bits of a (n, k) binary code, and partition them into n/b subblocks (assume n/b is an integer) of b bits each, without regard to whether the bits are data or check bits. Then let the second sending be as subblocks of check bits of a $(2b, b)$ code, where the corresponding first subblock holds the b "data" bits. See [METZ79]. If this $(2b, b)$ code has minimum distance greater than 2, there is potentially an improvement over repetition. Also, if b is no more than about 6 or 7 bits, the number of code words is small enough to consider making a maximum likelihood decision among the 2^b code words based on the two exact receptions. It is also important that the *b* data bits be extractable from the second sending as well as from the first sending.

There are not many good block codes meeting this criterion. One outstanding choice is an $(8, 4)$ Reed-Muller code with a minimum distance of 4. The four check bits of this code are derivable from the four data bits by the invertible matrix

$$P = \begin{bmatrix} 0 & 1 & 1 & 1 \\ 1 & 0 & 1 & 1 \\ 1 & 1 & 0 & 1 \\ 1 & 1 & 1 & 0 \end{bmatrix} \tag{7.1}$$

Asymptotically for high SNR, the minimum distance of 4 creates a 6 dB improvement over the original sending, compared to 3 dB for repetition. However, at lower SNR the improvement is somewhat less, because there are 14 code words at distance 4 from the correct code word, whereas there are only 4 code words at distance 2 with repetition.

This $(8, 4)$ code has the further useful property that P is its own inverse. The value of this property will be discussed in Section 7.7.

7.5.3   Whole Block Invertible Mapping

Let **v** be the first transmitted *n*-bit code vector of an (n, k) code. The second sending must be an invertible transform $g(\mathbf{v})$ of **v**. The following has been suggested [LIN83, WANG83]: Send successively $\mathbf{v}, g(\mathbf{v}), \mathbf{v}, g(\mathbf{v}), \mathbf{v}, \ldots$ until the block is acknowledged. At each point only the current reception and the preceding are used for decision. Use $g(\mathbf{v})$ or **v** alone just for error detection, and in combination as a powerful rate $1/2$ code. If no errors are detected in the current reception, take this as correct, inverse transforming if it is $g(\mathbf{v})$. If both halves detect errors, use the rate $1/2$ code for error correction.

The ideas of using just the last two receptions and trying both cases are attractive; this is because the case where the channel has recovered is allowed for, and the rate $1/2$ code usually will be powerful enough to correct residual errors. Greater decoding power could be attained with the more general approach of sending $\mathbf{v}, g_1(\mathbf{v}), g_2(\mathbf{v}), \ldots$, using the structure of an (in, k) code for *i* transmissions. If the $i * n$ symbols remain part of a cyclic code, the ability to derive the data from any one of the *i* sendings is ensured. If the full power of this method is used, the decoder has to work with code of length $i * n$, and be capable of correcting large numbers of bit errors. Some codes for carrying this approach to $i = 3$ are described in [ALFA94] and for larger *i* in [KRIS87].

Another alternative for enhancement is to combine Type I and Type II combinational techniques. The alternating $\mathbf{v}, g(\mathbf{v})$ scheme can be enhanced by incorporating Type I memory when more than two transmissions are required. The multiple copies of receptions for **v** can be symbol-by-symbol combined in Type I fashion, as well as multiple copies of receptions for $g(v)$. At any point, the symbol-by-symbol combined record for v can be code-block combined with the symbol-by-symbol combined record for $g(v)$. Attempts could be made to decode the most recent reception alone as well as various combinations with memory.

7.6 Concatenation and Erasure Subblocks

Concatenated coding is a versatile encoding/decoding method. The overall code tends to be rather large, so they are most suitable for sending large files of data. Individual inner blocks (subblocks) can either be error-detecting or error-correcting or both. Memory can be employed at the subblock level or at the outer (overall) code level.

The improved sequential signaling and subblock mapping techniques involve memory at the subblock level. In general, incremental redundancy techniques could be used on a per-subblock basis. The outer code treats the subblocks as symbols, and might be subblock-error-correcting as well as error-detecting.

An interesting application with memory ARQ at the outer code level is where the subblock codes are used for error detection. Then subblocks with errors detected can be marked as erasures [KASA86]. Another possibility is that lost inner blocks could be called erasures. An important potential application is in ATM systems. For this purpose, the inner blocks could be standard 53 byte cells. The overall code block would consist of n cells: the data cells plus redundant cells for erasure filling. The major source of error is cell loss due to buffer overflow. These losses can be recognizable through sequence numbering, and can be treated as erased subblocks. Up to k erased subblocks can be filled in with possibly as little as $k + 1$ redundant subblocks (one for error detection, and only k additional for erasure filling if Reed-Solomon codes are used). If more than k subblocks are erased, there are the following alternatives:

1. All n cells could be retransmitted, and with memory, the number of erased cells after two transmissions is just the number of cells that were erased both times.

2. A number r of additional redundant cells could be sent via incremental redundancy, after which as many as $k + r$ erased cells could be filled in.

3. Selective repeat of some or all of the erased cells could be requested.

The first of these alternatives is simplest and is compatible with memoryless receivers, but is the least efficient. The second and third are comparable in efficiency, but the second saves in feedback capacity because only the quantity of needed cells has to be specified, not their positions. The number of cells sent the second time in alternative 2 might exceed somewhat the number needed, to allow for additional erasures on retransmission.

7.7   Noisy Return Channels and Similarity/Difference Tests

Combining strategies need to consider two risks: one is that information relating to two different data packets might erroneously be combined as if belonging to one. This problem can occur in either Type I or Type II memory ARQ. A second danger, unique to Type II, is that the receiver may not be sure which part it currently is receiving out of the succession of transmissions regarding a given data packet.

7.7.1   Type I Memory ARQ

When both forward and return channels are noisy, there will be times when an unrequested repeat is sent and cannot be properly decoded. The receiver might then retain a memory of this reception, but the sender might belatedly learn of the previous block having been received correctly, and start sending a new block. The receiver might then think this is a retransmission to be combined with what is already in memory, and attempt to combine two receptions that really arise from different messages. Related problems also can arise in multiaccess networks, where different packets may be sent by different senders.

In consideration of this problem, Metzner and Morgan [Metz63] suggested two tests: a similarity test and a difference test. Actually, it seems preferable to use just one term, *similarity test*, but with two different purposes.

Test Against a Prior Decoded Block   Compare a nondecodable block to a block previously decoded. Depending on the protocol and time of arrival, there might only be one such block, or there might be more. Discard the information in the nondecodable block if it is too *similar* to a previous one.

The similarity test against one prior block is basically a matter of extracting just one bit of information, whether it is the prior block repeated or not. Note that a new block at the very least has to have a different sequence number. Any difference in the data, including the sequence number, will produce a pattern difference at least as great as the code minimum distance. It should be possible to make this decision reliably. Even if the decision is erroneous, usually the only harm is to impact decoding efficiency by causing the combined record to be a mixture of old and new blocks. Eventually the false start will be filtered out in a finite state Type I combiner. Failure to note similarity normally would occur only in a very noisy situation, in which receptions would be given low likelihood numbers.

Comparison of Two Nondecodable Blocks   If the similarity test with past blocks failed or if the receiver was not sure whether the current and past block came from the same data, a similarity test could be performed. If the current reception is too different from receiver memory, this suggests that the memory and current reception probably come from different blocks. This is true because the number of errors rarely is so great as to cause differences comparable to the difference between different blocks. If the difference test exceeds some threshold, the blocks should not be combined.

7.7.2 Type II Memory ARQ

Consider the strategy of alternating sending $\mathbf{v}, \mathbf{g(v)}, \mathbf{v}, \mathbf{g(v)}, \mathbf{v}, \ldots$ It is possible that the receiver, through loss of a frame reception, might not be sure whether the current frame represents $\mathbf{v}$ or $\mathbf{g(v)}$, in addition to not being sure whether it comes from an old or a new packet of data. The similarity test could be made with the old $\mathbf{v}$ and/or $\mathbf{g(v)}$ to check if it came from the old. The other ambiguity might be solved by adding protected bits identifying each sending [ALFA94]. If this is not done, one must be careful in designing the invertible transform to protect against an undetected error. To see this, let us compare two different recommended methods [METZ85A].

Following [LIN83, p. 479], one method of deriving $\mathbf{g(v)}$ from $\mathbf{v}$ is to take the original data vector $\mathbf{u}$, of k bits, derive a k-bit vector $\mathbf{q(u)}$ by an invertible transform, and use this as the data bits for the second sending. $\mathbf{u}, \mathbf{q(u)}$ are related by a $(2k, k)$ code. The first transmitted vector is a code word $\mathbf{v} = \mathbf{f(u)}$ from an (n, k) code. The second transmitted vector is a code word $\mathbf{v}^* = \mathbf{f(q(u))}$ from the same (n, k) code. This approach has a weakness if the receiver is not sure when the new block transmission starts. Since $\mathbf{q(u)}$ is just as valid data as $\mathbf{u}$, an error free $\mathbf{v}^*$ could be mistakenly interpreted as $\mathbf{v}$, resulting in a significant possibility of decoding the data as $\mathbf{q(u)}$ instead of as $\mathbf{u}$.

A modification of the above technique [WANG83] is, instead of transforming the k data bits of the first sending, to transform the whole n bits (both data and check) by an invertible matrix transformation:

$$\mathbf{v}^* = \mathbf{Mv}. \tag{7.2}$$

Now $\mathbf{v}^*$ and $\mathbf{v}$ form a $(2n, n)$ rate $1/2$ code. This code is not related to the (n, k) code of the individual block sending. Thus $\mathbf{v}^*$ would rarely be a code word of the (n, k) code containing $\mathbf{v}$ (for most choices of codes). Thus, if $\mathbf{v}^*$ were received error free but mistakenly tested as a $\mathbf{v}$, it normally would not check in the (n, k) code. But if it were inverted it would yield $\mathbf{v}$, which would check. Thus this second approach is more immune to uncertainty about when this new block transmission started than is the first approach.

The invertible subblocks method using the $(8, 4)$ Reed-Muller code also is immune to uncertainty between $\mathbf{v}$ and $\mathbf{g(v)}$. Within a subblock, the second sending $\mathbf{s}_i^*$ of the ith subblock is related to the first sending $\mathbf{s}_i$ by

$$\mathbf{s}_i^* = \mathbf{Ps}_i, \tag{7.3}$$

where $\mathbf{P}$ is given by (6.17). It was noted previously that $\mathbf{P}$ is its own inverse. The set of code vectors $(\mathbf{s}_i^*, \mathbf{s}_i)$ is thus the same set as $(\mathbf{s}_i, \mathbf{s}_i^*)$. (This property is also true of all rate $1/2$ cyclic codes). Thus this code has the remarkable property that even if the receiver has confused the reception as coming from $\mathbf{v}^*$ instead of $\mathbf{v}$, it will still make the maximum likelihood comparisons with the right set of 16 code words. (But it will not be sure of the associated data at this point). If a misinterpretation is made, the same misinterpretation will be made in all subblocks. By testing both alternatives, only the correct interpretation has significant probability of checking. It is shown in [METZ85] that the chance of false checking over all (n, k) codes using error detection is $2^{-(n-k)}$.

7.8   Some Comparisons

It is interesting to make a comparison between ideal Type I memory ARQ and ideal Type II memory ARQ with same size increments. Binary symbols, constant signal-to-noise ratio, and independent Gaussian noise will be assumed. Also, we will assume the Type II system needs to make hard binary decisions. By "ideal Type I" we mean that analog combinations can be made for each individual binary symbol. By "ideal Type II" we mean that whenever the effective data rate falls below the binary channel capacity the decoder will correct the errors. The ideal Type I system also assumes the overall (n, k) block code is similarly an ideal decoder.

Let p be the bit error probability without combinations. The channel capacity is

$$C = 1 + p * \log(p) + (1 - p) * \log(1 - p) \text{ bits/symbol.} \qquad (7.4)$$

Let $R = k/n$ bits/symbol be the initial rate. After i transmissions the effective rate is R/i. Thus the ideal Type II coder will be successful at the first i for which

$$R/i < C. \qquad (7.5)$$

The Type I memory system reduces p to p_i (define $p_1 = p$). The original rate R encoder then effectively sees a channel of apparent capacity C_i after i transmissions, where

$$C_i = 1 + p_i * \log(p_i) + (1 - p_i) * \log(1 - p_i) \text{ bits/symbol.} \qquad (7.6)$$

The Type I system is successful for the first i for which

$$C_i > R. \qquad (7.7)$$

Figure 7.11 shows the variation of C_i with i for various signal-to-noise ratios. Also shown is the effective rate if the initial $R = .9$. The most important case to compare is $i = 2$.

There is never a case where Type II fails after two sendings but Type I succeeds. This is because $C_2 < 2C$ in all cases, so if $C_2 > R$, then $2C > R$, which satisfies (7.5). However, there is a rather wide range where both would be equally effective. For example, if $C = .6$ and the original rate is between .6 and .83 (points A and B on the curve), both will be successful after two sendings. If the original rate is between .83 and .95 (point C), Type I will take 3 sendings, but Type II will need only two.

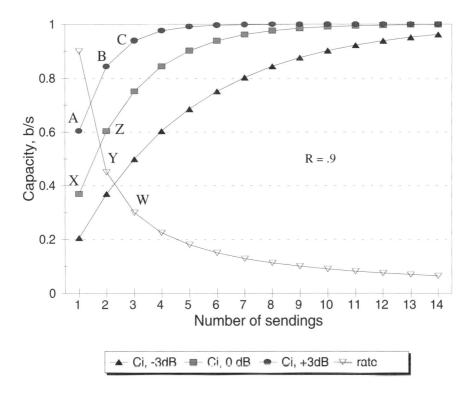

Figure 7.11: Rate and capacity variations with number of sendings.

The efficiency of ideal Type II memory could be further improved through use of smaller increments, since the effective rate would then more closely match capacity. Also, the advantage of Type II over Type I would be enhanced if the Type II system could use soft decisions. Soft decision operation is possible using improved sequential signalling for M-ary PAM or PPM, subblock mapping, or convolutional codes.

Varying channel conditions favor the use of soft decision techniques, because the variations can be accounted for in likelihood computations. A modified hard decision decoder could make use of erasures as an additional decision alternative, since combined error/erasure decoders are feasible.

Graphs like Figure 7.11 can also be used for other comparisons. The curve labeled "rate" is just a plot of R/i for $R = .9$. Suppose the channel capacity is only .37 (point X). After two Type II transmissions we are at point Y, which is above X, and thus decoding is unsuccessful. After three transmissions we reach point W and decoding is successful. Suppose we used the alternating $\mathbf{v}, \mathbf{g(v)}$ technique. If we only save the last two sendings, decoding would never be successful after any number of transmissions, assuming an abrupt threshold success probability of 1 or 0 according to whether the effective rate is below or above the channel capacity, respectively. If we combined this with Type I memory on $\mathbf{v}$ and $\mathbf{g}(\mathbf{v})$ separately, then the effective rate stays at point Y for 2 or more transmissions, while the capacity moves up the curve that starts at point X. Clearly after four transmissions we would be at point Z, which is above Y, meaning success. After three transmissions the bit error probability would be the average of p_1 and p_2. Assuming the decoder does not make use of the information that at this point $\mathbf{v}$ is more reliable than $\mathbf{g}(\mathbf{v})$, the effective capacity would be somewhat below the average of points X and Z, which turns out to be above Y, so the decoder would be successful.

7.9   Convolutional Code Memory ARQ

Convolutional codes can be utilized in either Type I or Type II memory ARQ schemes, sometimes in combination with block codes.

7.9.1   Type I Memory ARQ

With block coding, memory combination of an undecodable block with its retransmission is a natural extension. As mentioned in the beginning of this chapter, it is strictly an option of the decoder whether to employ memory or discard the prior reception. Convolutional codes are not usually organized in fixed block sizes, although at some point the code transmission is terminated into a block. The terminated block could be used as the retransmission unit, though it may be too long for some applications. Instead, individual symbols or subblocks of symbols could be retransmitted when the convolutional decoder gets into trouble due to excessive errors or excessive computation time. In the extreme case the decoder could request to retransmit from the start when this happens, but usually does not need to get data transmitted that are much further back than the order of a constraint length.

Chapter 4 mentioned two schemes for retransmitting some symbols when using Viterbi decoding or majority logic decoding. Memory was not suggested for those schemes, but could be used to some advantage.

For the case of Viterbi decoding, a likelihood metric is computed for received symbols, so it is a fairly simple matter to adjust a symbol metric based on reception of two copies of a received signal and redo the survivor computations.

Majority logic decoding is a simpler procedure that works after hard decisions and does not normally retain likelihood information. This information could be retained, however, at the cost of extra complexity. Alternatively, hard decisions could be used along with a memory of the vote score; the vote could then be recomputed based on scores on both receptions.

Sequential decoding with Type I memory is described and evaluated in [KALL88]. A convolutional code is terminated into a block code after a prescribed number of bits. If sequential decoding fails to decode, the whole block is retransmitted. A combined metric is recomputed for each symbol based on the two sendings. If necessary, there are additional sendings and combined metric adjustments are made by the decoder until successful. The effective rate is R_0/n after n transmissions, where R_0 is the initial rate in bits per transmitted symbol. As with block Type I memory ARQ, the rate steps down about to the point where R_0/n first is below the current capacity, at which it usually is first successful. However, sequential decoding uses likelihood information, whereas the block coder uses hard binary decisions (other than in the combining process), so the capacity with sequential decoding is somewhat higher. Retransmission of the whole block has one disadvantage over a more incremental approach in that the first retransmission reduces the rate by one-half, which would be inefficient if the original rate was only slightly above the capacity. Because the sequential decoder often can successfully decode a beginning portion of the block before running into trouble, efficiency could be improved somewhat by requiring only retransmission of the uncertain portion of the block.

7.9.2 Type II Memory ARQ

Convolutional codes are very well suited for schemes that send additional information rather than just retransmit symbols. They can be employed in cooperation with block codes or entirely as convolutional codes.

Use of Punctured Convolutional Codes [HAGE88, KALL90]   One idea is to design a basic low rate   1/2 or less—code, puncture many check symbols to convert it into a high rate code, and begin by sending the high rate code. Then, if the decoder has trouble, some of the punctured check symbols are sent; thus, only about as many check symbols as needed are sent, consistent with the incremental redundancy concept.

Block Code Initial Transmission [METZ79]   Suppose we send a block (n, k) code as a first transmission, where the symbols could either be binary or blocks of binary digits. Suppose this code has capability for near perfect error detection, although it could be given some error correction capability as well. If the first sending is not decodable, let the second sending be derived as the check symbols of a $(2, 1, m)$ systematic convolutional code. Let m be very small such as $m = 1$ or 2. It is necessary to add m additional symbols to terminate the convolutional code. For example, suppose $m = 1$. Define the first transmission symbols as $f_1, f_2, \ldots, f_N$, the second sending as $s_1, s_2, \ldots, s_{n+1}$. Then let

$$s_i = f_i + f_{i-1}, \qquad i = 1, 2, \ldots, n + 1, \tag{7.8}$$

where f_0 and f_{n+1} are defined to be zero.

In the binary symbol case, exact likelihood ratios could be remembered and used in a combined decision, using Viterbi decoding. After the combination, block error detection/correction could be performed to see if there is a success. Note that all the information is in the second sending as well as the first, so the decoder has the option of performing error detection on the second sending alone as well as the combined sendings. For the case where the signal-to-noise ratio is the same on both sendings, Viterbi decoding using likelihood ratios reduces bit error probability equivalent to a signal-to-noise ratio improvement of 4.5–5 dB for $m = 1$ and 6.5–7 dB for $m = 2$, compared to only 3 dB for Type I memory. This could also be compared to the nonbinary symbol/short subblock techniques described in Section 7.5.

Technique	dB Gain for Two Sendings
simple repetition	3
4-level PAM scrambled	6.9
8-phase PSK scrambled	8.3
$(8, 4)$ subblocks	5–6
$m = 1$ convolutional	4.5–5
$m = 2$ convolutional	6.5–7

The convolutional codes compare quite well considering that these are the simplest possible rate $1/2$ convolutional codes, the $(8, 4)$ subblock idea does not have a practical extension to longer codes, and the PAM/PSK cases are restricted to where nonbinary transmission is appropriate.

Performance is more difficult to analyze for the case of a time-varying channel. An analysis of performance for a two-state Markov channel model and an $m = 6$ convolutional code appears in [LUGA89].

Performance for an erasure channel is also discussed in [METZ79]. The assumption of erasures without errors is not realistic for binary symbols. However, the erasure channel could be appropriate if the basic block code in the first transmission were a concatenated code whose basic symbols were rather large subblocks with their own error detection. They could even each be the contents of an ATM cell, as another example. Then any detection of errors or loss of cell would lead to erasure of the block symbol. The equation (7.8) could still define a memory $m = 1$ convolutional code, but the $\{f_i\}$ symbols would each be a multibit vector representing one of the blocks. This case is described in [METZ82] in a description of an alternative to replication for memory protection. The convolutional code with $m = 1$ or 2 would allow filling in many more erasures than straight repetition. Decoding is extremely simple. It is necessary only to slide along with the basic relation as Equation (7.8) and fill in any case where only one of the terms in the equation is an erasure. It is shown in [METZ79] that only two passes—left to right and then right to left—is always sufficient to decode anything that can be decoded for the $m = 1$ and $m = 2$ systematic codes. Of course it could not do as well as a punctured Reed-Solomon block code, where the second sending consists of punctured check symbols—the rate $1/2$ Reed-Solomon code can fill in up to 50 percent erasures—but the short constraint convolutional code is far simpler.

Turbo Code Approach   The turbo code approach mentioned in Section 4.5 uses two codes operating on the same data, except the data is permuted for the check bits of one code relative to the other. The component codes usually are rather simple convolutional codes. This structure is ideally suited to use with Type II memory ARQ. The first transmission can be a block-terminated convolutional code corresponding to the first component code. If the channel happens to be good this might be successful. The termination point could actually be made variable, dependent on when the decoder reports trouble. If decoding is not successful, the second transmission could be the check bits for the second component code. A third sending, if necessary, could be check bits for a third component code. The number of check bits in the second or third sendings need not be the same as the number of check bits in the first sending. They could be the same number, however, and even the same code could be used, except for different data permutations.

7.10   Summary

Type I memory ARQ is defined as retransmitting, and at the receiver combining the retransmission with a memory of the first reception. In Type II memory ARQ the additional transmission(s) are not identical to the original, but provide additional redundancy to be used by the receiver in making a combined decision. Although in general Type II is superior, Type I has the advantages of allowing simple soft decision combinations and being compatible with memoryless ARQ.

In Type I memory ARQ with combinations per binary symbol and independent additive noise, ideal combined binary decision can be made by addition of log likelihood ratios; in constant strength Gaussian noise this just amounts to adding the received values and comparing to a threshold. For simplicity, coarse quantization of likelihoods into three levels (single-null-zone) or four levels (double-null-zone) can be used at a cost of only about 1 dB or less compared to ideal analog combinations.

In Type II memory ARQ, one approach is to send small additional increments of redundancy, equivalent to including more check symbols, until the block can be decoded. Reed-Solomon codes are ideal for this purpose, because the maximum minimum distance property holds at each stage. An important advantage is that only slightly more than the minimum redundancy needed is transmitted. A disadvantage of doing this with block codes is that decoding complexity requires that hard symbol decisions be made, which results in some loss of information. Type II memory ARQ with equal increments has the feature common to Type I that each sending can be devised to contain all the data. It has the advantage that code words close in the first transmission will almost always be far apart in the second transmission. By using the transformation idea at the nonbinary symbol or small subblock level, combined soft decisions for the first and transformed symbols yield an improvement far greater than the 3dB gain in effective signal-to-noise ratio obtained from simple repetition. Examples are about 7 dB with 4-level PAM, about 8.34 dB with 8-phase PSK, and asymptotically about a 6 dB improvement with (8, 4) Reed-Muller code subblocks.

In concatenated codes with erasure subblocks, memory of unerased symbols could be used in combination with additional redundancy transmissions to decode efficiently.

The similarity test can be used in Type I memory ARQ to ensure that proper combinations are being made. It could be used to discard an unrequested but non-decodable retransmission, or to combine only blocks that were similar enough to indicate they came from the same information transmission. The use with Type II is not as simple, but can be used with some transformation tests; this is easiest to do when the transform is its own inverse.

Convolutional codes need ARQ when error events cause excessive decoding complexity. Individual symbols or subblocks could be retransmitted and combined in a Type I fashion, or could just replace the original. Convolutional codes could be used in various ways in Type II memory ARQ. Alternatives could be: (1) first transmission treated like the data symbols of a rate $1/2$ convolutional code, and then second transmission like the check symbols; (2) second transmission symbols derived from the first by short constraint length convolutional codes; and (3) small incremental redundancy via punctured convolutional codes.

7.11   Problems

7.1.   For Type I memory ARQ with ideal analog combinations of retransmitted binary symbols, what is the optimum combination rule if the first bit sending encounters Gaussian noise at a signal-to-noise ratio of 0 dB, and the second bit sending encounters independent Gaussian noise at a signal-to-noise ratio of 6 dB?

7.2.   State how the following techniques regarding coding and decoding of a block of digits are similar and how they are different: Type I memory ARQ, space diversity reception, and time diversity coding by block repetition.

7.3.   Type I memory ARQ is used for transmitting and retransmitting if necessary a block of n symbols. Assume the channel has the property that each symbol independently is either received correctly with probability $1 - p$, or is erased with probability p. The memory consists simply of remembering all nonerased symbol decisions. Assume the receiver is not capable of filling in erased symbols or requesting individual symbol retransmissions. If the block is received with erasures, the receiver asks the sender to retransmit the whole block. The feedback channel is assumed error-free.

a.   Write an expression for the probability that there is no need for a retransmission.

b.   Write an expression for the probability that exactly two transmissions are required.

c.   Write an expression for the probability that exactly i transmissions are required.

d.   If $n = 100$ and $p = .1$, evaluate these expressions for $i = 1, 2,$ and 3.

e.   If instead, the receiver could request at each step (over an error-free feedback channel) exactly which symbols should be retransmitted over the channel, and the symbol retransmissions would still be erased with probability p, would the number of steps change? Would the total number of transmitted symbols change?

7.4.   In the example of 8-level PAM in Figure 7.9, show that the minimum separation after 3 sendings (3 dimensions) is $a\sqrt{14}$, as stated.

7.5. An $(8, 4)$ Reed-Muller code has the following generator matrix:

$$\begin{bmatrix} 1 & 0 & 0 & 0 & 0 & 1 & 1 & 1 \\ 0 & 1 & 0 & 0 & 1 & 0 & 1 & 1 \\ 0 & 0 & 1 & 0 & 1 & 1 & 0 & 1 \\ 0 & 0 & 0 & 1 & 1 & 1 & 1 & 0 \end{bmatrix}.$$

    a. Verify that the method in Section 7.5 [see Equation (7.1)] of using a Reed-Muller code to derive the second sending from the first agrees with the philosophy of making signals that are close on the first sending and far apart on the second.

    b. Show that the data are uniquely derivable from the second sending.

7.6. **a.** A frame that has detected errors needs to be compared against an old frame of which it might possibly be an unrequested repeat. Assume all frames are the same length, $L = 400$ bits. The decision of similarity will be made after hard binary decisions, based on the number of bit positions that disagree being less than n. Suppose the minimum Hamming distance of two different code words of the error-detecting code in each frame is 10. The average Hamming distance between two different code words is 200.

        Comment on the advisability of setting $n = 3$; $n = 9$; $n = 100$. Make some rough quantitative estimates of the chances of a false similarity or a missed similarity for the different cases.

    b. Repeat the problem with the only difference being that the comparison is between two frames that both have detected errors, and it is not known whether the two are retransmissions that should be combined or whether they relate to different data.

7.7. One possible Type II memory scheme uses a short constraint length convolutional code in the following manner. In the first block N symbols, $\{s_1, s_2, \ldots, s_N\}$, are transmitted using a block error detecting concatenated code. The symbols are inner codes that can perform error detection, so they are presumed to supply either an erasure or a correct symbol to the outer error detecting code. If there are any erasures, a second transmission is made of $N + 2$ symbols, $\{t_1, t_2, \ldots, t_{N+2}\}$, is derived from the first by the rule that $t_i = s_i + s_{i-1} + s_{i-2}$. Addition is vector sum modulo-2, and s_i is taken to be zero if $i < 1$ or $i > N$.

    Suppose $N = 10$, and in the first sending symbols 3, 4, 5, 6, 8, 9 are erased, and in the second sending symbols 1, 3, 5, 9, 12 are erased.

    a. Show that all erased symbols can be reconstructed.

    b. Show a different pattern with only four total erased symbols among the two sendings that cannot be reconstructed.

Appendix 7A

Derivation of the Null Zone Combining Performance Curves

7A.1 State Transition Probability Matrices

Suppose that the correct bit value is a one, and define $q(i)$, $q_N(i)$, $p_N(i)$, $p(i)$ as the probabilities that the individual decision regions for the ith sending will be b_1, a_1, a_0, and b_0, respectively. The i index is necessary when we wish to use a different threshold for different sendings. Where the values are independent of i the indexing can be omitted. The state transition probability matrix with 8 states, double-null-zone reception, and fixed threshold is given by ($i > 1$):

$$M(i) = \begin{bmatrix} q+q_N & q+q_N & q & 0 & 0 & 0 & 0 & 0 \\ p_N & 0 & q_N & q & 0 & 0 & 0 & 0 \\ p & p_N & 0 & q_N & q & 0 & 0 & 0 \\ 0 & p & p_N & 0 & q_N & q & 0 & 0 \\ 0 & 0 & p & p_N & 0 & q_N & q & 0 \\ 0 & 0 & 0 & p & p_N & 0 & q_N & q \\ 0 & 0 & 0 & 0 & p & p_N & 0 & q_N \\ 0 & 0 & 0 & 0 & 0 & p & p+p_N & p+p_N \end{bmatrix} \quad (7A.1)$$

For variable threshold, the terms should all have the index i added for transition from $i - 1$ sendings to i sendings.

The initial state vector for one sending is

$$S(1) = \begin{bmatrix} 0 \\ 0 \\ q(1) \\ q_N(1) \\ p_N(1) \\ p(1) \\ 0 \\ 0 \end{bmatrix}.$$

For $i > 1$,

$$S(i) = M(i)S(i - 1). \tag{7A.2}$$

Repeated application of Equation (7A.2) then allows computation of state probabilities for all i. For a given i, the sum of all state probabilities with positive subscripts is the probability of correct bit decision on the ith sending.

For single-null-zone reception (except double-null-zone on first sending), the transition probability matrix ($i > 1$) is given by

$$M(i) - \begin{bmatrix} q+u & q & 0 & 0 & 0 & 0 & 0 & 0 \\ p & u & q & 0 & 0 & 0 & 0 & 0 \\ 0 & p & u & q & 0 & 0 & 0 & 0 \\ 0 & 0 & p & u & q & 0 & 0 & 0 \\ 0 & 0 & 0 & p & u & q & 0 & 0 \\ 0 & 0 & 0 & 0 & p & u & q & 0 \\ 0 & 0 & 0 & 0 & 0 & p & u & q \\ 0 & 0 & 0 & 0 & 0 & 0 & p & u+p \end{bmatrix}. \tag{7A.3}$$

In (7A.3) for $M(i)$, $u(i) = q_N(i) + p_N(i)$, and the i index is omitted for simplicity.

The initial state vector is the same as for double-null-zone reception, and repeated application of (7A.2) again allows computation of state probabilities for all i.

7A.2 Maximum Initial Error Probability Reduction

One interesting problem is that of finding the threshold settings that yield the smallest error probability after two sendings. Consider the case of double null zone with threshold level t_1 on the first sending and t_2 on the second sending. The objective is to select t_1 and t_2 so as to minimize the probability of binary decision error for the two combined receptions. (Note that the first binary decision is independent of the null zone threshold level.)

The error paths for this case are shown in Figure 7A.1.

Adding the error paths, we obtain

$$P(\text{error in 2 sendings}) = p(2) + (1 - q(1)) * p_N(2) + p(1) * q_N(2). \tag{7A.4}$$

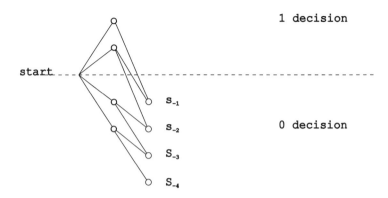

Figure 7A.1: Error events, double-null-zone.

Let t_1 and t_2 be the normalized threshold levels on the first and second sendings.

$$\frac{\partial p}{\partial t_1} = -p_N(2) * \frac{\partial q(1)}{\partial t_1} + q_N(2) * \frac{\partial p(1)}{\partial t_1} \tag{7A.5}$$

Setting to zero, we obtain

$$\frac{q_N(2)}{p_N(2)} = \frac{\dfrac{\partial q(1)}{\partial t_1}}{\dfrac{\partial p(1)}{\partial t_1}}. \tag{7A.6}$$

Using

$$q(1) = \frac{1}{\sqrt{2\pi}} \int_{-\infty}^{A-t_1} \exp \frac{-\lambda^2}{2} d\lambda,$$

$$p(1) = \frac{1}{\sqrt{2\pi}} \int_{A+t_1}^{\infty} \exp \frac{-\lambda^2}{2} d\lambda \tag{7A.7}$$

where $\pm A$ are the signal levels normalized to the noise standard deviation, we find

$$\frac{q_N(2)}{p_N(2)} = \exp[2At_1]. \tag{7A.8}$$

Differentiating with respect to t_2,

$$\frac{\partial p}{\partial t_2} = \frac{\partial p(2)}{\partial t_2} + (1 - q(1))\frac{\partial p_N(2)}{\partial t_2} + p(1)\frac{\partial q_N(2)}{\partial t_2}. \tag{7A.9}$$

By steps similar to those leading to (7A.8), we find

$$\frac{q(1)}{p(1)} = \exp[2At_2]. \tag{7A.10}$$

Equations (7A.8) and (7A.10) are transcendental equations that can be solved simultaneously for t_1 and t_2.

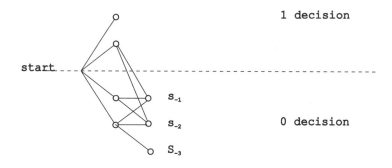

Figure 7A.2: Error events, single null zone.

Single Null Zone on Second Sending The error paths for this case are shown in Figure 7A.2.

$$P(\text{error in 2 sendings}) = p(1) + (1 - q(2)) * p_N(1) + p(2) * q_N(1) \qquad (7\text{A}.11)$$

Note that (7A.11) differs from (7A.4) only in that the indices 1 and 2 are reversed. Thus the optimum threshold pair (t_1, t_2) will be the same two numbers as in the previous case, but reversed. For example, at a 3 dB signal-to-noise ratio, the optimum (t_1, t_2) pair is $(1.23, .545)$ in the single null zone on second sending case, and $(.545, 1.23)$ in the strict double-null-zone case. Both will have the same error probability optimized for two sendings.

Optimization for Additional Sendings Given the optimum thresholds for two sendings, we can easily find the condition for optimum third sending threshold. Similarly, we can extend this result to the optimum ith sending threshold setting. For the **single-null-zone case,**

$$P(\text{error in }i\text{th step}) = P_{i-1}(S_1)p(i) + P_{i-1}(S_{-1})[1 - q(i)] + \sum_{j \geq 2} P_{i-1}(S_{-j})$$

$$= P_{i-1}(S_1)p(i) - P_{i-1}(S_{-1})q(i) + P(\text{error in }(i-1)\text{th step})$$

$$(7\text{A}.12)$$

Differentiating (7A.12) and setting to zero,

$$t_i = \frac{1}{2A} \ln \frac{p_{i-1}(S_1)}{p_{i-1}(S_{-1})}. \qquad (7\text{A}.13)$$

From (7A.13) it is a routine matter to compute successive optimum values of t_i. Note that (7A.13) is also valid for the previously derived $i = 2$ case.

For the **double-null-zone case**,

$$P(\text{error in } i\text{th step}) = P_{i-1}(S_2)p(i) + P_{i-1}(S_1)[p(i) + p_N(i)]$$

$$+ P_{i-1}(S_{-1})[1 - q(i) - q_N(i)]$$

$$+ P_{i-1}(S_{-2})(1 - q(i)) + \sum_{j>2} P_{i-1}(S_{-j})$$

$$= -P_{i-1}(S_{-2})q(i) + P_{i-1}(S_2)p(i) + P_{i-1}(S_1)[p(i) + p_N(i)]$$

$$- P_{i-1}(S_{-1})[q(i) + q_N(i)] + P[\text{error in } (i-1)\text{th step}]$$

$$(7A.14)$$

The last three terms in (7A.14) are independent of t_i. Differentiating and setting to zero,

$$t_i = \frac{1}{2A} \ln \frac{p_{i-1}(S_2)}{p_{i-1}(S_{-2})}. \qquad (7A.15)$$

Again, this checks with the $i = 2$ case.

7A.3   Asymptotic Results

Consider now the case of a fixed threshold, to see its effect on the asymptotic performance as k increases. In actual practice there would not be much interest in a system that requires a very large number of retransmissions for success. However, the asymptotic results are easy to obtain and provide some additional insight. Whereas for ideal analog combinations and discrete combinations with an infinite number of combination states the bit error probability approaches zero with increasing k, finite state combinations at a fixed threshold level approach some positive probability of bit error with increasing k. We will see that the limiting error probability decreases with increasing threshold level. This reinforces the strategy of widening the threshold level with increasing k.

If M is the state transition matrix and $\mathbf{P}$ is the column vector of asymptotic state probabilities when a one is sent, $\mathbf{P}$ is the solution of

$$(I - M)\mathbf{P} = 0, \qquad (7A.16)$$

together with the equation that the state probabilities add to 1.

Single Null Zone Case   Equation (7A.16) with M from (7A.3) could be used, but it is easier to see the solution from an N-state Markov chain diagram (Figure 7A.3). Letting $r = p/q$, solving for the state probabilities, and adding the probabilities of states leading to 0 decision, the asymptotic error probability is given by

$$p(\text{error}) \Rightarrow r^{N/2}/(1 + r^{N/2}). \qquad (7A.17)$$

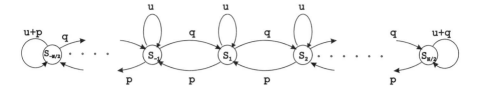

Figure 7A.3: State transition probabilities, single-null-zone case.

For a fixed threshold and number of states this is a strictly positive quantity that limits the minimum error probability. However, r decreases toward zero as the threshold is widened, so any arbitrarily small probability of error can be approached with a sufficiently wide null zone. Also interesting to note is the exponential reduction with the number of states.

Double-Null-Zone Case   In the single-null-zone case we saw that by gradually widening the null zone we could achieve asymptotically as low a bit error probability as desired. A perhaps surprising result for the double-null-zone case with the stated transitions is that this cannot be done given a fixed number of states. The reason is that a transition is required in every case that has a polarity opposite to the current consensus decision. Note that $p_0 - p_N + p$ is the probability of a wrong polarity decision, and is independent of the choice of null threshold. Then, no matter what the current state, the probability of a wrong combined decision $N/2$ steps later is at least $p_0^{N/2}$, since even starting in the highest state, $N/2$ transitions of at least one step each in the wrong direction will lead to a wrong decision. This asymptotic defect could be removed, however, by using single null transition rules when in the highest state.

Chapter 8

Reliable Transmission Over Time-Varying Channels

If one thinks of a communication channel between *A* and *B* as a single dedicated wire or optical fiber, it is reasonable to think of the channel as having constant characteristics and constant capacity to carry information. However, communication resources generally have to be shared, and then it is more the rule than the exception that communication channel conditions will vary. In a packet data network, circuits are not dedicated, and the interfering traffic a packet meets will vary statistically. Sometimes a packet may be held up excessively in a queue due to congestion, resulting in timeout and retransmission of the packet, even though it might eventually arrive; alternatively, the packet might be discarded at a node due to a full buffer. In a multiaccess network where many users share a common cable or radio channel, variations in traffic load create variations in occurrence of collisions and retransmissions. In these situations retransmissions themselves add to the traffic and tend to make congestion worse unless controls are applied. (Multiaccess networks will be discussed in Chapters 9 and 11).

Wireless communication is subject to still greater variation. In addition to the sharing problem, variations occur due to propagation/fading fluctuations, transmitter or receiver motion, atmospheric noise variation, multiuser interference, and intentional interference (jamming). There is even meteor burst communication [MILS87], where data transmission occurs only when reflection off a small meteor permits a brief period of communication. Also, use of moving earth satellites has been proposed [WERN95], which create varying, but mostly predictable, channel conditions.

8.1 Modeling Time-Varying Channels

Statistical models of how channels vary are desirable for system design and evaluation of prospective communication strategies. It should be clear from the previous comments that there are many different ways channel conditions can vary. Thus no one model is the best for all cases.

Models often seek to describe the variation of one key parameter of the channel. Most common choices are power signal-to-noise ratio (SNR), channel capacity and, for binary channels, bit probability of error. Often the bit error probability and channel capacity are deterministic functions of SNR. These parameters are good for something like a single radio link, but they are not suitable (except channel capacity) for communication through a network. For a network, the parameter might be expected delay, channel traffic load, or probability a packet is lost.

The variations with time of the parameter being modeled constitute a random process, and it can often be modeled as a stationary random process. One exception would be the case of channels with moving receivers or transmitters, which may introduce partially predictable and possibly periodic time fluctuations. For stationary random processes, the first order probability distribution of the parameter is a key item of interest.

For communication over a fading radio channel, distortion and spread of the signal shape must be considered as well as the first order probability distribution and time variation of the received energy. It is useful to look at the narrowband and wideband cases separately.

8.1.1 First Order Models of a Narrowband Fading Radio Channel

The extreme case of a narrowband signal is a continuous single tone. Narrowband signals that change slowly by a few orders of magnitude relative to the carrier frequency will behave approximately as this model. Variation of the received signal strength occurs mostly because the received signal is the sum of electromagnetic reflections of signals arriving via different paths. Ionospheric reflection is one example in long distance communication. Random motions of ions and different ionospheric layers create changes in interfering path lengths. In shorter distance communication, the phenomenon occurs through reflections off buildings and other objects, when there is motion of transmitter, receiver, or reflecting objects.

In ionospheric reflection, for example, path lengths change slightly with time, which creates very large fluctuations in received carrier phase because of the high frequency of the carrier. What is received thus can be approximated as the sum of many phasors whose phases vary independently with a uniform probability distribution. This is illustrated in Figure 8.1.

The sum can be at times constructive and at times destructive, so net amplitudes varying from zero to an extremely large value are possible. The x and y components of the phasors can be taken as zero mean approximately independent random variables, for which the central limit theorem justifies the assumption [BECK67, PROA89] they

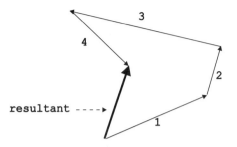

Figure 8.1: Phasor addition leading to Rayleigh fading.

are normally distributed random variables with mean zero and standard deviation σ. This yields a joint distribution

$$p(x, y) = \frac{1}{2\pi\sigma^2} e^{-(x^2+y^2)/2\sigma^2} \tag{8.1}$$

Converting to polar coordinates r, Θ, it is easily shown that the resultant phase distribution is uniform and the amplitude probability density function is

$$p(r) = \frac{r}{\sigma^2} e^{-\frac{r^2}{2\sigma^2}}. \tag{8.2}$$

Equation (8.2) is known as the Rayleigh amplitude probability density function. Examples that follow are expressed in terms of variation in power signal-to-noise ratio. Let S be the random variable power SNR, assume Rayleigh fading and a mean power signal-to-noise ratio of P. If we convert the amplitude density in (8.2) to a density in S, we find

$$f(s) = \frac{1}{p} e^{-\frac{s}{p}} \tag{8.3}$$

Sometimes the received signal needs to be considered as the sum of a fixed signal and a collection of random phasors, such as if there is one dominant phasor component. If C is the magnitude of the constant component, then the amplitude probability density function is given by

$$p(r) = \frac{r}{\sigma^2} e^{-\frac{(r^2+C^2)}{2\sigma^2}} I_0\left(\frac{rC}{\sigma^2}\right) \tag{8.4}$$

where I_0 is the zero order modified Bessel function. This is known as the *Rice distribution*.

8.1.2 Wideband Signals

If a signal consisting of the sum of two sufficiently different frequency tones were sent, the addition of phasors at one frequency would in general come out different from the addition at the other, because the amount of phase shift for a given propagation distance change depends on frequency. At a given time one could be in a destructive, fading condition, while the other could be in a constructive condition. This is known as *frequency selective fading*. Thus the shape of their composite signal would be distorted in different ways at different times. The net energy of a received signal composed of many individual tones would not obey a Rayleigh distribution even if each individual tone would. The net energy would tend to have a much smaller deviation about the mean than the Rayleigh distribution.

Wideband signals might be thought of as a composite of many tones, but it is also instructive to view them in terms of the radio channel impulse response. The channel can be approximated closely as a linear, time-varying system. However, at high data rates, the response is approximately time invariant during a given pulse transmission.

Suppose for simplicity that there are just three propagation paths from the sender to the receiver. If we sent a very short carrier pulse, duration τ, much shorter than the propagation time difference of the different paths, we would get a reception of three separate pulses, of relative strengths depending on the attenuations on the three paths, as illustrated in Figure 8.2. At first this looks good. The receiver certainly can detect the transmitted pulse; in fact it receives three copies of it. However, keep in mind that transmitted bandwidth is at a premium in radio transmission, and if enough bandwidth is being used to send τ-second pulses, one would like to send about one every τ seconds; but because of the reflections, we would need to send less often than once every T seconds to avoid energy overlap. If we sent a pulse a little less often than every T seconds we would want to use a bandwidth of the order of $1/T$, not $1/\tau$. Then we would send broader pulses, and their responses would overlap as indicated in Figure 8.3. The constructive/destructive effects would be different for the different pairs of overlapping response components, and would vary slowly from pulse to pulse with fluctuations in path lengths. Thus, transmitted pulses would be distorted, but in different ways at different times. If we spaced the pulses by $2T$, at least successive pulse responses would not overlap. If there are many paths rather than the three illustrated, the received energy in a pulse interval would not vary greatly because there would be a mix of mostly independent destructive and constructive

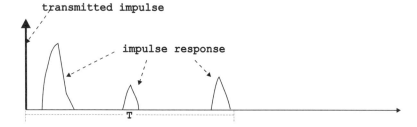

Figure 8.2: Response to a transmitted impulse with three propagation paths.

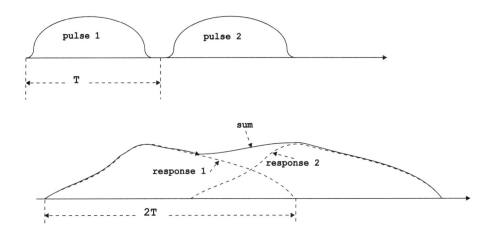

Figure 8.3: Response to a broader data pulse.

interferences from the different paths. This can also be seen from the viewpoint of frequency selective fading; some components of the signal will reinforce while others cancel, creating little net change in the average received energy.

Thus, on-off pulse transmission with decision based on received energy would not suffer as greatly as modulation techniques depending on signal shape and phase.

Parameter Time Variation In addition to first order distribution, the rapidity of the variation of channel characteristics is important. The narrowband model assumes a slow enough data rate. If the changes are rapid or the signaling rate is too high, more complex factors influence how the parameter in question changes or even if the single parameter model is adequate. If the fading is very rapid, the channel response characteristic can change during the transmission of a pulse, distorting its received shape. If the signaling rate is too high and the resulting bandwidth too wide, it causes severe distortion of the pulse shape due to frequency selective fading. Statistical descriptions of these variations have been made, but the details are beyond the intended scope of this book. A good discussion can be found in Chapter 7 of [PROA89].

The most convenient model to analyze is one where fading is both slow and frequency nonselective. In [PROA89], data on a number of types of radio channels are given; it is demonstrated that for several types of such channels there is a range of data rates where both assumptions can be made simultaneously. Also, even if the fading is frequency selective, if slow fading is valid, an ideal receiver can learn the fading channel response and properly combine the path signals in what is known as a RAKE receiver. The effects of distortion mostly are eliminated in this way. The details of this receiver design are given in Chapter 7 of [PROA89].

The average bit error probability for binary transmission over a Rayleigh fading channel is poor. The error probability falls only inversely with average SNR [PROA89], while in nonfading channels it falls exponentially with SNR. Despite the poor average error probability performance of fading channels, however, reliable and efficient communication is possible using ARQ or memory ARQ techniques. This will be shown in Section 8.2.

8.1.3 Markov Chain Modeling of Parameter Time Variation

The concept of a Markov chain has been described in Chapter 2. One of the earliest uses of a Markov chain to describe channel condition variations was the two-state Gilbert model [GILB60] for the binary symmetric channel. In this model there are two states—a good state (G) and a bad state (B). In the good state the probability of error is assumed to be zero, whereas in the bad state it is some probability p, $0 < p \le 1/2$. We limit p to $1/2$ because, even if the channel were complete noise, we could always guess the bit with error probability $1/2$. The state transitions are shown in Figure 8.4.

The model could be generalized slightly to allow some probability greater than 0 but less than p in the good state.

The long term frequencies of the states are easily found to be

$$P(G) = \alpha/(\alpha + \beta); \qquad P(B) = \beta/(\alpha + \beta). \qquad (8.5)$$

Normally α and β are both small and $\alpha \gg \beta$. This model exhibits the clustering of errors, a phenomenon often observed in communication channels. It is too crude to model many real channels accurately, but it still has some usefulness as a general guide because it models the essence of burstiness.

The Gilbert model need not be restricted to the binary symmetric channel. For example, in a data network the units could be packets instead of bits, and p could represent the probability of a lost packet. In this case the value of p need not be restricted to less than $1/2$, and might even be as large as 1. In the good state, packets would not be lost or would have a very low probability of loss.

An obvious extension of the Gilbert model is to have many states with different channel condition parameter values in different states. A slowly varying channel generally has a continuous range of parameter values. However, the model can be

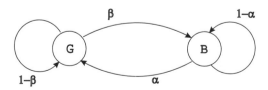

Figure 8.4: The two-state Gilbert model.

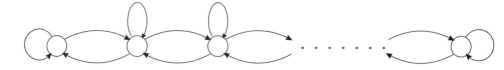

Figure 8.5: A Multistate chain model of a slowly varying channel.

discretized with little loss in accuracy. Most convenient would be a chain of states from best condition to worst condition, with transitions only between adjacent states, as illustrated in Figure 8.5.

In many real situations, channel statistics are not known accurately. It would be nice to introduce models that take this into account. Sometimes the current channel state can be estimated quite accurately and rapidly by observation of the received signal and noise. However, often the cause of the state and its likely duration are unknown. When a particular state exists for some time but its cause is unknown, it seems to be fundamental that the longer it has persisted, the longer it will be expected to continue to persist. Take the example of weather, and consider the two states as rain or no rain. Let us ignore the question of rain intensity, and just assume an individual only cares whether it is raining or not. When rain (the bad state) begins, the expected duration varies very greatly. There are many kinds of rain conditions, some of which have long expected durations and some short durations. To a naïve observer with no familiarity with weather analysis, either rain or no rain is occurring, and there appears to be only two states. Suppose this "naïve" observer is not so naïve in statistical analysis, and also knows there are different rain modes of different durations; but he/she does not know how to tell the mode from meteorological information, how the clouds developed, and so on. As the rain begins, the observer might expect it to be of short duration, because overall, the average duration is short. However, the longer the rain continues, the more likely it will seem to the observer that the rain is in one of those longer duration modes, and will continue much longer.

The data communicator often is in the position of the naïve observer. The communicator sees, for example, either a low SNR or a high SNR, but does not know what caused it. The communicator may know the possible causes, but does not observe the cause.

The author has made two attempts at modeling this phenomenon. In one model [METZ84A] there is a set of bad substates, each with the same bad conditions but different expected duration due to different physical causes. The communicator can observe a bad state, may have some idea of the statistical model of the different mode substates and transition probabilities, but does not know the substate. The longer the bad state persists, the more likely it is one of the longer expected duration substates. The other model [METZ65] involves an infinite chain of bad substates. Additional details of the two models are given in Appendix 8A.

A model that shows increasing expected duration of a state can influence a sender's transmission strategy. Suppose the desire is to minimize a function that weighs both transmitted energy utilization and delay cost. If the state is bad, the sender might be willing to wait a little while if the expected bad duration is short, but if it is longer, the delay cost may rise while the likelihood of the state getting better may fall. The variation of expected bad state duration will influence the point at which it becomes more cost effective to use the transmitted energy immediately rather than wait for a better state. An example is that of a satellite data transmission encountering high attenuation caused by a heavy rainstorm. If the transmission must get through without delay, it may require very high transmitted energy, with resulting battery energy drain and possible increased interference with other transmissions, whereas if transmission was delayed until the rain lightened much less energy would be needed. Wireless multiaccess communication in heavy traffic is another example. Both interference energy and battery consumption are energy costs in this case.

8.1.4 Arbitrarily Varying Channels and the Unfolding Channel Concept

Another approach has been taken that assumes there are states, but the channel state can change in an unknown and arbitrary manner. The idea apparently originated in [BLAC60], and was intended for study of communication subject to intentional interference or jamming. Papers such as [AHLS86], [CSIS88] and [ERIC85] derive various capacities and error probabilities, depending on permissible coding strategies and assumed state knowledge. An interesting result to note is that strategies that change the encoder randomly achieve higher rates than a strategy using always the same code.

The interest here is more on natural channel variations or unintentional interference rather than on intentional interference, so we will not discuss the previously mentioned work further. However, we will make use of the idea that there is a finite set of channel states that change in an arbitrary manner.

Often channel conditions vary slowly enough that the current state of a channel can be measured rather accurately at the receiver. Sometimes the channel state is a function simply of the received signal-to-noise power ratio. This parameter can be estimated reasonably well in a few symbol periods. Although we can measure current state accurately, there may be great uncertainty as to how this state will change in the future. Markov models with assumed transition probabilities might be postulated, but one possible approach is to make no attempt to predict how the state varies with time, but rather only say some state history unfolds. This approach was taken in [METZ70A], where a quantity called unfolding capacity was defined as follows: Assume a set of r channel states. Let C_i be the capacity if state S_i were always the state, $i = 1$ to r. Suppose State S_i occurs k_i times out of n transmissions. Then the unfolding capacity $C_F(n)$ is defined as

$$C_F(n) = \sum_{i=1}^{r} \{k_i C_i / n\}. \qquad (8.6)$$

There is a Type II memory ARQ scheme (to be described in Section 8.2) that ideally can send reliably at a rate arbitrarily close to whatever capacity unfolds. This achievement is not possible without feedback, because without feedback we would have to gamble, pick a rate and hope for the best. If a capacity unfolded that happened to be above the chosen rate then we would be successful, but if it unfolded below the rate we would fail.

8.2   Strategies for Time-Varying Channels

The prior statement about unfolding capacity makes it clear that when communication channels vary in an unpredictable fashion, the use of some form of feedback is critical to achieving reliable and efficient data communication. Without feedback, one might try to use interleaving or very long codes to increase the averaging period, which would reduce the variance of channel capacity. Still, even statistics about longer term averages are rarely known with confidence comparable to the block error probability ordinarily sought for reliable data communication. In most estimation problems, if we estimate a range and are off 1% of the time, this is considered pretty good. However, in selecting a rate without feedback, even being out of range one time in a million is not acceptable if we cannot tolerate one block error in a million. Given a history of time T to estimate the future average over a time τ, one has available roughly T/τ past samples. Thus, the longer is τ, the fewer are the available samples from past history. Also, there is no assurance that underlying factors that determined past statistics will remain constant. In certain rare cases, such as communication with a deterministically moving satellite or other object, variations in short-term averages are partially predictable.

There are two basic ways that feedback could be used to improve efficiency. One is to report channel condition as estimated at the receiver, so that the sender can adjust its rate to match channel conditions, or obtain additional or alternate communication resources if this is possible. The other is to use ARQ techniques. Also, both techniques could be used together. Observation of the frequency of retransmission requests even provides a crude estimate of channel condition that could be used as a basis for rate adjustment.

8.2.1   Adjusting Rate to Channel Conditions

If the communication channel conditions are varying very slowly, then it may be feasible to adjust the data rate to suit current conditions. This could be done through instructions or other information fed back about the current channel state. It could also be done indirectly in response to the number of retransmission requests. If there were too many, the sender could reduce its rate; if retransmissions were rare, the sender could increase its rate. The adjustments would have to be made in discrete amounts, would need to consider the synchronization problem, and would need to ensure the receiver was aware of the sender's rate. Memoryless ARQ could work fairly efficiently with this strategy, because the rate ideally would be selected just low enough that retransmissions are infrequent.

   If channel conditions vary rapidly enough to be likely to change over a code block interval or less, then data rate adjustments to follow conditions are not practical. However, ARQ with memory has the feature of adapting to channel conditions by supplying automatically just about the amount of redundancy needed. Rate changing could be used infrequently to correct for long-term average fluctuations, whereas memory ARQ could be used for automatic adaptation to the more rapid variations.

8.2.2   Use of Alternate or Additional Communication Resources

When a communication medium or network is shared, there is the possibility of using other resources if a channel condition deteriorates. For important data, priority rules could be employed to preempt other users on alternate channels, or other free channels or better network paths could be acquired. In radio networks, the possibility exists of increasing transmitted power to increase capacity under fading conditions. In shared radio networks this can work because of the capture effect that allows the strongest of a set of interfering signals to be received successfully, but the resulting greater interference seen by others deteriorates their performance. If there are no good alternatives but delay can be tolerated, it might be better to delay sending until conditions improve. More detailed discussion of these factors are best reserved for subsequent chapters, which deal with networks.

8.2.3   Achieving Unfolding Channel Capacity

Type II memory ARQ with small packets of incremental redundancy is the method that can be used to adapt the successful rate to whatever capacity unfolds. With this technique, one can start by sending at the highest practical rate, corresponding to close to the highest channel capacity anticipated. If the receiver cannot decode, as indicated by the return signal, send an increment of additional check symbols. Continue sending increments until the block can be decoded. (If the round trip time to return an acknowledgment were much less than a block length, the sender could just keep sending additional check bits until told to stop by a receiver acknowledgment.) It is shown in [METZ70A] that, for sufficiently long block codes, decoding will almost surely be successful for the first case where the effective rate falls slightly below the capacity that has unfolded [see Equation (8.6)]. This is illustrated in Figure 8.6.

   Note that each additional transmitted increment reduces the effective rate. After the fifth transmission, rate falls below capacity, and the block usually will be accepted at this point. The capacity can be approached more closely on average by using smaller increments, but at the cost of requiring more frequent acknowledgments.

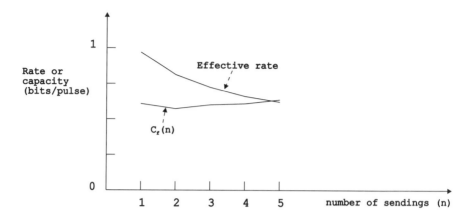

Figure 8.6: Incremental redundancy with unfolding channel statistics.

8.2.4   An Example with Rayleigh Fading

This example illustrates the kind of potential for reliable and efficient communication using memory ARQ techniques over a time-varying channel. Assume the variations are very slow relative to the data rate; so slow that with ARQ all transmissions relating to a particular block occur at the same SNR. This condition is not necessarily realistic for a time-varying channel, nor is it necessary for effective use of memory ARQ techniques; it is simply a convenient assumption for illustrative purposes.

Three schemes to be compared are memoryless block coded ARQ, ideal Type II memory ARQ, and Type I memory ARQ, all using binary transmission and hard binary decisions at the block code level, although the Type I system uses ideal analog combining at the binary symbol retransmission level. The coding/decoding is assumed to be ideal, such that once the rate falls below capacity the decoder will be successful. The channel is considered binary symmetric. An error-free feedback channel with negligible round-trip delay compared to a block length also is assumed. In this example we seek the average successful rate for each system. Because of the very slow fading rate assumed, the only role of the Rayleigh assumption is the first order density of power SNR, X, as given in Equation (8.3).

Type I System   The system initially transmits an (n, k) binary block code at rate $R = k/n$ bits/symbol. If the current power SNR X corresponds to a binary symmetric channel capacity exceeding R, we assume the sender will be successful. If not, the block is retransmitted. The effective power SNR after 2 sendings and ideal analog combining will be $2X$; after i sendings it will be iX. Success is assumed to come after the first i for which the capacity for power SNR iX exceeds R.

The bit error probability for an SNR of iX is[1]

---

[1]This relation applies assuming binary PSK with ideal coherent detection. For other types of modulation and demodulation the relation would be different (see [PROA89], pp. 716–719).

$$p(iX) = \frac{1}{\sqrt{2\pi}} \int_{\sqrt{iX}}^{\infty} \exp \frac{-\lambda^2}{2} d\lambda \qquad (8.7)$$

The corresponding capacity is given by substituting p from (8.7) into

$$C = 1 + p \log_2 p + (1 - p) \log_2(1 - p). \qquad (8.8)$$

Let P_0 be the SNR for which $C = R$. Then only one transmission will be required if $X > P_0$. In general, i transmissions will be required if

$$P_0/i < X \le P_0/(i - 1).$$

Let $r = P_0/P$. From integration of Equation (8.3), it is readily shown that

$$P(i \text{ transmissions}) = e^{-r/i} - e^{-r/(i-1)}, \qquad i > 1,$$
$$= e^{-r}, \qquad i = 1. \qquad (8.9)$$

The rate is R/i when i sendings are needed. The average successful rate in the Type I system is then

$$R_{\mathrm{I}} = R\{e^{-r} + \sum_{i=2}^{\infty} [e^{-r/i} - e^{-r/(i-1)}]/i\} \qquad (8.10)$$

R_{I} depends on the choice of R. If P is only a few dB, the optimum choice of R is found to be the value for which P_0 is close to but slightly higher than P.

Type II System   The system initially transmits at a rate close to 1 bit/symbol, but sufficiently less to protect against undetected error. Small increments of redundancy are sent until the rate falls just below the capacity corresponding to the current X, at which the decoder is assumed successful. Thus the effective rate will just about match the current capacity, which is theoretically optimum for this example. Weighing over all X, we obtain the expression

$$R_{\mathrm{II}} = \int_0^{\infty} f(X)C(X) \, dX. \qquad (8.11)$$

Memoryless ARQ   As the third system, consider memoryless ARQ that holds a fixed rate R, without any attempt to adjust to current channel conditions. For a given rate R, there is some $P_0(R)$ such that if $X > P_0$ the sending is successful. The effective throughput is then

$$R_{mless} = R \exp\{-P_0/P\}. \qquad (8.12)$$

Assume we select for each P the R that maximizes R_{mless} in Equation (8.12).

Throughput Comparisons   Figure 8.7 shows a comparison of the average success-ful rates of Type I and Type II memory ARQ and memoryless ARQ as a function of mean SNR for ideal slow Rayleigh fading. The dashed line is for a different assumption to be discussed shortly. The Type II memory results represent the best that can be achieved using binary transmission and hard binary decisions. Type I is inferior for two reasons. One is that having all transmissions the same size reduces the rate in increments that are too coarse. The other is that retransmission basically is not as effective as sending transformed information. As expected, memoryless ARQ is less efficient, but still allows significant throughput at low SNR, considering that it allows reliable transmission using the fundamental ARQ protocol principles described in Section 5.2. However, with slow fading, memoryless ARQ would experience protracted periods of basically zero throughput while the current capacity held below R, whereas with memory positive throughput occurs at any $C > 0$.

One alternative with memoryless ARQ could be to adjust the data rate. Under the very slow fading assumption of this example, adjusting the data rate based on feedback instructions could approach the same ideal approached by Type II memory ARQ. However, if the fading were more rapid, adjusting data rate would lose most of its effectiveness, while Type II memory ARQ would continue to do well.

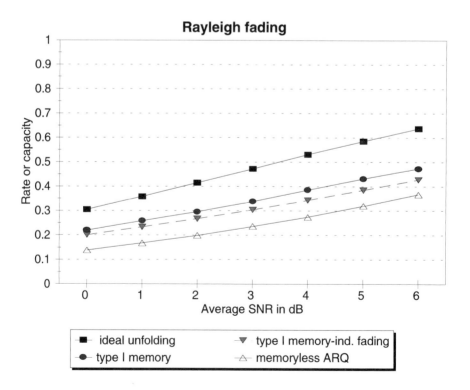

Figure 8.7: Memory and memoryless ARQ comparisons for slow Rayleigh fading.

8.2.5 Bit Error Probability Under More Rapid Fading Conditions

Note that the average error rate is high mostly because of errors during fades; at other times the error rate is very low. The Rayleigh fading example given previously assumed the fading was so slow that signal strength almost never changed during a code block duration and its retransmissions. This is too slow to be realistic in most cases. However, it is very realistic to assume that fading is slow relative to a bit duration. Thus, it is reasonable to assume that a receiver is capable of estimating fairly accurately the received signal strength in each bit interval based on measurements over several prior bit intervals. One crude approach would be to record erasures for all bits received when the SNR was below a certain level, and make binary decisions only at other times. To see that even this crude approach has some advantage, consider a simple example where $1/2$ of the bits are erased, and suppose the probability of error would have been $1/2$ if we had not erased them. Also suppose the error probability is zero for the unerased bits. (This is like the good/bad state model where the receiver knows the state.) If all bits were treated alike and the likelihood of error clustering ignored, the error probability would be $1/4$, corresponding to a channel capacity of

$$C_b = 1 + (1/4)\log_2(1/4) + (3/4)\log_2(3/4) = .189 \text{ bits/symbol}.$$

With erasures, the capacity of a binary erasure channel with erasure probability $1/2$ is

$$C_e = 1 - 1/2, \quad \text{or} \quad 0.5 \text{ bits/symbol}$$

in this example. Thus we see an increase from .189 to .5 in the limiting achievable rate for reliable communication.

A more sophisticated and effective method would be to record likelihood ratios for each binary reception, taking into account both received signal and estimated SNR, and then use soft decision decoding. This would allow successful decoding at higher transmitted rates.

No matter how sophisticated the decoding, however, the fading conditions may often fall below a threshold average during a certain period of time corresponding to a code block length with block codes or some duration related to constraint length with convolutional codes. Without ARQ, reliability then might still be quite poor, and the rate would have to be set low enough so this rarely happened. With memoryless ARQ, falling below the threshold would just mean retransmission, so reliability could be high. With memory ARQ efficiency could be much higher.

Let us consider another example of using Type I memory ARQ. Previously, we assumed the signal strength remained constant for successive retransmissions. Now we will assume that Rayleigh fading is independent for successive retransmissions of a bit in a block. Because there are many bit transmissions between two successive sendings of the same bit, this is a reasonable approximation in some cases. The Rayleigh distribution of power signal-to-noise ratio X given in (8.3) is assumed to apply. Further, assume that coherent binary PSK can be used, with normalized levels

$\pm\rho = \pm\sqrt{X}$. With the variable transformation $\rho = +\sqrt{X}$, the probability density of normalized level is

$$f(\rho) = (2\rho/P)\exp\{-\rho^2/P\}, \tag{8.13}$$

where P is the mean power SNR.

Assume the receiver can make an accurate estimate of the value ρ at a given bit time. The ideal receiver observes the random variable y:

$$y = \pm\rho + n,$$

where n is a Gaussian random variable of mean zero and unit variance (because of the normalization of level to signal-to-noise ratio).

For a single received sample, the probability of error averaged over the Rayleigh density is

$$P(err) = \int_0^\infty 2\frac{\rho}{P}\exp\left(-\frac{\rho^2}{P}\right)P_e(\rho)\,d\rho \tag{8.14}$$

where

$$P_e(\rho) = \frac{1}{\sqrt{2\pi}}\int_\rho^\infty \exp\left(\frac{-\lambda^2}{2}\right)d\lambda \tag{8.15}$$

In the event of inability to decode, the information stored is, ideally, the log likelihood ratio, which, for the Gaussian noise density, is

$$\log\frac{f(y/+)}{f(y/-)} = 2\rho y. \tag{8.16}$$

For successive receptions of a bit, the ideal receiver would add the log likelihood ratios to obtain

$$\sum_i \rho_i y_i$$

and would compare this to zero. Note that this is an addition of independent identically distributed random variables. Let us look at the sum of two of these random variables.

$$\rho_1 y_1 + \rho_2 y_2 = \rho_1(\rho_1 + n_1) + \rho_2(\rho_2 + n_2),$$

where n_1 and n_2 are (assumed Gaussian) independent noise random variables of unit variance. Given ρ_1, ρ_2, the conditional mean is $\pm(\rho_1^2 + \rho_2^2)$, and the conditional variance also is $\rho_1^2 + \rho_2^2$. The error probability based on observing the sum of these random variables is

$$P_e = Q(d/2\sigma) = Q\left(\sqrt{\rho_1^2 + \rho_2^2}\right).$$

Averaging over ρ_1, ρ_2,

$$P(err) = \int_0^\infty \int_0^\infty \frac{4\rho_2\rho_1}{P^2} \exp\left(-\frac{\rho_{eq}^2}{P}\right) Q(\rho_{eq}) \, d\rho_1 \, d\rho_2 \qquad (8.17)$$

where

$$\rho_{eq}^2 = \rho_1^2 + \rho_2^2.$$

Equation (8.17) can be reduced to a single integral by a polar coordinate transformation. It becomes

$$P(err) = \int_0^\infty 2\frac{\rho^3}{P^2} \exp\left(-\frac{\rho^2}{P}\right) Q(\rho) \, d\rho. \qquad (8.18)$$

Similarly, error probability for n independently faded transmissions combined can be expressed as an n-fold integral, which can be reduced to a single integral by a coordinate transformation (see Problem 8.6). The result for n sendings is

$$P(err) = \int_0^\infty \frac{2\rho^{2n-1}}{(n-1)!P^n} \exp\left(\frac{-\rho^2}{P}\right) Q(\rho) \, d\rho. \qquad (8.19)$$

It is interesting to compare bit error probability with very slow Rayleigh fading, where the SNR remains constant for a block and its retransmissions, with the case of more rapid Rayleigh fading where the SNR is independent for successive transmissions of a particular bit. The actual situation will lie somewhere in between these extremes. For the slow fading case, after n sendings,

$$P(err) = \int_0^\infty \frac{2\rho}{P} \exp\left(-\frac{\rho^2}{P}\right) Q(\rho\sqrt{n}) \, d\rho. \qquad (8.20)$$

Figure 8.8 shows how the probability of error decreases with the number of transmissions in the two cases. Note that the performance is much better if the fading is more rapid (but still not so rapid that the received SNR cannot be estimated accurately). This can be explained as follows: In the rapid fading case, if there are several transmissions there is a good chance one of them will come in at a good SNR, and this best reception will dominate in the decision making. In the slow fading case, if the first sending is at a bad SNR, so will be the retransmissions, and these cases of bad SNR are the main contributors to error events.

It is interesting to observe that the mathematical results displayed in Figure 8.8 also apply to diversity reception with multiple antennas, having the property that different antennas experience independent fading events. Probability of success with n repetitive transmissions at n different times with independent fading is the same as combining receptions of one transmission at n antennas with independent fading. In general there is a close behavioral relationship between (space) diversity reception and (time) diversity multiple repetition.

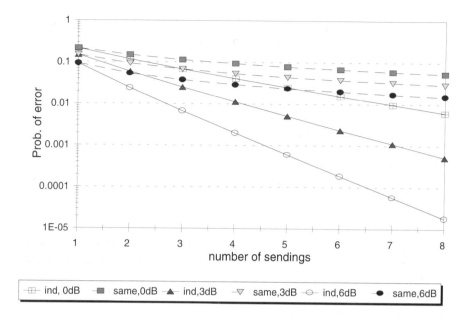

Figure 8.8: Bit error probability comparison between identical and independent fading on successive retransmissions.

8.2.6 Data Rates with the More Rapid Fading Model

Having noted the improvement in bit error probability with retransmissions at independent signal-to-noise ratio, it may be surprising to learn that this does not translate into better throughput for reliable communication. In this case we still assume that, although retransmissions come in at independent signal-to-noise ratio, for a given block transmission the signal-to-noise ratio remains constant. Also, the receiver is assumed to know the current signal-to-noise ratio.

For one thing, in memoryless ARQ the capacity would be the same as the Figure 8.7 result, because each sending sees the same first order distribution of signal-to-noise ratio, and it does not matter as to success frequency whether the block is a new transmission or a retransmission. Also, the unfolding channel Type II result would not be affected because the same average capacity unfolds.

Now let's look at the Type I memory case. For Type I memory we can use the same nth order density used in (8.19). Define this as

$$f_n(\rho) = 2 \frac{\rho^{2n-1}}{(n-1)!\, P^n} \exp\left(-\frac{\rho^2}{P}\right). \tag{8.21}$$

If we choose a power P_0 that corresponds to some rate R, the rate achievable is R/T, where T is the average number of sendings per success, given by

$$T = \sum_{i=2}^{\infty} i \int_{\sqrt{P_0}}^{\infty} [f_i(\rho) - f_{i-1}(\rho)] d\rho + \int_{\sqrt{P_0}}^{\infty} f_1(\rho) \, d\rho$$

$$= 1 + \sum_{i=1}^{\infty} \int_{0}^{\sqrt{P_0}} f_i(\rho) \, d\rho. \tag{8.22}$$

By bringing the summation inside the integral, a simple infinite series expansion for an exponential can be recognized, which exactly cancels the other exponential term in the integral. Then (8.22) reduces to the greatly simplified result:

$$T = 1 + P_0/P. \tag{8.23}$$

If P_0 is chosen to optimize R/T for each P, the dashed curve in Figure 8.7 is obtained. It is actually slightly inferior to the case where all retransmissions are at identical signal strength.

8.2.7   Multilevel Signaling

A channel subject to fading or other varying conditions may at times be so good as to support multilevel signaling, thereby allowing transfer of more than one bit per pulse. For example, suppose we risk sending two bits per sample, because sometimes the channel is good enough for this. Suppose it turns out we guessed wrong and the channel was not that good, and we should have used binary signaling. It would be nice if the 4-level sending was not wasted. If we send the second sending by scrambling the four levels as in Figure 7.7, we see from the figure that the combined decision has a reliability ideally as good as if we used binary transmission in the first place. Thus we succeed in getting through the two bits in two time intervals, just as we would have if we sent binary to begin with. Thus, nothing has been lost by our trying to get through at a higher rate. On the other hand, if the guess was right, we would have successfully sent at double the rate.

If we used ARQ without memory, the 4-level attempt in the previous example would have been wasted if the channel were not in a good enough state. Under slowly varying conditions, ARQ without memory would benefit in efficiency from the ability to change data rate according to channel conditions. Under more rapidly varying conditions it would suffer in efficiency compared to memory ARQ, but it would at least operate reliably.

8.3   Delay and Time Constraint Factors

Delay is an important consideration in data communication. The amount of delay that can be tolerated varies widely with applications. Analyses of network performance often use average delay as a performance parameter that should be minimized.

However, average system delay is not a good measure of network performance from the viewpoint of a particular user. One reason is that cost to the user is not a linear function of delay; another is that the delay cost function is different for different types of messages. For a given type of message, it generally is true that there is little or no cost to delay up to some critical point, and then the cost rises rapidly, being even a step function for some time-constrained applications. The point at which this cost rises rapidly differs widely with the application. In real-time digitized voice transmission (although this is not a high reliability application unless the signal is compressed), a fixed delay usually is designed in with some acceptable value. Any digitized sample that suffers a delay exceeding the fixed designed amount must be discarded. This incurs some cost, but the cost is perhaps not too high because loss of an occasional voice sample is tolerable. In some real-time control systems, the cost of not receiving an item of data by some specified time might be very high and could be set at infinity in some models. In file transfer, much longer delays are tolerated and the cost of delay increases more gradually. In ARQ systems, excessive delays lead to timeouts, which cost in efficiency and more serious problems if the delays continue to be in excess of the timeout interval.

One possible assumption is an exponential delay cost function [METZ84A]. The cost of delay τ is given by

$$C_1(\tau) = K[e^{\tau/d} - 1] \tag{8.24}$$

or

$$C_2(\tau) = Ke^{\tau/d}, \tag{8.25}$$

where d is a time constant appropriate to the application. The exponential is chosen because it exhibits about the right variation and is mathematically convenient. As an example of mathematical convenience, for two waiting messages with equal time constants, the ratio of their costs using the (8.25) function is dependent only on their time difference of arrival, not on how long they both have been waiting. The cost function might need to be truncated at some maximum, because no cost is infinite. This maximum could correspond to cost of complete loss of the data, which is another cost parameter of interest.

ARQ techniques ensure reliability at the expense of not putting a limit on the delay to obtain final acceptance. However, efficient memory ARQ systems almost always obtain that acceptance as early as the channel conditions permit. We saw that with the Type II memory ARQ technique, where if by time T the effective rate falls below the capacity that has unfolded, the communication statistically is nearly certain to be successful. If this does not happen by time T, no system with or without feedback could succeed in delivering the message successfully, short of changing the communication parameters.

Actually, changing the communication parameters may be the only way of solving a requirement that a fixed amount I of information be delivered very reliably in a fixed time T under variable channel conditions. If I/T is anywhere close to the expected channel capacity for the next T seconds, the estimated probability that the channel conditions will be equivalent to capacity above I/T over the next T seconds may be less than the desired probability of success. In a shared resource network, more current resources could be devoted to the communication that has the time constraint. An urgent message under a time constraint could, for example, be given more bandwidth, more transmitter power, extra network paths, or ability to preempt other messages waiting in a queue. Feedback could be useful provided that the round trip acknowledgment time is several times shorter than the time T to the deadline. Then, if a sender learns it is successful early, he or she does not need to continue to use the extra resources for the rest of the time interval T: otherwise the sender could continue to use resources, even more if necessary, to ensure success by time T. An illustration of such a strategy to minimize utilization of communication resources while striving to meet a time constraint is given in [METZ70B].

Whereas an urgent message might be given more power or resources to get through under poor channel conditions, an opposite behavior might be called for by a message with a low delay cost. Attempts to use more power or resources under poor conditions will increase interference or congestion for other users; thus it may be better for the delay-tolerant sender to wait for better conditions to prevail before sending. A cost function that weighs both resource utilization and delay cost could be useful as a decision aid.

8.4 Summary

Channel conditions vary for numerous reasons: fading and motion in wireless communication; varying congestion conditions in statistically multiplexed switched networks; varying congestion, interference, and collision in sharing a common cable or radio channel; burst noise or varying noise strength.

Varying channels can be modeled in terms of first and higher order densities of parameters such as **signal-to-noise ratio** or **channel capacity**. To model variations with time, **Markov models** of channel states are useful. **Arbitrarily varying** channel state also can be assumed.

Some form of feedback is essential for efficient and reliable communication under varying conditions. The feedback could allow either change of rate according to channel conditions or sending of additional **incremental redundancy** or retransmission if data are not received correctly. With incremental redundancy techniques (a form of Type II memory ARQ) it is possible to communicate reliably at a rate close to whatever capacity unfolds, if the receiver can make a good estimate of channel state. **Multilevel signalling** with second sending scrambling can help in approaching the unfolding rate. Type II memory ARQ is more efficient than Type I memory ARQ, which in turn is more efficient than memoryless ARQ.

In a fading environment, memoryless ARQ performs better when successive transmissions are at independent conditions (relatively rapid fading) than under slower fading conditions, because there is more chance one of the retransmissions will come in at a high enough signal-to-noise ratio to be successful. This is related to the advantage of independent fading in diversity reception.

Under varying conditions, there is a cost tradeoff between using excess energy to get data through under bad conditions, versus waiting to send more effectively when conditions improve, but at the cost of additional delay.

8.5   Problems

8.1. **a.** Perform the polar coordinate transform to derive Equation (8.2) from (8.1).
b. Also do the conversion of (8.2) into (8.3).

8.2. Suppose a signal propagates over three paths, and for transmission of a single tone at angular frequency ω_1 the three received components are

$$\cos[\omega_1 t], \qquad \cos\left[\omega_1 t - \frac{8\pi}{3}\right], \qquad \cos\left[\omega_1 t - \frac{34\pi}{3}\right].$$

This results in perfect cancellation. The phase angles represent $\omega_1 \Delta\tau$, where $\Delta\tau$ is the propagation time delay difference. Suppose the frequency were increased by 10%, with no change in the path time delays and attenuations. What would be the magnitude of the resultant component?

8.3. Suppose a channel obeys the Gilbert model of Figure 8.4 with $\alpha = \beta = .1$. The sender is ready to transmit a packet in the next interval, and learns the previous state interval was bad. The next state will be whatever occurs according to the Gilbert model. The packet must be received correctly in the next interval, else a cost of C_{LOSS} is incurred. There is a cost of C_T of sending the packet. If the state happens to be bad when the packet is sent the probability of success will be 0.1. If the state happens to be good when the packet is sent the probability of success is 1. For what range of C_{LOSS}/C_T would it be optimum not to send if the previous state were bad? For what range would it be optimum not to send if the previous state were unknown?

8.4. Consider binary transmission with incremental redundancy ARQ in a binary symmetric channel that obeys the unfolding model where the receiver knows the state. Suppose the sender initially sends a $(1000, 900)$ block code, and sends as many additional 100-bit blocks of check bits as needed. Assume the channel capacity is a constant 0.6 bits/symbol on the first block reception, and is a constant 0.8 bits/symbol on all the subsequent incremental transmissions. Ideally, how many additional incremental transmissions are needed to be successful? What would be the resultant ratio of rate to unfolded capacity in this case?

8.5. Derive Equation (8.9) from Equation (8.3).

8.6. Derive Equation (8.19) for combining n independently fading transmissions.

8.7. Assume an unfolding channel with 3 states, where the capacities are .5 bits/binary symbol in state 1, .8 bits/binary symbol in state 2, and .94 bits/binary symbol in state 3. The sender originally sends a $(1.1k, k)$ binary code block, and for each case the block is nondecodable based on an error-free return NAK/ACK signal, the sender sends another .1k check bits of an incremental redundancy code. Assume for each sending the channel capacity for that sending holds in the state indicated in the accompanying table. For the following chain of states that would unfold on the successive sendings, show the effective rate and unfolding capacity, and find the effective successful rate, assuming success comes as soon as the rate falls below unfolding capacity.

Sending No.	Eff. Rate	Channel State	Unfolding Capacity
1	1/1.1	2	.8
2		1	
3		3	
4		2	
5		1	

Caution: The unfolding capacity average must be computed as a per-bit average. Thus the first sending has a higher weighting in the average because more bits are sent in the first sending.

8.8. In the independent fading case, suppose that instead of combining log likelihood ratios, the decoder's decision after n sendings is the binary decision based only on that reception out of the n that came in at the maximum signal-to-noise ratio.

　a. Find the probability density function of the maximum of n Rayleigh distributed random variables. Hint: An easy method is to convert the one-reception density function equation (8.13) to the cumulative distribution function, and then obtain the cumulative distribution function for the maximum among n. Then convert back to density.

　b. Numerically compute the error probability at 6 dB average signal-to-noise ratio for n between 1 and 8, and compare with Figure 8.8.

8.9. Equation 8.14 with 8.15 can be integrated in closed form. Do this and see that the average error probability drops very slowly with P. Hint: Use parts integration of udv, where

$$u = P_e(\rho) \quad \text{and} \quad dv = \frac{2\rho}{P}e^{-\frac{\rho^2}{P}}d\rho$$

8.10. Suppose two sources, A and B, have the delay cost function (8.25). Suppose both have the same time constant $d = 2$ seconds, but for A, $K = 4$, while for B, $K = 1$. B arrives at $t = 0$, and A arrives at $t = 3$. If there is a choice whether to send B or A at time $t = 4$, which one should be sent based on minimizing average delay cost?

8.11. Suppose you have two chances to send a message, and the message must be successful after at most two sendings. With this constraint, you are trying to minimize expected total transmitted energy.

　Assume the following:

　1. You have time to get an acknowledgment back for the first try (on an error-free feedback channel).

　2. The receiver cannot use memory in case the first try fails.

　3. You must use either 2 units of energy or 6 units of energy with each try. It is certain that 6 units of energy will be successful. Due to lack of knowledge of current channel condition, you are not certain of success if you use 2 units of energy, but the probability of success if you use 2 units is known to be p.

　What is the largest value of p for which the best strategy would be to use 6 units the first try?

Appendix 8A

Models of Increasing
Persistence of Channel States

This appendix describes two models exhibiting the property that the longer one remains in a state, the greater is the expected remaining duration.

8A.1 First Model—Multimode States

Figure 8A.1 [METZ84A] illustrates the state diagram for this model. There is one good state and N bad states. The N bad states differ only in that they have different probabilities $\{\alpha_1, \alpha_2, \ldots, \alpha_n\}$ of returning to the good state, and thus different expected durations. The set of transition probabilities from the good state to the bad states is $\{\beta_1, \beta_2, \ldots, \beta_n\}$. The observer is assumed to know the statistical model, and be able to determine whether a state is good or bad, but is not able to distinguish among $\{B_1, B_2, \ldots, B_n\}$ other than by inference from the number of consecutive occurrences.

The probability of a sequence of $j + 1$ events: $GB_kB_k \ldots B_k$ is

$$p(G)\beta_k\overline{\alpha}_k^{j-1}$$

where $p(G)$ is the first order probability of the good state. Given a good state followed by j consecutive bad states, the conditional probability that the state is B_k is as follows:

$$P_i(j) = \frac{\beta_k\overline{\alpha}_k^{j-1}}{\displaystyle\sum_{i=1}^{N}\beta_i\overline{\alpha}_i^{j-1}} \qquad (8A.1)$$

The expected duration of state B_k is $1/\alpha_k$. Averaging over (8A.1), the expected remaining duration of the bad state after having been in the bad state for j consecutive

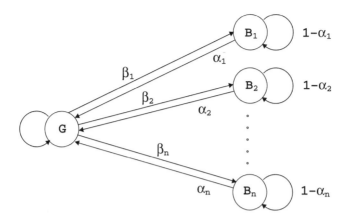

Figure 8A.1: Multimode bad state model. *Source:* Adapted from J. J. Metzner, "Message scheduling for efficient data communication under varying channel conditions," *IEEE Trans. Commun.*, vol. COM-32, pp. 48–55, January 1984.

times after a good state is

$$E_j = \frac{\sum_{k=1}^{N} \frac{\beta_k}{\alpha_k} \overline{\alpha}_k^{j-1}}{\sum_{i=1}^{N} \beta_i \overline{\alpha}_i^{j-1}} \tag{8A.2}$$

Suppose $\alpha_i > \alpha_j$ if $i < j$, so α_n is smallest and N is the longest average duration state. Computation will show that E_j increases with j. Asymptotically it approaches the largest individual state expected duration $1/\alpha_N$, which can be seen from the observation that the exponential term with the largest $(1 - \alpha_k)$ will prevail with increasing j in both summations.

8A.2 Second Model—Infinite Chain of Bad States

Figure 8A.2 illustrates this model—the infinite chain of bad states [METZ65]. The probabilities are chosen such that $p_i > p_{i-1}$, for all i, which has the effect that the longer one stays in the bad state the more likely one is to remain there. The mean recurrence time for state G can be shown to be

$$T = 1 + \beta[1 + p_1 + p_1 p_2 + p_1 p_2 p_3 + \cdots]. \tag{8A.3}$$

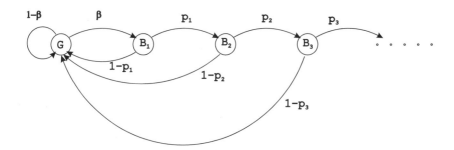

Figure 8A.2: An infinite state model. *Source:* Adapted from J. J. Metzner, "An interesting property of some infinite-state channels," *IEEE Trans. Inform. Theory,* vol. IT-11, pp. 310–311, April 1965. © 1998 IEEE.

In order to have a finite recurrence time for state G, the rate of increase of p_i with i must be sufficiently slow to permit convergence of the series in (8A.3). Choose

$$p_i = \left(\frac{i}{i+1} \right)^{\alpha} \tag{8A.4}$$

where $\alpha > 1$. The series

$$[1 + p_1 + p_1 p_2 + p_1 p_2 p_3 + \cdots]$$

then becomes

$$\sum_{i=1}^{\infty} i^{-\alpha}$$

which is convergent for $\alpha > 1$. The state probabilities are

$$P_G = \frac{1}{T}; \qquad P_{B_i} = \frac{\beta}{i^{\alpha} T} \tag{8A.5}$$

An interesting property of this model is that it gives a more pessimistic evaluation of the ability of long codes to reduce the probability of error. For most statistical models the probability of block error can be reduced exponentially with code length n if the rate is below capacity. Consider binary transmission with error probability 0 in the good state and $1/2$ in the bad states. Assume the decoder can tell if the state is good or bad for each symbol, and the state transitions are per-symbol time. With this model, error probability can be reduced at only a small inverse power of n. To see this, consider that when a state B_{2n} occurs there is a string of $2n$ consecutive informationless symbols. This will completely destroy at least one code block of n symbols, causing an average of $n/2$ binary errors. Thus the bit error probability is lower bounded by $n/2$ times the probability of state B_{2n}. From (8A.5),

$$P[\text{bit error}] > \left(\frac{n}{2}\right) \left(\frac{1}{2n}\right)^{\alpha} \frac{\beta}{T}$$

or

$$P[\text{bit error}] > \frac{1}{2^{1+\alpha} n^{\alpha-1}} \frac{\beta}{T} \tag{8A.6}$$

which decays only inversely as a power of n; a fractional power if $\alpha < 2$. For example, if $\beta = .1$ and $\alpha = 1.5$, $P_G = .793$, the channel is a binary erasure channel (since the state is assumed known) with capacity .793 bits/symbol. Yet the bit probability of error using coding without feedback cannot be reduced any faster than inversely with the square root of n at *any* transmitted rate. However, with feedback and no delay constraint, almost perfect reliability at rates near .793 bits per symbol could be attained by simply retransmitting erased bits.

Chapter 9

Multiaccess Networks

Thus far the discussion has concentrated on the problem of reliable communication for one sender over a single communication link. The fact that communication usually occurs over a network shared by many users has been given only passing mention, mainly with regard to a cause of interference and channel variations for the sender of interest. In this and subsequent chapters we will turn our attention to the problems of sharing a network.

Let the term *user* denote a communicator using the network to send and/or receive data. If data streams from a set of users all appear at a single node location for transmission over a common cable from that link to another, their transmissions can be coordinated in time and/or frequency for noninterference with each other. This process is referred to as *multiplexing*. One approach is to give each user a dedicated time slot in a repetitive, synchronized frame. This is referred to as *time division multiplexing*. Alternatively, each user could be given a dedicated frequency band. This is referred to as *frequency division multiplexing*. Both schemes can also be used together, because each frequency band can be divided into time slots. However, much data communication is sporadic, so it is usually preferred to avoid giving a user exclusive use of a dedicated time slot or frequency band. Most commonly this is done by *statistical packet time multiplexing*. Each user's packet is queued up for transmission if the channel is currently busy, and usually sent out on a first-come, first-served basis, though priorities also can be used. It is also possible to break the channel into subchannels by frequency division and/or time division (slotting), and to use statistical multiplexing within each subchannel; also, some subchannels could be dedicated.

It often is the case that separately located senders share access to a common communication medium. Dedicated time or frequency slots could still be used, though the time slots may have to be a little larger than needed due to propagation time differences. Also, coordination of user assignments would require additional communication overhead. If we want to use statistical packet multiplexing, coordination for noninterference is not as easy to accomplish. Nevertheless, statistical packet multiplexing is highly desirable for efficient multiuser data communication, so we need to investigate the performance of such systems with separately located users.

The common medium for statistical multiplexing of separately located senders is referred to as a *multiaccess channel* or a *multiaccess network*, and the methods by which the users share the medium are called *multiaccess protocols*. The protocols vary from tightly controlled, such as polling and reservation schemes, to loosely controlled, among which the ALOHA schemes are the loosest. Interference among users will occur frequently in the more loosely controlled schemes, so these schemes need careful attention to the reliability problem.

The most common assumption for a multiaccess channel is that when any user sends, all other users and destinations can hear the signal, but with some possibly significant time delay. This often is reasonable for the following configurations (see Figure 9.1):

a. All users are attached to a common cable or tree-connected cables, such that if any user sends a signal, the electrical signal propagates in both directions and is received with sufficient strength by all users connected to the tree. There are absorbing terminations at the unattached cable ends so that no electrical energy is reflected back onto the network.

b. Optical fibers employ unidirectional light signal transmission. If a fiber with uni-directional transmission is looped around so that each station has two connections or if each station is connected to two unidirectional fibers and sends on both, all stations can receive all signals. (See Figure 9.1b.)

c. Radio communication in a common band where the users all have transmitters and receivers and all are within receiving range of the others.

d. Radio (or wire) communication where each user sends its signal directly to a common central station, and that station broadcasts to all users whatever it receives.

A common simplifying assumption is that all received signals have about the same strength, and if two users send a packet of data at the same time or even in overlapping intervals, there will be a collision and neither will be successful. These assumptions are not too realistic, and tend to be somewhat pessimistic. Unequal received powers, signal design, and sophisticated signal processing techniques can allow a good probability of some success in a collision.

The assumption that all senders can tell by observing the common channel whether their sending is successful is optimistic. Using the common channel obser-vation as acknowledgment does not carry the very high reliability feature of ARQ protocols; in some applications, particularly radio communication, there may be frequent cases where some senders are very uncertain whether their transmissions suffered a collision. Thus some overlay of an ARQ protocol is usually needed.

In a general network, not all senders are directly connected to their destinations. Switching and routing decisions are needed to communicate effectively in such cases. The discussion of networks that require switching and routing will begin in Chapter 10. Wireless networks or networks with a wireless portion often exhibit

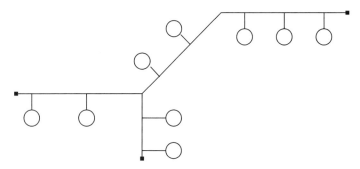

a) Common tree of cables (bidirectional).

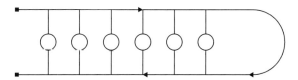

b) unidirectional optical fiber.

c) Radio - all in range.

d) Central station broadcast.

Figure 9.1: Multiaccess configurations.

a combination of single medium multiaccess and routing. Such networks will be discussed in Chapter 11.

Most multiaccess protocol design neglects background noise because the effect of interferers (collisions) is the main concern. The effects of background noise will be considered in Chapter 11, but in this chapter background noise will be neglected other than to recognize the need for error detection.

9.1 ALOHA Communication

Unslotted ALOHA is the most uncoordinated protocol, where any user that has a packet to send sends it, independent of what other users are doing. It is then assumed that the user learns whether the packet has been successfully received at its destination. There are two ways the sender can learn this: (1) If all users are assumed to observe all transmissions, the sender can observe whether its packet has collided or not with any others; or (2) an acknowledgment packet can be sent back from the destination, or from the central station in configuration d. If the packet has not been successful it usually needs to be retransmitted. Here there needs to be a little consideration of other senders, because if two colliders wait the same time to retransmit, they will collide again. Usually this is solved by waiting a random time before retransmission.

ALOHA communication is very attractive for use in a light traffic situation. A sender has in most cases immediate use of the full data-carrying capacity of the channel. However, we will see that in heavy traffic the efficiency attainable is discouragingly low and there are some potential instability problems.

Slotted ALOHA has one additional degree of coordination in that time is divided into slots, and all packets are sent entirely within a slot. Often, equal-size packets are assumed, approximately the same size as the slot (they may need to be a little shorter, to allow for different propagation times). In the central station configuration, it is possible for each station to offset its transmission time in proportion to the propagation time to the central station, such that all transmissions arrive exactly centered in a synchronized slot.

9.1.1 Quantitative Analysis of Idealized ALOHA Communication

Suppose slotted ALOHA is being used and all users can hear each other. Models have assumed either (a) an infinite number of users having a finite total message arrival rate, or (b) a finite number of users.

The Infinite Number of Users Model Packets are presumed to be generated by the infinite set of all users at a total finite rate of λ packets per time slot. The number of arrivals in a slot is assumed to obey a Poisson distribution:

$$P[k] = \frac{\lambda^k}{k!} e^{-\lambda} \qquad (9.1)$$

A newly arrived packet is transmitted in the first available slot. By assuming an infinite number of users and memoryless packet generation per user, we do not have to worry about a particular user having two packets to send at the same time, because the infinity of users makes the probability zero that a newly generated packet belongs to one of the finite set of busy users. If a packet needs to be retransmitted, we assume it goes back into the pot of potential arrivals, such that the class of new packets and retransmitted packets still obeys a Poisson distribution. Admittedly these are rather far-fetched assumptions. Particularly disturbing is the retransmission distribution assumption, because it does not properly reflect the dynamics of variations in retransmission rate. Also, individual user's packets actually tend to arrive in bursts. However, the analysis leads to simple and useful performance guidelines, and the behavior of average throughput with offered load is in general agreement with finite user models (although the finite user models also usually ignore generation burstiness).

Let G be the total Poisson arrival rate of new packets plus retransmitted packets. There is a successful transmission in a slot if and only if exactly one transmission occurs. Let S be the fraction of successful slots, also called the throughput per slot. Letting $k = 1$ and replacing λ by G in (9.1),

$$S = Ge^{-G}. \tag{9.2}$$

S is maximum at $G = 1$, where it equals e^{-1} or .368. A plot of (9.2) is shown in Figure 9.2.

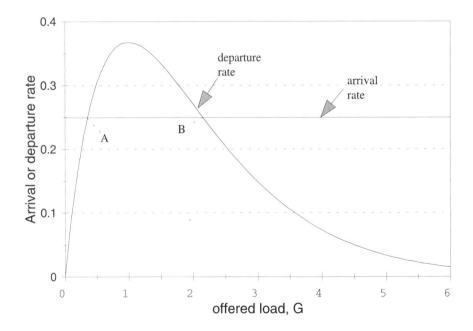

Figure 9.2: Slotted ALOHA throughput.

There is no possibility of an efficiency greater than 36.8% for ALOHA transmission under the given assumptions. Moreover, it is not easy to come close to this maximum because of the instability implied by the negative slope range of the curve. To see this, suppose there is a fixed arrival rate parameter λ as indicated by the horizontal line in the figure. When arrival rate exceeds success rate the backlog increases, and when success rate exceeds arrival rate the backlog decreases. The S curve represents the success rate. Between points A and B, success rate exceeds arrival rate, so the backlog and G decrease, bringing the system back to A. However, if any statistical fluctuation should bring the operating point beyond B, which eventually is certain to happen, arrival rate will exceed success rate, retransmissions and G will increase, and the system operating point will slide down toward zero throughput and infinite G, implying that the backlog of packets needing retransmission grows indefinitely and almost nothing ever is successful. For this reason the uncontrolled slotted ALOHA infinite user system model is said to be unstable at any input rate. It could be stabilized, however, by allowing control of the arrival acceptance rate and/or retransmission delay.

The Finite Number of Users Model In this model there are a fixed number M of sending users. If a sending user suffers a collision and must retransmit, it is referred to as a *backlogged* user. Others are referred to as *thinking* users. Each thinking user has a probability P_A that a packet arrives during a slot, to be transmitted in the next slot. Either no packet or one packet arrives at each thinking user per slot time, and the arrival probability is independent of past arrivals. Each backlogged user does not accept any newly arrived packet, and retransmits its backlogged packet with probability P_R, assumed to be independent of how many times it has been retransmitted.

This model also appears to depart significantly from realism. For one thing, there is not in practice a fixed number of "active" users; users initiate and terminate sessions at varying times, so the actual number will fluctuate about an average M value. Also, active users are bursty and have buffers; given one sends a packet, it is more likely to send another packet shortly afterward, and it will not block another packet when busy, but will place it in its buffer. A large number of users tends to average out the behavior, however, so that the number of arrivals may behave close to as if there were M users with each having arrival probability P_A in each slot.

Suppose at a given time there are K backlogged users. We will call this system state K. There will be a success if and only if exactly one user, backlogged or not, happens to send. The probability of this, which is equal to S, is

$$S = (M - K)P_A(1 - P_A)^{M-K-1}(1 - P_R)^K + KP_R(1 - P_R)^{K-1}(1 - P_A)^{M-K}. \quad (9.3)$$

The offered load in state K is

$$G(K) = (M - K)P_A + KP_R. \quad (9.4)$$

Consider for a moment the case $P_A = P_R = P$. Then we have the simpler relation

$$S = MP(1 - P)^{M-1}. \quad (9.5)$$

This expression is maximized at $MP = 1$, where it is

$$S_{MAX} = (1 - 1/M)^{M-1}. \tag{9.6}$$

With $G = MP$, Equation (9.6) approaches the infinite model result (9.2) exactly as M goes to infinity, and agrees within a few percent at $M = 20$.

Returning to the case where P_A and P_R are not equal, S and G depend on the state K (number of backlogged users). Although a Markov chain analysis could be applied, a drift analysis is recommended by Bertsekas and Gallager ([BERT92], Chapter 4) as being more useful. The key idea is that when the average arrival rate, $(M - K)P_A$, is greater than $S(K)$, the success or "departure" rate in state K, K tends to increase, while K tends to decrease if the inequality is reversed. It is shown by Bertsekas and Gallager that $S(K)$ can be approximated by

$$S(K) \cong G(K)e^{-G(K)} \tag{9.7}$$

where $G(K)$ is given by (9.4).

If one plots $S(K)$ and the arrival rate $(M - K)P_A$ versus $G(K)$, assuming $P_A < P_R$, the figure permits some important observations about performance. This is shown in Figure 9.3.

The arrows along the departure curve denote the drift direction. Point A is a desirable stable operating point. However, a short-term high fluctuation in arrival rate can easily move the system past the unstable equilibrium point B, after which K increases to send the system to the undesired stable operating point C.

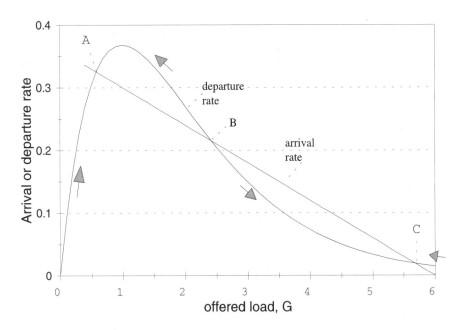

Figure 9.3: Arrival-departure curves for Slotted Aloha.

For very small P_R it is possible to have only the single desirable stable point, but very small P_R means long delay on retransmission; for example, if $P_R = .01$, one would have to wait an average of 100 slots before retransmitting a collided packet. If P_R is made too large the margin of safety from the unstable point is reduced.

Ideal operation would be to control P_R as a function of K so as to keep $G(K)$ as close to 1 as possible, since this is the point of maximum throughput. The state is difficult to know exactly. Various control schemes are possible. The main idea of such control schemes is to increase P_R when an idle slot is observed and to decrease P_R when a collision is observed.

9.1.2 More Efficient Alternatives

Slotted ALOHA with destruction on collision has a maximum throughput of $1/e$ or .368. Unslotted ALOHA with equal-size packets can be shown to have a maximum throughput of only $1/2e$ or .184, assuming two interfering packets are lost if any part of them overlaps. If the packets are of randomly different sizes unslotted ALOHA does a little better, but not much.

There are two avenues for modifying ALOHA communication to improve its efficiency:

1. Use protocols to eliminate or reduce collision frequency.
2. Tolerate collision through signal design and signal processing.

Techniques in the first avenue include: (a) send only when no activity is sensed on the channel (called *carrier sense multiple access*); (b) stop sending if a collision is detected (called *collision detection*); (c) reservations; or (d) polling.

The second avenue is based on multiuser information theory, which shows the possibility of correctly receiving many uncoordinated senders' signals simultaneously. More specifically, gains can come from: (a) the capture effect where the stronger of two received signals can be decoded successfully in a collision; (b) in radio, the possibility of using antenna directivity and space diversity; and (c) various sophisticated signal processing receiver techniques allowing simultaneous detection of several signals received at the same time. This last avenue will be investigated further in Chapter 11, which emphasizes multiaccess communication under conditions of significant noise and interference.

9.2   Collision Avoidance

As mentioned earlier, carrier sense multiple access[1] (CSMA) is one technique that may reduce the frequency of collisions. It assumes the multiaccess channel model in

---

[1] It seems a little strange to use the term "carrier," when there isn't any high-frequency carrier in wired baseband systems. Apparently the term evolved because ALOHA was originally a radio system and thus used high-frequency carrier signals for propagation.

which all senders can observe the signals on the channel, so a potential sender can sense whether the channel is actively being used, and refrain from sending its packet.

The sensing of the channel does not result in perfect collision avoidance because of the nonzero propagation time between potential senders. This is illustrated in Figure 9.4 for the case of two senders, A and B. Suppose it takes τ seconds for the signal from A to propagate to B. If A senses the channel as idle and starts to send a packet, there is a 2τ second period of vulnerability during which B might send and collide with A's signal. This is from the points labeled t_1 and t_2 in the figure. B did not start before t_1 or else A would have sensed it and would not have started. After t_2, B would have sensed A's sending and would have refrained from sending. This has a significant effect on efficiency when the propagation time is a significant fraction of the packet duration, as can occur due to long distances or short packet durations.

There are various possible rules for the waiting strategy of the sender that finds the channel busy. One extreme, called the *nonpersistent strategy*, is for the sender to wait a random time and then sense the channel again. Each time the channel is sensed busy, the sender waits a random time again, but if no activity is found at the time of sensing, the sender will transmit its packet. The other extreme, called the *1-persistent strategy*, is for the potential sender to continue to sense the channel until it shows no activity, and then send immediately. This latter strategy reduces the average waiting time to send, but increases the probability of a collision because two or more that arrive while the channel is busy are almost certain to collide when the channel activity stops.

CSMA reduces collisions but does not eliminate them entirely, since two senders could start sending at any time difference within the propagation time between them,

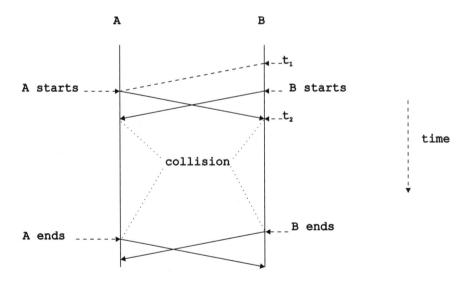

Figure 9.4: The effect of propagation time on CSMA.

and not discover the near simultaneous transmission until too late to avoid collision. A further improvement can be obtained if somehow the senders can learn of the collision very shortly after it starts and immediately stop sending, thereby reducing the time wasted in collision. This is called *collision detection* (CD). The popular Ethernet protocol employs CSMA/CD. CSMA/CD allows utilization efficiencies much higher than straight slotted or unslotted ALOHA, provided that the longest propagation delay is much less than the average packet length. An approximate maximum throughput, assuming $\beta < 1$, is about $1/[1 + k\beta]$, where β is the ratio of maximum (propagation + detection) delay to average packet duration. The parameter k is somewhat dependent on the assumed model (for example, $k = 6.2$ in [BERT92], Chapter 4). Thus, when $\beta \ll 1$, efficiency is near 100%, whereas if β is large CSMA/CD is no better than unslotted ALOHA. β increases, and efficiency decreases, either because of longer cable lengths or higher bit rates (for a fixed number of bits/packet).

9.2.1 Retransmission and ARQ in Ethernet

If a collision is detected, Ethernet uses what is called an exponential backoff to determine the next attempted retry. On the first retry attempt, some random waiting time from 0 to T before retry is selected; for each additional needed retry of the packet the random next waiting time interval is doubled. This continues until the number of attempts reaches some maximum. The intent of this backoff is to help stabilize the system by reducing P_R. The word "retry" is used here instead of retransmission, since a complete packet is not actually sent unless no collision of the first part is detected. The collision detection protocol actually can be viewed as a type of reservation, whereby the initial part of the packet transmission is like an implicit reservation request, which is satisfied if no other such request interferes.

Layers and Packet Structure   Although networks in general have not yet been discussed, it is useful at this point to introduce something about the layered architecture concept in network communication. The communication task is divided into seven layers, where each layer performs services for all the layers above it. The layered concept is similar to modular design in engineering. A systems designer employs certain modules as part of the system, where the performance characteristics of each module are known or specified. Some other designer will have the task of designing a module (A) to meet the specifications. That designer may also, in turn, use smaller modular components as part of the design of module A.

The three lowest communication layers, from top down, are the network, link, and physical layers. The network layer deals primarily with routing in a network. If all communication is between pairs in a multiaccess network such as Ethernet, there is no routing involved, because each pair has a direct link communication, though shared in time, with each other. Thus the network layer does not come into play for communication entirely within the multiaccess network. Often, Ethernet users also are connected to other networks through an external connection from the Ethernet; then a networking layer function (actually internetworking) would be present.

The link layer of communication within the Ethernet has two aspects. One is the Medium Access Control aspect, called MAC sublayer, which deals with the problems of obtaining noninterfering use of the channel, through the CSMA/CD protocols described. The other is the communication between the two end users that have the link through the multiaccess network. This is called the logic link control (LLC) sublayer.

An Ethernet packet contains a 32-bit CRC sequence for error detection. If errors are detected, the LLC sublayer handles the appropriate actions. This includes ARQ protocols and possible sequence numbering. In fact the LLC is very similar to HDLC, and basically the same LLC can be used for a wide variety of multiaccess methods, not just restricted to Ethernet.

Thus, the MAC sublayer controls retries due to collisions, but the LLC sublayer controls retransmissions between the communicating pairs due to error detection. Errors in noncollided packets are rare in most Ethernets, so the communicating pairs might choose not even to use error detection/ARQ.

A brief description of the Ethernet packet follows. More complete details of Ethernet operation are contained in textbooks such as [STAL97]. Figure 9.5 shows the standard packet format.

The 7-byte preamble consists of the pattern 10101010 repeated to ensure bit synchronization, and is followed by start-of-frame delimiter 10101011, and a length indicator for the logic link control field. The logic link control field contains the data and a control field to perform functions similar to HDLC, such as providing send and receive sequence numbers. It also may contain padding to ensure a minimum 64-byte packet size.

9.2.2   Reservations and Polling

Reservation is a collision avoidance technique that can improve efficiency if β is too large for efficient CSMA/CD. Reservation is a three-step process: a reservation request signal is transmitted, the sender learns the request is successful, and the sender then transmits data in the reserved interval. Actually, CSMA/CD can be thought of as a crude type of reservation when $\beta \ll 1$. Transmission of the first 2β fraction

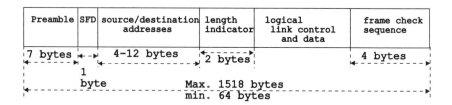

Figure 9.5: The Ethernet packet.

of the packet could be thought of as a request to send the whole packet. Collision detection would be a denial of the request. If no collision is detected during the first 2β fraction, this is an implied successful reservation. If β is close to or greater than 1, however, there is no concept of reservation.

The central station or star-wired configuration of Figure 9.1d is the most convenient one for reservation schemes. Otherwise, it is difficult to obtain a common time reference for the reservations. Figure 9.6 shows how a common time reference can be established even though stations may be different distances from the central connecting point. Assume full duplex connections from each station to the central point, so that each station receives the sum of all transmitted signals, including its own. Suppose a periodic slot boundary reference signal is broadcast from the central point, as indicated by the dashed lines in Figure 9.6b. Stations A and B, at different distances, can determine their reference packet starting point by experiment with their own reflected signal. Note from Figure 9.6b that their actual packet starting times are different, but are the same on the signals that propagate out from the central connecting point. In radio transmission, the same effect can be had by directed transmission to the central station (which could be a communications satellite, for example) in one frequency band, followed by an omnidirectional broadcast from the central station in a different band.

Many reservation schemes exist. The most common is to have a short reservation interval alternating periodically with long packet intervals (see Figure 9.7).

Since the purpose is to operate efficiently with a large β value, the reservation interval cannot refer to the immediately following packet interval because there is not

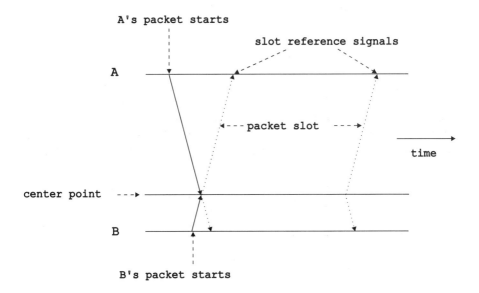

Figure 9.6: Establishing a common slot reference.

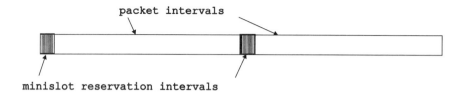

Figure 9.7: Minislot reservation intervals.

enough time for senders to get the feedback of what reservation(s) is/are successful. Usually, it refers to the second packet interval after the reservation interval. Since the reservation requests carry very little data, the reservation interval usually can be subdivided into a number of minislots. Each requestor could send at random in one of the minislots, in an ALOHA fashion, or minislots could be assigned if the number of active senders is small. If two senders pick the same minislot there will be a collision. In that case, if there were no other requestors, both could decide with probability $1/2$ whether to send in the related packet interval, with a 50% chance exactly one will send and thus be successful. With a number of minislots and random selection of minislot, a reservation collision with two or three requestors will be infrequent. If, say two are successful, a convention could be that whichever sent in the earlier minislot gets to send the packet, or the convention could be that the first requestor gets the next packet slot and the second gets the one after.

This scheme uses fixed size packets. Some users may need to send more data at a time than others. The reservation scheme just described could be modified to allow a reservation of more than one packet at a time. One way to do this would be to include in the reservation a count of number of packets needed, but this might make the reservation requests longer than desired. Another would be for a station that has won a reservation to include a "more packets bit" either in the start of its packet or in a specially reserved minislot position. Then others could reserve successfully only if the indication was that no more packets were being sent.

Being given a dedicated channel is also like a reservation. However, it is often best to avoid giving dedicated channels because they may often go unused by the reserver. One way to have some of the advantages of both dedicated and nondedicated channels is to give a particular user a priority reservation of a channel. Others can use the channel if it is inactive, but if a collision occurs they must defer for some interval, whereas if the collision is due to the priority user, that user will resend while the others are deferring. This will ensure availability to the priority reserver at any time needed, but allow use by others when not needed.

Polling is another method of avoiding collisions. Polling can be done from a fixed primary point, which gives permission in turn to each of a group of potential senders. It also can be done in a more distributed fashion: permission to send can be passed on from one member to the next in sequence, a procedure known as token passing or hub polling. The amount of data each can send on receiving permission can be fixed or variable, perhaps subject to some maximum or perhaps dependent on user priority. Polling is very efficient when most members of the polling group have something to send most of the time. Since the polling itself takes significant overhead time, it causes extra delay when there are many users to poll and very few have something to send. It also can be inefficient in this case if there is a maximum amount of permitted data per user per cycle, and a particular user has more than this amount to send. Schemes of polling less active users less frequently can reduce the polling overhead and time waiting for permission. Also, users can leave the polled group if inactive and rejoin when necessary.

The token bus is a standard token passing media access protocol (IEEE 802.4). All stations are connected to a common bus or tree, as in Ethernet. A station with the token sends data if it has data to send, and then sends the token to the next station in turn. The order does not have to have any relation to the physical location of the stations on the bus. Packets are somewhat similar to Ethernet packets. Preambles and 32-bit frame check sequences are similar, but the control field is different. The control field designates a token packet, which is a packet with no data field used to pass the token to the address specified in the destination field. Each token sender (source address) knows its successor (destination address of token packet). Since all stations see what is being sent, the token sender can see if the successor has successfully received the token based on its response (which should be either sending data or passing on the token) and take corrective action if necessary. Protocols provide also for removing or adding stations to the token cycle.

9.2.3   Collision Resolution Algorithms

In ordinary ALOHA or in CSMA/CD, if a collision occurs, the colliders retransmit at random later times and compete with newly arriving traffic. It has been found that the efficiency and stability of ALOHA can be significantly improved by limiting future transmissions to the colliders until these colliders are successful [BERT92, CAPE79]. The usual assumption is that time is slotted and that all users observe a collision (although the number of colliders is not assumed to be known), a success, or an unused slot. Also, it is assumed that they are able to observe this event before the occurrence of the next slot. For large β this is not realistic, but the same efficiency improvement could be achieved by interlacing slot streams or channels, as in time division multiplexing. A collision in a channel slot would be resolved within the same channel; the next slot for that channel would be arranged to occur after all had learned of the prior collision result for that channel.

The goal is to have an algorithm that resolves a collision in as few slots as possible, on average, while also allowing all users to know when the collision has been resolved. The basic idea is called a splitting algorithm [BERT92]. Each collider picks a number, which could be just a random number between 0 and 1, or, preferably in most cases, a number representing time of arrival. The range of numbers is divided into (assume two) subsets, and a collider whose number is in a particular subset (such as those who arrived before a certain time) will retransmit, but others whose number is in the other subset will defer. In the event of a success or idle in the permitted subset, that subset is resolved, and only those in the other half remain to be resolved.

In the event of a collision in the first subset, that subset must be split into two parts. Transmissions are then restricted to that first subset until it becomes resolved.

As an illustration, suppose there are three colliders whose selected numbers are: $A = .3$, $B = .4$, and $C = .6$. Let .5 divide the subsets, so A and B will transmit in the next slot and collide again, as shown in Figure 9.8. The 0–.5 interval is further subdivided, so the next set to transmit is 0–.25. There are none in this interval, so the next slot is idle. Thus 0–.25 is resolved, and the next interval to look at is .25–.5. The algorithm could work by having all with numbers in the .25–.5 range transmit, but in this case there is certain to be another collision, so to be more efficient the algorithm splits this interval so that only those with numbers in the .25–.375 range transmit. This is only A, so A transmits successfully in the next slot. Then those with numbers in the .375–.5 range transmit, which is only B, so B also transmits successfully. Now everyone knows that the 0–.5 range has been resolved, so all in the .5–1 range will send. C is the only one in that range, so C sends successfully, and now all users know the collision has been resolved.

There are various improvements to the algorithm, such as allowing newly arrived users to join in the resolution subdivisions. This is especially important in a long resolution interval, where many may arrive during the interval, making a collision after the end of the resolution interval nearly a certainty. An object is to manage to control the subdivision into subsets in such a way that the expected number of senders per subinterval is as close to 1 as possible, since statistically this gives the greatest probability of a successful slot transmission.

Collision resolution algorithms permit stable throughput with arrival rate λ packets/second provided that, for large n, the average time to resolve n colliders is less than the average number of arrivals in the average resolution time. Maximum throughputs of about .487 have been achieved with collision [BERT92], compared to

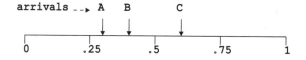

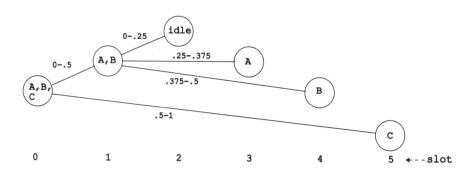

Figure 9.8: Example of the collision avoidance splitting algorithm.

.368 for ordinary ALOHA. The maximum throughput achievable by any algorithm is unknown, but has been proven to be less than .587.

9.3   Ring Networks

The ring topology is a closed loop to which all stations are connected. Figure 9.9a illustrates this for a unidirectional ring, that is more common than a bidirectional ring. Each station (square box) needs to be connected to an interface node (circle) that contains at least a one-bit delay. This allows a station to alter the signal traveling around the ring. Obviously some ability to change the signal is necessary, since otherwise a signal once transmitted would continue to circulate. In addition, the delay permits any station to alter the signal. In particular, any signal source station can have the ability to remove its own signal from the ring when it returns to it, or it could be arranged that any destination station has the ability to remove the signal from the ring.

Physically, it often is preferable for maintenance and addition/deletion of stations to have the interface nodes nearby in a centrally located ring, with stations at a greater distance, each connected to its interface node. This *star-ring* arrangement is shown in Figure 9.9b. If a station is not active or fails, a simple bypass can be performed at its associated interface node.

Ring networks are generally considered in the multiaccess category because of the sharing of the common ring. Contention is easier to resolve because each station is visited in turn as the signals circulate around the ring. The common methods of using a ring (token, slotted, and register insertion) do not need to worry about collisions.

9.3.1   The Token Ring

One way of preventing collision in a ring network is to pass around a token that gives permission to send data. This is similar to the concept of a token bus that was described previously, but with the differences that the stations are active rather than

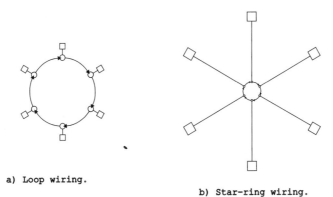

a) Loop wiring.

b) Star-ring wiring.

Figure 9.9: The unidirectional ring.

passive, in the sense that they can alter the signal going around the ring, and the order of token passing is prescribed by the physical position around the ring.

For a ring network, the token is simply free (also called idle) or busy as it circulates. An idle token automatically visits successive physical locations on the ring until some station changes it to busy, and does not need a destination address. A station observing an idle token can change the token from idle to busy and then start sending data. This can be done with only a single bit delay per station to change a bit indicating idle to busy. Although there is a one-bit delay, the token unit is many bits, 24 in the token ring standard, in order to carry synchronization and other information. Artificial delay can be added at any point in the ring, if necessary, to ensure the round-trip delay around the ring is at least the duration of a token unit. The data packets can be of variable length, but some maximum size may be specified to prevent hogging of the ring.

Normally, a packet is allowed to circulate the ring before being removed by the sender. This provides a means of acknowledgment, because if the return agrees with what was sent there probably were no received errors.[2] The sender can release the token in one of two ways. One way is to send a free token immediately following completion of sending its packet. This allows another station to start sending its own packet with minimum further delay, but it means that if the original sender discovers its packet did not come back correctly, it could not retransmit until it got an idle token again. The other way is to wait until the transmitted packet returns completely before sending out an idle token. This could allow retransmission without releasing the idle token in case what was returned was not correct. The two alternatives are illustrated in Figure 9.10, adapted from [BERT92]. The figure depicts the transmitted data (upper stream) and received data (lower stream) for one particular ring interface unit. Part (a) illustrates the case where the idle token is generated immediately following transmission of the packet, whereas part (b) illustrates the case where the sender waits for a complete return of the packet before generating an idle token.

9.3.2   The IEEE 802.5 Standard Token Ring

A standard for a token ring multiple access protocol has been defined as IEEE 802.5. Such rings have been designed for rates of 1, 4, and 16 megabits/second. Figure 9.11 shows the token and data frame formats. Actually, a token frame is an idle token; a busy token is incorporated with the data frame. Note that the first byte is the same for both token and data frames. It is the starting delimiter pattern. This pattern provides identification of the start of a token or data frame by creating an abnormal bit signalling waveform. The normally bit waveform is Manchester coding, where a bit is encoded as a two-level pattern, high-low or low-high per bit interval. In the delimiter pattern, some bit positions are instead coded all high or all low. This is illustrated in Figure 9.12.

---

[2]It is not certain that there were no errors, because a single bit could be altered on the source-to-destination route, and altered back to the correct value on the return trip.

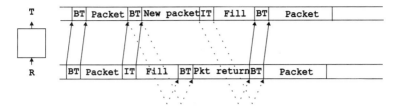

a) Immediate token release.

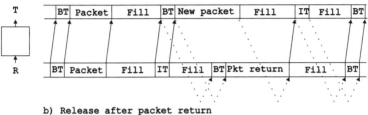

b) Release after packet return

Figure 9.10: Two alternatives for idle token generation. *Source:* DATA NETWORKS, 2/E by Bertksekas/Gallagher, © 1992. Adapted by permission of Prentice-Hall, Inc., Upper Saddle River, NJ.

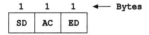

a) Token format.

SD	AC	FC	source/destination addresses	Data	Checksum	ED	FS
1	1	1	2-6		4	1	1 ← Bytes

b) Data frame format.

Figure 9.11: Token and data frame formats.

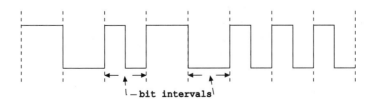

Figure 9.12: Start delimiter field.

A bit in the access control field distinguishes idle token from busy token per data frame. Bits are also provided in the access control field for priority (3 bits), reservation (3 bits), and monitoring (1 bit). The reservation bits set a priority level for a station wanting to obtain a token, and the priority bits indicate a token can only be used by a station with an equal or higher priority.

The end delimiter field includes a bit that can be set by any station to indicate an error has been detected. The frame status at the end of the frame contains address recognized (*A* bits) and frame copied (*C* bits). This helps the sender learn of these two events. Since these bits do not have the protection of the frame check sequence, there are two duplicate *A* bits and two duplicate *C* bits for error protection. If there turns out to be one error in the *C* bits, the sender could play safe and retransmit, on the assumption the frame was not copied. However, ultimate error control does not have to be carried out on the ring. At the higher logical link level, ARQ protocols with send/receive sequence numbers and the included frame check sequence can be used for end-to-end error control of the communication.

Error Effects and Problems   Most bit errors can be recovered from using the logical link end-to-end ARQ protocol. However, special problems occur due to lost or multiple tokens or due to station failures. As to the bit error aspect, note that only one bit position in the access control field distinguishes between a token frame and a data frame. An error in this one bit could then potentially cause a lost or added token. The station could usually learn of this error by subsequent reception (i.e., whether the next field is the frame control field of a data frame or the end delimiter), but with only a one-bit delay it is too late to avoid passing on the error. Also, the sending frame has the responsibility of removing its data and regenerating an idle token. If the sending station somehow fails to do this, its data will continue to circulate with no new idle token generated. A monitor station is assigned (which can be any station if the current monitor fails), which has the task of restoring lost tokens or removing multiple tokens. Since any station has the capability to regenerate or change all incoming bits, the monitor station can simply clear out and not send anything until all circulating bits have been received, and then send out an idle token.

9.3.3   The FDDI Token Ring

The FDDI (Fiber Distributed Data Interface) ring is a token ring designed for use with fiber optic links [JAIN94]. It operates at 100 megabits/second, and over much longer distances (up to 200 km) than Ethernet or the 802.5 token ring. The ring can contain up to 1000 stations.

The ring is bidirectional, but primarily for failure tolerance. If a bidirectional link should fail, such as by being physically broken, traffic can be redirected to make a loop that passes through each station twice. Figure 9.13 illustrates the bidirectional ring architecture and the rerouting due to a link failure.

The frame format is similar to the 802.5 token ring. The start delimiter is phys-ically different because Manchester coding is not used. Fiber optic communication

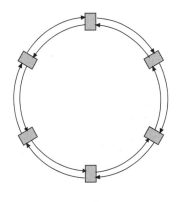
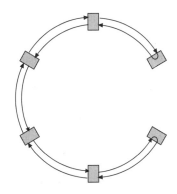

a) Basic bidirectional
   architecture.

b) Redirection on link
   failure.

Figure 9.13: The FDDI ring.

uses intensity modulation, so AC coupling factors are not relevant. Instead, groups of 5 binary pulses are used to convey 4 bits of data. This means that only 16 of the 32 combinations have data significance. These 16 are selected to have a varied mix of 0's and 1's to improve bit synchronization, and the 16 unused patterns can be used as part of the start delimiter and for other purposes. The 4 of 5 code only increases the signalling rate relative to bit rate by 25%, compared to 100% for Manchester coding. Another difference is that immediate token release (Figure 9.10a) is used for better efficiency in a ring with long round-trip propagation time.

9.3.4 Efficiency Limitation of the Token Ring

Since there is just one token, only one station can be transmitting new data into the ring at a given absolute time in the standard protocol. Thus, the total transfer rate of the token ring cannot be faster than the bit rate on one of its links. This may seem good enough, since the same could be said about Ethernet. However, in the ring the different links are isolated, so it is physically possible to be sending new data simultaneously on different links. Consider, for example, a ring of four stations: A, B, C, and D, in clockwise order. Suppose each link could carry 10 MB/s. If it just happened that A was sending data exclusively to B, B to C, C to D, and D to A, a total of 40 MB/s could ideally be transferred, but a ring with a single token does not allow a transfer rate higher than 10 MB/s. There are ring protocols, however, that do allow transfer of the full 40 MB/s.

9.3.5 The Slotted Ring with Destination Removal

Another type of ring is the slotted ring. The slotted ring normally requires that all packets be the same size. This is somewhat of a disadvantage in that a larger packet will have to be segmented, and a small packet may not fill the slot, resulting in some efficiency loss. In compensation, however, we will see that the ability to send more than one new packet simultaneously in a simple manner can more than compensate for this efficiency loss. Also, the prevalence of fixed-cell-size ATM could fit well with the fixed-size slotted ring structure, since a slot size could be made just the size to hold one ATM cell or an integer multiple of cells.

Figure 9.14 illustrates a slotted ring with two different amounts of interface delay.

The slotted ring in Figure 9.14b has a full slot length delay at each interface. This has the feature of allowing a destination to completely decode a received packet before deciding what to send out. This allows both destination removal and an efficient

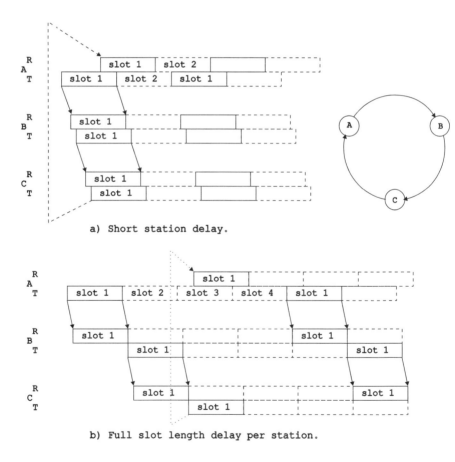

a) Short station delay.

b) Full slot length delay per station.

Figure 9.14: A slotted ring with different amounts of station delay.

means of acknowledgment. It is assumed that a CRC is included in each slot packet for error detection. This may add up to 4 bytes to the packet size.

If the destination can remove a packet from a slot and replace it with either an idle slot or one destined for another channel, multiple uses of slots are possible, and the overall transfer rate can exceed the single link capacity. Usually, this is not done, because the return of a packet back to the source serves as an acknowledgment that the packet was received correctly.

Use of the New Word Policy   The new word policy described in Section 5.3 extends directly to a slotted ring with destination removal and replacement with a new frame [METZ73]. It allows acknowledgment of everyone's packet with use of only one extra bit per packet. Each slot acts as a separate stop-and-wait process, somewhat like the interlaced memory technique described in Section 6.1. A station always keeps a memory of the last frame sent out in each slot and the alternating bit status for that slot. If the station does not receive an error-free frame with a new alternating bit value it is required to send out the frame memory of its last transmission in that slot. If it does receive an error-free frame with a new alternating bit, it will either relay the frame if not the destination, or accept it and replace it with its own frame or an idle frame, in each case with the new alternating bit value.

This technique has not been implemented to the author's knowledge. One drawback is the trend in high-speed communications to do the error control ARQ end-to-end, whereas this slotted ring protocol does error control directly on the ring. If there is a move to using nonbinary transmission rate for higher data rates, coupled with higher symbol error rates, it could prove useful for its error control feature. Another drawback is that it requires a whole packet length delay at each repeater station. This would tend to limit the number of stations on the ring. It can be pointed out, however, that at high bit rates this delay still could be quite short. The delay could be compared to time multiplexing packets in a multipacket frame or frequency multiplexing. In time multiplexing, a given packet must wait to be placed in its position in the frame, which requires a delay on average of $N/2$ packets, if there are N packets per frame. In N-channel frequency multiplexing, each packet is time lengthened by N, which multiplies by N the packet length delay. Thus if the number of stations is a comparable value N, the ring delay in repeaters from source to destination is of comparable size to N-channel multiplexing delay. The higher maximum throughput stemming from destination removal should allow smaller buffering delays for a given offered load.

It is possible to place acknowledgments in a frame without having a full frame delay, but the acknowledgment strategy is not as simple or as naturally protective. End-to-end logical link error control would then be needed to ensure high reliability. A technique we have seen used in the token ring is to reserve the last or near last bits in a frame to indicate the most recent received frame has a detected error. Since the sender has already started sending its frame, it is too late to change whether it was relaying a frame or sending its own, but not too late to change the last frame bit. Because this last bit has no parity protection, a return path change from error detected to no error detected is not well protected against.

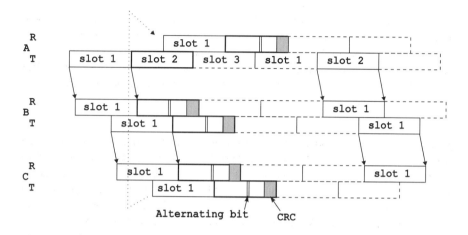

Figure 9.15: Timing for the new-word policy with 1/2 slot-time delay.

An interesting feature of the slotted ring new word policy with whole frame station delay is that the number of slots is always at least one more than the number of stations. This could allow each station to have priority use of one of the slots, which would help to satisfy fairness requirements.

The new word policy could be modified to give full error protection with a delay reduced to slightly more than 1/2 of a slot length. The destination address must be in the first half, the check sequence in the last half, and the alternating bit exactly in the middle. The timing is illustrated in Figure 9.15. After reading the destination address and the alternating bit value, the station could begin sending as if the incoming frame were correct. Error detection then is performed prior to transmission of the alternating bit value and the CRC check sequence. If error is detected and the station has done the actions based on a new alternating bit, the old alternating bit value would be inserted and the CRC sequence scrambled to ensure error detection. If error is detected and the station has begun the action (resend old frame) based on an old alternating bit, no change in transmission is made.

Voice-Data Integration in the New-Word-Policy Slotted Ring   Voice packets require immediate delivery, but error detection for possible retransmission usually is not feasible. Data packets usually can tolerate variable delay. The error protection feature of the acknowledgment policy makes it very simple to allow a voice packet to interrupt the flow of data in a slot at any time without doing any more harm than to cause a delay of at most one ring round-trip time in the progression toward its destination of data in the particular slot. When a voice packet needs to be sent by some station X, X can ignore (or save) a data reception in a slot (it will automatically be retransmitted later) and send out the voice packet, while retaining its memory of the data transmission state. Voice packets would need identification as such, and a destination address, but wouldn't need error detection. The destination would remove the voice packet and replace it with its previous data or idle packet with the previous alternating bit, thereby letting the acknowledgment/data flow process to resume automatically. Voice packets couldn't interrupt other voice packets, but unless the traffic were heavy, with mostly all voice packets, it would be rare to have a voice packet lost due to excessive delay.

Destination Removal Efficiency Improvement   In the extreme case that every source has a stream of packets just for the next station, the throughput with destination removal could be up to N times the link rate, where N is the number of stations in the ring. For less extreme cases, efficiency limit can be readily evaluated for a symmetrical traffic assumption. Figure 9.16 shows the contributions that each sender makes to the traffic on one particular link. Suppose the N stations experience data arrival at a rate R_0 each. Suppose each node needs to send a fraction f_i of its traffic i clockwise hops, $1 \le i \le N - 1$.

Let the links have capacity C each. Adding all the traffics:

$$C > R_0 \left[\sum_{k=1}^{N-1} \sum_{i=k}^{N-1} f_i \right] \tag{9.8}$$

$$Throughput < \frac{NC}{\sum_{k=1}^{N-1} \sum_{i=k}^{N-1} f_i}. \tag{9.9}$$

If all destinations are equally likely, $f_i = 1/(N - 1)$, (9.9) evaluates to $2C$. If a greater proportion of traffic goes to closer stations, the throughput could be greater.

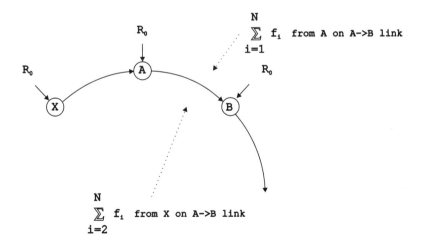

Figure 9.16: Contributing traffic on a particular link.

Even better efficiency is achieved if the ring is bidirectional, because then the shorter of the two routes can be selected. Similar traffic source destination assumptions as those that lead to (9.8) for the unidirectional ring, but applied to a bidirectional ring with capacity C per link in each direction and with the special case $f_i = 1/(N - 1)$, lead to the result as follows for the case of N odd (see Problem 9.7).

$$Throughput < \frac{8NC}{N + 1}. \tag{9.10}$$

The throughput approaches $8C$ for large N. This is four times the limiting total capacity of a bidirectional ring without destination removal. This corresponds to an average of close to four uses of the slot per round-trip.

9.4 Bus and Dual Bus Networks

Distributed Queue Dual Bus   Fiber optical and carrier band transmissions using amplification tend to be one-way, due to the one-way nature of amplification. The requirement to send to all connected stations can be satisfied by using dual unidirectional busses or a folded bus where every station is connected twice, as shown in Figure 9.17.

The distributed queue dual bus is of particular interest, as it is the IEEE standard 802.6 network. Data transmission is in fixed-size 53-byte frames (for ATM compatibility). A slot generator at the end of each bus generates fixed-length slots for frames. This is shown in Figure 9.18.

Data can be sent on the left or right bus, depending on destination location. A request bit is added to the header of a frame. When a station wants to send a frame to the right and there is a queue ahead of it, it sets a request bit on a frame to the left.

All stations keep a count of unfilled request bits; from the right for sending data to the right, and from the left for sending data to the left.

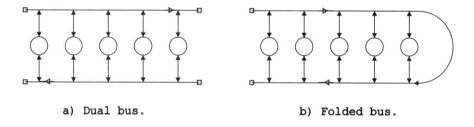

a) Dual bus.   b) Folded bus.

Figure 9.17: Dual bus and folded bus topology.

Slot generator

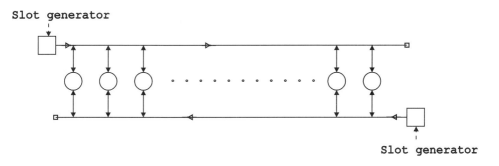

Slot generator

Figure 9.18: The DQDB topology.

Each station keeps virtual queues (actually counts) for both directions. The station must let empty slots pass by, decrementing virtual queue count once per bypass, until the queue of requests ahead of its own request is emptied. Then it can send its packet in the next empty slot.

To prevent hogging, a station cannot have more than one outstanding request at a time. If it has additional packets to send, they must be kept in a separate queue, and a request for the next can be entered only after the current packet is sent.

If the virtual queue is empty when a station needs to send a packet, it can send it immediately in the first empty slot, without sending a request. In this way, if no one downstream needs to send on the same bus, the station can keep sending a long string of packets with no waiting.

Slot Reuse in DQDB   Just as was noted for a slotted ring, if a packet in a slot reaches its destination but has not reached the end of the bus, ideally it could be removed by the destination and the slot reused if any downstream station was waiting to send a packet further downstream.

There is quite a bit of interest in slot reuse in DQDB. The October 1993 issue of the *Journal on Selected Areas on Communications* is devoted to metropolitan area networks (MANs). Most of the articles deal with DQDB, and 5 of the 15 articles in the journal mention slot reuse, 3 in great detail. Slot reuse requires something like a slot delay at a station to give the station the ability to recognize itself as the destination and either use the slot for sending data out itself or passing along an empty slot. It is called an "erasure node," since it has the ability to erase anything on the bus that already has reached its destination, and replace it with an empty slot. A few erasure nodes at well-placed locations can realize most of the potential efficiency gain.

Actually, the DQDB is much like a slotted ring if one considers the slot generators as part of the ring. There is a difference though, in that each station has two connections to the "ring," and no packet crosses the slot generators. The slot generators perform the equivalent of destination removal, as do the erasure nodes, if used. It is possible for one of the slot generators to adjust the outgoing versus incoming slot times to create the effect of a fixed number of interlaced slots as in the slotted ring, although there ordinarily would be no incentive to do this. The new-word policy slotted ring acknowledgment protocol requires in effect that every station act as an erasure node.

9.5   Summary

The multiaccess networks considered in this chapter are mostly of the broadcast type, where all stations can receive signals sent by any one station. Possible configurations with this property were shown in Figure 9.1. ALOHA communication is an uncoordinated protocol (except for having slots in the slotted case). **Slotted ALOHA** has an efficiency limited to about .368 successful transmissions per slot, and has stability problems if not controlled. **Unslotted ALOHA** has even a lower efficiency if it is assumed that colliding packets are lost if they overlap in any portion. Two avenues for improving ALOHA efficiency are access controls to reduce collision frequency and signal design and processing to decode in the face of collision. The first avenue includes **CSMA** (carrier sense multiple access) and **CD** (collision detection), both features of Ethernet. These improve ALOHA throughput from .368 to values that approach 1 if propagation time becomes negligible compared to frame length. The first avenue also includes collision resolution algorithms, which improve the theoretical limit of slotted ALOHA from .368 to about .5 while also solving the stability problem. The second avenue includes using the capture effect, power control, antenna directivity, and signal processing. This avenue, which is closer to the problem of communication in noise, is pursued further in Chapter 11.

Collision avoidance can also be attained by **time division/frequency division multiplexing** (TDM/FDM), or by polling/reservation. **Polling** and **reservation** are more appropriate than TDM/FDM for statistically varying data communication because of the potential waste of unused dedicated channels. CSMA/CD becomes inefficient when propagation times become a significant proportion of data frame length; this favors polling or reservation techniques. However, CSMA/CD is desirable under light loads because immediate response is obtained if no one else is sending; with polling it is necessary to wait for one's turn to come up, while with reservation it is necessary to wait until the reservation is confirmed. The standard token bus protocol is basically a polling scheme.

A **ring structure** loosely fits into the broadcast network category, although in schemes where destination removal is allowed it is not always true that all stations receive a transmitted frame. A ring structure avoids collision by the fact that only the receiver of a free token can send a frame, and as with polling it can approach 100% efficiency. In a **token ring**, when a station sends a frame, one possibility is to wait until the frame has completely returned to the original sender before releasing the token, and another is to release the token immediately after completing frame transmission. The standard token ring uses the first of these, while the **FDDI ring**, designed for longer distances and higher speed, uses the second.

A **slotted ring** uses fixed-size packets, usually the same size in each slot. Data can flow independently in different slots. If at least a $1/2$ slot time delay can be tolerated at each station, the **new-word policy** can be implemented in each slot to allow destination removal and automatic acknowledgment of all packets. With **destination removal**, network throughputs on a unidirectional ring approach twice the basic link data rate assuming random source/destinations; in a bidirectional ring the throughput can approach eight times the basic link data rate because shorter average paths to the destination can be chosen. The error-tolerant progression of the new-word acknowledgment policy allows interruption by voice packets for **voice–data integration**.

Dual-bus architecture is a good means of using optical transmission efficiently over fairly long distances in a broadcast-like network—Distributed Queue Dual Bus (**DQDB**) is the accepted standard for doing this. DQDB uses fixed-sized slots and a reservation-type scheme. The use of an erasure node for DQDB to allow reuse of a slot is somewhat like destination removal in a slotted ring.

9.6 Problems

9.1. In slotted ALOHA, if there are 5 backlogged senders that transmit with probability p_b, and 10 other senders that transmit with probability p_n, what is the probability of a successful transmission?

9.2. A and B are both sending to C according to the slotted ALOHA protocol.
  a. Suppose A and B send independently, each with probability $1/2$ in each slot. Suppose that if both send at the same time, both fail. Show that each achieves an average throughput of $1/4$ per slot.
  b. Suppose A uses much higher power, such that if A and B both send at the same time then A is successful, but not B. Assume the same probabilities $1/2$ of sending. What now is the average throughput, individually and total?
  c. If A uses higher power as in (b), show that A can use a different probability of sending that will make both A and B more successful than in case (a); that is, not only is the higher power user more successful, but so is the lower power one.

9.3. Three senders A, B, and C are using a common communication medium and the nonpersistent CSMA protocol. Each pair of senders is separated by τ seconds of propagation time. Each independently experiences a Poisson arrival rate of G packets per second. Suppose A sends a packet at time t. Packet durations are T, which is much larger than τ. Assume all three have sensed the channel to be idle for some time up to time $t - \tau$. Answer the following:
  a. Draw a time-line diagram with time going down and with A in the middle. Mark off the intervals at which B or C could cause a collision with A's packet sent at time t.
  b. What is the probability A's packet will suffer a collision?

   c. On the condition that B and C did not start sending before time $t + \tau$, what is the probability A's packet will suffer a collision?

   d. On the condition that B and C did not start sending before time t, what is the probability A's packet will suffer a collision?

9.4. The efficiency of a multiaccess protocol scheme can be analyzed in terms of a busy-idle cycle. Suppose it is found that the expected duration of the idle period in a cycle is 0.5 time units. A successful packet occupies one time unit of useful data. Two-thirds of the busy periods lead to successful reception of a packet; the others are collisions. The expected duration of a busy period is found to be 1.24 time units. What fraction of the time does the channel deliver successful useful data?

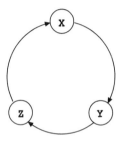

a) ring

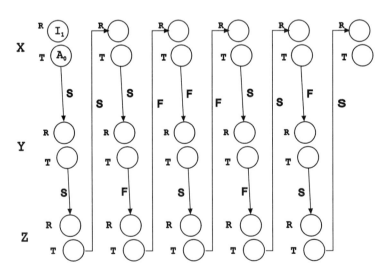

b) Progression of packets.

Figure P9.1: Slotted ring for Problem 9.8.

9.5. Repeat the method of Figure 9.8 if four colliding packets, *A*, *B*, *C*, and *D*, arrived at times 0.2, 0.4, 0.8, and 0.9, respectively. Show the steps leading to a resolution of the collision. What are the total number of additional slot times (not counting the original collision slot) to complete the collision resolution?

9.6. Consider a 3-node token ring using 24-bit tokens. Suppose there is a 16-bit delay at each node for reading a token or start of message, and a 2-bit-length propagation delay between each successive node. Suppose *A* receives a token, sends an 80-bit message frame to *C*, and follows it immediately with a token. *B* then accepts the token and sends a 128-bit message frame to *A*.

   a. Draw a space–time sketch of the events up through *A* receiving *B*'s message.

   b. Show that there is a time in this example when two different messages are being sent on different links during the same real-time interval.

   c. Despite this ability to be sending more than one message on different links at the same time, show that for a token ring the total transferred data rate cannot exceed the single link bit rate.

9.7. **a.** Derive Equation (9.13) for the slotted bidirectional ring and destination removal, *N* odd.

   b. Derive a similar expression for *N* even, assuming that for the station equidistant clockwise and counterclockwise the traffic is divided equally.

9.8. Consider one slot of a slotted ring of three stations, *X*, *Y*, and *Z*, implementing the new-word policy. Suppose *X* has a long string of packets *A*, *B*, *C*, *D*,... to send to *Z*, and there is no other traffic in the slot. If a packet has reached its destination and the destination has nothing to send, it sends an idle packet, denoted *I*.

   Fill in the progression of packets around the ring given the indicated succession of channel link events in Figure P9.1: *S* = success, *F* = failure. With each capital letter identifying the packet sent, **include a subscript** identifying the value of the alternating bit.

Chapter 10

Reliable Communication in Data Networks

In the previous chapter we considered the case of multiaccess networks, where all users share a common medium, and usually all can observe everyone's signal. The routing problem normally is not present in multiaccess networks. In a general network, there usually are alternate paths from source to destination, so the question enters as to how to route data.

The problems of sharing media that were met for multiaccess networks become even more complex in a network with routing. There is different sharing on different links of the network, and the routing strategy interacts with other factors to determine system reliability and efficiency.

Acknowledgment strategies also are more difficult in a network than over a direct link. Acknowledgments could be restricted to end-to-end only, or they could be applied at each link, or at certain intermediate points on the path from source to destination. The acknowledgments might be carried out on a packet-by-packet basis, or on a larger message-unit basis. When the path or circuit used is not dedicated, statistically varying delays occur that complicate ARQ strategies, particularly with regard to the timeout mechanism.

10.1 The Traditional Dedicated Circuit

The voice telephone network was for a long time the dominant communication network. Originally, the voice signals were transmitted in analog fashion, allowing 4khz of bandwidth per signal. Links were divided into a number of channels using frequency division multiplexing, with a standard organization of groups of channels and groups of groups according to available bandwidth. Each connection was given a specific dedicated two-way path through the network, denoted a *circuit*. The circuit follows specific links and specific channels on each link. Gradually the network has converted to digital format, using PCM to digitize voice and also allowing more convenient use of the network for data communication. Then, time division multiplexing became more practical than frequency division multiplexing. Due to the standard 8000 per second sampling rate for digitizing voice, most transmission was standardized at a basic 125 microsecond frame rate. A PCM voice signal needs about 8 bits per sample for quantization, and thus needs one 8-bit time slot per frame. With a dedicated circuit, no special overhead is needed to identify the data flowing through the given circuit, since anything in the assigned time slot is automatically switched at each node according to the circuit path set up on connection. Also, since a synchronized fixed-size frame is used, very little overhead is needed to keep track of the start of each frame. Frames are sent continuously in synchronous TDM, independently of whether data are being sent.

As data and image/video communication has expanded greatly, the need for much higher rates became clear. Fiber optic communication is the best means for providing these high rates, and has led to the SONET (Synchronous Optical Network) standard [OMID93]. This continues to use a 125 microsecond frame, but the basic frame is much larger (810 bytes compared to 24 bytes). These basic frames can be themselves time-multiplexed through a hierarchy of rates ranging (including overhead) from the basic 51.84 megabits/second to 2488.32 megabits/second. At each level of the hierarchy the basic frame time is maintained at 125 microseconds, but the number of bytes per frame increases.

10.2   Virtual Circuits

In *circuit switching* a path is assigned to a source–destination pair for the duration of the communication, referred to as a *session* or a *conversation*. Switches are set at each intermediate node to ensure the session data follows the assigned path. A return path also is assigned, which usually but not necessarily follows the exact reverse of the forward path. In conventional circuit switching the forward and return paths are dedicated, as described in Section 10.1. For many forms of data communication dedicated circuits are highly wasteful of communication resources.

The term *virtual circuit switching* denotes the setting up of a particular path (circuit) and switch connections for the session, except that the links along the path do not have completely dedicated allocations for that session. The choice of route usually is based on information about the session user's expected data rate needs, as well as the current network traffic state. The data must be divided into units, referred to as *packets*. (However, in ATM networks the units are called *cells*.) Since each link is not dedicated, when a session packet arrives at a node to be switched to a certain outgoing link, it may find at the moment that that line is busy and may have to wait in a buffer for its turn to use the line. If a buffer at some node becomes full, it may be necessary to discard either incoming or stored packets. Thus a reliable data protocol must account for possible lost packets as well as varying delays.

After a dedicated circuit has been set up, sessions sharing a common line do not need circuit or user identification bits, because each session is given specific time slots or a specific frequency band for its sole use. However, in a virtual circuit, different users sharing a common line must carry sufficient identification to distinguish them from each other. The size of this identification number has to be large enough to distinguish all the different sessions sharing a common transmission line. This is called the logical channel number. The logical channel number space usually is far less than the set of currently active sessions on the network, and even less than the address space of all network users.

Figures 10.1a and b illustrate the similarities and differences of dedicated and virtual circuits. For a dedicated circuit employing TDM, data from a session assigned to time slot 4 on line X arrives at a node where circuit switching information is stored to switch whatever is in slot 4 on line X into slot 6 on outgoing line A. For a virtual circuit, data from a session assigned logical channel 7 on line X arrives at a node where circuit switching information is tabulated to take whatever comes in on line X with logic channel number 7, replace its channel number by an assigned channel number 9 for outgoing line A, and place it in A's outgoing transmission buffer. Packets can be transmitted from A's buffer on a first-come, first-served basis, or a system of priorities

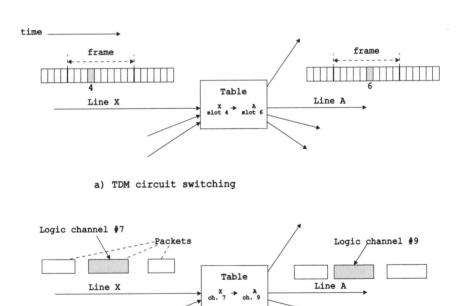

a) TDM circuit switching

b) Virtual circuit switching.

Figure 10.1: Comparison of TDM circuit switching and virtual circuit switching.

can be used. The virtual circuit approach can be used independent of whether A's transmission is in the form of synchronized frames or asynchronously as packets arrive for transmission; in either case logic channel numbers can be included for identification in the statistically multiplexed packets. When a virtual circuit session terminates, its various logic channel numbers are freed for reuse by a new connection. When a dedicated circuit terminates, its various time slots become idle for reuse by a new connection. It is also possible to set up a *permanent virtual circuit*. In a permanent virtual circuit the numbers and associations for the virtual circuit are retained, even when the virtual circuit is not being used. While it is not being used, the virtual circuit is not using network resources other than retaining the channel numbers.

It is also possible to provide a partially dedicated circuit to a connection or to combine dedicated circuits with virtual circuits in a network. For example, in the synchronized frame format some time slots could be reserved for dedicated traffic and others could be shared statistically. The proportion devoted to dedicated traffic could vary. Also, by a system of priorities, "dedicated" portions of circuits not currently in use by the preferred user could be used temporarily by statistically shared connections.

10.3 Datagrams, Multiple Virtual Circuits, and the Time-Ordering Problem

In making either a dedicated or a virtual circuit connection, a decision must be made as to what path should be taken through the network, if any acceptable path is available. Routing strategies assign costs to each link dependent on link capacity, current link traffic, delays, and other factors. Usually, the router attempts to select for a new connection a least-cost path between source and destination. In the dedicated circuit case it is known how much capacity is given up and how much remains available on each link. In the virtual circuit case there is the additional complication that it cannot be predicted in advance of the connection exactly how much capacity will actually be used by the connection.

One problem with the virtual circuit approach is that a circuit may be set up, and then it will turn out that buffering becomes excessive on certain links. Although some attempt may be made to match expected data rate needs with network capacities at setup time, short term fluctuations are unpredictable, because much data communication is sporadic; this sporadic nature of data communication is, in fact, the main reason for having virtual circuits rather than dedicated circuits. A solution that could come to mind is to let a packet that encounters delay go out on a less busy route on its way to the destination. One possibility is to change the path, but the change is hard to do without disrupting the flow of data. Another possibility is to give a connection multiple alternate circuits initially. The logic channel associations could be set up for each alternative at initiation of the session. Then if one path was found congested, subsequent data for the session could be sent over an alternate path, or the data could be apportioned on different paths. Packets of the session would not need destination addresses; they would only need the assigned logic channel numbers for the links traversed.

The multiple alternate circuit idea probably is not a good one except for special applications. Reasons are the rather elaborate connection setup and the loss of the ability to ensure ordered arrival of the session's packets at the destination node. However, if data are distributed in a regular pattern over the multiple circuits, order can be maintained (see Problem 10.2). If possible out-of-order arrival can be tolerated, a better solution in many cases would be to do away with the connection setup entirely and let each packet find its own route. This is the approach known as *datagram* communication. No circuit connection setup is made, so there are no virtual circuit numbers. Each datagram packet needs to carry the destination address (a slight disadvantage because the destination address has more bits than the logic channel number), and at each node would be switched on to the currently best next node toward the destination. Since the best routing path to the destination can change dynamically, successive datagrams may follow different paths and may arrive out of order.

The reordering that may be needed in datagram communication could be done by the destination user, or it could be done by the network destination node prior to delivery. This latter alternative allows the network to deliver the packets in order, giving the appearance, externally to the network, of having a virtual circuit connection. This method is referred to as *external virtual circuit, internal datagram.*

Packets arriving out of order create a need for a larger sequence number size to ensure proper packet reordering. In the ARQ protocols of Chapters 5 and 6, we assumed that packets were received in the order sent, if they were received at all. The sequence number size was then governed by needing to have enough different numbers to send packets continuously and yet have acknowledgment come back before the range of allowed new sequence numbers was exhausted. Round-trip time to acknowledgment was the principal influence on sequence number size. The variable and usually longer round trip delay in networks is in itself a cause for needing larger sequence numbers. Out-of-order reception possibilities increase the required size even more. Consider, for example, that a particular packet may take a route that causes an excessive delay; as a result it fails the timeout and gets retransmitted. It may be that after it is retransmitted successfully and the sequence numbers proceed through a new cycle, the long delayed packet finally arrives, and is mistaken for a new packet with the same sequence number in the next cycle. This is illustrated in Figure 10.2.

The transport protocol layer has the task of ensuring reliable end-to-end communication over a network. The reordering problem can be virtually eliminated by using extremely large sequence numbers. Transport layer protocols over networks have been using 31- or 32-bit sequence numbers. These protocols will be described further in Section 10.7. The large number of bits employed practically eliminates the sequence number reuse ambiguity problem. Also, limitations on the time a packet can remain in the network and random starting sequences for new connections protect against old sequence numbers reappearing when they might be misinterpreted.

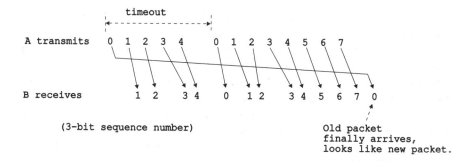

Figure 10.2: Effect of an excessively delayed packet in a network.

As long as packets are large, say 1000 bits or more, the sequence number overhead is not excessive. Occasional short packets would be individually inefficient if using large sequence numbers, but occasional short packets might not contribute much to the traffic of a variable-packet-size network; a large data transfer would use large size packets by choice.

10.3.1 Incorporating Extra Information in the Check Computation

It has been pointed out (see p. 116 of [BERT92]) that the ambiguity protection of a large sequence number can be obtained while using a much smaller number of bits. This idea has not been used in the standard transport protocols, however.

Each frame is associated with a b-bit sequence number that advances with each new frame. The trick is to send only the i least significant bits of the sequence number and incorporate the remaining $b - i$ bits of the large b-bit sequence number into the computation of the frame check sequence. This is illustrated in Figure 10.3 for $i = 4$ and $b \gg i$. Since frames may be accepted out of order, the general selective repeat transmitted window limit $W = 2^{i-1} = 8$ or less should be used. The receiver's window and record of accepted frames are shown. All frames up to #2049 (transmitted #1) have been accepted, and the receiver window extends from #2042 (transmitted #10) through #2057 (transmitted #9), with only frames between #2050

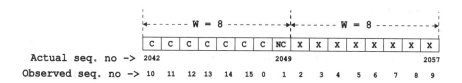

Frame 162 then is received.

Figure 10.3: Receiver window with partial incorporation of sequence number in check computation ($i = 4$, $b \gg i$).

through #2057 (#2 through #9) acceptable as new frames. If old frame #162 then is received with transmitted #2, it could be mistaken for #2050, but it almost certainly will not, because the number 160 is included in its check computation. However, the decoder will check assuming #2048 is in the check computation instead, so the frame will almost certainly be rejected due to detected apparent error.

This saving of transmitted bits by incorporating them with the check computation is an important basic principle; sometimes it is used to save transmission of parts of addresses or frame-to-frame repetitive information currently unique to the session of interest. Including the address helps protect against misrouting, since a misrouted frame would have the wrong address and as a result almost surely would be discarded due to check failure.

The check sequence can also be used to incorporate information feedback about what an acknowledgment is responding to. Suppose A wants to know if a return is a response to a specific transmitted frame, which itself has a long sequence number. The receiver B can incorporate in the check sequence of its response the sequence number of A's frame or by agreement any other contents of A's frame that would uniquely identify it. Then A would make the same incorporation in doing error detection (it also could attempt error detection without doing this, in case this was a response to something else). It probably would not be advisable to extend this idea to identifying all acknowledgments because the large number of detection modes needed would be too complex and the probability of undetected error would be multiplied by the number of possible acknowledgments.

10.4   Mixed Media Communication

The principal emphasis in this book is on communicating data with very small probability of error. However, not all digital communication has this requirement, and a network is likely to carry a mixture of data requiring different degrees of reliability. Design of a particular process for reliable and efficient communication cannot ignore the effects of sharing communication resources with mixed classes of traffic. Digitized voice and image signals can tolerate more frequent errors, although if data compression is used the error tolerance becomes more stringent. Voice and motion video usually have the constraint that the digital signal delay cannot exceed some maximum, or else the data become useless. Most data communication falls within one of the following three general classes:

Class I: a strict time constraint but less strict error tolerance, such as voice and motion video.

Class II: a less strict time constraint but very strict error tolerance.

Class III: a strict time constraint and a strict error tolerance.

One solution would be to provide separate networks for the different network classes; however, this is not necessary and would probably be less efficient. It is not fundamentally difficult for the different classes of data communication to share a network.

Voice and motion video generally are considered examples of class I traffic. However, data compressed voice or video also have some class III aspects because certain parts of the data are very critical to reception quality.

There are also classes of data with neither a strict time constraint nor a strict error tolerance, but we will omit these as not being worthy of much concern.

Class III was discussed briefly when communication over variable channel conditions was discussed. When channel conditions vary, sometimes it may not be possible to satisfy the requirements of class III. Even if it is possible, priority and permission to use extra network resources may be necessary to meet the requirements.

Sharing of the different classes of data is readily accomplished through a system of priorities. Following are some examples assuming virtual circuits.

1. **One class I session with multiple class II sessions.** Make sure that every link used in the connection has capacity to carry at least the peak rate of the class I session. If no such path exists, the connection is not accepted. Set up a priority rule so that class I has priority over class II. Then a class II session assigned a virtual circuit can use any free capacity for its transmissions over the circuit. However, it is not realistic that no other class I session would exist needing a common link. Thus consider the second example.

2. **Multiple class I and class II sessions.** Make sure every link used has a capacity such that, statistically, the probability is small that the short-term data rate of the composite class I sessions would exceed capacity of any link used. A rule could be established to fairly distribute discards of packets among the class I users in the rare cases when capacity temporarily is exceeded, and to discard any class I packet that has already been delayed such that it cannot arrive by its deadline.

   Since the allotted capacity would be significantly above the average rate of the class I traffic, there would be a great deal of additional capacity for class II traffic.

   In the preceding examples a class II session can encounter congestion on particular links of its route due to temporary class I usage. This can create rather large buffer requirements at each node. Buffer storage is not as much a problem as it once was due to greater memory capacities, but the resulting delay is still a potential problem. This might favor using the datagram approach or provision of multiple alternate circuits for class II sessions; that is, datagrams could be mingled with "dedicated" circuits, with datagrams permitted to be sent on momentarily idle dedicated circuits as well as on any currently unassigned facility.

3. **Mixed class I and class III sources.** In compressed video some of the information is especially critical. The loss of certain reference information would cause severe degradation of the reception, while occasional loss of fine detail would not have much effect. Thus the signals could be thought of as part class I and part class III. It is possible to partition data compressed video [CHIA94, PANC94] such that the critical portions of the data are clearly separated from the other portions. The

class III part could be given special treatment in terms of higher priority or use of extra redundancy or extra energy for greater error protection. Since the class III part is generally a small portion of the total information transmission, the extra resources used would not diminish utilization significantly. The extra resources for the class III portion could come in the form of added redundancy for error correction.

Video signals, a major source of capacity demand, can allow enormous reductions in required capacity when statistically packet multiplexed if appropriate measures are taken. Data compression of an individual signal seeks to allow use of a channel whose capacity is well below the peak data generation rate of the video signal, ideally closer to the average. Although significant data compression of a single video signal is achievable, it is not practical to get very close to the average due to the large delays and storage needed to time-average the rate of generation of data, particularly with regard to frame-to-frame motion changes. With multiplexed signals, this averaging can occur over the ensemble of signals as well as over time. The ensemble average has the further advantage that different signals are almost statistically independent at a given time, whereas successive time samples are highly correlated. For example, it is rare that most scenes among a set of different signals will experience rapid motion at the same time. Also, there is some flexibility as to which frame the detail needs to be put into, since the human receptor cannot make use of detail and rapid motion at the same time. Thus it is feasible to tolerate a capacity much closer percentagewise to the total average generation rate for a given time delay than the capacity provided for individual signal data compression alone.

10.5   Network Structures and Internetworking

The networks of Chapter 9 have a specific network structure and specific communication procedures. Communication is between a limited set of endpoints, usually in a common local area. Communication over a wider number of endpoints usually involves a network of smaller component networks, as illustrated in Figure 10.4. Communication in this case is called internetworking. The component networks generally were developed for different organizations at different times and have different structural and procedural characteristics. The connections between component networks (square boxes) have particular significance. They need to have the ability to make changes to adapt to the different component network specifications and participate in routing. The devices that perform this are known as gateways or multiprotocol routers. Note that each of the component networks may have its own routing strategy within the network. Thus routing is best divided into two stages: internet routing between the gateways, and routing within a component network. Figure 10.4b illustrates how the internetwork links appear (solid lines) from the viewpoint of gateway routing. The actual link between two adjacent gateways is through a common network, as indicated by the dashed lines. For example, the link between A and D actually is through network N_4.

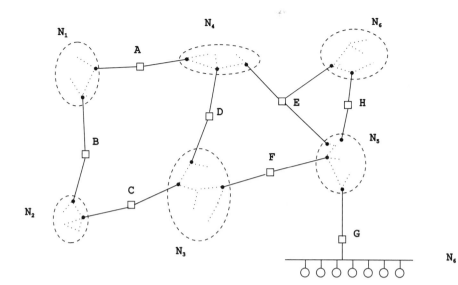

a) Internetwork configuration.

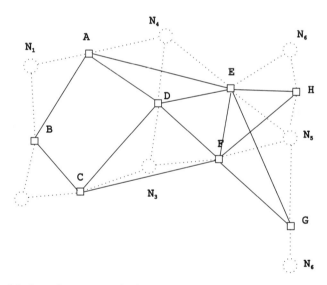

b) Routing network from the gateway viewpoint.

Figure 10.4: A network structure with component networks.

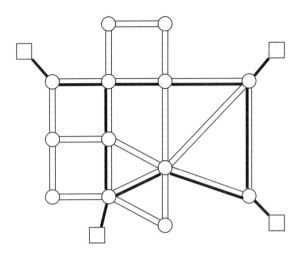

Figure 10.5: A network within a network.

Also, a group of users, such as a corporation or government organization, can construct their own network within a network by using leased lines or permanent virtual circuits inside the overall network, as illustrated by the thicker lines in Figure 10.5.

The current structure of internetworking known as the Internet is built on the two-stage routing between component networks and inside component networks. One major reason for the division is the existence of diverse networks that have widely different internal communication methods. However, the Internet technique is not the only feasible alternative. Refer to Figure 10.4b. The solid line apparent network among gateway routers could actually be constructed as a separate "backbone" network, such as the current telephone system for voice communication. This network, with the nodes A, B, C, D, E, F, G, and H in Figure 10.4b, could deliver data to any of the subnetworks $N_1, \ldots, N_7$ by some of the connections shown in dashed lines. The component networks still could do their own routing by their own methods, but would not participate in intermediate routing and would need to connect to only one backbone node.

10.5.1 The Internet Protocol (IP)

The Internet Protocol uses the connectionless datagram approach. Each datagram is processed and routed individually. IP manages the routing of datagrams among gateway routers, as illustrated in Figure 10.4. Routing inside a subnetwork is performed according to the methods of the particular subnetwork. The subnetwork might use datagrams, virtual circuits, or it could be a type of multiaccess network. The subnetwork also might have a maximum packet size that is less than the size of a datagram.

If the subnetwork is an intermediary in the communication rather than the destination subnetwork, there may be special provisions controlling transfer of the datagram to the next gateway router.

Reliable and ordered delivery of datagrams is not guaranteed. It is the task of the higher transport layer to provide reliable and ordered delivery. Most commonly, the transport layer protocol denoted TCP is used for that purpose. In the combined protocol denoted TCP/IP, each IP datagram encapsulates a TCP data unit.

IP datagrams contain a rather large header. Part of the reason for this is that the datagram approach requires retention of complete address information within the datagram. A few different versions of the header format have been developed. Version IPv4 was the main version, but it is being replaced by version IPv6. Version IPv4 has a header of 20 bytes minimum. It contains the following fields:

32-bit source address and 32-bit destination address

Fragment identification

Length of header (20 byte minimum) and total datagram length

IP options subheader if used

Time to live

16-bit header checksum

Version field

Other fields

IP packet lengths are variable, and can be as large as 65,535 bytes. The fragment provision was included to accommodate passing the datagram through networks for which the datagram is larger than the allowed packet size of the network. Fragments are given full headers, and once fragmented are not reassembled until the destination is reached. If all fragments of a datagram are not received the datagram is discarded. Any datagram or fragment for which the checksum fails is discarded as soon as the failure is discovered. This is because it is a waste of network resources to communicate something that is sure to be discarded. The time to live field is decremented with time and hops. If it goes to zero the datagram is discarded, thereby preventing it from arriving so much later that it might be mistaken for a different datagram with a similar sequence number.

IPv6 is being introduced because some features of IPv4 were becoming obsolete or needed improvement. (1) The large growth of networks requires longer address fields. (2) There is a need for special handling of data that has strict delay and rate requirements. (3) Fragmenting is better avoided as much as possible because of excess processing and greater chances of datagram loss. (4) Some simplification of the header for faster processing is desired.

IPv6 has a 40-byte basic header. The header includes the following fields:

128-bit source address and 128-bit destination address

28-bit flow label

16-bit payload length field

Next header field to indicate a following optional header or TCP header

Version

Hop limit

The use of 128 bits per address is more than adequate for any future needs. The flow label includes 4 bits of priority specification, including time sensitivity. The other 24 bits are a flow identifier that identifies the source using the particular flow. A particular flow is associated with information about resource allocation and quality of service that routers can use in making routing decisions. The checksum field is eliminated because the transport protocol will do the necessary checking. Fragmentation is done only at the source node, and is preceded by a path discovery technique to ensure the fragment size chosen will be able to pass through a network route. This reduces processing requirements at the various routers. A fragment extension header is used, in addition to the base header, to carry a fragment.

10.6   Standard Transport Layer Protocols

The transport layer in the layered OSI/ISO model used to describe network operations has among its tasks the responsibility to ensure reliable and efficient end-to-end data transfer. Although a specific network could be designed to ensure reliable communication to any destination node of any data it can accept from the source node, a user-to-user connection often has to connect through networks that do not have such a capability. In fact, it is common for the communication to occur through a network of smaller component networks, with different reliability and characteristics in the different networks. Thus, it is important to have a reliable data communication protocol layer above the network layer.

The ISO has specified five classes of transport protocol standards: TP 0, 1, 2, 3, and 4. Of these, only TP-4 is designed to ensure end-to-end reliable communication. However, a different protocol, called TCP (transmission control protocol) has proven to be much more widely used. The protocol developed from funding by the Defense Advanced Research Projects Agency (now ARPA) of an experimental computer network. The network was the foundation for the development of the current Internet, which is a collection of diverse subnetworks. TCP was designed to work with IP. The combination is denoted TCP/IP.

We will not go into all the details of TCP/IP and other protocols. The book [COME95] is devoted entirely to TCP/IP, and other recent books such as [TANE96] and [STAL97] have good explanations of TCP/IP and other transport protocols. However, it seems worth discussing some features relating to the use of ARQ and communication efficiency.

TCP data units, called segments, all contain a header that has a minimum size of 20 bytes. In TCP/IP the segment is encapsulated in an IP datagram. Thus, an IP datagram actually contains a minimum of 40 bytes of overhead (IPv4) or 60 bytes (IPv6). This is very inefficient for small messages. The argument can be made that small messages do not contribute much to traffic anyway; it is the large messages that are more important contributors to traffic load. For datagrams carrying thousands of bytes, an overhead of 40–60 bytes is a small percentage. However, some networks share capacity in small packet increments. ATM cells, which will be discussed in Section 10.7, are an example of this. This can be handled by breaking the transport frames into cells and reassembling them on leaving the ATM network.

The TCP header includes a 32-bit send sequence number, a 32-bit received sequence number, 16-bit source and destination addresses, a 16-bit checksum, a 16-bit window control field, other control bits, and possible options beyond the 20-byte minimum.

The sequence number actually is a count of bytes, referred to as octets. It is the number m of the first data octet in the packet. If the packet contains n octets, the next packet will have sequence number $m + n$. The received sequence number specifies the next expected octet. If the packet is purely acknowledgment, it still needs to be the minimum 20-byte header size, even though the 32-bit send sequence number is not needed.

The window field is a statement of how many octets beyond the most recently acknowledged octet are permitted to be sent without waiting for a new acknowledgment. This can be used for flow control to keep the destination from being overwhelmed by data, and for congestion control to keep the network circuits from being overloaded. Figure 10.6 shows an example of data transfer between A and B. To simplify the illustration, window instructions from A to B are not shown. B's first packet shown contains 192 bytes of data along with a piggybacked acknowledgment of bytes 5001–6000 from A, plus a window of 3000 additional bytes that A would be permitted to send.

Note that after B receives (6001–8000) it acknowledges them but for some reason decides to give no advanced permission by changing the window to 1000, which does not change the advance limit of permissions that has already been given to A. Then B decides to increase the window, and sends a separate packet to A with the new window instruction. Note that a station does not have to wait for acknowledgment of each individual packet before sending another, as long as its window is not exceeded.

It seems strange that only 16 bits are used for checking considering the general overkill used for most parts of the header and the much greater protection that a 32-bit field would provide. Also, the checksum was chosen because it was easier to compute than the CRC, although CRC computation is rather simple. One byte of the checksum is simply a modulo 255 sum of all the bytes; the other is a weighted sum of these bytes. The single mod 255 sum is not very protective, since a single bit error in the same position of two different bytes would cancel out; however, it most likely would not cancel out in the weighted sum that comprises the other check byte. So maybe the error detection is comparable to a 16-bit CRC. Of course the 2^{-16} fail-safe ratio is the same. There is some protection due to inconsistencies that errors might produce. An error in an acknowledgement number could be recognized as out of place—it might refer to some byte in the middle of a packet. A packet full of errors that were undetected by the checksum would almost surely have many inconsistencies.

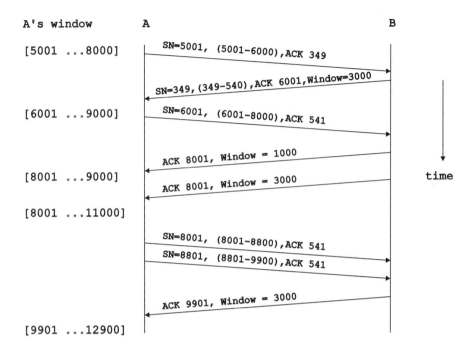

Figure 10.6: TCP acknowledgment/data transfer also showing window instructions from *B*. (Window instructions from *A* are not shown.)

TP-4 uses an option of either 7- or 31-bit sequence numbers, but the numbering is by packets, not by octets. There are different types of packets in TP-4, as opposed to one type in TCP. Acknowledgments are sent as separate acknowledgment packets. They carry the next expected sequence number, and a credit value, which specifies the maximum number of packets the sender can send without obtaining further acknowledgment.

10.6.1 Establishing and Terminating a Transport Connection

Establishing a Connection   Starting a communication is a nontrivial process, particularly when the communication is carried over a network that is not 100% reliable. Since the datagram approach of TCP/IP is being discussed, the question of setting up a virtual circuit connection does not arise. Between two communicators *A* and *B*, the initiation of data communication from *A* to *B* and from *B* to *A* are treated as two different processes, even though there is two-way communication in both cases. If *A* wants to establish a transport connection sending data to *B*, the first thing necessary is for *A* to send a message to *B* indicating the desire to do this. The message might also include various parameter information such as data rate and maximum TCP segment size. The desired parameters might also have to be acceptable to the network, or else the network could refuse to establish the connection. Assuming the specifications are acceptable to the network, A must learn via a message from B that it is acceptable to begin. Thus B sends such a message. Because B would like to be assured that A has gotten its approval, it is standard for A to acknowledge B's acknowledgment. This completes what is called the *three-way handshake*. Under noisy channel conditions this could be continued indefinitely without the latest responder ever being sure that the other has received the latest acknowledgment; but after the third step in the handshake, A will begin sending data, retransmitting upon timeout after not receiving acknowledgment. Receipt of any of thse data by B will ensure B that A has gotten its initial acknowledgment of data establishment. If nothing gets acknowledged after many tries, it would be time to consider terminating the connection. The termination problem will be discussed later.

The standard flow of messages in establishing a TCP connection of data from A to B is shown in Figure 10.7. The handshake messages are denoted as SYN segments. A's SYN segment contains a send sequence number x. This is counted as a 1-byte message for byte numbering purposes, so the subsequent data segment will start at $x + 1$. The initiating number x is selected at random, to protect against the reappearance of old delayed segments from a previous TCP connection that may have been closed a short time ago. Because of the large alphabet size (2^{32}) of sequence numbers, the chance of the old sequence number falling in the window of currently valid sequences is remote due to the random choice. Similarly, B chooses a random sequence number y to initiate the sending of data from B to A.

A may send several SYN retransmissions before getting a response. Only after getting back ACK $= x + 1$ will A be able to send data. B could continue to repeat its response if it doesn't get ACK $= y + 1$. However, if the convention is that A will resend its SYN, B could wait for the next SYN to make another response. The process is somewhat akin to the new-word policy—each new message allows a transition to a new response.

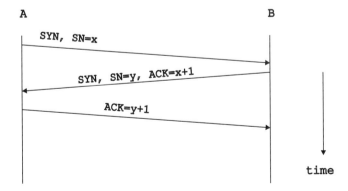

Figure 10.7: Establishing a TCP connection with a three-way handshake.

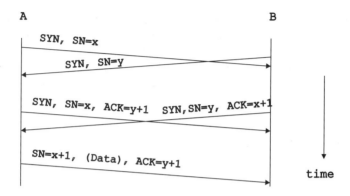

Figure 10.8: Events where both initiate simultaneously.

Initiation of data transmission from *A* to *B* can occur at different times or simultaneously. Figure 10.8 illustrates a case where both initiate a connection simultaneously.

Terminating a Connection The two separate data flows can be terminated separately, as well as initiated separately. If *A* wants to terminate sending data to *B*, *A* sends a segment with a FIN command, with a sequence number *x*. Assuming *B* receives the message, it returns an ACK with sequence number *x* + 1. If the ACK is not returned by a certain timeout, *A* would repeat FIN until an ACK is obtained. *A* would then stop sending anything (except ACKs to *B* if *B* is still sending data). Although *A* never ACKs *B*'s ACK, passage of time with no further FIN commands implies the *A*-to-*B* data flow connection is closed. Similar steps are taken to close the data flow from *B* to *A*.

Occasionally a failure may break all connection between *A* and *B*. The solution is to restart a new connection. The rule of initiating a connection with a new random 32-bit sequence number, as well as the passage of time, will make it highly unlikely that old segments from the old connection will arrive and be mistaken for parts of the new data connection transmission. There might be a problem of how much of the old data needs to be repeated. Some of it may have already been acknowledged, but with the old sequence numbers. Possibly retransmission of all or some of his these could be saved via messages to determine receiver reference points.

10.6.2   Retransmission Timeout

The TCP protocol specifies that an acknowledgment be returned for each reception of a new set of octets. There is a wide and rapid variation in the round-trip time of datagrams through the internet and the subsequent return acknowledgement. This variation is due to different routes, variable amount of buffering at each node, and variable time to when the destination includes an acknowledgment in a return packet.

The latter time is variable because the destination may wait up to a certain maximum amount of time until it has data to send so it can piggyback an acknowledgment rather than devote a packet to acknowledgment alone. Also, forward or return packets can be lost. Thus it is difficult to estimate how long the sender should wait (timeout) for a response before retransmitting. Rather than discuss specific TCP timeout algorithms at this point, the problem will be investigated in more general terms in Section 10.10.

10.7 Asynchronous Transfer Mode (ATM)

The Integrated Services Digital Network (ISDN) is being implemented to serve as a worldwide public telecommunications network to carry all types of communication traffic through digital communication and digital switching. Originally it was planned based on several 64 kb/s channels between the users and the network, with control information on separate channels. With the need for higher rates and flexibility of mixing various types of communication, what is called broadband ISDN, or B-ISDN, was introduced. Transmission speeds of 155.5 mb/s, 622 mb/s and higher are planned for. It was decided that a packet switched mode, using fixed-size packets and virtual circuits, would be used. This is called ATM. Since a given session always follows the same path, switching could be done faster and more efficiently. Signals requiring periodic transmission could be allocated near periodic space on each link of the virtual circuit on circuit setup, thereby giving them effectively a dedicated circuit, whereas other types of traffic could be given space as available, with buffering. Although originally developed for a public telecommunications network, ATM is finding application in many smaller networks requiring high-speed multimedia traffic.

10.7.1 ATM Cells

The size of the packets, called cells, was chosen as 53 bytes, including 5 bytes of header. This was a compromise, taking into account voice PCM requirements. PCM voice would require an inherent delay equal to the time needed to assemble 48 bytes of data from successive quantized samples. This amounts to about 6 ms of delay (48 samples at 8000 samples per second) with the standard packet, which is well within an acceptable range for voice conversation. Longer packets would mean longer inherent delay, which could be unacceptable when added to propagation delays.

The 5-byte ATM header within the network contains the following fields:

12-bit virtual path identifier (VPI)

16-bit virtual channel identifier (VCI)

3-bit payload type

1-bit priority

8-bit CRC check on header

There is a slight modification replacing four of the VPI bits for user to network cells.

The separation of VPI and VCI in the virtual circuit identification is intended to allow faster switching of circuits that all follow a common path. These can be switched together, and the routing switch need look only at the VPI until the path ends. Also, with 28 bits devoted to identification, it is not necessary to use the method described in Section 10.2 of changing logic channel numbers at each node.

The 3 bits of payload type are used to specify congestion and management information as well as data type and indication of last cell in an AAL5 frame (to be described). The priority bit provides information that allows less important cells to be discarded in case of congestion.

ATM is designed for fast switching, so hop-by-hop ARQ is avoided. The CRC bits provide some error detection/correction for the header. This is because a misdirected packet is more serious than a lost packet, and packets with detected errors can be discarded to protect against misdirection, whereas if an error is corrected its possible misdirection is avoided without discarding. An 8-bit CRC is used with polynomial $D^8 + D^2 + D + 1$. The single error correction mode is used until an error is corrected or detected. When this happens the system switches to a pure error detection mode until no errors are detected for a while. The reason for this is that on the high-speed fiber optic network, errors are extremely rare and usually random. However, if an error should occur, there is a possibility that the error is due to some bursty effect that might cause more errors, so the switch to the safer error detection is made. When an error has just been experienced, there is more chance the channel is in a bad state that will cause more errors. If an error is detected without correction, the cell is discarded.

Data checking and retransmission are handled at higher levels: the ATM adaptation layer to be described, and the transport layer.

The cell structure does not specify how the links actually carry the cells. This is considered part of the physical layer. In fact, the cells themselves do not have direct means of defining their beginning and end, so this is left to the physical layer. In most cases they can be placed in a synchronized format, which will define their beginning and end points and possibly place idle cell information as needed. For example, they can be placed in the SONET (Synchronous Optical NETwork) format described in Section 10.1. This format has a basic 125 microsecond frame rate that by design corresponds to the standard voice PCM sampling rate.

A point worth mentioning is that a packet can be a fixed number of bits, and yet its time duration can vary if it is switched onto a lower capacity link. For example, suppose a node has a 150 mb/s incoming link and one of its outgoing links has 15 mb/s rate. A packet that is switched to the 15 mb/s link would be lengthened in time by a factor of 10. However, only some of the incoming packets on the high rate line would be going out on the low rate line, since it obviously is not designed to carry more than 15 mb/s. The time diagram would look somewhat like Figure 10.9.

10.7.2   The ATM Adaptation Layer

Information supplied for transmission into the ATM network is not normally organized into ATM-size cells. Thus there is an adaptation layer that segments data into

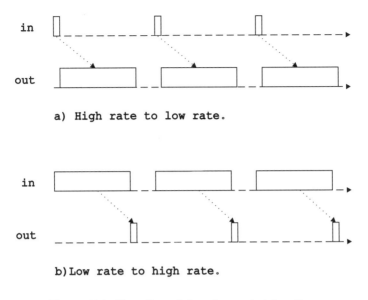

a) **High rate to low rate.**

b)**Low rate to high rate.**

Figure 10.9: The effect of changing packet duration.

cells and reassembles them at the destination node. Some error checking also is provided to detect lost or missing cells and other errors. Two steps or sublayers are used for this purpose. There are mainly two protocol types, AAL1 for constant bit rate timed data such as PCM voice, and AAL5 for variable bit rate communication. AAL1 simply places the data directly into cells, 47 bytes at a time, with 1 byte reserved for sequence numbering (4 bits) and its protection (4 bits). AAL5 accepts up to 65,535 bytes at a time into a frame, and adds an 8-byte trailer, which includes a 32-bit CRC for error detection and a 2-byte data length indicator, in number of bytes. With AAL5 there is a segmentation and reassembly sublayer to place the data frame into cells and reassemble the frame from the cells received at the destination node. The process of segmentation is illustrated in Figure 10.10.

The trailer with length indicator aids in reassembly. It appears in the last part of the last cell, and the length indicator allows the reassembler to identify padded bits that were entered because the data frame was not an integral number of cells.

A Remark on Missing Cells In AAL5, if even one cell in a data frame is lost, the entire frame will be lost. Recovery and retransmission can be left to the transport layer. If cell loss is extremely rare this is not a serious disadvantage. However, if cell loss were more frequent it would be better to reduce this waste of discarded good cells. Erasure-correcting-codes with cells as the basic symbol unit could be used to replace missing cells. This could be done at the transport layer if that layer supplied sequence-numbered cells directly to ATM without an adaptation layer, somewhat as with AAL1. For example, a single cell included every $N + 1$ cells whose data

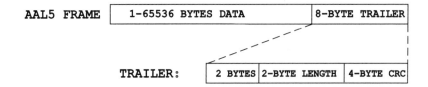

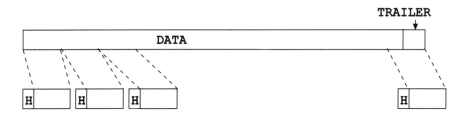

Figure 10.10: Segmentation into cells with AAL5.

part was the vector modulo 2 sum of the other N cells could allow reconstruction of any one missing cell. The sequence numbering is needed to identify which cell is missing. Since order is preserved in a virtual circuit, the identification of missing cells is unambiguous provided that no more than $2^b - 1$ consecutive cells are missing, where b is the number of bits in the sequence number.

One approach to the missing cell waste problem that has been considered is that, if a cell must be discarded due to congestion, all following cells belonging to the same frame should be discarded, because they will have to be retransmitted anyway. (The last cell bit lets the network know the end of the current frame.) This will reduce the load on congested links on the remainder of the virtual circuit. Also, it would be preferable to discard a cell at the beginning of a frame, where not much resource has been wasted yet, rather than near the end of a frame. This line of reasoning would not apply if the transport layer bypassed AAL5 by supplying its own sequence-numbered cells, as suggested in the previous paragraph.

10.7.3   Network Traffic Management

ATM uses virtual circuits, which have the characteristic that traffic offered on a virtual circuit varies statistically, and often the statistical laws are not known prior to making the connection. This makes it difficult not only to decide when to accept a connection and how to route it, but also how to reduce the traffic intensity of existing circuits when congestion occurs. Congestion generally occurs on a subset of network links, but possible solutions of rerouting a connection or providing multiple alternate virtual circuits to a connection are considered undesirable.

The first thing to recognize is that an ATM network will carry different classes of traffic, as described in Section 10.4, with different sensitivities to rate changes, cell losses, and delays. Fortunately, the classes that are most critical to requiring a constant bit rate, such as voice and video, have demands that are known fairly well at connection time, while other classes have less precisely known and more sporadic demands, but can more easily tolerate rate control.

Traffic management is broken into two problems: *call admission control* and *rate control* for existing circuits.

Call Admission Control Call admission control [PERR96] includes the specification of type of service, specified allowed rate and quality of service parameters, and the decision whether or not to accept a connection. The types of service are called *constant bit rate* (CBR), *variable bit rate* (VBR), *available bit rate* (ABR), and *unspecified bit rate* (UBR).

For CBR, a fixed cell rate allocation is provided, referred to as *peak cell rate* (PCR). A route is selected that guarantees the PCR can be handled with an acceptable *cell loss rate* (a quality of service specification). Digitized voice is often given as an example of a source needing CBR service, since voice signals are sampled at a fixed rate with a fixed number of bits per sample. There are silent periods in voice conversation that could be omitted in cell generation in order to provide more capacity for others, but this might not be done in the interest of simplicity.

VBR specifies a peak rate and also an average rate. The network strives to guarantee that at least the average rate can always be attained, and with high probability the peak rate can be accommodated. This is designed for sources that have a high peak-to-average information rate and have a real time constraint. Uncompressed digital video could be considered a CBR source, but because of the high peak rate and large ratio of peak information generation rate to average information generation rate it is more efficient to treat video as a VBR source. Also, data compression techniques can greatly reduce required average transmitted bit rate, but do not eliminate variability in bit rate requirements. VBR sources specify both a peak rate and an average rate. In multiplexing several video signals, the network capacity can be significantly less than the sum of the peak rates, but must be comfortably above the sum of the average rates.

ABR is for sources that can tolerate data rate variations because they do not have a strict time constraint, but would like to transmit as fast as possible in some range between a minimum cell rate and a peak cell rate. The network will reserve enough bandwidth for the minimum cell rate, but will allow transmission at rates above and up to the peak only as available without causing congestion problems. It is this category that is most amenable to congestion control strategies for existing virtual circuits.

Rate Control Because of statistical variations in traffic, periods of congestion will occur in parts or all of the network. If not controlled, quality of service specifications will get violated. Also, congestion tends to get worse if a significant part of the traffic requires acknowledgment, as increasing delays will lead to more timeouts and more capacity-wasting retransmissions. The most effective control is to reduce the traffic input. Prior to ATM, input was most commonly managed by the window mechanism or some other permissions mechanism, which limited average rate by reducing the window size or the number of permissions generated per second; that is, when a source had a number of permissions, it could send as fast as it could until it had exhausted its permissions or its window, at which point it would have to pause until new permissions or acknowledgments were obtained. However, it was decided that instead of using permissions and windows, the allowed rate of generation of ATM cells would be controlled dynamically [FEND96]. Given an allowed cell rate, the source could generate cells regularly at no more than the allowed cell rate.

The changes in rate are specified in resource management (RM) cells, which pass around the loop between source and destination, or in some cases might be sent back from intermediate nodes in the circuit. Depending on congestion conditions, these cells contain information to change to some specified rate. Because delays during severe congestion might slow these cells, there are rules for the ABR sources to reduce their rate if no RM cells arrive in a certain interval. An ABR source is required to generate these cells once every N data cells, where N is specified, or sometimes according to other rules. Details of ABR strategies can be found in [SAIT96, JAIN96, and ARUL96].

Cell Loss Priority One additional tool for traffic management is the cell loss priority bit: (1 = low priority, 0 = high priority). The 1 value might be used by the source to send cells above its allocation, or the network could change from 0 to 1 the priority bit in cells that were in violation of agreed parameters. In cases of congestion that causes buffers to fill, cells with priority bit 1 would be discarded prior to discarding any priority 0 cells. One way this could be used is to allow a source to send high bursts of data above its rate allocation if the circuit is currently lightly used.

10.8 Frame Relay

Frame relay is a popular virtual circuit packet switching technique. Unlike ATM, which switches fixed-size cells and segments variable-length frames into cells, frame relay switches variable-length cells. Prior to frame relay, packet switching networks employed HDLC and X.25 protocols, which made use of significant internal network error control, including hop-by-hop acknowledgment. Frame relay leaves error control to the end user, allowing higher speed processing within the network. However, the variable length frames do not allow the high switching speeds achievable by ATM, so frame relay communication generally is in the 1–2 megabit/second range.

FLAG	ADDRESS	INFORMATION	FCS	FLAG
1	2-4	UP TO 1600	2	1	← BYTES

Figure 10.11: Frame relay frame contents.

Only a brief description is given here. Detailed information can be found in [SMIT93] and Chapter 10 of [STAL97]. Figure 10.11 shows the makeup of a frame.

The 16-bit frame check sequence serves about the same purpose as the 8-bit header CRC in an ATM cell. This is checked at each node and the frame is discarded if it does not check. No other error control is performed within the network. Sequence numbering and acknowledgment/error control functions are done at the transport level. Whatever overhead is needed for this purpose can be included in the information field.

Congestion control is aided by two bits in the address field; one for forward congestion and the other for backward congestion. The network sets these congestion bits, and users are supposed to react by slowing down on learning of congestion, which can be done by reducing the window size. Discarding of frames may become necessary due to buffer overflow. Frequency of discard also serves as implicit congestion information. To ensure fairness, another option is to agree on certain rate parameters on connection, somewhat as in ATM, and if congestion occurs to discard frames of senders that are exceeding their agreements.

10.9 High-Speed Network Protocols

In some networks, particularly fiber optic networks, channel capacities are extremely high and error rates extremely low. For such networks, processing speed and buffer capacity rather than channel capacity may be the principal bottleneck. With 100 mb/s–1 gb/s bit rates, enormous amounts of data may get transferred before there is time to get back an acknowledgment. One saving factor is that memory capacities also are increasing greatly. However, processing time can also be a large contribution to round-trip time if error detection cannot be computed as fast as the absorbed data rate. Also, bit errors are very low on such networks, although packet loss due to buffer capacity limitations may be significant in some cases. If both losses and errors are rare, acknowledgments can be less frequent. Since conditions can change, an ability to adapt the frequency of acknowledgment to current conditions is desirable.

Light-weight transport protocols have been proposed to reduce acknowledgment protocol processing time. A good summary of these is contained in [DOER90]. Since a massive amount of data might be transferred before information about an error is returned, selective repeat is preferred over go-back. In essence, the ATM network satisfies a good part of the needs of a lightweight protocol, in that error control processing is minimal within the network.

Three techniques of interest are XTP, wormhole routing, and file comparison. The third of these approaches will be discussed in Section 10.11.

10.9.1   XTP (Express Transfer Protocol)

One of the proposed lightweight protocols is denoted XTP [NETR90], [STAL94], [PROT89]. For error checking, an XTP packet has a 32-bit checksum for the header only, and a separate 32-bit checksum for the data. The header checksum is used within the network to avoid misrouting of packets, much as is done with ATM. Data checking is done end-to-end. The checksum method is not as protective against undetected errors as a CRC, but is easier to generate. Considering that the header checksum was eliminated in IPv6, it would seem not that critical to have this large a header checksum, or even any header checksum. It would seem to be better to use all 64 checking bits for the whole frame (but probably check it only at the destination). Then the chance of an undetected error could almost always be ignored. The destination address could be incorporated into the check so as to filter out misrouted packets.

The XTP header has a bit for requesting a response from the receiver relating to status and flow control or rate parameters. Thus the sender can adjust frequency of acknowledgments and the rate of sending based on responses. The receiver also responds when errors are detected. The idea of using negative acknowledgments with an infrequent positive acknowledgment is a good one, because the negative acknowledgment gives a rapid retransmission response, whereas the occasional positive acknowledgment gives assurance of reliable transmission. The sender must retain a record for retransmission of anything prior to a positive acknowledgment.

Detailed selective repeat is provided for in responses. The receiver can list up to 16 pairs of sequence numbers. Each sequence number pair defines a span of consecutive packets that have been received correctly. Missing packets between the spans are the ones that must be retransmitted.

10.9.2   Wormhole Routing

A connection-oriented network such as ATM is at a disadvantage if one wants to send a fast burst of information to some destination to which a connection has not previously been set up. In multiprocessor communication and some local networks the concept of wormhole routing has been adopted. In wormhole routing, a large packet is sent through a network without a prior connection setup. The packet (the worm) contains a small "head" and a small "tail" at the end. When the head of a packet is received at a node it is forwarded immediately to a next node. As long as the first piece is successful, remaining pieces follow the head along the route without further delay. Occasionally buffering is required due to conflicts. The buffering for a worm packet can be distributed along its route or all at one node. Although this scheme allows fast connectionless communication, there are serious congestion problems under high utilization, which remain to be studied and ameliorated [LEON96]. Actually, with a permissions management strategy ATM could provide fast bursty transmission from a particular source to a particular destination by setting up a permanent virtual circuit that is used only sporadically. However, if a source was sending bursts each time to a randomly different choice among many destinations, the permanent virtual circuit idea would not be practical.

10.10 Transport Layer ARQ Design Factors

Three important related factors are window sizes, retransmission timeouts, and frequency and type of acknowledgment. We begin by summarizing the features of each of these individually.

10.10.1 Window Size

Window size refers to the sender's window of the maximum extent from the oldest unacknowledged transmitted information through the newest information the sender is allowed to send. This could be measured in number of octets, as illustrated in Figure 10.6 for TCP, or in number of frames. There are three different constraints that could be set on the window size.

1. There is an absolute constraint on maximum window size to prevent ambiguity based on the number of bits in a sequence number, as discussed in Chapters 5 and 6. However, with the 32-bit sequence numbers often used in transport protocols this constraint is not encountered.

2. A maximum window size can be set to prevent the data rate from exceeding the buffering and processing capability of the receiver.

3. There can be a maximum window to reduce network congestion by limiting the session data input. When a sender has sent a full window of packets or octets, it must stop until acknowledgment allows it to advance the window.

The last two of these constraints can vary according to conditions. Constraint (2) is varied by destination instructions (the window field in TCP). Constraint (3) can be varied by instructions from the network to the source.

10.10.2 Retransmission Timeout

This is the limit on how long the sender waits for a response before sending a retransmission of unacknowledged data. The wrong action will result either in unnecessary retransmission or excessive waiting. Unnecessary retransmission (short timeout) is bad for the wastage of network resources; excessive waiting (long timeout beyond the window size) is bad for communicators that want low delay and high average data rate.

The proper timeout setting is closely related to the round-trip time from sending a packet until receiving its acknowledgment. However, this time is not known in advance and varies rapidly and widely in time in a wide-area internetwork. The information available is measurements of packet acknowledgment times, but these can sometimes be ambiguous if retransmission has occurred. In TCP, a version of what is called Karn's algorithm is used to determine timeout setting [COME95]. Basically, timeout adjustments are based on most recent round-trip measurements only for cases where no retransmissions were attempted prior to the acknowledgment (since then the round-trip time is known unambiguously); otherwise, the timeout value is multiplied by a factor of two or more every time a retransmission is required, up to some maximum timeout value.

10.10.3 Frequency and Type of Acknowledgment

There are various options.

1. Acknowledgments (positive or negative) can be made for each individual trans-mitted data unit or packet.

2. Positive acknowledgments can be sent once per group of n packets or irregularly.

3. Acknowledgments can be deferred until they can be piggybacked in a return packet containing data, or they can be sent as soon as possible using an acknowledgment-only packet.

4. Acknowledgments can be cumulative, with the sequence number confirming all packets or octets prior to the stated number, or they could refer to individual packets (as with a selective repeat list).

5. Negative acknowledgments can be used to indicate specific packets needing rep-etition. This can be coupled with infrequent positive acknowledgments.

6. Irregular positive acknowledgments could be sent only as the source commands a response.

10.10.4 Stop-and-Wait or ACK at End of Window

Suppose A has a long sequence of frames to send to B, as in file transfer. The case where A sends a window of frames and then stops and waits for a single cumulative acknowledgment is equivalent to the stop-and-wait strategy with multiple frames outstanding discussed in Section 5.4. The cumulative acknowledgment can be either for the whole window of frames or for an initial subset of the frames as defined by the ACK sequence number. Selective repeat of specific frames in the window is also possible, but more complex to implement.

For a single dedicated channel, stop-and-wait or a single acknowledgment at the end of the window is generally thought of as inefficient because A cannot send while waiting acknowledgment. The fraction of the time spent waiting is just $T_r/(T_r + W)$, where T_r is the round-trip acknowledgment time and W is the time duration of the frame window.

In a statistically shared network, an individual session is almost never given the full capacity of any of the links it uses, except in the short bursts of packet time multiplexing. A particular session cannot and does not need to make full use of the network capacity. The time spent waiting for acknowledgment is available for others and should not be considered as wasted. Also, the reduced acknowledgment frequency of one acknowledgement per window reduces return channel traffic compared to per-frame acknowledgment.

Since ACK at the end of the window is simple and not necessarily inefficient in statistically shared networks, it is worth consideration. Let us consider for this method the interplay of timeout duration, window size, and variable round-trip acknowledgment time. Define the following parameters:

W = the time duration of a window of frames. The exact number of frames in the window is not specified. It is assumed fairly large, as will become evident, but this assumption does not have a critical bearing on the conclusions.

t_r = the round-trip time, measured from the end of the window to the time the acknowledgment is returned and decoded.

T_r = expected value of t_r.

T_{rmax} = maximum round-trip time beyond which acknowledgment is deemed lost.

$f(t_r)$ = the probability density of the round-trip time t_r, conditional that the acknowledgment is not lost.

$e(t_r)$ = excess channel use in a cycle when the round-trip acknowledgment time is t_r.

T_0 = the timeout period, measured from the end of the window. The sender will retransmit at this time if $t_r > T_0$ or if the acknowledgment is lost.

R = A's average successful data rate.

E = A's average excess transmission rate.

C = expected cycle duration.

p = probability an acknowledgment is lost or a decoding failure occurs. Acknowledgments that would take more than some very large time T_{rmax} to return can be counted as lost and included in p.

At the end of a window reception, the receiver B sends back just one acknowledgment. Assume for mathematical convenience that B can accept only the whole window or nothing, and if there is a failure to decode any of the window frames this is equivalent to a lost acknowledgment. This assumption is somewhat pessimistic, because an early negative acknowledgment ($t_r < T_0$) could allow A to start retransmitting sooner. However, if $t_r \geq T_0$ the negative acknowledgment would have the same effect as a lost acknowledgment. Negative acknowledgments are easy to implement in the virtual circuit case when frames are known to arrive in order if they arrive, because an out-of-order reception would indicate a frame has been lost or in error.

However, in datagram networks with out-of-order reception a common occurrence, the receiver will not be sure whether a missing frame has been lost or is just late.

To justify the renewal process assumption we have to assume that if an acknowledgment is lost despite a successful window reception at B, B will respond to the retransmission of that window with a positive acknowledgment only if it receives the retransmission entirely correct; that is, B does not make use of its prior successful reception. Again, this is pessimistic, because a "next expected" response would provide the desired acknowledgment even if the retransmission was not decoded but the original transmission was decoded.

If A has begun to resend a window due to a timeout and the acknowledgment arrives, A is assumed to stop the retransmission immediately and start sending the next window of frames. Actually, it would be more realistic to wait for the end of the frame currently in transmission, but if the number of frames per window is large this is a good approximation.

With these assumptions, the method of renewal cycles can be used. If an acknowledgment is lost the cycle is of length $W + T_0$, and no useful transmission is accomplished with W time units of channel use. If $t_r \leq T_0$ the cycle is of length $W + t_r$, W units of useful data are transferred with W time units of channel use. If $T_0 < t_r < T_0 + W$ the cycle is of length $W + t_r$, W units of useful data are transferred with $W + t_r - T_0$ time units of channel use. This is illustrated in Figure 10.12.

For values of t_r exceeding $T_0 + W$, the receiver might be sending a second acknowledgment. We will ignore the rather rare possibility that the second acknowledgment might arrive sooner than the first. The event would improve performance slightly but is difficult to include mathematically. Once the original acknowledgment gets back, any acknowledgments of retransmissions of the same data will be irrelevant. Thus the cycle ends and the sender begins to send new data. Figure 10.13 shows a plot of the excess channel use, $e(t_r)$; also shown in dashed lines is some hypothetical $f(t_r)$ density.

It now is possible to derive equations for two key parameters of interest: A's effective data rate R and the ratio E/R of excess transmission to successful transmission. Averaging over the cases of loss and no loss,

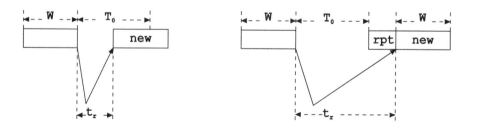

Figure 10.12: Timing for two t_r ranges.

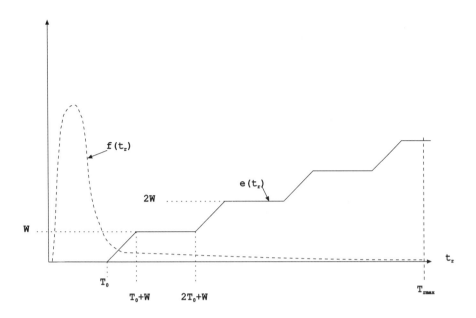

Figure 10.13: Excess channel use as function of acknowledgment round-trip time.

Expected cycle duration,

$$C = W + pT_0 + (1 - p)T_r \qquad (10.1)$$

Average successful data per cycle $= (1 - p)W$.

$$R = \frac{1 - p}{1 + (1 - p)\dfrac{T_r}{W} + p\dfrac{T_0}{W}} \qquad (10.2)$$

$$E = \frac{pW + (1 - p)\int_0^{T_{rmax}} e(t_r)f(t_r)\,dt_r}{C} \qquad (10.3)$$

$$\frac{E}{R} = \frac{p}{1 - p} + \frac{1}{W}\int_0^{T_{rmax}} e(t_r)f(t_r)\,dt_r \qquad (10.4)$$

Certainly the timeout period should be larger than the average round-trip time T_r. It is evident from Figure 10.13 together with the integral in (10.4) that if T_0 is set out near the tail of the $f(t_r)$ round-trip distribution, most of the excess transmission will be just the minimum due to lost acknowledgments. Also, from (10.2), A's success rate will not be much affected by the timeout setting as long as

$$T_0/T_r < (1 - p)/p. \qquad (10.5)$$

Because it is not likely that as much as 10% of the frame window acknowledgments will be lost ($p = .1$), T_0 would have to get to almost 9 times the average round-trip time before A's rate would be significantly affected at $p = .1$. If T_0 were 5–8 times T_r, the tail of $f(t_r)$ that overlaps $e(t_r)$ in the (10.4) integral would in most cases be too small to affect E/R significantly. Thus, at least for the case of the ACK at end of window protocol, timeout settings are not too critical if set on the long side compared to estimated average round-trip time. Of course $f(t_r)$ will change as network congestion varies, so algorithms for changing timeout settings, such as used in TCP, are needed.

The command/response form of acknowledgment is closely related to the ACK at end of window protocol. When the window ends, the last frame can contain a command to respond, and only at that point does an acknowledgment need to be sent. The acknowledgment can be of the cumulative type, acknowledging all frames up to a particular point, ideally to the end of the window.

10.10.5 Higher ACK Frequency and Sliding Window Protocols

Although increasing the frequency of acknowledgments has the undesirable feature of increasing return channel traffic, it carries benefits for the forward channel.

1. It allows continuous transmission if return acknowledgments occur before the window is exhausted.

2. If the next expected sequence number is used to provide cumulative acknowl-edgment, a lost acknowledgment on the return channel is less likely to cause an unnecessary retransmission, because the next acknowledgment will include the information in the lost acknowledgment.

The sliding window protocol is to send back an acknowledgment of every frame, and to set a timeout for each individual frame, rather than at the end of a window. TCP provides for an acknowledgment return for each segment, or frame, but a lost or skipped acknowledgment does not cause an unnecessary retransmission as long as at least one acknowledgment that includes the segment in question arrives before that segment's timeout expires. Selection of acknowledgment frequency is a tradeoff between shorter round-trip acknowledgment time versus increased acknowledgment traffic. Acknowledgments that can be piggybacked on segments going in the reverse direction do not add to traffic.

10.10.6 Selective Repeat Strategies

The cumulative acknowledgment of all frames up to a certain number (indicated by the statement of next expected number) is very useful, but there are times when more feedback information could improve efficiency. The receiver may, for example, be missing only frames numbered 1002 and 1009, but otherwise have received all frames up through 1070. The sender would be informed only "expecting number 1002." (Actually, in TCP it is a byte number rather than a frame number, but this does not change the basic concept.) Assuming the timeout was reached for frame 1002, the sender would begin resending 1002. If the sender sent only frame 1002 and then waited for further feedback information, it might have to wait a long time for the round-trip acknowledgment. This does not cause wasted transmission, but impacts individual user delay and throughput. If the sender continued resending all subsequent frames until a further acknowledgment is returned, there would be a good deal of unnecessary retransmission. In HDLC there is a "selective reject" command in a supervisory frame that allows the receiver to specify a specific frame that needs repeating. This is fine in a virtual circuit connection where frames are known to arrive in the order sent if they arrive at all, but in a datagram network where frames may arrive out of order, a receiver may have a temporary missing frame that will arrive late, and a retransmission request would prove wasteful.

Efficiency thus could be improved if more information were incorporated with the acknowledgment. An example of this was seen in XTP in Section 10.8. It is interesting to speculate on how TCP might be modified for this purpose. The next-expected-byte sequence number is 32 bits in TCP. We have already seen in Section 10.3 that some of these 32 bits could be incorporated into the check sequence without endangering ambiguity protection. If this were done, the bits saved could be used to provide extra feedback information. It would only be important to specify a small number of frames over a rather small number of subsequent frames to gain most of the benefit in saved retransmission.

It would be better for this idea if frames were numbered instead of bytes, because if bytes are missing the receiver is not sure how many frames they represent, and the frame number takes less information than the byte range. Possible solutions are:

1. Incorporate a frame number in the data field, in addition to the standard byte send sequence number. The frame number needs only to be a small number of bits because the byte number provides the ambiguity protection and only a small range of next frames ordinarily is under consideration.

2. When using selective repeat, send a stream of fixed-length frames; then the byte number automatically determines the frame number.

Following is a speculative description of how acknowledgment could be performed with knowledge of frame numbers. Assuming timeout is set on a frame number basis, the extent of subsequent frames would be of the order of the maximum timeout period, since the sender wouldn't be sending any frame later than this time after the next expected frame had been sent. Suppose we set the maximum number of allowed missing frame specifications to be 2. Suppose we used 10 bits as position information, and one bit to identify as selective reject, allowing 21 of the 32 bits of the next expected byte to be stated explicitly, and the rest incorporated in the check sequence. This is illustrated in Figure 10.14.

The byte number would define the first selective reject frame. The first 5-bit group could indicate the span of error-free frames (between 0 and 30) before the next frame needing selective repeat, with the code 11111 reserved to mean there is not a second

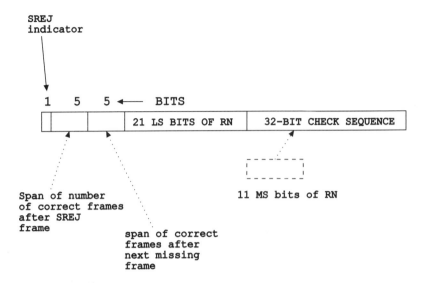

Figure 10.14: Hypothetical incorporation of both frame and byte numbers in a selective repeat scheme. RN = received sequence number (next expected byte); LS = least significant; MS = most significant.

selective reject frame. If the first number is between 0 and 30, the second number is then the number of acknowledged frames after the second selective reject. If the first number is 11111, the second number would be the number of acknowledged frames after the only selective reject. In the previous example where frames 1002 and 1009 were missing, the information would be the next expected byte, a 5-bit block 00110 to indicate six consecutive decoded frames (1003–1008) with 1009 missing, and a 5-bit block 11111 to indicate at least the 31 frames (1010–1040) were received correctly.

If instead only frame 1002 were missing up through 1070, the first 5 bits could be 11111 and the last five 11111, implying the need to repeat 1002 and acknowledgment of frames 1003–1033. The sender would thus repeat frame 1002 immediately. There is not enough information to determine if 1034 and following have been received, but if timeout for 1034 has not expired, the sender could send new frames beyond 1070, or wait.

This example is efficient if gaps are usually single isolated frames. If gaps are often large clusters of frames, the XTP idea (Section 10.8) of specifying spans of correct packets by pairs of numbers would be more effective.

For high-speed data transmission of massive amounts of information the XTP protocol described in Section 10.8 also makes use of selective repeat. There the amount of feedback information is much greater, but the justification is that the amount of forward information to which it refers also is far greater, so the proportion of data transfer devoted to acknowledgment remains small. The following section presents some other ideas related to transfer of massive amounts of information.

10.11   A Transport Protocol Based on Replicated File Comparison

If one sends a large amount of data, such as a file, the task of seeing if it was received entirely correctly, and if not where the error locations are, is similar to the replicated remote file comparison problem, because the receiver now has a copy and would like to verify if it is the same as the one sent.

This idea on handling the problem of selective repeat after mass transmission of information arose from some work by the author [METZ83, METZ90, METZ91] on efficient replicated remote file comparison. Again, it should be noted that this idea has not been implemented to the author's knowledge, although there have been some further studies reported by others [ABDE94A, BARB88, FUCH86] on the file comparison application aspect. The data being sent are presumed to be in units, perhaps called blocks or pages, which might have sequence numbers, but no error detection, in each page unit. The sender computes a parity sequence, sometimes called a signature, for each page, but does not send all the individual page signatures.[1] The signatures are recommended to be about 40 bits. The receiver computes these signatures from its received data, using the same parity rules as the sender. After transfer of the entire file is complete, information about the signatures is exchanged. This information exchange can be done once or in steps, and there is flexibility of the direction of transmission of the extra information. One possible simple first step is that both sender and receiver compute the vector sum of all signatures; then either the sender could include this at the end of its transmission, or, if preferred, the receiver could report back its computed sum. Either way, if the sums agree, it is virtually certain that there are no errors. The original suggestion was that different pages have different parity rules in order to reduce the probability that the vector sum could mask certain common events such as an interchange of two pages. It was suggested that the page address be used as a seed number in a feedback shift register parity sum calculation; then different pages would have pseudorandomly different parity rules on the actual data. In that way, the chance of a false masking is about 2^{-c}, where c is the number of bits in the signature. For 40 bits this is about 10^{-12}.

10.11.1   Finding the Disagreeing Pages

Suppose the overall signatures do not check. Then the task is to find which pages do not agree using as little communication as possible. Perhaps surprisingly, the number of 40-bit signature combinations that need to be sent to determine the locations of the disagreeing signatures is only slightly more than the number of erroneous pages.

---

[1]In some cases it would be easier to send the signature for each page or block and use error detection to find the bad pages. However, if the number of blocks is very large, there can be a substantial communication saving. Also, block size can be adapted to the desired fineness of the error search.

However, this number is not known prior to the search for the disagreeing page locations.

A Parity Check Code Method   Begin with the assumption that the number of disagreeing pages is not likely to exceed some value t. Each site computes a set of syndrome vectors from combinations of its computed page signatures according to the parity check matrix, as in Equation (3.26). One site (could be the source or the destination, but assume it is the destination) sends the syndrome vectors to the other (the source in this case). The source then forms the differences of the syndrome vectors. These differences are related to the signature differences in the same way that the syndrome vectors are related to the error vectors in the Section 3.10 error control coding application. The signature differences play the role of vector symbol errors.

If the disagreeing pages are located, the exact signature disagreements can be found by the decoder as a byproduct. Knowing these actual signature disagreements normally is not needed, although if the block/page units were the same number of bits as the signatures, the receiver could actually derive the correct data from the signature difference information with no further retransmission.

For the case of a maximum distance code structure, the number of page signatures that need to be transmitted could be as small as $t + 1$ [METZ90].

If the assumption is wrong, one approach is to send additional combinations until the code is able to find all the disagreements or until the number of disagreements is so great that it is better to resend the whole file.

Another approach for where the number of disagreements is too great is to apply the combinational method to any level of the tree in Figure 10.15 to find disagreeing sets of pages, which generally would be fewer than the total number of pages that disagree; then further steps could isolate disagreeing pages among disagreeing sets.

It is also possible to carry the procedure into the page by subdividing the page into blocks.

A Binary Tree Structured Method   A simpler approach is to use a binary tree structure of signature combinations. Assume the number of pages is 2^P, a power of two, although if it is not it can be modified simply by assigning zero signatures to unused pages. The tree will have $P + 1$ levels including the root level, which will be designated level 0. Figure 10.15 illustrates the notation being used for the tree structure. The page signatures will be at level P at the ends of the leaves.

Page i data will have a c-bit signature $S[P, i]$. Level k will have 2^k nodes, numbered from $(k, 0)$ to $(k, 2^k - 1)$. The signature at node (k, j) will be denoted $S[k, j]$, and, for $k < P$,

$$S[k, j] = S[k + 1, 2j + 1],$$ (10.6)

where sequences are added as vectors with components over GF(2).

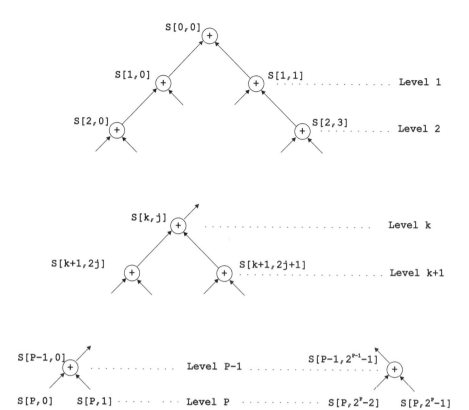

Figure 10.15: Notation for the binary tree structure. *Source:* Adapted from J. J. Metzner, "Efficient replicated remote file comparison," *IEEE Trans. Comput.*, vol. 40, pp. 651–660, May 1991, © 1998 IEEE.

If there is only one disagreeing page, it is shown in [METZ91] that it is sufficient to send only two signature-size units:

$$S[0,0] \quad \text{and} \quad \sum_{i=0}^{2^P-1} \beta^i S[P,i] \tag{10.7}$$

where β is a field element of order greater than 2^P (assume $c > P$), and operations are in $GF(2^c)$.

If there is more than one disagreeing page the two-signature-size approach is not of further help. There is another approach in [METZ91] that is more hierarchical and also does not require any operations in a field other than $GF(2)$. Send, for each level, the vector sum of the signatures at the even numbered nodes for that level. For level

k, this is

$$\sum_{j \text{ even}} S[k, j].$$

This requires $P + 1$ signatures, and it can be shown that it allows immediate discovery of the location of up to two disagreeing pages. However, in the event there are more than two, it still provides useful information. Suppose, at level i of the tree, all the disagreements are confined to at most two branches down to level $i + 1$. The decoder will locate those two branches, and will only need more information when it gets to a level where three or four branches contain page errors. Then, after it gets information to resolve one of the two subtrees from which excessive disagreeing branches arose, it is able to advance further on the other subtree, because that subtree will now have only one or two disagreeing branches at the current level. Thus the errors may be narrowed to much smaller subsets, with the option at any step of either sending more information (using a similar structured sending within a subset) to locate the trouble more precisely or to just resend everything in the disagreeing subsets. In fact, one could even break down the page units themselves in a similar manner, if this proved cost effective. If carried down to signature-sized units, location discovery, if done at the receiver, would lead to immediate correction based on the discovered signature values.

The parameter r corresponds to the number of bits in the signature, and t corresponds to the number of disagreeing pages. An error in a page is reflected in a pseudorandom pattern in the signature differences, so the probability the error vectors will have the linear independence property needed for decoding success is well approximated by $1 - 2^{-(r-t)}$, as in (3.27). The previous procedure will not work if $t > r$ or if the number and position of the errors violates the successful decoding conditions described in Section 3.10. If a maximum distance code such as a Reed-Solomon code is used for the code structure, any case of t or fewer linearly independent page signature disagreements can be located and evaluated for which t is less than the number of transmitted page signature combinations.

10.12   Summary

The traditional use of **dedicated circuits**, as in telephone calls, is less desirable for data transmission because of its sporadic communication over a connection period. **Virtual circuits** provide a nondedicated network path for packetized data transmission. They have the desirable characteristics of greater data transmission efficiency and ordered transmission. A disadvantage is variable delay and occasional unexpected congestion. The **datagram** approach is for each packet or message unit to be separately switched through the network. This has the advantages of requiring no circuit setup, and allowing fast adaptivity to changes in network condition and traffic. The disadvantages are possible out-of-order reception and more source/destination address overhead per message unit. Frame relay and ATM networks use virtual circuit switching, but internet communication uses datagrams.

Networks are required to carry a variety of data traffic types, referred to as **mixed media communication**. Traffic types vary as to reliability and time constraint requirements, but this variation must be considered in designing for efficient as well as reliable communication. In systems with time deadline constraints, some parts of the data may be more critical and should be given added error protection or resources.

Transport protocols are the main tool for ensuring reliable communication. Where networks have low internal bit error rates and high data transmission rates, the trend is to eliminate all or most error control at the link layer and do it at the transport layer. Where all or some links are noisy, however, link error control will remain important for efficiency. Consideration of networks with noisier channels is reserved for Chapter 11. **TCP** is the most popular transport layer protocol. It is most commonly linked with the internet protocol **IP** for communication over a large internet of component subnetworks. IP uses the datagram approach for routing of TCP segments from subnetwork to subnetwork, but within a subnetwork this routing depends on the rules for the particular subnetwork. TCP uses octet numbering, but only the number of the first octet in a segment is reported. Another protocol, TP-4, uses frame numbering.

Transport protocols that can work in a datagram network must deal with the problem of out-of-order receptions and wide delays. Unambiguous segment identification is maintained by the use of large alphabet sequence numbers—31 or 32 bits. Important factors in transport layer design are window size control, retransmission timeout settings, and frequency and type of acknowledgment. The multibit sequences essentially eliminate concern of ambiguity as a limit on window size, but window size can be used as a permission mechanism for rate control.

10.13 Problems

10.1. Refer to Figure 10.1a. Suppose a frame is of duration 1 millisecond and contains 20 slots. Assume the starting times of all frames are synchronized.

    a. If a dedicated circuit instructs that slot 3 on line X is to be switched to slot 2 on line A, how much delay is experienced at the switch?

    b. Repeat part (a) for switching slot 2 to slot 3.

10.2. Suppose a stream of data packets from a source is distributed in round-robin fashion to n buffers, each feeding one of n parallel two-way paths to the destination. Suppose that each path uses stop-and-wait alternating bit transmission. Each path is a virtual circuit, so packets sent on an individual circuit can be assumed to arrive in order if they ever arrive. However, delays and retransmission requests vary differently and randomly on the different paths, so packets do not arrive at the destination in the order generated by the source.

    a. Show that no sequence numbering beyond the alternating bit is needed for the receiver to unambiguously reorder the packets correctly, assuming there are no undirected errors, the receiver knows the order in which the source distributes packets among the n circuits, and the receiver knows which path each packet took. Possibly a path identification number could be used for this purpose if the path was not otherwise obvious.

b. One problem with the above strategy is that the throughput would be limited by the capacity of the slowest path. Suppose the paths have different but known capacities. Devise a modification that more closely maps the different path capacities while retaining the unambiguous reordering capability.

10.3. Refer to Figure 10.3 and the associated discussion. Suppose $i = 4$, $W = 6$, $b = 24$, and there is a 32-bit check sequence in the frame. If an older frame prior to the window arrives, what is the approximate probability the frame will check, thereby possibly causing an error?

10.4. Ten information sources share a common communication link. For each source the data rate generated in each interval is determined by a two-state Markov chain as shown in Figure P10.1. In state A the rate generated is R, while in state B the rate is $0.1R$. After each interval a transition to the same or other state occurs with the probabilities indicated. The 10 sources have identical but independent statistics.

a. What is the average total generated rate?

b. In what fraction of intervals will the total generated rate be $6R$ or higher?

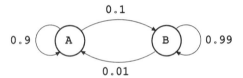

Figure P10.1: Markov chain model for two data rate states.

10.5. Refer to Figure 10.6. Explain whether there would be any confusion if the two ACK 8001 messages from B to A arrived out of order.

10.6. Refer to Figure 10.6. What would be two possible effects of losing ACK 9901?

10.7. Comment on the practicality of conveying conversational digitized voice signals via IPv6 packets.

10.8. If an ATM cell header has a random pattern of errors (all possible patterns equally likely), what would be the probability of undetected error in

a. The error detection mode?

b. The single error correction mode?

If undetected error did occur, make a rough estimate, based on some additional assumptions, of the probability that the cell would be delivered to some wrong destination.

10.9. Since the AAL1 adaptation layer has sequence numbers, there is the possibility of using this mode to allow insertion of redundant cells to correct for lost cells.

In ATM adaptation, consider the following two alternatives for sending a long stream of data:

1. Using AAL1, but including one redundant cell for every 99 true cells, so that one missing cell out of a block of 100 could be reconstructed without a need for retransmission.
2. Using AAL5, including 99 cells in a data frame, and retransmitting the whole frame if one or more cells are lost.

a. Assuming cell losses are random and independent, what is the smallest cell loss probability for which alternative 1 can improve on the efficiency of alternative 2, even if cell losses in excess of one block per 100 can be retransmitted with ideal selective repeat of the lost cells only? Ignore the overheads of the 8-byte AAL5 trailer and the 1-byte AAL1 sequence numbers.

b. Actually, cell losses can be highly correlated, especially when due to congestion. How would this affect the comparison?

10.10. In a stop-and-wait protocol, packets of average duration one millisecond are sent one at a time. One-third of the time an acknowledgment is returned 2 milliseconds after the end of transmission ($t_r = 2$ ms in Figure 10.12a), and a new packet is sent. One-third of the time an acknowledgment is returned 4 milliseconds after the end of transmission, and a new packet is sent. The other one-third of the time the packet is lost or erroneously received, and after timeout $T_0 = 5$ milliseconds the packet is retransmitted.

a. Find the average cycle duration for a packet transmitted.

b. Find the average rate of successful packet transmissions/second.

Chapter 11

Wireless and Noisy Link Multiuser Data Communication

Wireless and noisy link multiuser data communication is a severe challenge to reliable and efficient communication. Wireless communication is one of rapidly growing commercial interest. Also, wireless communication channels are by nature noisy and time varying. Noisy channels also can arise when nonbinary transmission is employed in order to increase the capacity of wired links.

Solutions to the noisy link challenge can draw on principles discussed in all the previous chapters. One big difference from the networks described in Chapters 9 and 10 is the need to pay more attention to symbol transmission errors caused by channel noise. Other important differences are fading, mobility, and different directions of arrival of different received signals. The broadcast feature of wireless networks was given some attention in Chapter 9. However, the assumption that all senders can hear all other senders is often violated in wireless networks. The sender will usually not know, without being informed separately, as to success or collision. Thus, techniques of carrier sense, collision detection, observation of success, and collision resolution may not be appropriate. Also, there is the possibility of successfully decoding some data packets despite collisions.

The noisy and variable conditions result in a much more pervasive role for ARQ and feedback control in system design. Error control coding can reduce the need for retransmissions, but because of the variability of conditions it cannot be predicted in advance how much error correction redundancy is needed to attain a desired reliability. Supplemented with feedback information, additional redundancy can be provided as needed through further information transmission. Also, a feedback channel is needed anyway for power control and other purposes.

Radio transmission space is shared by many uses and users. Thus, wireless communication is subject to strict regulation on permitted bandwidth and transmitted power. Typically, a wireless data network would be allocated a particular band of frequencies and a power constraint. The network itself may choose to divide its resources, such as by frequency (FDM), time (TDM) multiplexing, or code division multiplexing (CDMA). Also, the network may place more severe power constraints on its users to control intranetwork user interference.

Wireless data communication in a network may be a mix of pure data with digitized sound and image transmission, that is, multimedia. Voice and video data usually must be received within a fixed maximum delay, but can tolerate occasional errors. However, if data compression is used, tolerance to error is much less. The usefulness of ARQ techniques is limited by the delay constraint. However, there may be time for several retransmissions during the tolerable delay interval. Pure data can usually tolerate variable delay, but normally cannot tolerate error; thus ARQ is appropriate to such a communication.

A key consideration in mixed media communication is the apportioning of dedicated versus nondedicated communication resources. Nondedicated circuits are more efficient for sporadic data communication that can tolerate variable delay, while dedicated circuits are generally preferred for steady stream data with a delay constraint, such as some voice or video communication. However, it is possible to have a mix of dedicated and nondedicated resources. For example, some channels could be dedicated and some shared. As another alternative, a channel could be dedicated by priority, such that the priority user can have the channel whenever needed, whereas others could use the channel only when the priority user was inactive; for example, if the priority user was a voice conversation, the silent periods could be used to transmit variable delay data. Also, in data compressed voice or video, data generation rate varies with time, and some parts of the message are more critical than others. The more critical parts of the transmitted information can be given extra protection of more redundancy with possibly error correction, or priority against discarding under congestion conditions.

Another important factor in wireless and mobile data communications is the great deal of variability of channel conditions that occurs in addition to the variability of traffic and number of interferers. As explained in Chapter 8, a propagated signal travels from the sender to the receiver via various paths, and these paths change due to motions of the communicators and other objects in the communication path. In narrowband transmission, slight changes in path lengths can easily cause large angular shifts in the carrier phases of the different path receptions. The resultant signal, illustrated in Figure 8.1, can vary greatly in amplitude. In wideband transmission, as exemplified by transmission of a short carrier pulse, the effect of multiple paths is a spreading out of the transmitted pulse; if the pulse is extremely short and there are just a few main reflections, the received response may be a train of pulses of different amplitude, as illustrated in Figure 8.2. These pulses are spread out over the maximum time difference between the significant propagation paths. If the transmitted pulse is broader than this time distance, it appears as a single pulse that is distorted and somewhat broadened, as illustrated in Figure 8.3.

11.1   Limits to Multiuser Channel Efficiency

In a multiaccess network as described in Chapter 9, the principal limitation appears to be other user interference rather than background noise. However, theory shows that the ultimate limit still is background noise.

We have seen from information theory that, for a channel with band limitation to highest frequency F hz and white Gaussian noise of spectral density N_0 at the receiver, the information capacity for a single user with received power P is

$$C = F * \log\left(1 + \frac{P}{N_0 F}\right) \text{ bits/second.} \tag{11.1}$$

For fixed F and fixed N_0, we can write $C(P)$ to emphasize its dependence on the sender's received signal power. A perhaps remarkable result of information theory ([COVE91], Chapter 14) is that if a number of uncoordinated users transmit to the same receiver, the maximum total composite rate at which all users could send reliably to the same receiver is this same $C(P)$ expression, but here P is the total of the received average powers for all receivers (the receiver is assumed to know the codes used by all senders). Thus, introduction of additional senders increases $C(P)$ through the increase in total received power, despite the increasing interference. This is contrary to the practical experience that total system throughput falls off rather rapidly as the interference level increases beyond some point.

Though the result seems surprising, it is easy to see that this could be achieved with perfectly coordinated time multiplexing. Let n users each transmit separately in turn, creating a received power of P during their allotted time slot. Then each could send at rate $C(P)/n$ with an average power over all time of P/n each, yielding a total average throughput of $C(P)$.

It is not obvious that such a high total rate of reliable data transfer rates could be approached in practice without time coordination. There is a great deal of complexity involved with knowing every user's codes and using that information to decode each user's signal. Code division multiple access, to be discussed in Sections 11.4–11.5, allows simultaneous transmission through user code discrimination, but falls far short of the $C(P)$ limit. Two principles that can aid in the goal of decoding multiple interfering signals are: (1) If one signal can be decoded, then subtracting its effect might allow another to be decoded; and (2) In certain cases, the interfering signal effects are approximately equivalent to random noise whose power is equal to the interference power.

To illustrate possible use of these two principles, suppose there are n senders to a common receiver. The senders are presumed to be in symbol synchronism and are sending in the same band of width F with error-correcting codes at rates R_1,

$R_2, \ldots, R_n$ and received powers $P_1, P_2, \ldots, P_n$, respectively. Let the receiver noise be white Gaussian with power density $N_0/2$. If, say one sender i is sending at a rate such that

$$R_i < F * \log \left(1 + \frac{P_i}{N_0 F + \sum_{j \neq i} P_j} \right) \text{ bits/second} \tag{11.2}$$

i's signal can be reliably decoded, in theory, if sufficiently long codes are used. Then, if i's effect could be subtracted out, the effective noise the other senders would see would be reduced by P_i. Thus, if there is a sender k such that

$$R_k < F * \log \left(1 + \frac{P_k}{N_0 F + \sum_{j \neq i,k} P_j} \right) \text{ bits/second} \tag{11.3}$$

then k's signal can be decoded.

This is an idealization. In addition to the complex encoding to achieve these results, the subtraction cannot be perfect. Knowing the particular message does not define its effect exactly unless the channel noise-free response characteristic is known exactly. However, the principle of decoding a signal and subtracting its effect to decode another is an important one in the search for schemes to improve multiaccess efficiency.

For many multiaccess systems, such as wired local networks, the $P/N_0 F$ ratio is quite high, and the main limitation appears to be the interference. However, the information theory result stated previously shows this is not so; the main limitation to total throughput is $C(P)$.

Systems using binary transmission at high signal-to-noise ratio could substantially improve their throughput by using nonbinary transmission. Since both dB and $C(P)$ are proportional to $\log(P)$ for moderately high $P/N_0 F$, achievable capacity is roughly proportional to signal-to-noise ratio in dB. That is, if binary transmission needs 8 dB signal-to-noise ratio to communicate reliably, it should be possible to transmit reliably 5 times as fast at a 40 dB signal-to-noise ratio.

Wired local networks have almost universally used binary transmission and reception in multiple access networks because of the great simplicity and usually adequate channel capacity. Signal-to-noise ratios are ordinarily extremely high in such systems. Thus, there is the possibility of multiplying transmitted rates by 5–10 times by employing nonbinary transmission. There has been little incentive to do this in most past systems, since nonbinary transmission could require high complexity modems at all connected nodes and high complexity repeaters. It is worth noting, however, that high complexity nonbinary transmission modems have proven cost effective for communication over telephone voice channels and other dedicated channels where limited bandwidth makes it important to send more than 1 bit/hz.

Although it may be very complex to decode multiple signals simultaneously, simple slotted ALOHA using nonbinary transmission can achieve up to about 36% of the theoretical limit without the need for multiple simultaneous decoding. Even higher efficiencies are possible if CSMA or collision resolution protocols can be employed. If we take the previous 40 dB example, 36% of 5 yields a slotted ALOHA maximum throughput of 1.8 times what a binary transmission could achieve with perfect coordination. Even in a system such as Ethernet, it might be feasible with some modifications to allow a subset of senders (who have the capability, with suitable modems) to send and receive nonbinary signals during their acquisition of the channel. Others could send binary in the normal manner.

11.1.1 Strongest Signal Capture and Multiple Signal Demodulation

Another possibility of improving efficiency toward the $C(P)$ limit referred to previously is to simultaneously decode interfering signals. One possibility is a capture effect in signal demodulation/detection such as might allow successful decoding of the strongest of several signals. An example of this is the capture effect of wide deviation frequency modulation, where, for two received signals of different strength, the dominant phasor controls the net received phase, whereas the smaller phasor produces only a small perturbation in the resultant phasor. This is also evident if the two interferers both use binary phase shift keying. Assuming the receiver is able to synchronize to the phase and bit timing of the stronger signal, the resultant phase of the two interfering signals can never differ by as much as 90° from the true phase of the stronger (see Figure 11.1), so in the absence of noise this stronger signal could always be correctly decoded. Once the stronger signal has been successfully decoded, it may be possible to decode the other by subtracting the decoded signal from the received signal.

Slight differences in starting time also can be used to discriminate between different signals. This would be particularly valuable in the unslotted case. Signals

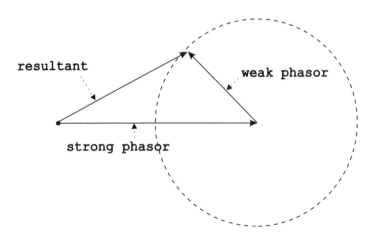

Figure 11.1: Capture of the stronger phasor, binary PSK.

could have short preambles that, if not interfered with, could provide aid in locking onto that signal.

If we could assume that two simultaneous packets could be decoded successfully, but not more than two, the throughput of a system such as slotted ALOHA could be substantially increased. To get a rough idea of the potential, for the infinite number of users model, the throughput would be, instead of (9.2),

$$S = Ge^{-G} + G^2 e^{-G} \qquad (11.4)$$

S is maximized at $G = (1 + \sqrt{5})/2$ and is

$$S_{max} = .840 \text{ packets/slot.} \qquad (11.5)$$

One simple way of using the capture phenomenon to increase the throughput of slotted ALOHA while retaining binary transmission per sender is to use two different packet transmission power levels. Assume that if exactly one strong signal packet is sent in a slot, along with any number of weak signal packets, the strong signal packet is successfully decoded, but the weak one(s) will be lost. Also, assume that it is never possible to decode more than one packet in a slot. This allows a higher efficiency than ALOHA without capture, and it has been shown [METZ76B] that for an optimum proportion of high power senders the maximum throughput is increased from $1/e$ or .368 to about .53 (exact value $e^{-(1-1/e)}$).

Another method of allowing simultaneous decoding of different signals is to use CDMA (code division multiple access), also known as *spread spectrum*. These techniques will be described in Sections 11.4 and 11.5.

Strongest signal capture and multiple signal demodulation techniques are applicable to both wired and wireless communication, but are of greater interest in wireless communication.

11.1.2   Use of Antenna Directivity

In radio communication, antenna directivity and physical location allow creation of additional capacity through spatial separation. Reduction of interference and improved signal capture ability can be created through antenna directivity. Directivity of a multielement antenna can be controlled electronically without any physical motion by changing the weighted sum of signals picked up by the different elements so as to favor signals coming from a certain direction. This is illustrated in Figure 11.2. It is possible to have two different weighting outputs so as to pick up simultaneously two different signals coming from two different directions, as shown in Figure 11.2b.

Directivity can be used to create isolated spatial sectors, so that interference occurs only among senders located in the same sector. It also can be used adaptively to direct the antenna into a narrow beam in the direction of a particular sender.

Arriving electromagnetic wave

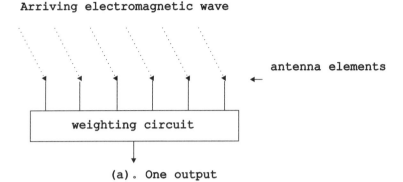

antenna elements

(a). One output

Arriving electromagnetic waves

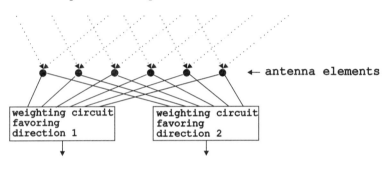

← antenna elements

(b). Two simultaneous outputs.

Figure 11.2: Directivity by phase weighting.

11.2   The Cellular Concept in Mobile Communication

A wireless network can share space as well as frequency and time. Transmitted radio signals are received with power inversely with the square of distance in free space, although in different environments the power falls off differently, usually more rapidly with distance. Thus two transmitters sending in the same frequency band will not interfere significantly at a receiving point if one is sufficiently closer to the receiver than the other and both exercise some constraint on transmitted power. This obvious principle has been applied for a long time in the assignment of AM/FM broadcast licenses in different cities or regions. A station in New York, for example, can transmit in the same frequency band as one in California, with no danger of interference.

Mobile communication systems evolved primarily for telephone communication of voice signals. This meant dedicated circuits, initially using FDM. To provide a larger number of available channels, spacial separation is used in terms of a cell structure. Each cell contains one base station, ideally centrally located. Normally the base stations are stationary, and may be connected through a wired network or directed microwave beams. The cellular arrangement most commonly follows an approximation to a hexagonal pattern, as indicated in Figure 11.3. This is an efficient arrangement that requires only $k = 7$ different kinds of cells with three-cell separation for cells using the same band. Thus cells that use the same frequency bands do not interfere to a significant extent. Of course cell boundaries cannot follow such a regular pattern in areas such as cities with large buildings.

Say the bandwidth available to all cells could support N users if they were frequency division multiplexed. Suppose there are k different cell bands. A cell with a base station is assigned one of the k groups so no two adjacent channels are in the same group. Cells with the same group assignment are spaced sufficiently far apart as to have an interference level below a maximum acceptable amount. Then each cell with its base station could support $\lfloor N/k \rfloor$ users in its region by providing each with a channel using FDM or TDM. With C total cells, a total of $C * \lfloor N/k \rfloor$ channels are available. Thus, the smaller is k, the greater is the number of available channels. The actual channel utilization would rarely be this high because the distribution of users over cells would rarely be uniform at peak capacity.

As density increases, sometimes cells are subdivided into "microcells." Within a microcell, transmitted power would need to be reduced to reduce range and prevent interference.

As a mobile station moves out of a cell, its call needs to be handed off to a new cell and base station. Clearly the system is highly complex, with a need for handoff, frequency assignments, power control, and need to reserve free channels for handoff so calls do not get lost while in progress. Also, at the microcell level, rapid mobility between cells may make the cellular handoff approach impractical.

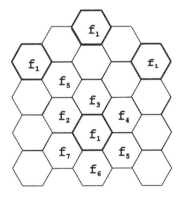

Figure 11.3: Idealized arrangement of cells in mobile radio.

11.3   Packet Radio Communication

With the trend toward digitization of all networks, mobile communication is likely to be on a packetized basis. The packets possibly will conform to the standard ATM format of 48 data bytes in a 53-byte packet. The overhead in a radio transmitted packet might be different than the standard in a wired ATM network, however, because of different requirements and different channel conditions. As a wireless link connection to an ATM network, it does not matter to the rest of the network how much or in what way additional redundancy is added to the radio packet for error control, as long as the rest of the network gets delivered to it the correct 48 bytes of data and the appropriate 5-byte header for communication through the rest of the network.

ARQ could be used on the radio link, as long as the resulting delay did not exceed a given constraint. Several retransmissions may be possible even with voice and video, as long as they can be completed by the specified deadline. It is not current practice to do this, but as packet radio communications goes to higher data rates it may become practical to use ARQ in short distance propagation of voice and video signals. In this case, the object of ARQ is to reduce the proportion of lost packets to an acceptable level, not perfect reliability. Forward error correction can be combined with ARQ in this task; error correction will reduce the average number of required retransmissions, whereas ARQ will provide efficient adaptivity to changing channel conditions. For data transmission, more protection against undetected error is required. The amount provided should be enough to make the probability of packet error comparable to the rest of the network. Otherwise, end-to-end retransmissions that add to the load of the whole network may be required. These excess end-to-end retransmissions would not be needed if the wireless link was made more reliable.

Type I memory ARQ can provide still further benefits to reducing the number of packet retransmissions. In a multiaccess situation, however, there may be a problem of knowing what is a repeat of what. How much of a problem this is would depend on the multiaccess method, the amount of interference, and the physical environment. If retransmissions are known to occur at regular intervals, it should be possible to make the right combinations. The similarity test described in Section 7.7 could be used to see if a combination decision should be attempted. In cases where there is a reservation or dedicated channel, the still more efficient Type II memory ARQ techniques could be used. In some cases antenna directivity could be used to create a dedicated or near-dedicated channel. The effectiveness of memory techniques under varying conditions was discussed in Chapter 8 from the viewpoint of the efficiency for a single user. In a multiuser channel, any scheme that reduces the average transmitted energy per successful bit of a given user has the further benefit of reducing interference seen by other users.

11.4   Direct Sequence CDMA and Spread ALOHA

Spread spectrum techniques originally were developed by the military to overcome jamming and interception of signals. Spread spectrum has the characteristic that the bandwidth used is much greater than would be required by the sender bit rate, so the signal energy is *spread* over a wide frequency *spectrum*. By spreading the signal over the whole band using some pseudorandom code, it becomes immune to jamming by a narrow band tone, and spreading the jamming signal over the whole band requires excessive power unless the jammer knows the code. Most important to the multiaccess situation is that it is possible to send and decode several different signals simultaneously by using different codes for different signals. This technique is called *Code Division Multiple Access* (CDMA). For use in cellular networks, it has the advantage that interference from nearby cells in the same band is less disturbing. There are two types of code division multiple access, called direct sequence and frequency hopping. In this section the direct sequence method will be discussed.

In sending a bit of data in the direct sequence approach, one sends not just a binary signal, but a certain "spreading code" sequence of L binary values, called *chips*. The sending of a data 0 or 1 is accomplished by sending the L-chip sequence or the sequence inverted. Thus bandwidth is spread by a factor of L relative to what would be required by binary transmission at the sender's effective data rate. L is called the *bandwidth expansion factor*. The spreading code is assigned differently for different potentially interfering senders. Different spreading codes are designed to be orthogonal or nearly so. Thus a receiver can decode a particular sender by correlating with a stored copy of the known code for that sender. Other sender's signals each will appear at the correlator output approximately as random noise with power reduced by about a $1/L$ factor compared to its received power.

If all M signals are received at the same power, the desired signal power at the correlator output will be about $L/(M - 1)$ times the net interfering received power. If a competing signal is k times as strong as the desired signal, its noise equivalent effect will be multiplied by k. Thus, in servicing a number of senders to a common base station, power control is used to keep the received powers from the different senders at approximately the same level. To do this, mobile stations far from the receiving base station need to use much greater power than those nearby, which may create greater interference to other base stations operating in the same band.

The spreading is achieved at a considerable cost in data rate. For example, if $L = 128$, which is a common case, the data rate per user is slower by a factor of 128 compared using those 128 bit values for sending data. In exchange, one can have a number of simultaneous users, but not nearly as many as 128. If M users can send reliably, the efficiency is M/L bits/chip. The maximum throughput at an acceptable error rate of a multiple code CDMA system communicating to a single base receiver without use of sectorization by antenna directivity has been estimated to be in the range between 0.1 and 0.2 bits per basic "chip" [TURI84]. A chip is defined as the duration of one of the binary pulses that make up the code. This compares to a limit of .186 for equal packet size unslotted ALOHA.

Capacity of the system can be increased by the use of sectorized antennas. Also, because of the greater tolerance against interference, cells using the same band have less interference effect, except possibly if the same or excessively correlated codes are used by senders in the other cell.

Fading creates both negative and positive effects in CDMA. A negative effect is that it may be very difficult to keep the received powers equalized. A positive effect arises from some signal processing capabilities. With multipath fading, components of the desired signal arriving over multiple paths can be combined by their correlation properties to enhance the probability of successful decoding. A receiver that performs this combination is known as a rake receiver [PRIC58].

11.4.1 Orthogonal Codes

Since the sending of just one bit in L intervals is a rather extravagant use of bandwidth, a possible option is to send k bits, $k > 1$, in L intervals by selecting from one of 2^L length L sequences that are chosen to be orthogonal. This improves the bandwidth efficiency but at the cost of greater complexity. An analysis of such orthogonal codes and their bandwidth efficiency appears in Section 9.6.6 of [PAHL95].

11.4.2 Spread ALOHA

This section describes some interesting relationships between spread spectrum and ALOHA communication. It may seem surprising to see a connection, since ALOHA ordinarily is designed to avoid simultaneous transmission, whereas spread spectrum plans for simultaneous transmission.

Abramson [ABRA94] has suggested an idea of everyone using one code, in a scheme he calls "spread ALOHA." Assume that different users are not synchronized as to starting time. Figure 11.4 shows the output of a receiver after correlation when two senders are transmitting with a different starting times d seconds apart. The result is two interleaved streams of spikes, which represent the two data streams. As

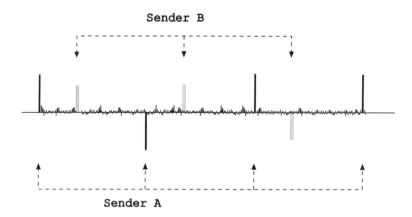

Figure 11.4: Spread ALOHA with two interferers. *Source:* Adapted from N. Abramson, "Multiple access in wireless digital networks," *Proc. IEEE,* vol. 82, pp. 1360–1369, September, 1994. © 1998 IEEE.

long as the starting times of the interfering signals are not too close, which is usually the case, they can be separated, as shown. In packetized transmission, ID or circuit numbers in the packet will identify the sources of the different streams. Abramson makes a good case that using a single code is about as good as the multiple code case, and is much simpler. He points out one exception, however. In the case of multipath fading, there is a method whereby the multicode receiver can combine the different delay paths belonging to the desired code so as to reinforce it, whereas the single code could not distinguish between the different delay paths and other senders with different delay times, unless the starting times were well separated.

This idea leads the author to observe the following: A similar effect can be had by not using any code at all! Suppose a particular user sends a pulse train for a packet at a high bandwidth, pulse width τ, but much lower duty cycle, $T \gg \tau$. Figure 11.5 illustrates two different data pulse trains.

If two different senders use almost exactly the same T values but have a random fixed time difference they will in most cases not overlap over a long sequence of bits. The probability of interference is roughly the ratio $2\tau/T$, because the closest pulse spacing that can be distinguished is of the order of τ. Thus, the different senders often can be simultaneously decoded by their separation in time and known spacing T between successive pulses in a packet, without a spreading code. In contrast to *spread ALOHA multiple access* and CDMA, the deconvolution already exists through the short time-separated pulses. Also, even partial overlaps have a possibility of successful decoding based on timing, power differences, and other simultaneous decoding methods.

If the pulse trains drift slightly by an amount Δt per cycle, there is a probability of about the lesser of $(n\Delta t + 2\tau)/T$ and 1 that they will overlap somewhere. However, if the sender can lock on entirely to the time spacing of the desired signal, this overlap may affect only one, none, or a small number of bits. For $\Delta t < \tau$ it would affect roughly $\lfloor 2\tau/\Delta t \rfloor$ bits, whereas for $\Delta t > \tau$ it might affect only 0, 1, or 2 bits. The

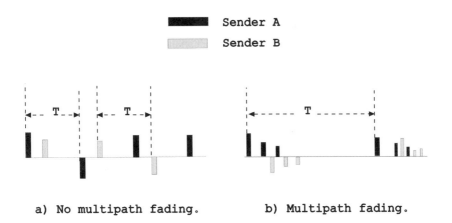

a) No multipath fading.   b) Multipath fading.

Figure 11.5: Two senders in pulse time spread ALOHA.

capture possibility due to unequal powers could reduce the chance of error for the higher power interferer; it could result in erased bits rather than error bits for the low power interferer.

Perhaps this technique could be called *pulse time spread ALOHA*. As with CDMA, performance would degrade with increasing number of users, although error statistics would be somewhat different. Pulse time spread ALOHA, and also spread ALOHA, need to rely more on ARQ, because there is a small but significant probability that one interferer will cause a packet loss, whereas in CDMA it is highly unlikely that just one other interferer will cause a packet loss. The high peak-to-average power ratio for individual senders also is a disadvantage of the pulse time spread ALOHA technique.

Another way of viewing pulse time spread ALOHA is as a sort of unorganized time division multiplexing. If a time slotted frame organization were created, with random selection of a time slot and when to send, it would be similar to a multichannel ALOHA system. Other methods of organization would be to require a reservation to send, or a command to adjust timing if two senders were too close in time.

It is interesting to look at the effects of fading in pulse time spread ALOHA, which is illustrated in Figure 11.5b. If the randomly interleaved pulse trains have a very small value of pulse duration τ, they will look like impulses to the fading channel. Each pulse will produce a fading multipath channel response [PROA89] approximating several impulses, one for each significant propagation path. In many cases one will dominate. The data pulse response components will be of varying size, delay, and number, though varying at a relatively slow rate. The dominant component will vary slowly with time, but is likely to prevail during a packet transmission. Another user causes a train of pulses whose main peak usually will occur at a different time, though its echoes also may interfere with the desired user's signal. How the interference varies from bit to bit will depend on the channel variations and on how closely the bit periods of the different users are synchronized. To lock onto a particular user, the receiver can search for its strongest impulse point, and follow that every T seconds. Most of the samples observed will come primarily from the desired signal. A more sophisticated decoder could make use of the echoes also, by following displaced trains that correlate well with the principal train. This is somewhat like the Rake receiver idea in CDMA. Just as with CDMA, several users can be decoded simultaneously, but also as in CDMA, the rate of a particular user is far below the pulse rate $1/\tau$.

11.5   Frequency-Hopping CDMA

There is a distinction made between fast and slow frequency hopping. In fast frequency hopping there are a number of hops per bit or per basic nonbinary symbol; in slow frequency hopping there are several bits or nonbinary basic symbols per hop, but the next hop involves a new set of bits. We will look first at a popular form of fast frequency hopping.

11.5.1 Fast Frequency Hopping with Q-FSK Basic Symbols

In this scheme the code sends a basic k-bit symbol using a length L hopping pattern among Q frequencies in L τ-second pulse times. $Q = 2^k$, and k bits are sent in time $T = L\tau$. The process is best visualized as a two-dimensional frequency-time array, as shown in Figure 11.6. In the figure example, $Q = 8$, $k = 3$ bits and $L = 7$. A chip is defined as one of the $QL = 56$ boxes in this array, and a chip duration is τ. If, instead, a single user put a bit of information into each chip, a total of 56 bits could be sent, but only 3 (in general k) bits will be sent. Thus, the spreading factor is $QL/k = 56/3$. To send 3 bits of data, one of the eight tones is selected, say tone 4, as indicated in Figure 11.6a. A random sequence (the hopping pattern) of seven octal numbers is added modulo 8 to the selected tone number. Then the frequency hopped pattern of Figure 11.6b is transmitted (shaded boxes indicate the transmissions).

The receiver makes a presence/absence (hit/miss) decision in each chip, and then translates the positions of the decisions by subtracting the hopping pattern modulo 8. If there are no other senders and no errors, the pattern of Figure 11.6a should appear, revealing the data value 4. With other interfering senders, several chips may show a hit in each time slot. Usually, the effect of interfering senders will be just to add hits, though on rarer occasions there can be destructive interference that could cause a hit-to-miss error in a chip. Also, background noise could cause either type of error.

Figure 11.7 shows the received pattern with the same desired signal transmission as in Figure 11.6, but with an additional interferer using a different hopping pattern (in this example there is no destructive interference or noise; also, the interferer is

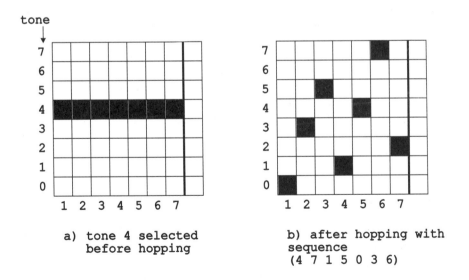

a) tone 4 selected
before hopping

b) after hopping with
sequence
(4 7 1 5 0 3 6)

Figure 11.6: Frequency hopping as a two-dimensional array.

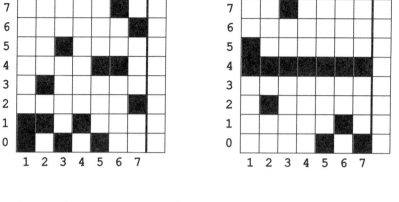

a) received   tone matrix
   with an interferer

b) after dehopping by
   subtracting sequence
   (4 7 1 5 0 3 6)

Figure 11.7: Two-dimensional frequency hopping array with interferer.

assumed to be in chip synchronism). After dehopping, the desired signal creates a row 4 with all hits. The interfering signal has its hits scattered. The receiver decision will be the row with the greatest number of hits. Without destructive interference or noise, the correct row will be all hits; however, with many interferers there is a significant chance of another row of all hits. With destructive interference and noise, the correct row can also have misses.

A Simple Upper Bound on Performance   The case of interference only, no hit-to-miss destructive interference, no fading, chip synchronism, and randomly chosen codes is a simple one to analyze. It is overly optimistic, and can serve as an upper bound to efficiency performance.

Suppose there are M simultaneous users. Assuming acceptable reliability, the efficiency is

$$\eta = Mk/QL \text{ bits/chip.} \tag{11.6}$$

Obviously, η cannot exceed 1 with hit-miss binary chip decisions.

A given interferer has probability Q^{-1} of using a particular tone at a particular time slot (although chip synchronism is assumed, it does not matter under the random hopping pattern assumption whether the interferer is in L-symbol frame synchronism). The probability that a particular chip has at least one signal due to the $M - 1$ interfering users is $[1 - (1 - Q^{-1})^{M-1}]$, and the probability that a random wrong row is all filled with hits is

$$P_1 = [1 - (1 - Q^{-1})^{M-1}]^L. \tag{11.7}$$

If more than one row has all hits, the receiver is assumed to make a random choice among the candidate tones. With this procedure, it can be shown [HASK81] that the probability of deciding the wrong sequence is upper bounded by $QP_1/2$. Because about $1/2$ of the bits, on average, will be decided in error if the wrong symbol is chosen, the postdecoding bit error probability is about $1/2$ of this, or

$$P_b = QP_1/4. \tag{11.8}$$

Equations (11.6–11.8) allow simple calculation of efficiencies that can be achieved for desired bit error probability. For example, if $Q = 256$, $L = 20$, and $P_b = 10^{-3}$, η is about .34, which corresponds to about 217 simultaneous users. Figure 11.8 shows how bit error probability varies with efficiency $\eta = Mk/LQ$ when $Q = 256$ and $L = 20$. The $h = 0$ labelled curve is the one applicable; the meaning of the $h = 6$ curve will be explained shortly.

Of course this bound on performance is very optimistic, given the idealized assumptions. With noise, fading, or destructive interference, there may be a significant probability that the right tone will not show all hits, in which case there is a much greater chance that some wrong tone will get an equal or greater score. Without chip synchronism, there is a likelihood that an interferer's chip transmission will influence two successive chip decisions; in the worst case this could double the effective interference.

In direct sequence CDMA there is considerable concern about the choice of code sequences, which are orthogonal or nearly orthogonal. In frequency hopping with a Q as large as 256 and $L = 20$ this is not of much concern. Let $\mathbf{v_i}$ be the interferer's hopping sequence, let $\mathbf{v_d}$ be the desired signal's hopping sequence, and let $\oplus$ represent modulo Q vector addition. Then the maximum interferer contribution to a false row will be the maximum number of identical values in the vector $\mathbf{v_i} \oplus \mathbf{v_d}$. With each component having 256 possible values, the maximum repetitions in L components will almost always be a small fraction of L. Unless a very careless method were used for generating the hopping patterns, one individual interferer rarely would make a significant difference; it is the number of other interferers that is of most concern. Note also in this case there are 2^{160} different frequency hopping patterns!

Spread spectrum communication deteriorates gradually in the presence of increasing amount of interference. This is reflected in the postdecoding bit error probability increase with M, as shown in Figure 11.8. Data communication requires lower final bit error probabilities, but error correcting codes and/or ARQ can bring the error probability down to acceptable levels. One must be careful to take into account, however, that increased redundancy means increased transmission time and increased interference, which can be counterproductive if not done in an efficient manner. In the case of frequency hopping with $Q = 256$, correction is more effectively carried out on an 8-bit symbol basis than on a binary basis, since the errors occur in these 8-bit clusters, which would count as just one symbol error, instead of an average of about 4 bit errors. Thus Reed-Solomon codes or other nonbinary codes would be most appropriate.

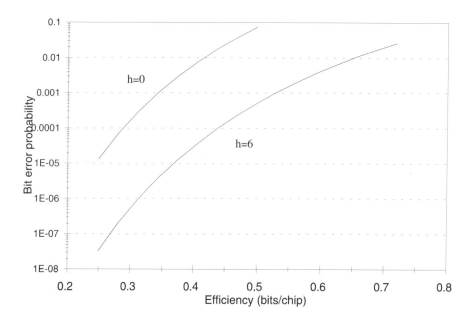

Figure 11.8: Bit error probability versus efficiency.

Thoughts on Use of Memory ARQ Suppose ARQ is being employed based on error detection in a block of n Q-ary symbols, which possibly employs error correction as well. When an error is made on a Q-ary symbol with frequency hopping, usually the correct symbol value was a close contender. Thus it can be wasteful to discard the undecodable transmission information. One memory scheme proposed by [KIM91] is to save the QL presence-absence decisions and do a logical AND with the corresponding symbol decisions in the retransmitted block. The argument is that the retransmission should still all be present in the correct row, while the interference will be randomly different. In the absence of erased symbols, the correct row will be filled both times and lose nothing by the ANDing, while the incorrect row will likely lose a great deal.

Where there is a great deal of fading or otherwise erased symbols this procedure will be less effective, since different parts of the correct row may be lost each time and the ANDing will reduce the number of hits. In this case, a better method might be to remember just the number of hits per row each time and add this number per row for successive transmissions. Then a competing wrong decision that had a high score the first time can expect only an average score the second time.

A Thought on Two-Power-Level Transmission We have seen in Section 11.1 that the use of two power levels can increase the limiting efficiency of slotted ALOHA from 36% to 53%. Also, direct sequence spread spectrum communication from mobiles to a common base station normally utilizes power control to ensure about equal received power from all senders. Although equal received power is less critical in frequency hopping spread spectrum, it could be employed. This suggests the possibility to allow a user two levels of power; each user would be allowed use of high power for h of the L chip intervals, in randomly assigned positions, as an additional property of the hopping code. The other $L - h$ positions would be at low power. If interference is the main consideration, the separation between powers can be great enough so that in each of the QL chip positions the following three events can be distinguished reliably: (1) One or more high power transmissions occurred; (2) no high power transmission has occurred, but at least one low power transmission has occurred; (3) no transmissions have occurred in the chip. With these assumptions, it is shown [METZ84C] that, for the same idealized assumptions just mentioned, efficiency can be improved substantially. For $Q = 256$, $L = 20$, the optimum h is 6. The improvement is indicated by the $h = 6$ labelled curve in Figure 11.8. For a bit error probability of .001, the efficiency in bits/chip is raised from .34 to .53.

A Pulse-Position Modulation Equivalent If hopping among 256 frequencies happens to be impractical, a possible alternative is to have frames of 256 time slots and to hop in time position over L successive frames. To express this analytically, let the time slot be one unit duration, and let $p(t)$ be a pulse in time 0 to 1. Then a byte value k can be communicated in an L-frame interval by sending the pulse position modulation chain

$$\sum_{i=0}^{L-1} p(t - k - 256i - d_i) \tag{11.9}$$

where a delay hopping value d_i is between 0 and 255, according to the given hopping pattern. Assume the demodulator knows the starting time of the frame and L-frame interval. Possibly this could be learned through a preamble. The demodulator can first make a present–absent decision in each slot and regenerate a clean fixed-size pulse or zero in that slot. It then applies a delay $256 - d_i + 256(L - i)$ to the clean pulses in frame i, producing the response to the desired signal of:

$$\sum_{i=0}^{L-1} p(t - k - 256i - d_i) - (256 - d_i) - 256(L - i)$$

$$= \sum_{i=0}^{L-1} p(t - k - 256(L + 1)) = Lp(t - k - 256(L + 1)) \tag{11.10}$$

Interference will produce pulse values in the other positions with magnitude proportional to the number of interfering hits in the positions, usually much less than L. Thus a decision on k corresponding to the largest pulse of 256 will usually be correct. Alternatively, a delay of $256 - d_i$ could be employed; this would produce the train of L pulses

$$\sum_{i=0}^{L-1} p(t - k - 256(i + 1)). \tag{11.11}$$

Then the number of hits out of L could be counted for each position (ideally, L for the correct position). Proper identification of the position value requires knowledge of the starting point of the frames of the sender being decoded. Possibly a differential form of modulation could be used if the starting point was not accurately known.

The same idealized analysis leading to the same results as Figure 11.8 can be performed for the pulse position modulation method. In the two-power case, the frames in the sequence of L devoted to high power are known as part of the code designation, so in those frames the presence decision threshold is set at a higher level, because any lower power pulses can be presumed to be interference.

Actually, the pulse position modulation hopping is related to the orthogonal signals version of direct sequence CDMA described in Section 11.4. The alternative PPM hopped signals of a given user are orthogonal because they have no common time overlap. Correspondingly, in fast frequency hopping the Q alternatives of a sender also are orthogonal because they do not overlap in any frequency-time chip.

11.5.2   Slow Frequency Hopping

In slow frequency hopping, one of Q frequencies is selected at random, and b bits are sent over some time T at that frequency in the selected band, using any appropriate modulation method confined to the selected band. In the next interval, another b bits are sent at time T, but in a probably different band, according to the hopping pattern. There is no special relationship between b and Q. This differs substantially from fast frequency hopping as to the effect of a hit; a hit basically destroys the b bits sent in the interval T, but does not affect the other b-bit sending intervals. An error- or erasure-correcting code is needed to reconstruct the bit groups that are hit.

The performance of slow frequency hopping can be likened to Q parallel channels of slotted ALOHA, except the slots would only be parts of packets. Given $M - 1$ interferers, it is approximately as if the interferers decide randomly and independently at which frequency to be at a given time. Thus, the probability a sending of b bits does not get interfered with is

$$P_{NI} = (1 - 1/Q)^{M-1}. \tag{11.12}$$

For large Q and M, this is approximately $e^{-M/Q}$. Thus the total successful throughput is

$$MP_{NI} = Me^{-M/Q} = Q(M/Q)e^{-M/Q}. \tag{11.13}$$

The maximum of (11.13) occurs at $M/Q = 1$, and is Qe^{-1}. Because there are Q channels, this represents a maximum efficiency of e^{-1}, just as with slotted ALOHA.

However, at the maximum throughput point, about $1 - e^{-1} = .632$ of the transmitted b-bit units will be destroyed, which requires a considerable amount of error/erasure correction. Erasure correction could be done by using a Reed-Solomon code with sufficient redundant symbols to fill in the erased symbols; this has been suggested by [KIM92]. However, this is more inefficient than ALOHA, because not only are the erased symbols lost (because the code must add as many redundant symbols to reconstruct them), but also the information in the nonerased symbols is lost if the number of erasures exceeds the correcting capability. This latter lost information could be recovered, however, if incremental redundancy memory techniques were used.

11.6 Reservation in Packet Radio Networks

ALOHA and CDMA are in the collision tolerance category. ALOHA tolerates collision in the sense that ARQ and retransmission are used to remedy the effect, or capture of the strongest signal might be used. CDMA tolerates collision by using individual codes to decode in the presence of simultaneous transmission.

The other solution is to try to avoid any simultaneous transmission within the range of a base station. The use of dedicated channels is generally to be avoided in data networks because data communication is very sporadic. Even voice signals encounter silent periods that take up a large proportion of conversation time, and with video the data generated can vary widely with different amounts of picture detail and motion. These silent or low-rate periods could be used for other communication.

CSMA can be difficult to implement over wireless networks, because the senders can only learn of channel status and communication success through base station feedback information. Because the base station is providing feedback anyway, it makes sense to use the base station as a control for reservation schemes, as discussed in Section 9.2, to get rather efficient communication with almost no collisions. This also allows giving short-time dedicated access to a particular communication and implementation of priority rules. These capabilities are especially important to delay-constrained communication, such as voice or video.

Thus, there are packet reservation multiple access schemes (PRMA) [GOOD89] for packet radio networks. All participating stations are presumed to be sending to some central base station. The base station broadcasts slot timing and reservation acknowledgment results to all in its control range. In these schemes priority is given to the user having strict delay constraint, such as packetized voice, over other data transmissions. Time is divided into frames with a number of slots, each slot being the correct size for a voice packet, at a one-slot-per-frame rate. If a sender needs to send a stream of packets for a while, at a rate of one slot per frame, this is referred to as periodic traffic. Senders needing to continue to use the slot place a reservation 1 bit in their packets; others place a reservation 0 bit. Senders contend in slotted ALOHA fashion for one of the currently idle slots. If a sender with a reservation 1 bit wins the slot contention, it continues to be given exclusive use of the slot until it stops using the slot. Then the slot becomes available for contention. If a sender with a reservation 0 succeeds, the slot it used can be contended for next time by any sender.

There are still some collisions in the contention slots, but these are relatively rare. If one allowed voice packets to send at a higher power than data packets (but just in the contention mode) a voice packet would almost always win the contention over any data packet, and could then obtain the slot reservation immediately. New voice conversations could avoid slots that currently are carrying a conversation, thereby minimizing any chance of two voice requests colliding and both being lost.

Reservation methods have good potential efficiency. There are some problems, however, when one considers effects of fading, noise, and channel interference outside of the base station's control. If a stream of packets encounters an error due to noise or interference, it is not known whether the reservation should be continued. With varying signal strengths due to fading, if two senders send at the time, it often happens that only the stronger one of the two can be decoded, and which is stronger may vary rather rapidly with time. A sender of a stream of data that encounters a fade may fail to be received, whereas another sender may have been successful if it had tried. Possibly power control could be used to allow the reserving sender to increase its power during a fade.

11.7   A Multibase ALOHA Scheme

A shortcoming of reservation systems is that they assume only one sender can be received successfully at a given time, and that a particular sender will be successful if the others under control will not send. Considering the powers of antenna directivity, space diversity, effects of fading, and sophisticated decoding techniques, collision avoidance is not always the best way to use communication resources efficiently. Although CDMA allows decoding of several senders that send simultaneously to a common base station, individual senders are limited to data rates that are a very small percentage of system capacity. CDMA can, however, increase system through-put through antenna directivity sectorization, diversity reception, and correlation of multipath reflections.

Also a problem in mobile communication is the need to handoff a connection as the position of the transmitter changes. In microcell layouts, where cells are very closely spaced, this chore might have to be done quite frequently. A great deal of coordination between the base stations is needed because of this handoff problem. Thus it is normal for base stations to communicate and cooperate.

11.7.1   The Random Forwarding Concept

With ALOHA, there is an alternative method of dealing with multiple base stations. Base stations need to intercommunicate, and have a fixed network for that purpose. This allows an idea that has been proposed [SIDI88] called random forwarding. The technique applies to the mobile-to-base link. This is generally the one of most concern, because fixed base stations can more easily coordinate their base-to-mobile transmissions. In random forwarding, there are no separate cells over a fairly large set of base stations. A mobile sends a packet, and if the packet is received correctly by any of the base stations, it is considered successful. The base station network is considered able to recognize duplicate packets, which should be easy to do since they arrive at almost the same time and will have the same identification.

Figure 11.9 illustrates a typical configuration. The base stations are denoted by squares and letters, while the mobiles are denoted by circles.

Suppose the five shaded mobiles are the ones currently transmitting. With the indicated positions, it is likely that three of the transmitters are likely to be successful, as indicated by the solid arrows. Mobile 5 is in fact successful to two base stations. Mobiles 3 and 4 may not be sufficiently closer to a base station than one of the others, so are likely to fail. With fading and different powers, the success events for this set of transmitters could be quite different at different times.

The acknowledgment can be returned by one of the receiving base stations, probably the one that received the strongest signal. Together with the acknowledgment, any necessary power control or other transmission control instruction for the next transmission can be communicated. This allows control of excessive interference power; it is not necessary, however, that powers be equalized, as unequal powers actually can be an advantage, as has frequently been pointed out [ARNB87, BORG96, HABB89, LAU92, LEE87, ROBE75, ROBE92, SAKA92, ZORZ94]. As the mobile moves, the acknowledging base station may change, but in most cases nothing special has to be done as long as the mobile does not leave the network of base stations. A single base station can act additionally as multiple stations through antenna sectoring, or can lock onto one or more particular senders through adaptive antenna directivity. Narrow beam adaptive directivity can be used to create a quasi-reservation channel

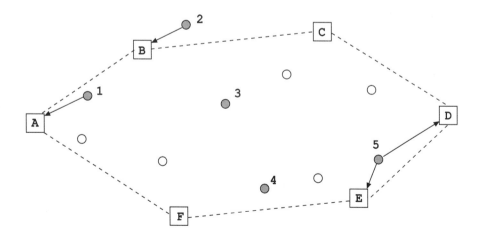

Figure 11.9: A typical configuration for random forwarding to multiple base stations.

for a given sender. This can also allow the sender to use less power and create less interference for others.

11.7.2   Power Control

Tight power control is employed in CDMA systems to equalize as much as possible the received power from the several simultaneous senders. This is because the objective is for all transmitting signals to have a high probability of success almost all the time. If one signal were much weaker than the others, interference would overwhelm the benefits of correlation with the weak signal's code and prevent decoding it successfully. Power control also is useful in ALOHA systems, but the objective is different. Because of the high individual rate when a sender is sending, ARQ can be used to allow the sender additional tries while maintaining a satisfactory successful throughput. Also, senders are sending at a much smaller fraction of the time due to using the full data rate when transmitting. Equalization of received power is neither critical nor desirable, because throughput with capture capability usually is better when received powers are unequal. However, power control could easily be incorporated into the acknowledgment signals to ensure that the amount of transmitted power is not much in excess of what is needed for success, so as to minimize interference. For example, if a steady rate mobile sender was accommodated by a highly directive base station beam, the mobile could be instructed to reduce its (omnidirectional) power to minimize interference with others.

Power control could be used for other purposes as well. A sender that is not getting any response could perhaps be allowed to increase power. Senders that are heard but continually violate a power reduction instruction could be controlled by returning a data refused signal. It also could be used to ensure success under a time constraint, and for other priority and fairness considerations.

In addition to instantaneous power, minimization of total transmitted energy per successful unit of data transmitted is of interest. This is related to the use of ARQ strategies, which will be discussed next.

11.7.3   ARQ in Multibase ALOHA

The uncertain nature of ALOHA transmission requires some form of acknowledgment. Under conditions of high mobile-to-base traffic, packet-by-packet acknowledgment may be needed. Although stop-and-wait ARQ is normally thought of as less efficient than continuous transmission, this is necessarily not the case in a multiuser environment, because no interference is generated during the wait period, and efficiency in terms of energy utilized per success is higher than in a go-back scheme in a noisy environment, and as high as selective repeat.

ARQ is potentially at a disadvantage for time-constrained traffic. However, since ALOHA can use the full band, packet transmissions can be much shorter than in more bandlimited systems, and propagation distances to base stations also are short in local area or in-building networks, which may be the most suitable types of networks for using ALOHA. Thus there may be time for several packet retransmissions in the time that a more bandlimited system would take to transmit the packet once. Thus ARQ could be used effectively in digitized voice transmission. Alternatively, the use of a directed antenna at the base station combined with power control might eliminate or ease the ARQ requirement.

Ideally, one would like to use memory ARQ, where the information in a nondecodable packet is not discarded, but is combined with future receptions of the packet. Incremental redundancy techniques are particularly efficient, because they can approach efficiency at whatever channel capacity "unfolds." Memory ARQ may not always be feasible in the multibase ALOHA system, because without decoding the packets it may not be clear which belong to the same packet data. There is the possibility of using a similarity test [METZ85A]: if two undecodable receptions correlate closely enough, combine them; otherwise do not combine them. This similarity test is very easy to do compared to error correction. In the case where all retransmissions are heard by one base station, combining would be easier to accomplish. Memory may be applicable in continuous flow as voice/video, with an "almost" reserved channel such as directivity could provide.

Many forward error correction schemes exhibit a coding gain, reducing the average energy needed for a given success probability. They can also be combined with ARQ.

11.7.4 Efficiency of ARQ without Combining

Even without combining, ARQ can be effective in reducing the energy utilized. Without ARQ, one might try to send more energy (either by more power or longer packet duration) to increase the success probability. Often this will result in sending more energy than needed.

As an illustration, say there is time to send up to N attempts with ARQ to meet a time constraint. Without ARQ, one might just send N copies. If an amount of energy E is used in one sending, suppose the probability of failure is p_0. If up to N attempts are made, assuming the same probability p_0 on each attempt, independently, the probability of failure is $p_0^N = P$. The expected energy utilization, assuming the sender always stops after a success, is readily shown to be

$$E_{N-ARQ} = \sum_{i=0}^{N-1} p_0^i E. \qquad (11.14)$$

If the sender did not stop but always sent N copies, the same failure probability P would be achieved, using total energy NE. Figure 11.10 shows a plot of the ratio

$$NE/E_{N-ARQ}$$

for $P = .01, .001, .0001$. It is seen that there is a large saving of energy for rather small values of N, and the value increases with N.

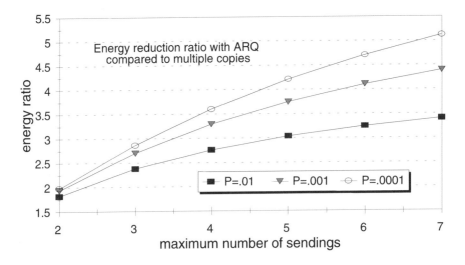

Figure 11.10: Energy reduction with ARQ compared to sending N copies. No combining is assumed for both cases.

Actually, just boosting the power would not generally decrease the failure probability as fast as exponentially with power in a fading/interference environment; with ARQ the probability would go down exponentially provided successive sendings were independently affected by noise, fading, and interference. Thus the comparison with ARQ would in most cases be even worse with the power-boosting strategy than indicated in Figure 11.10. However, if the extra energy were employed by sending a fixed N copies sufficiently spaced in time that the same ARQ assumption of independent failure probabilities per sending applied, then the comparison would be precisely as shown in Figure 11.10.

Further improvements can come from an ARQ strategy of increasing transmitted power as one approaches the deadline.

11.7.5   Diversity Reception and Combining

It is well known that multiple antennas or antenna elements at a receiving station can permit enhanced successful reception through combining information about a given signal and separation of different signals [BREN59]. The combining aspect is closely related to multirepetition combining in ARQ, but has the advantage that all copies are received at about the same time. Diversity occurs because the fading condition can be different at antennas that are not very far apart, and thus it is likely that at least one antenna gets a strong signal. The random forwarding idea also is a form of diversity reception among the multiple base stations. However, it would not normally be feasible for all the base stations to relay their exact receptions to a central point for processing. Most likely, the individual stations would do their own detection/correction for each packet, and report only packets with corrected or undetected errors. A more complex and demanding alternative for the base network would be for each base station to make preliminary binary or ternary decisions per bit reception for any sufficiently recognizable packet and feed all those to a central processing point. At the least, one has the diversity reception feature that the packet is successful if it is successful at any base station.

11.7.6 Fading Effects

Fading has both a positive and negative effect on ALOHA system performance. Positive is the capture effect, whereby the signal that happens to be the strongest gets to be successful, and at different times different senders will be successful, thereby contributing to fairness as well as greater throughput. A negative effect occurs due to high packet transmission rate, whereby frequency selective fading distorts the signal and causes more intersymbol interference within the packet and more sensitivity to interfering signals than at lower rate. This could be combatted by using a set of frequency multiplexed ALOHA channels from which a sender could select a channel at random.

11.7.7 A Simplified Multibase Example

The model to be presented is purely hypothetical, but it suggests something about the potential of multibase ALOHA communication under widely varying channel conditions, such as exemplified by fading. Let there be M mobiles and B base stations, and assume a slotted system. Define an $M \times B$ matrix, such that the (m, b) entry describes the current state of the channel from mobile m to base station b. For our simplified model we will assume the entry is simply 1, meaning b can hear m; or 0, meaning b cannot hear m. To model rapid fading in a simplified manner, we assume that in each time slot the entry assumes the value 1 with probability p_h and 0 with probability $1 - p_h$, independent of other matrix entry values. Also assume that if mobiles m_1 and m_2 send to base station b and both entries (m_1, b) and (m_2, b) are 1, both sendings fail. On the other hand, if m_1 sends and (m_1, b) is 1 but (m_i, b) is 0 for all m_i that currently send in that slot, b receives m_1's packet successfully. This model does not directly assume capture, but the assumption signals are heard or not heard implies indirectly that strong signals (heard) have some capture capability over weak signals (not heard). On the other hand, when two signals are "heard," the model is pessimistic in not allowing one to capture. The model of an $M \times B$ matrix of 1's and 0's was used in [SIDI88], but the matrix values were assumed to be fixed. The model described here is from [METZ94]. As a further simplification, assume each mobile sends in each slot with a fixed probability p_s, independent of other mobiles and its own past sendings.

With these assumptions, we can rather easily derive a formula for the average success rate in the system as a function of p_s, p_h, M, and B.

Consider the probability of success for a transmitting mobile to a given base b in a given slot. Suppose there are a total of i particular other transmissions in that time slot.

$$P_{succ}[b, i] = p_h(1 - p_h)^i. \tag{11.15}$$

The probability of success to any base is then

$$P_{succ}[i] = 1 - \{1 - P_{succ}[b, i]\}^B = 1 - [1 - p_h(1 - p_h)^i]^B. \tag{11.16}$$

Weighing over all other sending events,

$$P_{succ} = \sum_{i=0}^{M-1} p_s^i(1 - p_s)^{M-1-i}\{1 - [1 - p_h(1 - p_h)^i]^B\}. \tag{11.17}$$

On average there will be Mp_s attempts per slot. The average number of successes per slot, S, will then be

$$S = Mp_sP_{succ}. \tag{11.18}$$

Figure 11.11 shows a plot of S versus p_s, for $M = 20$, $B = 8$, and different values of p_h. Note the relative insensitivity to p_s, particularly for small values of p_h. For $p_h < .05$, the maximum is at $p_s = 1$. This is a valuable feature for maintaining system stability. Also, the throughputs are quite high for small values of p_h. For a wide range of cases, there are more than two successes per slot with only 8 base stations.

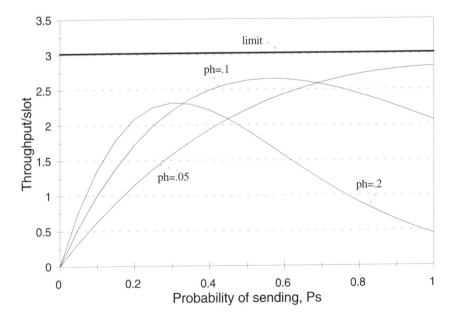

Figure 11.11: Throughput versus P_s for $M = 20$ mobiles and $B = 8$ base stations.

The results can be compared to a theoretical limit. Each base station sees a slotted ALOHA channel with M users apparently sending with a probability $p_s p_h$. The success rate for this one base station cannot exceed an average throughput of $(1 - 1/M)^{M-1}$, which is achieved when $p_s p_h = 1/M$.

Thus, even if the base stations were receiving independent packets, the overall throughput is bounded by

$$S < B * (1 - 1/M)^{M-1}. \tag{11.19}$$

Bound (11.19) is plotted ($B = 8, M = 20$) as a horizontal line in Figure 11.11. We see that the peak throughput comes rather close to this limit when p_h is about .1 or less. This is somewhat remarkable, considering that we do not actually have B independent channels. Most of the departure from the ideal can be ascribed to duplicate successes. When p_h is high, most of the successes occur when only one sender is sending, and there are several duplicate receptions of that one; thus peak performance is well below the ideal. When p_h is low, throughput is higher when many are sending, and usually different senders are successful to different bases, so there is less duplication; thus peak performance is closer to the ideal.

The peaks of the curves occur very near $p_s p_h = 1/M = .05$.

Variation of p_h   In a real situation each mobile is more likely to be heard by some base stations than others. We can model this by selecting a value $p_h(m, b)$ for each mobile-base pair. One way would be to select the p_h independently according to some fixed distribution. Once these values are assigned, average throughputs can be computed analytically. The analysis part is greatly simplified if we assume $p_s = 1$. The study of varying offered load can still be accomplished by changing the number of mobiles.

Let $p_{succ}(m, b)$ be the probability that mobile m is successful to base b, and let $P_{succ}(m)$ be the probability it is successful to at least one base.

$$Mp_{succ}(m, b) = p_h(m, b) * \prod_{\substack{k=1, \\ k \neq m}}^{M} (1 - p_h(k, b)) \tag{11.20}$$

$$P_{FAIL}(m) = \prod_{j=1}^{B} (1 - p_{succ}(m, j)) = 1 - P_{succ}(m) \tag{11.21}$$

The average total throughput per slot is then

$$S = \sum_{m=1}^{M} P_{succ}(m). \tag{11.22}$$

If random variables are statistically independent, the mean of their product is the product of their means. Because each $p_h(m, b)$ is selected independently according to some fixed distribution, $p_h(m, b)$ and all the product terms $(1 - p_h(k, b))$ in (11.20) are independent, and $p_{succ}(m, j)$ is independent of $p_{succ}(m, k)$, $k \neq j$, because they are derived from different columns of the matrix. Then the mean of $P_{FAIL}(m)$ averaged over all matrix choices is just the product of the means of the independent product terms in (7). Thus the average throughput over all matrix choices is *the same as* for fixed p_h equal to the average of the distribution used. For the case of $p_s = 1$ and fixed p_h, a simple formula can be derived for S by direct substitution in (11.20)–(11.22):

$$S = M\{1 - [1 - p_h(1 - p_h)^{M-1}]^B\}. \tag{11.23}$$

S in equation (11.23) is maximized for $p_h = 1/M$.

It is interesting that the average throughput with all sending is the same for the average of all matrix choices for any $p_h(m, b)$ distribution with a fixed average p_h. This broadens the result somewhat, because it is an average over many physical arrangements. Although the average is the same, however, variations about the average might be great for particular matrix choices, especially when m and b are small. This is because the average of the particular $\{p_h(m, b)\}$ numbers chosen for that matrix may depart significantly from p_h.

11.8   ARQ on Error-Prone Cascaded Channels

ARQ can be applied on cascaded channels from end-to-end, hop-by-hop, or both. Factors of efficiency, processing speed, and subnetwork characteristics and protocols influence the decisions as to how to apply ARQ.

Hop-by-hop has the disadvantage of more processing and buffer storage, thus slower operation. On relatively error-free networks it is not worth the extra trouble to do ARQ at each hop, and the trend for high-speed data communication is to do ARQ end-to-end. However, if the links are noisy, hop-by-hop acknowledgments have some efficiency advantages. Even if it is not worth doing ARQ on each hop, it still may be worthwhile doing error correction on each hop if error correction is simple enough not to cause excessive processing load or delay.

11.8.1   A Hop-by-Hop versus End-to-End ARQ Example

Suppose transmission is via frames with built-in error detection and possibly also error correction. As an example, consider a cascade of n links, where on each link a frame has a probability p of acquiring uncorrectable errors, independent of other links or other frames. We will disregard the probability that a block with errors has its errors cancelled on later links or that uncorrectable errors are undetected. Also assume for simplicity that feedback acknowledgments are error-free, and selective repeat is used so that only erroneous frames are retransmitted. If acknowledgments are end-to-end, the probability a frame will not have to be retransmitted is the probability $(1 - p)^n$ that it does not encounter uncorrectable errors on any link. The average number of sendings per successful transfer is thus

$$T_{e\text{-}e} = 1/(1 - p)^n. \tag{11.24}$$

Note that every link in the circuit must carry this many sendings. Hop-by-hop, the average number of frame sendings on any link per success is

$$T_{hbh} = 1/(1 - p). \qquad (11.25)$$

If there are 10 links and $p = .1$, the end-to-end protocol requires $(.9)^{-9} = 2.58$ times as much traffic on every link as the hop-by-hop protocol.

11.8.2 A Subnetwork of Noisy Links

Sometimes a network has a subnetwork of noisy links but is otherwise relatively noise-free. This could occur when the subnetwork is a wireless network, for example. In this case it would be desirable to apply some ARQ within the noisy subnetwork that was not used in the rest of the network. For example, referring to Figure 11.12, suppose it took an average of three transmissions to exchange a packet successfully from one point A in the subnetwork to a gateway B to the rest of the network, whereas from B to the destination C packets rarely need retransmission. It would seem to be preferable to use ARQ from A to B, resulting in an average of three sendings, and then send the successful result from B to C, rather than use ARQ from A to C, and send an average of 3 copies of the packet from A to C, thereby tripling its load on the network between B and C.

An alternative solution for the postulated noisy A to B subnetwork would be to use forward error correction at a reduced rate on the A to B channel; i.e., send initially at $1/3$ the rate or less. This might eliminate the need for ARQ on the individual A to B link, since uncorrectable errors might be rare enough to handle end-to-end. The extra redundancy could be stripped before sending from B to C, where it is not required. However, if conditions were variable on the A to B link, forward error correction without ARQ on the link would not be an efficient solution, for reasons explained in Chapter 8.

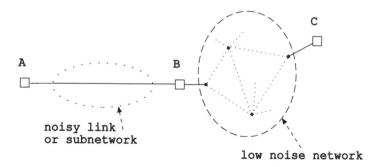

Figure 11.12: A network with a noisy link or subnetwork.

11.8.3   Forward Error Correction or Added Redundancy for Cascaded Noisy Channels

Binary signal regeneration at relay points is responsible for the reliability advantage of digital signalling over analog by preventing noise accumulation. This was cited in [OLIV48] as the basic justification for PCM. Similarly, the ability to correct small numbers of errors at each link can prevent errors from building up beyond what the destination receiver is able to correct.

Hop-by-hop forward error correction is related to the cited advantage of relay regeneration: the fact that binary digits can be regenerated at the relay stations, thereby preventing the noise accumulation that an amplified analog signal would acquire.

If, for example, coded blocks of N_b bits per block are sent, and bit errors are independent with probability p_b, such that $N_b p_b$ is significantly less than one, single error correction per hop will correct most erroneous blocks without a need for retransmission. Otherwise, these single errors would tend to accumulate. With n such identical links in cascade and no hop-by-hop single error correction, the average number of bit errors at the destination would be a little less than $n N_b p_b$ per block, which might be considerably greater than one. This would require a more complex decoder at the final receiver and probably also more error protection redundancy.

Hop-by-hop forward error correction seems to be an attractive alternative if the error correction is simple. Single error correction and burst error correction are simple operations that can be done at high speeds with special purpose hardware. ATM networks, in fact, provide for single error correction of header information. Delays somewhat greater than one frame length per hop are needed for whole block correction, but at high data rates these delays are relatively small. Also, if packets are being buffered, error correction can be done on waiting packets by a separate dedicated processor, often with no delay cost. Coded modulation is akin to error correction, and it can improve per-hop reliability with less per-hop delay than block code error correction.

Different links in the chain could employ different amounts of redundancy and error correction to suit their specific conditions. This would require stripping of and replacing redundancy of different amounts at each hop. This could be transparent to the rest of the network and to higher layers.

Even the simple act of slowing the bit rate or repeated bits can improve capacity for cascaded noisy channels [METZ59]. As an illustration, consider a cascade of s links that are independently disturbed by identical-strength white Gaussian noise. The overall probability of bit error with no forward error correction and per-link bit error probability p is

$$p_{ov} = \frac{1}{2}[1 - (1 - 2p)^s] \qquad (11.26)$$

If the bits are sent as $\pm a$ pulses of duration T and the two-sided noise power spectral density is $N_0/2$,

$$p = \frac{1}{\sqrt{2\pi}} \int_{a\sqrt{2\frac{T}{N_0}}}^{\infty} \exp \frac{-\lambda^2}{2} \, d\lambda \tag{11.27}$$

The end-to-end channel capacity is then given by

$$C = \frac{1}{T}[1 + p_{ov} \log_2 p_{ov} + q_{ov} \log_2 q_{ov}]. \tag{11.28}$$

For the case of a single link ($s = 1$), as $T \to 0$ (bit rate $\to \infty$), C asymptotically approaches the value

$$C_\infty = (2a^2/\pi N_0) \log_2 e. \tag{11.29}$$

It is convenient to define a capacity normalized to the single-link asymptotic capacity:

$$\frac{C}{C_\infty} = \frac{\pi}{2a^2 \dfrac{T}{N_0} \log_2 e}[1 + p_{ov} \log_2 p_{ov} + q_{ov} \log_2 q_{ov}]. \tag{11.30}$$

For constant a^2/N_0, Figure 11.13 shows a plot of normalized capacity from (11.30) versus per link bit error probability p for a fixed number of links s. For constant a^2/N_0, p and the right-hand side of (11.30) depend only on T. The behavior may look strange at first, seeing capacity increase with increasing p. Signal power and noise power

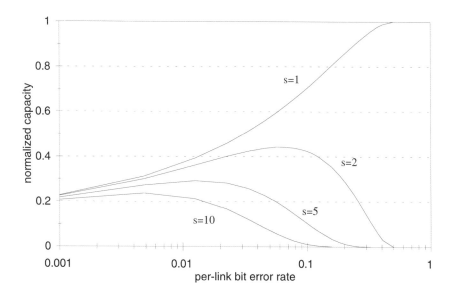

Figure 11.13: Cascaded noisy binary symmetric links.

density are being held constant, so increasing p corresponds to decreasing T, or increasing binary signalling rate.

Note that there is an optimum p for every case except $s = 1$, for which capacity increases with bit rate, approaching a constant asymptotically (the point $p = 1/2$ represents the asymptote as $T \to 0$.) For example, if there are five links, any bit rate for which p is somewhat above 0.01 should be reduced; in fact, there is a rather flat region, indicating that the bit rate could be reduced to where p is well below 0.01 with little loss in capacity, considerable gain in decoding ease, and less bandwidth. For a larger number of links, the optimum is at a still lower value of p_{ov}, and is still flatter. Reductions from operation at bit rates beyond the optimum simultaneously increase capacity, decrease decoding complexity, and decrease bandwidth!

11.8.4 Concatenated Codes on Cascaded Channels

If concatenated codes are used for end-to-end block correction, inner code error correction could be performed hop-by-hop, while the outer code decoding, which requires longer decoding delay, could be performed only end-to-end. Retransmission could be applied only end-to-end, and only when the block error events exceed the outer code's decoding capability.

An alternative to retransmission of all the blocks in the concatenated code is to send additional incremental redundancy blocks; if the locations of probably erroneous blocks are available from the inner decoder, such as by setting an erasure bit in the inner block, another alternative is retransmission of just the erased blocks; on receiving these erased blocks, the end-to-end decoder very likely would then be able to decode successfully.

Another alternative would be to use information feedback: that is, the destination could derive and send back information that would allow the source to compute the probable location of erroneous blocks and resend them. One way of doing this is by using the file comparison technique described in Section 10.11; that is, the transmitted and received copies of the data are the files to be compared.

11.9   Summary

Wireless multiuser channels are noisy and time-varying both in amount of interference and in signal-to-noise ratio. Both ARQ and error control coding are needed for reliable and efficient communication. Wireless data communication is likely to be primarily on a packetized basis. Also, noisy links in general involve different communication design than very low noise networks.

Chapters 9 and 10 were concerned primarily with networks where noise was not a major factor. Chapter 9 concentrated on multiaccess network users seeking to avoid collision (simultaneous transmission) as much as possible. Wireless networks are generally noisy and time varying, and in a shared medium senders usually cannot observe directly if there is a collision. There is, however, the possibility of collision tolerance; one or more signals may be successfully decoded at a receiving station despite "collisions." In theory, many simultaneous senders can all be decoded at a composite total successful rate equal to what a single sender could achieve using a power equal to the sum of all the received signal powers. In practice it is hard to come close to this rate.

When one signal is much stronger than another, the **capture effect** may provide a simple means of successfully decoding the stronger signal. Then subtraction can be used to decode the other. The principal of decoding one signal (usually the strongest) and then subtracting its effect to decode another is an important general principle.

One way of getting more throughput without trying to rely on simultaneous decoding is to send **nonbinary**, thereby allowing shorter packets. With k bits per pulse, simple **slotted ALOHA** is capable of approaching $.368k$ times the maximum throughput of conflict-free binary transmission. The value of k is limited only by the signal-to-noise ratio.

Antenna directivity and **spatial separation** of senders are important factors allowing increased system data transfer capacity. Signals coming from different directions can be decoded simultaneously in this way, or if the signals are received at different receiving stations they can both be decoded. The cellular concept achieves a space sharing; **random forwarding ALOHA** achieves a more randomized form of space sharing.

CDMA or spread spectrum achieves simultaneous user decoding capability by assigning different spreading codes to different users and using correlation demodulation. It has the advantage of suffering only graceful degradation as opposed to collision loss. However, individual senders are confined to rates far below system channel capacity. CDMA has the disadvantages of being complex and requiring tight power control. Antenna directivity and signal processing techniques can increase its capacity. **Direct Sequence CDMA** is the most popular form. Other alternatives are **fast frequency hopping** and **slow frequency hopping**. **Spread ALOHA** is a modification of direct sequence CDMA that needs only one common code. A hypothetical pulse-time spread ALOHA has a similar effect with no code at all, but suffers from high peak-to-average power ratio. Fast frequency hopping efficiency can be enhanced by using **memory techniques** and **two-power-level** techniques. Fast frequency hopping has a **pulse-position-modulation hopping** equivalent. Slow frequency hopping suffers from symbol unit collisions, which could be filled in by an erasure-correcting code. However, it is basically no more efficient than multichannel ALOHA.

Packet reservation multiple access is a good way to avoid collisions and be efficient in wireless multiple access. However, with **fading**, **multiple-base diversity reception** and **adaptive antenna directivity**, there is a question whether it is better to give sole reservation to one sender or allow senders to compete for simultaneous success.

Mobile communication involves a cooperating set of base stations. Normally, each has its own cell in some allocated frequency band. Each cell might use reservations, TDM, FDM, CDMA, or ALOHA. A mobile sender is assigned to a cell, but may be handed off to another cell as the sender moves. An interesting alternative is to have a large group of base stations without separate cells. **Random forwarding** can then be used, where, if a sender's packet can be decoded at any base station, it is successful and is forwarded to its destination. The base station network is able to recognize duplicates in case of multiple successes. This is also a form of **diversity reception**.

Power control to equalize power is important in DS CDMA. In ALOHA with capture or multibase random forwarding, power differences actually are an advantage in terms of more successful throughput, though there is a **fairness** question if high power signals are favored. **Intentional power differences** can be used to give priorities or improve fairness. Power control together with ARQ can be used to **minimize interference energy** by using no more energy than actually needed for success.

Hop-by-hop error correction and ARQ are not favored for very low-noise networks. On **cascaded noisy links**, link error correction performs a regenerative task that prevents multiple-error buildup, similar to the binary PCM regeneration advantage over analog relay amplification. With concatenated codes, hops could do the inner block correction part, or inner convolutional decoding. For one particular noisy link, error correction redundancy as needed can be added for that link and then stripped off at the end of the link so as to be transparent to the rest of the network. Where packet buffering is needed anyway, error correction can be done while a packet is waiting in the buffer. ARQ can also be used on a particularly noisy hop, so as to confine retransmissions to that hop rather than have the whole network path carry retransmissions.

11.10   Problems

11.1. Assume the method of decoding one signal and subtracting it could meet close to the bounds (11.2) and (11.3). Suppose $F = 10^6$ Hz, $N_0 = 10^{-6}$ microwatts/Hz, $P_2 = 1$ microwatt.

    a. What is the minimum P_1 if sender 1 wishes to send 3 megabits/second?

    b. Given that sender 1 uses power P_1 successfully, what is the maximum rate at which sender 2 can send successfully?

    c. With a reference P_1 for the above specification, the given P_2, and the transmission rates, how would each of the following actions affect the success of each of the two senders?

        1. Decrease P_1;

        2. Decrease P_2;

        3. Increase P_2.

11.2. Consider interference between two binary phase shift keying signals. If received signal A is k times the amplitude ($k > 1$) of received signal B, what is the maximum phase error due to B when trying to decode A? Ignore any effect of noise.

11.3. Continuing the idea of the two interfering binary phase shift keying signals, suppose A has twice the received amplitude as B and the two are 30° out of phase.

    a. Draw a phasor diagram showing four possible instantaneous resultant phases.

    b. Describe how you could decode both signals, assuming the pulse starting times are synchronized and the phase difference stays the same.

   c. If the pulse starting times were out of step by some fixed amount, say half a pulse duration, would this affect the ability to decode both signals? Explain.

   d. If the two signals were instead exactly in phase, redraw the phasor diagram of (a) and answer (b) and (c).

11.4. Suppose two signals $x(t)$ and $y(t)$ arrive at a two-element antenna from different directions as shown in Figure P11.1. The voltage outputs from the two elements are $x(t) + y(t - \tau_y)$ and $y(t) + x(t - \tau_x)$.

   a. Show how $x(t)$ can be completely cancelled out by some simple linear operations, given that the directions—and thus the values of τ_x and τ_y—are known.

   b. Can $y(t)$ then be extracted from the result by additional linear operations?

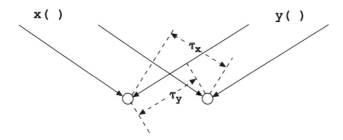

Figure P11.1: Received signals for Problem 11.4.

11.5. Compare the bandwidths of the following CDMA schemes:

   a. Direct sequence with 256 chips per bit.

   b. Fast frequency hopping with $Q = 256$ frequencies and $L = 20$ chips per 8-bit interval.

   c. The pulse position modulation equivalent of fast frequency hopping with the same Q and L.

11.6. Derive equation (11.14).

11.7. Suppose there are six mobiles and four base stations employing the random forwarding strategy. Transmission is packets in fixed-size slots. In the matrix of 1's and 0's that follows, let a "1" indicate that the base represented by the column can receive the sender represented by the row, and a "0" that the base cannot hear the sender. If two or more senders are heard by the same base station, assume neither can be decoded, but if only one is heard, that one is decoded successfully. To be successful, a sender must be decoded by at least one base station. Assume each mobile sends independently in each slot with probability p. Find the probability that mobile 3 is successful when it sends a packet. Evaluate for $p = 0.2$.

	Base → 1	2	3	4
Mobile				
1	1	0	1	1
2	0	1	1	0
3	0	1	1	1
4	1	0	0	1
5	1	0	0	0
6	0	0	1	0

11.8.   Derive equation (11.29) from (11.26)–(11.28).

11.9.   Data is sent from A to B in blocks of 20 symbols. Each symbol is a multibit subblock that contains redundancy for error detection. If error is detected in a symbol, the symbol is erased. One of the symbols is the sum of the other 19, so that a single erased symbol can be filled in.

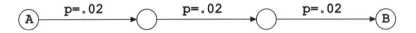

Figure P11.2: Cascaded channels for Problem 11.9.

Suppose the blocks are sent over a cascade of three links as in Figure P11.2. On each link the probability is .02, independently for different symbols or links, that a symbol will be erased as a result of having errors. Ignore as negligible the chance that a cancelling error will turn an erroneous symbol back to the correct value.

Find the probability of successfully delivering a 20 symbol block to B in one sending for each of the following procedures:

a.   On each hop, an erasure can be filled in, if there is only one, before relaying the block. If erasures cannot be filled in, the data are simply relayed as received, but of course the block will not be delivered successfully.

b.   The erasure-filling procedure is exercised only at the final destination.

Chapter 12

The Acknowledgment Problem in Multicasting

Data transmission is not always one-to-one. It often is desired to disseminate the same information to many destinations. It also may be important that every destination or some subset of destinations receive a correct copy. Then a feedback response at some level is needed from each destination for which correct reception is critical.

Generally, the term *broadcast* is taken to mean transmission to all destinations of a network, whereas *multicast* means transmission to some set of destinations, where the number in the set is greater than one and may include the broadcast case.

Two problems with multicast acknowledgments are that the acknowledgment traffic may be very great and that retransmission must continue until all destinations are satisfied. However, we will see that there are ways of organizing the process to make it efficient. Another problem in switched networks is the difficulty of setting up the routing and controlling congestion.

12.1 Noisy Networks with a Broadcast Architecture

Chapter 9 discussed networks where all potential destinations can hear what is sent. Examples are Ethernet, some ring networks, broadcast from stationary satellites, or a radio transmitter where all intended destinations are within range. This makes sending to all or some subset of stations about as simple as sending to one station, other than for the error and acknowledgment problem. If errors are rare, acknowledgments per destination can be at large intervals. Still, a great deal of acknowledgment traffic may be needed if there are many destinations.

For a multicast to some subset, it is best if the subset has some group ID such that each station knows if it is a member or not by the group ID; otherwise, a list of destination addresses might be needed, which is not practical if the subset is large.

311

The same idea of a group ID number could be used to identify which receivers are required to acknowledge.

Two major problems arise in attempting to deliver data reliably and efficiently to many destinations. One is the potential inefficiency of trying to satisfy all receivers' retransmission needs. The other is the large amount of acknowledgment traffic that might have to be handled.

Retransmissions would increase drastically if a go-back policy were used to many receivers in a noisy environment, since if any one of the receivers needed a repeat, the sender would have to go back. Even with selective repeat, different receivers would need different frames repeated, so the number of frames that needed repeating can be many times more what a typical, or even the worst, receiver requires. However, a partial solution to this problem will be discussed in the next subsection.

The large number of acknowledgers can cause excessive acknowledgment traffic, particularly at certain times. There have been various proposals for reducing acknowledgment traffic. If errors are rare, a good approach [RAMA87] would be to transmit only negative acknowledgments (which are rarely needed in a low noise environment), and then find out by polling at the end of a long transmission whether all have received a correct copy. Another possibility if periodic acknowledgments are needed is to stagger responses from different receivers to come at different times in the message stream. If acknowledgments cannot be coordinated this way, some kind of contention scheme might be used for the acknowledgments [CROW88]. In [CHAN84] a protocol is proposed that chooses a token receiving site. As a token site acknowledges, it passes on the token to some other site, which accepts it if it has received the messages to that point. This is designed to reduce acknowledgment traffic.

12.1.1 Satellite or Other Wireless Transfer from One Site to Multiple Sites

Consider transmission of a long stream of data frames to multiple sites. The frames are presumed to be individually error-detection protected and sequence numbered, so that any frame with undetected error is almost surely correct, and the decoder can thus determine the missing or erroneous frames by the sequence numbers of frames with undetected errors. For satellite file transfer, the long round-trip time necessitates that many frames of data be sent before an acknowledgment is returned. Thus a go-back strategy would be inefficient. Calo and Easton [CALO81] proposed sending the file as a sequence of frames or blocks, each with error detection, and then getting requests from each of the sites as to which frames were missing or erroneous; any frame missed or found in error by any site would be retransmitted. A difficulty with this is that the number of retransmitted frames increases rapidly with the number of sites.

A paper [METZ84B] suggested an improved retransmission protocol for this application. Recall the idea mentioned in Section 6.3 of specifying the number of missing frames, so then the sender sends a little more than that many frames, derived according to a Reed-Solomon code, to determine the missing frames. This generalizes very nicely to the multicast problem. Each destination responds simply with the number of missing frames, which is far less feedback information than identifying which frames are missing. The sender then sends a number of blocks that is equal to or slightly more than the maximum number of blocks requested. This will usually be enough to satisfy all receivers, with a few extra for safety if desired, and will often be far fewer retransmissions than with the [CALO81] scheme.

As an elementary example of the gain in efficiency, suppose there are 100 sites, and after sending 1000 frames 20 sites are missing one frame each, while the other 80 sites experience no error. With the Calo-Easton scheme, if errors at different receivers were independent, one would have to send probably close to 20 frames, since most frame requests would be different, whereas with the improved scheme only one extra frame would have to be sent. That frame could simply be the vector sum of all transmitted frames, and any site could find its missing frame by subtraction.

Furthermore, it is not essential to use Reed-Solomon codes if a slight reduction in efficiency is acceptable. With almost any binary matrix defining vector sum combinations of frames to resend, the number of retransmissions would be just slightly more than with Reed-Solomon coding, but simple modulo 2 vector addition could be used instead of complex operations in a large field.

Another alternative would be to send the extra combinations initially, a form of forward error correction. For example, in the prior case where each site is missing only one frame, the initial sending of the vector sum frame would result in no need for retransmissions. Generally, though, the sending of additional redundancy only as requested is more efficient since the redundancy is transmitted only as needed. A compromise could be to send initially a number of initial additional redundant frames of the order of the expected number of additional frames needed to satisfy all sites, assuming the statistics were known. This could be learned from past experience of transmissions of blocks of K data frames, assuming statistics remained relatively stable.

Often, many of the frames that need repeating contain only a few errors, rather than being "lost." The scheme in [METZ84B] can be further improved if one uses the information in frames with detected errors. This improvement has been proposed and simulated in [SAKA95]. Following is a description of the basic difference between the two schemes. The details of the [SAKA95] scheme differ slightly from the description given here, but the main idea is the same.

Since the basic symbol of a practical Reed-Solomon code would normally be much smaller than the number of bits in a frame, the frame could be considered a sequence of L code symbols. In both schemes, if there are K original frames and $N - K$ redundant frames, the encoding can be visualized as a product code of N by L symbols, with each row being a frame, and each column having the check symbols derived by the same Reed-Solomon (N, K) code. This is shown in Figure 12.1.

The difference is that in [METZ84B], a frame that is not received error-free is considered a row of erased symbols, regardless of whether it was received with errors detected or lost entirely, whereas in [SAKA95] the actual received symbols in frames

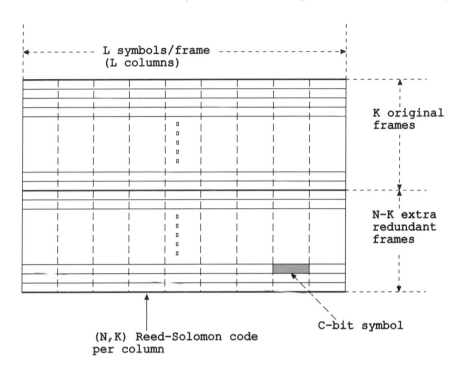

Figure 12.1: The product code structure for redundant frame transmission.

with detected errors are retained and made use of, in addition to the information as to which frames had detected errors and also the reliability of each frame if error correction within a frame has been used. Then, each column code can be used to correct symbol errors in that column until all frames (rows) check. A significant gain in throughput is found from using this extra information when the symbol error probability is greater than about 10^{-3}, with $L = 32$ symbols per frame. However, this is a rather high error rate for the likely range of application. With this high an error rate it would be advisable to include a number of redundant frames in the initial transmission, as mentioned before.

If frames do not arrive in order, there is the additional complication that a frame with detected errors may have the wrong sequence number. This does not matter in the [METZ84B] strategy of discarding frames with detected errors, assuming every frame in the block has a different sequence number, but it could have some effect on the [SAKA95] scheme of using information in frames with detected errors (see Problem 12.3).

Some Relevant Reed-Solomon Code Properties   Although a brief discussion of Reed-Solomon codes was given in Chapter 3, it is instructive to relate the code properties to the previous application. Let each symbol in Figure 12.1 have C bits.

Each column in Figure 12.1 represents a (N, K) code over $GF(2^C)$, where we assume $2^C > N$ for any N we use. Then this code can be considered as a punctured $(2^C - 1, K)$ Reed-Solomon code, with $2^C - 1 - N$ check symbols deleted. The code has minimum distance $N - K + 1$ and can fill in any $N - K$ or fewer erased symbols; i.e., if any K symbols in the column are known to be correct, the other $N - K$ can be found. Thus, if all but at most $N - K$ frames are received with undetected errors, all the symbols in the missing frames can be found symbol-by-symbol from the column Reed-Solomon code erasure decoding. However, if the information in frames with errors detected is retained, usually most of the symbols in these frames are error-free. Thus the maximum number of errors per column is usually less than the number of frames with detected errors, and the errors are known almost certainly to be confined to positions corresponding to frames with detected errors. In [SAKA95], the combined erasure-error decoding capabilities are used to increase the success probability compared to erasure decoding without using information in the error-detected frames.

A Random Coding Approach In [METZ84B] a simpler binary combinational alternative to Reed-Solomon codes was proposed. For each column in Figure 12.1, let the vector symbols in the data frames be

$$\overline{d}_1, \overline{d}_2, \dots, \overline{d}_K$$

Then derive the jth redundant frame by the modulo 2 vector sum

$$\overline{c}_j = \sum_{i=1}^{K} c_{ji} \overline{d}_i, \tag{12.1}$$

Where the $\{c_{ji}\}$ are 0 or 1. Decoding involves the equivalent of inverting an m by m binary matrix, where m is the number of missing frames, and then performing the m vector sums dictated by the inverted matrix.

This approach requires slightly more redundant frames than Reed-Solomon coding. Let R be the number of redundant frames needed for Reed-Solomon codes, and let E_R be the average number of redundant codes over all random combinational choices. It is shown in [METZ84B] that

$$E_R = R + \sum_{i=1}^{R} \frac{1}{2^i - 1}. \tag{12.2}$$

The average excess number $E_R - R$ ranges, as R varies, from 1 to 1.61.

Basic Limitation from the Unfolding Channel Viewpoint The papers referenced above assumed in their analysis that receiving sites encounter independent errors with identical error statistics. This is an idealization to allow for simple presentation of results. In practice, error statistics might vary greatly for different receiving sites and error events may be dependent. Another way of looking at the problem that has some general characteristics is to look at the problem from the unfolding channel viewpoint described in Section 8.1. In this case there are M channels, where channel states unfold in an unpredictable way for all sites. For each channel a certain capacity unfolds during transmission. The sender uses incremental redundancy; the initial transmission is a set of K frames at the highest rate, followed by a succession of redundant frames until all sites have acknowledged. The net effective rate is approximately the minimum capacity that unfolded for any of the channels during the transmission/retransmission cycle. Assuming a given site sees only its own channel, this conclusion does not depend on whether the different channel statistics are dependent. However, dependent statistics should improve the performance, for the simple fact that the average of the minimum of a set of identically distributed independent nonnegative random variables is $\leq$ the average of one of them. For time-varying channels, a longer period K of initial frames would be preferred to reduce the variance in unfolding capacity.

12.2   Broadcast to Locally Interconnected Receivers

Consider the problem of broadcasting a large file of data to a number of sites that are locally interconnected [METZ86B]. Suppose the cost of using the broadcast channel is high, but local communication cost is low. Physically, one example of this would be a satellite broadcast to a group of receiving stations connected via a local network. It is sufficient to deliver a correct copy to any one site; then local communication can supply the correct copy to the other sites. It may not even be necessary to deliver any individually correct copy directly by the broadcast. The set of local receivers can effectively perform diversity reception by exchanging their information about the reception. In a changing communication environment such as with fading, atmospheric effects, or transmission from moving satellites, different receivers may experience error-free communication in different intervals. In this way a correct copy may be derivable from multiple erroneous copies.

Whereas corrective retransmission broadcast to unconnected multiple sites takes more broadcast resources than sending to one site, as seen in the prior section, corrective broadcast to a set of interconnected cooperating multiple sites has the reverse effect; it incurs often less transmission from the original site than sending to one site, due to the diversity reception property. As a simple illustration of this observation, suppose a block of data is broadcast to M sites, and each site independently has probability P of receiving the block correctly. The block has to be repeated as many times as necessary. Let us compare the average number of sendings with no local communication to the case with local communication. With no local communication, the probability of success in j or fewer sendings is

$$(1 - P^j)^M.$$

From this, we obtain that the expected number of broadcasts, N_0, is given by

$$N_0 = 1 + \sum_{j=1}^{\infty}[1 - (1 - P^j)^M]. \tag{12.3}$$

With local communication, the expected number N_L of broadcasts to get a correct copy to at least one site is

$$N_L = \frac{1}{1 - P^M}. \tag{12.4}$$

Figure 12.2 shows N_0 and N_L as a function of P for $M = 10$. Also shown for comparison is the $M = 1$ case. Clearly there is a big difference between the two $M = 10$ cases. Figure 12.2 assumes all sites experience the same error rate. The difference would be even more pronounced if these error rates were unequal. If one site were error-free and one site very bad, only one transmission would be needed in the local communication case, while many transmissions would usually be needed in the case with no local communication.

The receiving sites still have to communicate over the local network. Where local communication cost is a consideration, methods can be devised that minimize the amount of local communication.

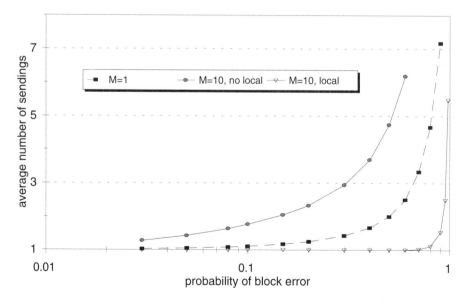

Figure 12.2: Expected number of sendings with and without local communication compared.

12.2.1   Local Communication When One or More Sites Receive Correct Copies

The case where one site receives a correct copy is closely related to multicasting within the local network. However, the site should not have to send the whole file to the other stations, since they usually all have partially correct copies. The site that has a correct copy needs to know what information to send. If more than one site has a correct copy, they may be able to cooperate to reduce the amount of communication, depending on the local network architecture. With a bus architecture, it does not matter which of the sites with correct copies sends the corrective information. In other network architectures, different correct sites can provide corrective information to separate domains of the network.

If it is decided to save sending the whole file from a correct site, the site has to learn what information is missing at the other sites. Assume the file data is divided into sequence numbered blocks. One possibility is that each block has its own error detection. Another possibility is that each block does not have error detection, but there is some overall parity check sequence or signature.

Each Block Has Own Error Detection   One possible approach could be the multicasting technique described in Section 12.1. Assume there is one correct site, site A. After A declares it has a correct copy, each site could report over the local network the number of blocks that are missing or have detected errors, and A could use a Reed-Solomon code or combinations rule to multicast redundant information sufficient to allow all sites to reconstruct the erroneous sites. This would be ideal if the local network had a broadcast or bus architecture. However, for more general networks this does not take advantage of the fact that correct copies of a given block may exist at many sites, even though only one site has a correct complete file copy. Thus in a distributed switched local network a site may be able to obtain a missing block from one of its neighbors, even though none of its neighbors has the whole correct file.

Overall Signature But No Error Detection in Blocks   For this case the file comparison technique described in Section 10.11 can be applied. The broadcaster should include one fairly large (perhaps 64 bits) master signature derived from the whole file and communicate this signature with high error protection and redundancy, so it will almost certainly be correctly received by at least one site. This can be multicast in the local network to all receiving sites to ensure all have a correct master signature copy; it will serve to verify any candidate for the correct file copy. Then a site that determines it has a correct copy can send various signature combinations computed in one of the ways discussed in Section 10.11. The other sites can compute signatures from their own blocks and use this to find the regions of disagreement with the correct file. These regions can be narrowed down with additional signature combination transmissions into precise blocks or small subsets of blocks. Then a site can obtain the true block values by requesting them from either neighboring sites or the known correct site. A final check is made with the master signature at each site to ensure the final result is correct.

12.2.2   Error Correction from Multiple Erroneous Copies

Even if no site has a completely correct copy, the multiple erroneous copies contain a great deal of redundancy, which may allow correct reconstruction of a correct copy. However, the copies are remotely located, and we would prefer to obtain the correct copy without having to deliver all erroneous copies over the local network. Following are some approaches, the first two of which are similar to what we just discussed for the case of one or more error-free sites.

Each Block Has Own Error Detection   If for each block there was at least one file that detected a correct copy, correct file copies could be obtained by all through intercommunication of correct blocks on the local network. Only blocks that did not have any error-free copy would need to be resent over the broadcast network. Alternatively, the broadcaster could initially transmit enough redundant blocks so that one or up to a certain number of blocks not received by any could be reconstructed.

Overall Signature But No Error Detection in Blocks   This procedure again requires for success that a correct copy of each block appears correctly somewhere in the set of sites, but in this case the sites do not know which blocks are erroneous. Assume, however, that all sites obtain a correct copy of the master signature. Comparison to find a tentatively correct copy of the whole file or some subset (like a subtree in Figure 10.15) of the file can be made by passing around computed signatures for file subsets. Discovery of any duplicate signature for a file subset tentatively makes that a candidate for being the correct subset. If the receptions were truly independent any duplicate discovery would almost certainly indicate a correct subset has been found. However, with dependent errors this is less certain, since two receptions might have the same error. If a duplication is not found for some subtree, further subdivision into subtrees may find duplicate subsubtrees, which together construct a tentative correct subtree. If coverage of the whole tree is obtained in this way, the associated tentative signatures can be combined and compared with the master signature for verification.

A method is described in [ABDE94B] for finding correct block copies based on signature disagreements. Comparisons could be made for the sites as a whole or pairwise between sites. Consider for simplicity a pairwise comparison. If we find n disagreeing blocks and want to test if in each case one of the n is correct, we might have to try 2^n combinations to verify this. If n is of the order of 20 or 30 this may be prohibitive. In [ABDE94B], a simpler method is shown. Write the $2n$ disagreeing signature values as rows of a matrix, and include another row, which is the difference between the master signature and the agreeing and presumed correct block signatures. Then by elementary column operations leading to a Gauss-Jordan reduction, we find, if certain linear independence conditions apply, the correct block combination if it

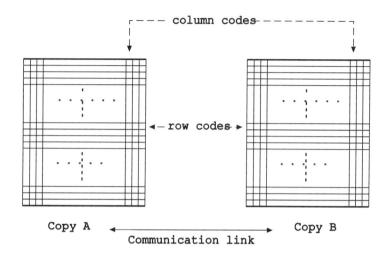

Figure 12.3: Two-dimensional code at two sites.

exists. The solution needs to show exactly one from each pair to be valid. The number of bits in the signature should be at least 30 bits greater than n to protect against false conclusions. Thus the number of computations to find a correct combination goes up only as n^3, rather than exponentially with n.

Two-Dimensional File Precoding   Instead of including separate error detection for each block, suppose each file or file subsection is encoded in a two-dimensional array [METZ86A, METZ86B]. The individual symbols could be binary or nonbinary. Each row and each column is an error-detecting code, possibly also with some error correction. For simplicity, consider the case of two file copies, A and B, to be compared, as illustrated in Figure 12.3.

In the first step, each reports to the other which rows do not check.[1] In the second step, if A has some rows that check for which B's do not check, A sends the symbols in that row to B, while B does the same relative to A. In the third step A and B report which columns do not check. In the fourth step, if A has some columns that check for which B's do not check, A sends the symbols in that column corresponding to rows of B that still do not check, while B does the same relative to A. This process continues, alternating between rows and columns, until everything checks or until no further corrections can be made. Error correction ability is quite high. Simulations for the case of a 100×100 array of symbols with single error correction per row

---

[1] Actually, if they also send at this time the columns that do not check, some communication could be saved, because then on sending a corrective row, only the symbols in nonchecking column positions would need to be sent.

indicate that in most cases a total of 600 total random symbol errors about equally proportioned among the two copies can be entirely corrected, usually after just 3 or 4 row-column rounds. With larger numbers of copies with independent errors, much larger proportions of errors could be corrected. If a site had an uncorrectable row or column, any site having a good copy of that row or column could provide the correction.

12.3 Ring Networks

A ring network is well-suited for multicasting. Without destination removal, it is just about as efficient to send to all other stations in the ring as to send to just one. With the slotted ring acknowledgment strategy described in Chapter 9 all acknowledgments can be gathered in the same slot rotation.

A Virtual Ring   Even in a general network a virtual ring using the new-word policy could be formed of any closed loop of stations that wanted to multicast. This is illustrated in Figure 12.4. No synchronized slot structure is needed. A nonparticipating node, such as the one between *C* and *D*, need only pass on what it receives on the virtual circuit, which is the normal procedure.

Each participating station would need to provide a delay of at least one packet duration to perform error detection and determine if it is a new packet. If errors are detected or if it is the old packet, the station sends out the old packet. If it is a new packet the station sends it out with the new alternating bit value, and also records it. Also, if nothing new is received by some timeout period the station resends the old packet.

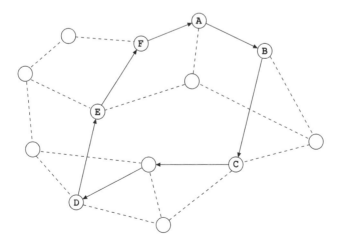

Figure 12.4: A virtual multicast ring in a general network.

Timeouts could occur at any of the participating stations due to the variable round-trip delay that occurs with queueing on a virtual circuit. This is not a reliability problem, because each station simply retransmits what it sent last if a timeout is reached, and each receiving station ignores any old (previously received) frame. For example, if B times out after receiving a packet on a broadcast from A, it retransmits the last packet sent, but when B finally receives a new packet it immediately goes ahead and relays the new packet.

Detected error on any link will cause source A to retransmit. For example, suppose an error is detected between D and E. A cannot tell that the packet has advanced to D, so it will retransmit if it does not get an acknowledgment back by its timeout. However, if A's retransmission should fail, this will not hold up progress at all, since the packet has already gotten to B (as well as to C and D). In a very noisy situation this is much better than if one had to start over. For example [METZ73], if there were n links in the ring with packet error probability p per link, starting all over on any round-trip error would require an average number of round-trip tries per packet N of

$$N = \frac{1}{(1 - p)^n}.$$

(12.5)

With the new-word policy, the average number N_{NW} of round-trip tries per packet is

$$N_{NW} = \frac{1 + (n - 1)p}{1 - p}.$$

(12.6)

Note that (12.5) exhibits an exponential increase with n, whereas (12.6) has a linear increase with n.

A virtual ring is limited by its weakest or slowest link. However the same can be said of a virtual circuit from a source to a destination.

12.4   Tree and General Network Multicast

Broadcast of data to all sites in a network can be accomplished efficiently through using just the links of a spanning tree subnetwork. Exactly one copy of a packet needs to be sent along each link of the tree, assuming no retransmissions. If a node is reached that has n links in the spanning tree, that node makes $n - 1$ copies of the received packet to send over each of the links except the one from which the packet arrived. Given the transmission costs for each link, for the case of equal cost in both directions of a link, there is a standard technique [BERT87] for finding a minimum cost spanning tree, which can be used to broadcast from any node to all the others at minimum communication cost. If not all the nodes are destinations (multicasting), finding the minimum cost tree to do the multicasting is a very difficult problem. Of course some tree that spans the multicast group could be used even though it is not optimum. Note that, provided that the cost is the same in both directions, the group multicast cost from any of the members to all the others is the same no matter which

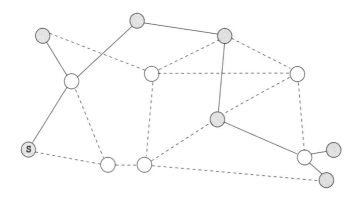

Figure 12.5: A tree for multicast among the shaded nodes.

member is the source, because in all cases a packet is sent exactly once on each link of the tree. Figure 12.5 shows a multicast tree. The source node is labeled S, the participating nodes are shown shaded, and the links used are shown as solid lines. Alternatively, any of the other shaded nodes might be the source, with the same tree under the prior bidirectional assumption.

12.4.1   Cable TV or Natural Tree Networks

A case of a natural tree network for multicasting from one source is a cable TV network, where the cable office is the source and subscribing homes are the destinations. In a natural tree network there is a simple way of distributing to the multicast group without referring to a complete table of "subscribers." Each node receives a report from each of its child nodes of 1 = subscriber or 0 = no subscriber. If there are no subscribers for any of its children it reports a 0 back to its parent; otherwise it reports a 1. This can be continued back to the source, where each node sends out a copy of the information on each link that has a 1 appended corresponding to that service.

12.4.2   Acknowledgment Gathering

Suppose we have found a tree by which to multicast from a source to all destinations on the tree, and wish to obtain acknowledgments. Refer to Figure 12.6. The 1 and 0 labelings have the meanings just described for natural tree networks. In the cable TV case only the leaf nodes are destinations. In general, some of the intermediate nodes, such as node A, also could be destinations. We could include this case in the natural tree representation by appending a "self leaf," shown as a dashed line coming from node A, if node A is a destination as well as an intermediate node.

We assume the nondestination nodes cooperate in the multicast distribution. For example, node B receives one copy and sends three copies, one to each outgoing line that needs one. The record of 1's for subscribers or group members mentioned

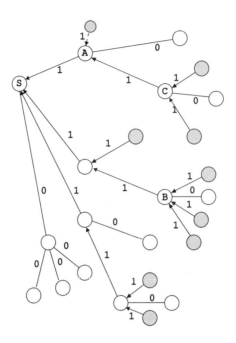

Figure 12.6: Multicast acknowledgment gathering in a tree network.

regarding to the natural cable TV tree structure could be used for both multicast distribution and acknowledgment-gathering in the reverse direction.

Similarly, nondestination node cooperation could help improve the efficiency of sending acknowledgments. Rather than having each destination individually send its acknowledgment back to the source, the following could be done. *B* waits to receive acknowledgment of all three destinations, and then sends an acknowledgment back to the source. *C* waits to receive acknowledgments from its outgoing lines and then sends an acknowledgment back to *A*. *A* then sends back an acknowledgment to *S*, assuming *A* also has a correct reception. That way only one acknowledgment per item traverses each link of the tree. Also, retransmissions do not have to be multicast to the whole group. If *S* receives an acknowledgment from *A* but not from *B*, it only has to send a retransmission to *B*.

The intermediate stations could help even more if given additional capabilities. Suppose the intermediate stations could retain a memory of all received packets that were not yet acknowledged by all of its children. This requires a greater degree of participation of network nodes than normally occurs. For example, if *A* receives a correct copy but gets a retransmission request from *C*, it could supply the retransmission, thus relieving the *S*-to-*A* link of this load. This is related to the hop-by-hop versus end-to-end acknowledgment choice for cascaded channels described in Section 11.8. As in that case, hop-by-hop is more efficient than end-to-end but requires more processing. For an intermediate node with large numbers of children, the efficiency gains are greater, because the chance that at least one of the children needs a retransmission may be high.

12.4.3 Internetworking and Diverse Networks

Ideal multicast organizations are not universally used in practice. Multicasting is natural in broadcast networks such as Ethernet and in ring networks. In general networks the IP protocol provides for group multicasts by sending to a group address in some subnetwork, so only one copy has to be sent to the subnetwork, and the subnetwork can multicast to the group by its own means.

ATM networks do not currently provide a very efficient multicast technique. Problems are the need control congestion and the high degree of cooperative node processing that is needed. The setting up of a multiple virtual circuit tree for a group is not inherently difficult, although finding the exact optimum tree is difficult [DEER88, WALL82]. Suppose we want to give m stations multicasting capability so each could send to the other $m - 1$. We saw in Section 10.1 how a virtual circuit is set up. This can be generalized to a multiple (m-ary) virtual circuit. A tree topology is found that will connect the m participants, as in Figure 12.5. Consider the case where there is one source and multiple destinations. A group number defines the multiple virtual circuit. Just as a single virtual circuit is set up by depositing in a table at each node which logic circuit input is switched to which logic circuit output, in the multiple virtual circuit there is a table for the group logic circuit input going to which sometimes multiple logic circuit outputs (but at most one logic circuit output per outgoing line). Figure 12.7 is an example of this at a node that has two outgoing lines in the tree. Comparing with Figure 10.1b, we see that the additional table memory for doing this is normally insignificant. The main complication is that every switching node needs to have multiple copy creation ability. The main advantage is that it is not necessary to send two copies of a packet over the same link. Now if any station is to be the

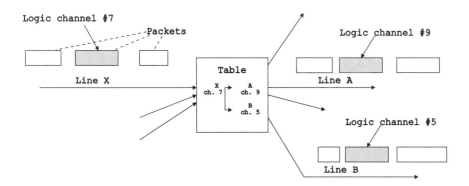

Figure 12.7: Node in a multiple virtual circuit with two participating output lines.

source, assuming the same tree can be used, the switch information is the list of logic circuits that go with the group number. The node simply relays each group packet to all participating attached links except the one it arrived on.

The multicast switching rule for a fixed group is easy to accomplish if the multicast has a group number and each node keeps a record of which attached links are part of the tree for each group number. However, if membership changes the problem is more difficult [BELK89] because a major change in the tree structure might have to be made in some cases. For example, in Figure 12.6, if A left the multicast group, there might be some other path from S to C that does not go through A, but is less costly. If a node joins the group, one way might be to connect it to the nearest tree member and add a "1" to the links along the path to that member. This may or may not lead to an inefficient tree after a number of joinings. A similar strategy could be used to improve the tree: if a member node occasionally searches for a lower cost path to the tree and finds one, under the bidirectional equal cost assumption, the node could make the change—add this path and delete the old one—yielding a lower cost tree.

12.4.4   Multicast Switching Networks

Multistage interconnection copy networks have been designed and are capable of fast switching [LEA93, TURN88, LEE88, TURN93]. Generally they are composed of a copy network that makes the required number of copies, followed by a routing network to properly distribute the copies. The intention is to have these work as part of an ATM switch. However, in the past multicast services have not been extensive enough to justify the extra expense of providing these multicast high-speed switching capabilities. Also, there is the higher level problem of ATM traffic management and congestion control, which would be strongly impacted by multicast traffic.

A thought is to consider combining a bus network with a multistage interconnection network (MIN), as illustrated in Figure 12.8. Unicast packets would use the MIN, while multicast packets would use the bus. The bus transmissions would contain the group number, and only output links recognizing the number would copy the packet into their link buffer. Since the number of multicast groups using a particular switch is likely to be small, the number of different groups that need recognition would usually be small.

12.5   Summary

Multicasting with acknowledgments has the problems of satisfying all receiving sites, gathering large numbers of acknowledgments, and network routing and switching. In a network with a **broadcast architecture**, routing is not a problem. The need for retransmission to satisfy all receivers can be reduced by providing common redundancy that all receivers can use, rather than retransmitting all specific parts that any receiver needs. The acknowledgment traffic can be reduced or spread out by

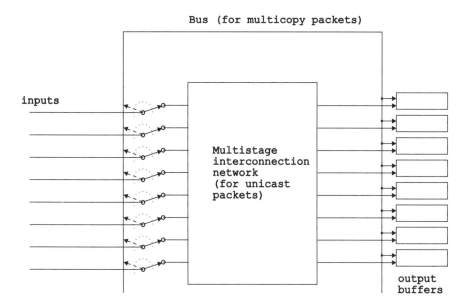

Figure 12.8: Possible combination of a bus and a MIN.

relying on negative acknowledgments combined with occasional staggered positive acknowledgments.

The problem was discussed of broadcasting over an expensive medium to multiple sites connected by a less expensive local communication network. The diversity reception characteristic cuts down greatly on the more expensive broadcasting. *Local corrective information* can be accomplished efficiently using error detection in sub-blocks or signature combination exchanges in cases where the exact error regions are unknown. It is even possible to reconstruct a correct copy from local communication when all received copies are erroneous. Another technique of possible use in this regard is a **two-dimensional precoding** of the broadcast information.

A **ring** is an ideal architecture for multicasting because it is a natural form for the purpose and allows automatic acknowledgment gathering. A **virtual ring** can be formed in a general switching network with not much more difficulty than setting up a virtual circuit.

A **natural** or **embedded tree network** can be used for efficient multicasting and acknowledgment gathering. It can be arranged that the multicast data traverse each of the tree links only once, excepting retransmissions. **Acknowledgment gathering** can be used to ensure acknowledgments also traverse each link only once, and retransmissions need not necessarily travel over all tree links. Even greater node participation can allow node cooperation to provide local retransmissions.

Multicast switching and multiple virtual circuit forming within a network such as ATM could be provided, but the extent to which this will be done and the methods used are not yet determined.

12.6 Problems

12.1. Consider a simple stop-and-wait system where a sender sends frames one at a time to M sites and retransmits until all sites have positively acknowledged the frame. Assume an error-free acknowledgment channel, and suppose each site independently has probability p of correctly receiving each frame transmission. Derive a formula for the expected number of transmissions of a frame to have acknowledgment by all frames, as a function of p and the number of sites, M.

12.2. Consider the binary combinational alternative (refer to Equation 12.1) for broadcasting additional information to multiple sites. Suppose there are blocks of 16 frames, and the first five combinations of the c_{ji} matrix are

$$
\begin{array}{cccccccccccccccc}
1 & 1 & 1 & 1 & 1 & 1 & 1 & 1 & 1 & 1 & 1 & 1 & 1 & 1 & 1 & 1 \\
1 & 1 & 1 & 1 & 1 & 1 & 1 & 1 & 0 & 0 & 0 & 0 & 0 & 0 & 0 & 0 \\
1 & 1 & 1 & 1 & 0 & 0 & 0 & 0 & 1 & 1 & 1 & 1 & 0 & 0 & 0 & 0 \\
1 & 1 & 0 & 0 & 1 & 1 & 0 & 0 & 1 & 1 & 0 & 0 & 1 & 1 & 0 & 0 \\
1 & 0 & 1 & 0 & 1 & 0 & 1 & 0 & 1 & 0 & 1 & 0 & 1 & 0 & 1 & 0 \\
\end{array}
$$

$$\cdots\cdots\cdots\cdots\cdots\cdots\cdots\cdots\cdots\cdots\cdots\cdots\cdots\cdots$$
$$\cdots\cdots\cdots\cdots\cdots\cdots\cdots\cdots\cdots\cdots\cdots\cdots\cdots\cdots$$

a. If a site is missing 2 frames in random positions, find the average number of frame combinations the site would need to reconstruct the missing frames.

b. Note (and show) that 5 is always sufficient for this example.

c. Does the site always know how many frame combinations it needs?

12.3. Consider the [SAKA95] approach of using information in frames with detected errors. Discuss the effect and likelihood of frames with detected errors that have incorrect sequence numbers. Factors to be considered are whether frames are received in order, symbol error probability, effect of not matching any frame number in the set, or of duplicating another prospective Q-member.

12.4. In the coding technique of Figure 12.1, suppose there are 10 frames with detected errors and it is known which frames they are. Let the probability that a symbol in an error-detected frame is erroneous be 0.01, independent of other symbols, and let $L = 32$. What is the probability that no column has more than one erroneous symbol?

12.5. **a.** If there are three possible capacities C_1, C_2, and C_3, where $C_1 > C_2 > C_3$, and a channel to a site has, independently, capacity C_i with probability p_i, what is the probability that the minimum capacity among N sites will be C_3?

b. For the parameters in (a), suppose there are two intervals, and each site channel has capacity C_i with probability p_i, independently for the two intervals. What is the probability that the minimum average capacity over the two intervals among the N sites will be C_3?

12.6. Derive Equation 12.3.

12.7. Suppose A, B, and C are three local sites receiving a file from a longer distance. Suppose C declares it has a correct copy, and by the method of signature combinations it is discovered that B has erroneous copies of pages 4, 8, and 16, whereas A has erroneous copies of pages 2, 4, and 10. Suppose it costs one unit to send a page between A and

B (either direction), and 5 units to send a page from *C* to *A* or from *C* to *B*. Determine the least cost of the exchange to get correct copies to both *A* and *B*. Ignore the cost of any request information.

12.8. Given the cost is the same in both directions on each link, prove that the forward link transmission cost, from a given source, of a multicast tree is always less than the forward cost of a multicast virtual unidirectional ring. How does the comparison change if acknowledgment costs are considered? Does the virtual ring have any advantages in terms of using the same configuration for different sources in the group?

12.9. Consider the tree network in Figure 12.6. Count the total network traffic created by a packet sent from a source node as one unit for each traversal of the packet over a link.

   a. With multiple copies made only as needed at the switching nodes, how much forward traffic is created by a packet to the indicated destinations?

   b. If, instead, a separate packet was sent individually to each destination on its own logical circuit, how much forward traffic would be created?

   c. Answer (a) and (b) for feedback acknowledgment packets if each destination sends a packet positive acknowledgment. Part (a) would use acknowledgment gathering.

   d. If just one of *C*'s children and one of *B*'s children reported a negative acknowledgment, how much packet retransmission traffic would be generated?

References

[ABDE94A] K.A.S. Abdel-Ghaffar and A. El Abbadi, "An optimal strategy for comparing file copies," *IEEE Trans. Parallel and Distrib. Systems*, vol. 5, pp. 87–93, Jan. 1994.

[ABDE94B] A. Abdennadher and J. Metzner, "Use of Gauss-Jordan matrix reduction in the reconstruction of a correct file copy from erroneous copies," *Proc. of the 27th Ann. Hawaii Conf. on Systems Sci.*, pp. 333–340, Jan. 1994.

[ABRA94] N. Abramson, "Multiple access in wireless digital networks," *Proc. IEEE*, vol. 82, pp. 1360–1369, Sept. 1994.

[AHLS86] R. Ahlswede, "Arbitrarily varying channels with states sequence known to the sender," *IEEE Trans. Inform. Theory*, vol. IT–32, pp. 621–629, Sept. 1986.

[ANAG86] M.E. Anagostou and E.N. Protonotarios, "Performance analysis of the selective repeat ARQ protocol," *IEEE Trans. Commun.*, vol. COM–34, pp. 127–135, Feb. 1986.

[ANCH79] T. Ancheta, "Convolutional parity check automatic repeat request," *IEEE Int. Symp. Inform. Theory*, Grignano, Italy, 1979.

[ARNB87] J. Arnbak and W. van Blitterswijk, "Capacity of slotted ALOHA in Rayleigh-fading channels," *IEEE J. Select. Areas Commun.*, vol. SAC–5, pp. 261–269, Feb. 1987.

[ARUL96] A. Arulambalam, X. Chen, and N. Ansari, "Allocating fair rates for available bit rate service in ATM networks," *IEEE Comm. Mag.*, vol. 34, pp. 92–101, Nov. 1996.

[BARB88] D. Barbara, H. Garcia-Molina, and B. Feijoo, "Exploiting symmetries for low-cost comparison of file copies," *Proc. Int. Conf. Distributed Comput. Syst.*, pp. 471–479, June 1988.

[BATT79] G. Battail, M.C. Decouvelaere, and P. Godlewski, "Replication decoding," *IEEE Trans. Inform. Theory*, vol. IT–25, pp. 332–345, May 1979.

[BECK67] P. Beckman, *Probability in Communication Engineering*. Harcourt, Brace and World, 1967.

[BELK89] N.E. Belkeir and M. Ahamad, "Low cost algorithms for message delivery in dynamic multicast groups," *Proc. IEEE Ninth Int. Conf. on Distributed Computing*, pp. 110–117, June 1989.

[BENE85] G. Benelli, "An ARQ scheme with memory and soft error detectors," *IEEE Trans. Commun.*, vol. COM–33, pp. 285–288, Mar. 1985.

[BENE87] G. Benelli, "An ARQ scheme with memory and integrated modulation," *IEEE Trans. Commun.*, vol. COM–35, pp. 689–697, July 1987.

[BERL83] E. Berlekamp, *Algebraic Coding Theory*. New York: McGraw-Hill, 1968.

[BERR93] C. Berrou, A. Glavieux, and P. Thitimajshima, "Near Shannon limit error-correcting coding and decoding: turbo-codes," *Proc. ICC'93*, pp. 1064–1070, May 1993.

[BERT92] D. Bertsekas and R. Gallager, *Data Networks, Second Ed.*, Englewood Cliffs, NJ: Prentice Hall, 1992.

[BLAC60] D. Blackwell, L. Breiman, and A.J. Thomasian, "The capacities of certain channel classes under random codings," *Ann. Math. Statist.*, vol. 31, pp. 558–567, 1960.

[BLAH83] R. Blahut, *Theory and Practice of Error Control Codes*. Reading, MA: Addison-Wesley, 1983.

[BLOO75] F.J. Bloom et al., "Improvement of binary transmission by null zone reception," *Proc. IRE*, vol. 45, pp. 963–975, July 1957.

[BORG96] F. Borgonovo, M. Zorzi, L. Fratta, V. Trecordi, and G. Bianchi, "Capture-division packet access for wireless personal communications," *IEEE J. Selected Areas in Commun.*, vol. 14, pp. 609–622, May 1996.

[BREN59] D.G. Brennan, "Linear diversity combining techniques," *Proc. IRE*, vol. 47, pp. 1075–1102, June 1959.

[BRUN88] H. Bruneel, "Throughput comparison for stop-and-wait ARQ schemes with memory," *Electron. Lett.*, vol. 24, no. 9, pp. 531–533, Apr. 1988.

[CAIN79] J.B. Cain, G.C. Clark, and J.M. Geist, "Punctured convolutional codes of rate $(n-1)/n$ and simplified maximum likelihood decoding," *IEEE Trans. Inform. Theory*, vol. IT–25, pp. 97–100, Jan. 1979.

[CALO81] S.B. Calo and M.C. Easton, "A broadcast protocol for file transfers to multiple sites," *IEEE Trans. Commun.*, vol. COM-29, pp. 1701–1706, Nov. 1981.

[CAPE79] J.I. Capetanakis, "The multiple access broadcast channel: protocol and capacity considerations," *IEEE Trans. Inform. Theory*, vol. IT–25, pp. 505–515, 1979.

[CARL80] D.E. Carlson, "Bit-oriented data link control procedures," *IEEE Trans. Commun.*, vol. COM–28, pp. 455–467, Apr. 1980.

[CHAN84] J. Chang and N.F. Maxemchuck, "Reliable broadcast protocols," *ACM Transactions on Computer Systems*, pp. 251–273, Aug. 1984.

[CHAN86] S.R. Chandran and S. Lin, "Selective repeat ARQ scheme for point to point communications and its throughput analysis," in *Proc. ACM SIGCOMM '86*, 1986.

[CHAN56] S.S.L. Chang, "Theory of information feedback systems," *IRE Trans. PGIT*, vol. 2, no. 3, pp. 29–40, 1956.

[CHAS85A] D. Chase, "Code combining—A maximum-likelihood decoding approach for combining an arbitrary number of noisy packets," *IEEE Trans. Commun.*, vol. COM–33, pp. 385–393, May 1985.

[CHAS85B] D. Chase, P.D. Mullers, and J.K. Wolf, "Application of code combining to a selective-repeat ARQ link," in *Proc. MILCOM'85 Conf. Rec.*, vol. 1, pp. 247–252, 1985.

[CHIA94] T. Chiang and D. Anastassiou, "Hierarchical coding of digital television," *IEEE Commun. Mag.*, vol. 32, pp. 38–45, May 1994.

[CHES88] G. Chesson, "XTP/PE overview," *Proc., 13th conf. on local computer networks*, Oct. 1988.

[CHIT82] D.M. Chitre, "A selective-repeat ARQ scheme and its throughput analysis," *Proc. IEEE ICC*, vol. 3, pp. 6G4.1–6G4.6, June 1982.

[COHN88] M. Cohn, "A lightweight transfer protocol for the U.S. Navy safenet local area network standard," *Proc., 13th conf. on local computer networks*, Oct. 1988.

[COME95] D.E. Comer, *Internetworking with TCP/IP, Volume 1, Third ed.* Englewood Cliffs, NJ: Prentice-Hall, 1995.

[COOP91] A. Cooper, "Fiber-radio: a new technique for delivering cordless access services," *Proc. ICC'91*, pp. 999–1005.

[CROW88] J. Crowcroft and K. Paliwoda, "A multicast transport protocol," *ACM SIGCOMM*, pp. 247–256, Aug. 1988.

[CSIS88] I. Csiszar and P. Narayan, "The capacity of the arbitrarily varying channel revisited: positivity, constraints," *IEEE Trans. Inform. Theory*, vol. 34, pp. 181–193, Mar. 1988.

[DAVA87] F. Davarian, "Channel simulation to facilitate mobile satellite communication research," *IEEE Trans. Commun.*, vol. COM–35, pp. 47–56, Jan. 1987.

[DEER88] S.E. Deering, "Multicast routing in internetworks and extended LANs," *ACM Computer Commun. Rev.*, vol. 18, pp. 55–64, 1988.

[DENG87] R.H. Deng and D.J. Costello, "Reliability and throughput analysis of a concatenated coding scheme," *IEEE Trans. Commun.*, vol. COM–35, pp. 698–705, July 1987.

[DOER90] W.A. Doeringer, D. Dykeman, M. Kaiserwerth, B. Meister, H. Rudin, and R. Williamson, "A survey of light-weight transport protocols for high-speed networks," *IEEE Trans. Commun.*, vol. 38, pp. 2025–3039, Nov 1990.

[DRUK83] A. Drukarev and D. F. Costello, Jr., "Hybrid ARQ control using sequential coding," *IEEE Trans. Inf. Theory*, vol. IT–29, pp. 521–535, July 1983.

[DU88] J. Du, M. Kasahare, and T. Namekawa, "Separable codes on type-II hybrid ARQ systems," *IEEE Trans. Commun.*, vol. COM–36, pp. 1089–1097, Oct. 1988.

[EAST80] M.C. Easton, "Batch throughput efficiency of ADCCP/HDLC/SDLC selective reject protocols," *IEEE Trans. Commun.*, vol. COM–28, pp. 187–195, Feb. 1980.

[EAST81] M.C. Easton, "Design choices for selective-repeat retransmission protocols," *IEEE Trans. Commun.*, vol. COM–29, pp. 944–953, July 1981.

[ERIC85] T. Ericson, "Exponential error bounds for random codes in the arbitrarily varying channel," *IEEE Trans. Inform. Theory*, vol. IT–31, pp. 42–48, Jan. 1985.

[FANG71] R.J. Fang, "Lower bounds on reliability functions of variable-length nonsystematic convolutional codes for channels with noiseless feedback," *IEEE Trans. Inf. Theory*, vol. IT–17, pp. 161–171, Oct. 1971.

[FANO63] R.M. Fano, "A heuristic discussion of probabilistic decoding," *IEEE Trans. Inform. Theory*, vol. IT–9, pp. 64–73, Apr. 1963.

[FEND96] K.W. Fendick, "Evolution of controls for the available bit rate service," *IEEE Commun. Mag.*, vol. 34, pp. 35–39, Nov. 1996.

[FUCH86] W. Fuchs, K.L. Wu, and J.A. Abraham, "Low-cost comparison and diagnosis of large remotely-located files," *Proc. Symp. on Reliability of Distributed Software and Database Systems*, pp. 67–73, Jan. 1986.

[GALL63] R. G. Gallager, *Low Density Parity Check Codes*. Cambridge, MA: MIT Press, 1963.

[GALL68] R. G. Gallager, *Information Theory and Reliable Communication*. New York: Wiley, 1968.

[GILB60] E.W. Gilbert, "Capacity of a burst noise channel," *Bell Sys. Tech. J.*, vol. 39, pp. 1253–1266, Sept. 1960.

[GOOD89] D.J. Goodman, R.A. Valenzuela, K.T. Gayliard, and B. Ramamurthi, "Packet reservation multiple access for local wireless communications," *IEEE Trans. Commun.*, vol. 37, pp. 885–890, Aug. 1989.

[HACC89] D. Haccoun, G. Begin, "High-rate punctured convolutional codes," *IEEE Trans. Commun.*, vol. 37, pp. 1113–1125, Nov. 1989.

[HABB89] I.M.I. Habbab, M. Kavehrad, and C.E. Sundberg, "ALOHA with capture over slow and fast fading radio channels with coding and diversity," *IEEE J. Select. Areas Commun.*, vol. SAC–7, pp.79–88, Jan. 1989.

[HAGE88] J. Hagenauer, "Rate-compatible punctured convolutional codes (RCPC) and their applications," *IEEE Trans. Commun.*, vol. 37, pp. 389–400, Apr. 1988.

[HAGE96] J. Hagenauer, E. Offer, and L. Papke, "Iterative decoding of binary block and convolutional codes," *IEEE Trans. Inform. Theory*, vol. 42, pp. 429–445, Mar. 1996.

[HASK81] B.G. Haskell, "Computer simulation results on frequency hopped MFSK mobile radio-noiseless case," *IEEE Trans. Commun.*, vol. COM-29, pp. 125–132, Feb. 1981.

[JAIN94] R. Jain, FDDI Handbook - *High speed networking using fiber and other media*, Reading, MA: Addison-Wesley, 1994.

[JAIN96] R. Jain, S. Kalyanaraman, S. Fahmy, R. Goyal, and S-C. Kim, "Source behavior for ATM ABR traffic management," *IEEE Comm. Mag.*, vol.34, pp. 50–57, Nov. 1996.

[JONE91] M.G. Jones et al., "Protocol design for large group multicasting: the message distribution protocol," *Computer Commun.*, pp. 287–297, June 1991.

[KALL88] S. Kallel and D. Haccoun, "Sequential decoding with ARQ code combining: a robust hybrid FEC/ARQ system," *IEEE Trans. Commun.*, vol. 36, pp. 773–780, July, 1988.

[KALL90] S. Kallel and D. Haccoun, "Generalized type II hybrid ARQ scheme using punctured convolutional coding," *IEEE Trans. Commun.*, vol. 38, pp. 1938–1947, Nov. 1990.

[KALL91] S. Kallel and C. Leung, "An adaptive incremental redundancy selective-repeat ARQ scheme for finite buffer receivers," *Proc. INFOCOM'91*, pp. 720–725, May 1991.

[KALL92] S. Kallel and C. Leung, "Efficient ARQ schemes with multiple copy decoding," *IEEE Trans. Commun.*, vol. COM–40, pp. 642–650, Mar. 1992.

[KANA78] L. Kanal and A.R.K. Sastry, "Models for channels with memory and their applications to error control," *Proc. IEEE*, vol. 66, pp. 724–744, July 1978.

[KASA86] T. Kasami, T. Fujiwara, and S. Lin, "A concatenated coding scheme for error control," *IEEE Trans. Commun.*, vol. COM–34, pp. 481–488, May 1986.

[KIM91] S. Kim and J.J. Metzner, "Performance improvement of a frequency hopping CDMA system utilizing memorized prior data," *IEEE Trans. Commun.*, vol. 39, pp. 496–502, Apr. 1991.

[KIM92] S.W. Kim, "Frequency-hopped multiple access communication with retransmission cutoff and rate adjustment," *IEEE J. Select. Areas Commun.*, vol. 10, pp. 344–349, Feb. 1992.

[KRIS87] H. Krishna and S.D. Morgera, "A new error control scheme for hybrid ARQ systems," *IEEE Trans. Commun.*, vol. COM–35, pp. 981–990, Oct. 1987.

[LAU92] C.T. Lau and C. Leung, "Capture Models for Mobile Packet Data Networks," *IEEE Trans. Commun.*, vol. 40, pp. 917–925, May 1992.

[LEA93] C-T. Lea, "A multicast broadband switch," *IEEE Trans. Commun.*, vol. 41, pp. 621–630, Apr. 1993.

[LEE87] C.C. Lee, "Random signal levels for channel access in packet broadcast networks," *IEEE J. Select. Areas Commun.*, vol. SAC–5, pp. 1026–1034, July 1987.

[LEE88] T.T. Lee, "Nonblocking copy networks for multicast packet switching," *IEEE J. Select. Areas Commun.*, vol. 6, pp. 1455–1467, Dec. 1988.

[LEON96] E. Leonardi, F. Neri, M. Gerla, and P. Palnati, "Congestion control in asynchronous, high-speed wormhole routing networks," *IEEE Comm. Mag.,* vol. 34, pp. 58–69, Nov. 1996.

[LIN79A] S. Lin and J.S. Ma, "A hybrid ARQ system with parity retransmission for error correction," *IBM Res. Rep. 7478 (32232),* Jan. 1979.

[LIN79B] S. Lin and P.S. Yu, "SPREC—An effective hybrid-ARQ scheme," *IBM Res. Rep. 7591 (32852),* Apr. 1979.

[LIN82] S. Lin and P.S. Yu, "A hybrid ARQ system with parity retransmission for error control of satellite channels," *IEEE Trans. Commun.*, vol. COM–30, pp. 1701–1719, July 1992.

[LIN83] S. Lin and D. J. Costello, Jr., *Error Control Coding*. Englewood Cliffs, NJ: Prentice-Hall, 1983.

[LIN84] S. Lin, D. J. Costello, Jr., and M.J. Miller, "Automatic repeat-request error control schemes," *IEEE Commun. Mag.,* vol. 22, pp. 5–17, Dec. 1984.

[LOCK75] A. Lockitt, A.G. Gatfield, and T.R. Dobyns, "A selective repeat ARQ system," *Proc. 3rd International Conf. Digital Satellite Commun.*, Tokyo, 1975.

[LUGA82] L. Lugand and D. J. Costello, Jr., "A comparison of three hybrid ARQ schemes on a non-stationary channel," in *Proc. GLOBECOM '82*, pp. C8.4.1–C8.4.5, 1982.

[LUGA89] L.R. Lugand, D.J. Costello Jr., and R.H. Deng, "Parity retransmission hybrid ARQ using rate 1/2 convolutional codes on a stationary channel," *IEEE Trans. Commun.*, vol. 37, pp. 755–765, July 1989.

[MAND74] D. Mandelbaum, "An adaptive-feedback coding scheme using incremental redundancy," *IEEE Trans. Inform. Theory*, vol. IT–20, pp. 388–389, May 1974.

[MAND75] D. Mandelbaum, "On forward error correction with adaptive decoding," *IEEE Trans. Inform. Theory*, vol. IT–21, pp. 230–233, Mar. 1975.

[MASO60] S. Mason and H. Zimmerman, *Electronic Circuits, Signals, and Systems*, New York: Wiley, 1960.

[MASS63] J.L. Massey, *Threshold Decoding*, Cambridge, MA: MIT Press, 1963.

[MASS68] J.L. Massey, "Inverses of linear sequential circuits," *IEEE Trans. Comput.*, vol. C–17, pp. 330–337, Apr. 1968.

[MASS72] J.L. Massey, "Variable length codes and the Fano metric," *IEEE Trans. Inform. Theory*, vol. IT–18, pp. 196–198, Jan. 1972.

[METZ59] J.J. Metzner, "Binary relay communication and decision feedback," *IRE National Convention Record*, part 4, pp. 112–122, 1959.

[METZ60] J.J. Metzner and K.C. Morgan, "Reliable fail-safe binary communication," in *IRE WESCON Conv. Rec.*, vol. 4, pt. 5, pp. 192–206, 1960.

[METZ63] J.J. Metzner and K.C. Morgan, "Cumulative decision feedback systems," New York Univ., New York, NY, *14th Sci. Rep.*, Contr. AF 19(604)–6168, July 1963.

[METZ65] J.J. Metzner, "An interesting property of some infinite-state channels," *IEEE Trans. Inform. Theory*, vol. IT–11, pp. 310–311, Apr. 1965.

[METZ68] J.J. Metzner and K.C. Morgan, "Variable-data-rate procedures for feedback communication systems," *Proc. Sixth Annual Allerton Conf. on Circuit and System Theory*, pp. 802–809, Oct. 1968.

[METZ66,67] J.J. Metzner and K.C. Morgan, "Analysis and Simulation of Word Selection Procedures in Error-Free Communication Systems," Part I, report AFCRL–66–747(I), Sept. 1966, Part II, report AFCRL–67–0594, Oct. 1967.

[METZ70A] J.J. Metzner, "A new viewpoint on communication channel capabilities," *IEEE Trans. Inform. Theory*, vol. IT–16, pp. 712–716, Nov. 1970.

[METZ70B] J.J. Metzner, "Optimization of time-constrained variable-energy decision feedback systems," *Proc. Fourth Annual Princeton Conf. on Information Sciences and Systems*, pp. 76–82, Mar. 1970.

[METZ73] J.J. Metzner, "The new-word policy and decision feedback in loop data communication networks," *IEEE Trans. Commun.*, vol. COM–21, pp. 727–730, June 1973.

[METZ76A] J.J. Metzner, "Variable-length block codes with internal sequential decoding and retransmission strategies," *Proc. Nat. Telecomm. Conf.*, pp. 24.2–1–24.2–5, 1976.

[METZ76B] J.J. Metzner, "On improving utilization efficiency in ALOHA networks," *IEEE Trans. Commun.*, vol. COM–24, pp. 447–448, Apr. 1976. Reprinted in *Multiple Access Communications*, ed. N. Abramson, pp. 298–299, IEEE Press, 1993.

[METZ77A] J.J. Metzner, "Improved sequential signaling and decision techniques for nonbinary block codes," *IEEE Trans. Commun.*, vol. COM–25, pp. 561–563, May 1977.

[METZ77B] J.J. Metzner, "A study of an efficient retransmission strategy for data links," *NTC'77 Conf. Rec.*, pp. 3B.1–1–3B.1–5, Nov. 1977.

[METZ79] J.J. Metzner, "Improvements in block retransmission schemes," *IEEE Trans. Commun.*, vol. COM–27, pp. 525–532, Feb. 1979.

[METZ82A] J.J. Metzner, "Convolutionally encoded memory protection," *IEEE Trans. Comput.*, vol. C–31, pp. 547–551, June 1982.

[METZ83] J.J. Metzner, "A Parity Structure for Large Remotely Located Replicated Data Files," *IEEE Trans. Comput.*, pp. 727–730, August 1983.

[METZ84A] J.J. Metzner, "Message scheduling for efficient data communication under varying channel conditions," *IEEE Trans. Commun.*, vol. COM–32, pp. 48–55, Jan. 1984

[METZ84B] J.J. Metzner, "An improved broadcast retransmission protocol," *IEEE Trans. Commun.*, vol. COM–32, pp. 679–683, June 1984.

[METZ84C] J.J. Metzner, "A two-power-level method for multiple access frequency-hopped spread-spectrum communication," *IEEE Trans. Commun.*, vol. COM–32, pp. 853–855, July 1984.

[METZ85A] J.J. Metzner and D. Chang, "Efficient selective repeat ARQ strategies for very noisy and fluctuating channels," *IEEE Trans. Commun.*, vol. COM–33, pp. 409–416, May 1985.

[METZ85B] J.J. Metzner, "A high efficiency acknowledgment protocol for the slotted Pierce ring," *Proc. INFOCOM 1985*, pp. 333–339.

[METZ86A] J.J. Metzner, "The use of two-dimensional codes in the reconstruction of a correct file copy from multiple erroneous copies," *IEEE International Symp. on Inf. Thy.*, abstracts only, p. 6, Oct. 1986.

[METZ86B] J.J. Metzner, "Reliable and efficient broadcast of files to a group of locally interconnected stations," *Proc. Globecom '86*, pp. 1762–1767, Dec. 1986.

[METZ90] J.J. Metzner and E.J. Kapturowski, "A general decoding technique applicable to replicated file disagreement location and concatenated code decoding," *IEEE Trans. Inform. Theory*, vol. 36, pp. 911–917, July 1990.

[METZ91] J.J. Metzner, "Efficient replicated remote file comparison," *IEEE Trans. Comput.*, vol. 40, pp. 651–660, May 1991.

[METZ94] J.J. Metzner, "On the benefits of fading in a multi-base packet radio network," *Proc. 1994 Princeton Conf. on Information Systems and Sciences*, pp. 456–461, Mar. 1994.

[METZ96A] J.J. Metzner, "Simulation of majority-logic-like vector symbol decoding for block codes," *Proc. 1996 Princeton Conf. on Information Systems and Sciences*, pp. 567–571, Mar. 1996.

[METZ96B] J.J. Metzner, "Majority-logic-like decoding of vector symbols," *IEEE Trans. Commun.*, vol. 44, pp. 1227–1230, Oct. 1996.

[MILL81] M.J. Miller and S. Lin, "The analysis of some selective-repeat ARQ schemes with finite receiver buffer," *IEEE Trans. Commun.*, vol. COM–29, pp. 1307–1315, Sept. 1981.

[MILS87] L.B. Milstein, D.L. Schilling, R.L. Pickholtz, J. Sellman, S. Davidovici, A. Pavelcheck, A. Achneider, and G. Eichmann, "Performance of meteor-burst communication channels," *IEEE J. Select. Areas Commun.*, vol. SAC–5, pp. 146–154, Feb. 1987.

[MOORE60] J.B. Moore, "Constant-ratio code and automatic-RQ on transoceanic HF radio services," *IRE Trans. on Commun. Sys.*, vol. CS-8, pp. 72–75, Mar. 1960.

[MORG89] S.D. Morgera and V.K. Odoul, "Soft-decision decoding applied to the generalized type-II hybrid-ARQ scheme," *IEEE Trans. Commun.*, vol. COM–37, pp. 393–396, Apr. 1989.

[MULH68] R.G. Mulholland, A.K. Joshi, and J.T. Chu, "Retransmission scheme for communication systems with applications to group codes," *IEEE Trans. Inform. Theory*, vol. IT–14, pp. 71–77, Jan. 1968.

[NETR90] A.N. Netravali, W.D. Roome, and K. Sabnani, "Design and implementation of a high-speed transport protocol," *IEEE Trans. Commun.*, vol. 38, pp. 2010–2024, Nov. 1990.

[OH94] K.T. Oh and J.J. Metzner, "Performance of a general decoding technique over the class of randomly chosen parity check codes," *IEEE Trans. Inform. Theory*, vol. 40, pp. 160–166, Jan. 1994.

[OLIV48] B.M. Oliver, J.R. Pierce, and C.E. Shannon, "The philosophy of PCM," *Proc. IRE*, vol. 36, pp. 1321–1331, 1948.

[OMID93] C.G. Omidyar and A. Aldridge, "Introduction to ADH/SONET," *IEEE Comm. Mag.*, vol. 31, pp. 30–33, Sept. 1993.

[PAHL95] K. Pahlavan and A. Levesque, *Wireless Information Networks*. New York: Wiley, 1995.

[PANC94] P. Pancha and M. El Zarki, "MPEG coding for variable bit rate video transmission," *IEEE Commun. Mag.*, vol. 32, pp. 54–66, May 1994.

[PAPO91] A. Papoulis, *Probability, Random Variables, and Stochastic Processes*, Third Ed. New York: McGraw-Hill, 1991.

[PERR96] H. G. Perros and K.M. Elsayed, "Call admission control schemes," *IEEE Commun. Mag.*, vol. 34, pp. 82–91, Nov. 1996.

[PETE71] W. Peterson and E. Weldon, Jr., *Error-Correcting Codes*. Cambridge, MA: MIT Press, 1971.

[PING91] S. Pingali and J.F. Kurose, "On scheduling two classes of real-time traffic with identical deadlines," *Proc. of Globecom '91*, pp. 14.4.1–14.4.6, 1991.

[PRIC58] R. Price and P.E. Green, Jr., "A communication technique for multipath channels," *Proc. IRE*, vol. 46, pp. 555–570, Mar. 1958.

[PROA89] J.G. Proakis, *Digital Communications*, Second Ed. New York: McGraw-Hill, 1989.

[PROT89] Protocol Engines, Inc., *XTP protocol definition*, revised 3.4, July 1989.

[REIF61] B. Reiffen, B.W. Schmidt, and H. Yudkin, "The design of an error-free data transmission system for telephone circuits," *Trans. AIEE (Commun. and Electron.)*, vol. 80, pp. 224–231, July 1961.

[RAMA87] S. Ramakrishnan and B. N. Jain, "A negative acknowledgement with periodic polling protocol for multicast over LANs," *IEEE INFOCOM*, pp. 502–507, 1987.

[ROBE75] L. G. Roberts, "ALOHA packet system with and without slots and capture," *Comput. Comm. Rev.*, vol. 5, pp. 28–42, Apr. 1975.

[ROBE92] R.C. Robertson and T.T. Ha, "A model for local/mobile radio communications with correct packet capture," *IEEE Trans. Commun.*, vol. 40, pp. 847–854, Apr. 1992.

[ROBI67] J.P. Robinson and A.J. Bernstein, "A class of binary recurrent codes with limited error propagation," *IEEE Trans. Inform. Theory*, vol. IT–11, pp. 90–100, Jan. 1967.

[ROCH70] E. Y. Rocher and R.L. Pickholtz, "An analysis of the effectiveness of hybrid transmission schemes," *IBM J. Res. Develop.*, pp. 426–433, July 1970.

[RUDO67] L.D. Rudolph, "A class of majority-logic decodable codes," *IEEE Trans. Inform. Theory*, vol. IT–13, pp. 305–307, Apr. 1967.

[ROSB89] Z. Rosberg and N. Shacham, "Resequencing delay and buffer occupancy under the selective repeat ARQ," *IEEE Trans. Inform. Theory*, vol. 35, pp. 166–173, Jan. 1989.

[SABN82] K. Sabnani and M. Schwartz, "Multidestination protocols for satellite broadcast channels," *IEEE Trans. Commun.*, pp. 232–239, Mar. 1985.

[SAIT96] H. Saito, K. Kawashima, H. Kitazume, A. Koike, M. Ishizuka, and A. Abe, "Performance issues in public ABR service," *IEEE Comm. Mag.*, vol. 34, pp. 40–49, Nov. 1996.

[SAKA92] K. Sakakibara, "Performance approximation of a multi-base station slotted ALOHA for wireless LANs," *IEEE Trans. Vehic. Tech.*, vol. 41, pp. 448–454, Nov. 1992.

[SAKA95] K. Sakakibara and M. Kasahara, "A multicast hybrid ARQ scheme using MDS codes and GMD decoding," *IEEE Trans. Commun.*, vol. 43, pp. 2933–2940, Dec. 1995.

[SAND90] S.D. Sandberg and M.B. Pursley, "Retransmission schemes for meteorburst communications," *Proc. Conf. on Computers and Commun.*, pp. 246–253, Mar. 1990.

[SAST75] A.R.K. Sastry, "Improving automatic repeat-request (ARQ) performance on satelite channels under high error rate conditions," *IEEE Trans. Commun.*, vol. COM–23, pp. 436–439, Apr. 1975.

[SHAC83] N. Shacham, "Performance of ARQ with sequential decoding over one-hop and two-hop radio links," *IEEE Trans. Commun.*, vol. COM–31, pp. 1172–1180, Oct. 1983.

[SHAN48] C.E. Shannon, "A mathematical theory of communicaton," *Bell Sys. Tech. J.*, vol. 27, pp. 379–423, 623–656, 1948.

[SIDI88] M. Sidi and I. Cidon, "A Multi-Station Packet Radio Network," *Performance Evaluation 8*, pp. 65–72, North-Holland, 1988.

[SIND77] P.J. Sindhu, "Retransmission error control with memory," *IEEE Trans. Commun.*, vol. COM–25, pp. 473–479, May 1977.

[SMIT93] P. Smith, *Frame Relay: Principles and Applications*. Reading, MA: Addison-Wesley, 1993.

[STAL94] W. Stallings, *Data and Computer Communications*, Fourth Ed. New York: Macmillan, 1994.

[STAL97] W. Stallings, *Data and Computer Communications*, Fifth Ed. Upper Saddle River, NJ: Prentice-Hall, 1997.

[STUA63] R.D. Stuart, "An insert system for use with feedback communication links," *IEEE Trans. Commun. Syst.*, vol. CS–11, pp. 142–143, 1963.

[SULL71] D. Sullivan, "A generalization of Gallager's adaptive error control scheme," *IEEE Trans. Inform. Theory*, vol. IT–17, pp. 727–735, Nov. 1971.

[SWAR93] F. Swartz and H.C. Ferreira, "Markov characterization of channels with soft decision outputs," *IEEE Trans. Commun.*, vol. 41, pp. 678–682, May 1993.

[TANE96] A.S. Tanenbaum, *Computer Networks, Third Ed.* Upper Saddle River, NJ. Prentice-Hall, 1996.

[TOWS87] D. Towsley and S. Mithal, "A selective repeat ARQ protocol for a point to multipoint channel," *INFOCOM*, pp. 521–526, Mar. 1987.

[TURI84] G.L. Turin, "The effects of multipath and fading on the performance of direct-sequence CDMA systems," *IEEE J. Select. Areas Commun.*, vol. SAC–2, pp. 597–603, July 1984.

[TURN88] J.S. Turner, "Design of a broadcast packet switch network," *IEEE Trans. Commun.*, vol. 36, pp. 734–743, June 1988.

[TURN93] J.S. Turner, "A practical version of Lee's Multicast switch architecture," *IEEE Trans. Commun.*, vol. 41, pp. 1166–1169, Aug. 1993.

[UNGE82] G. Ungerboeck, "Channel coding with multilevel/phase signals," *IEEE Trans. Inform. Theory*, vol. IT–28, pp. 55–66, Jan. 1982.

[UNGE87] G. Ungerboeck, "Trellis-coded modulation with redundant signal sets—Part I: Introduction, Part II: State of the art," *IEEE Commun. Mag.*, vol. 25, pp. 5–29, Feb. 1987.

[VAND43] H.C.A. van Duuren, "Printing telegraph systems," U.S. Patent no. 2,313,980; Mar. 1943.

[VUCE88] B. Vucetic, D. Drafic, and D. Perisic, "An algorithm for adaptive error control system synthesis," *Proc. IEE*, Part F, pp. 85–94, Feb. 1988.

[VUCE91] B. Vucetic, "An adaptive coding scheme for time-varying channels," *IEEE Trans. Commun.*, vol. 39, pp. 653–663, May 1991.

[WALL82] D.W. Wall, "Selective broadcast in packet-switched networks," *Proc. Sixth Berkeley Workshop on Distributed Data Management and Computer Networks*, pp. 239–258, Feb. 1982.

[WANG83] Y.M. Wang and S. Lin, "A modified selective repeat Type-II hybrid ARQ system and its performance analysis," *IEEE Trans. Commun.*, vol. COM–31, pp. 593–607, May 1983.

[WELD82] E.J. Weldon, Jr., "An improved selective-repeat ARQ strategy," *IEEE Trans. Commun.*, vol. COM–30, pp. 480–482, Mar. 1982.

[WERN95] M. Werner, A. Jahn, E. Lutz, and A. Bottcher, "Analysis of system parameters for LEO/ICO-Satellite communication networks," *IEEE J. Select. Areas Commun.*, vol. 13, pp. 371–381, Feb. 1995.

[WICK89] S.B. Wicker, "An error control technique for high data rate communication networks," in *Proc. INFOCOM*, 1989.

[WICK90A] S.B. Wicker, "Modified majority-logic decoders for use in convolutionally encoded hybrid-ARQ systems," *IEEE Trans. Commun.*, vol. 38, pp. 263–266, Mar. 1990.

[WICK90B] S.B. Wicker, "High reliability data transfer over the land mobile ratio channel using interleaved hybrid-ARQ error control," *IEEE Trans. Vehic. Tech.*, vol. 39, pp. 48–55, Feb. 1990.

[WICK94] S.B. Wicker, *Error Control Systems for Digital Communications and Storage*. Englewood Cliffs, NJ: Prentice-Hall, 1994.

[WILS96] S.G. Wilson, *Digital Modulation and Coding*. Englewood Cliffs, NJ: Prentice-Hall, 1996.

[WOZE59] J.M. Wozencraft, "Sequential decoding for reliable communication," *IRE National Convention Record*, Part II, pp. 11–25, 1959.

[WOZE60] J.M. Wozencraft and M. Horstein, "Digitalised communication over two-way channels," *Fourth London Symposium on Information Theory*, Aug. 29–Sept. 3, 1960.

[WU82] K. Wu, S. Lin, and M. Miller, "A hybrid ARQ scheme using multiple shortened cyclic codes," in *Proc. GLOBECOM'82*, pp. C8.61–C8.65, 1982.

[YAMA80] H. Yamamoto and K. Itoh, "Viterbi decoding algorithm for convolutional codes with repeat request," *IEEE Trans. Inform. Theory*, vol. IT–26, pp. 540–547, Sept. 1980.

[YASU84] Y. Yasuda, K. Kashiki, and Y. Hirata, "High rate punctured convolutional codes for soft decision Viterbi decoding," *IEEE Trans. Commun.*, vol. 36, pp. 315–319, Mar. 1984.

[YU81] P.S. Yu and S. Lin, "An efficient selective-repeat ARQ scheme for satellite channels and its throughput analysis," *IEEE Trans. Commun.*, vol. COM–29, pp. 353–363, Mar. 1981.

[ZORZ94] M. Zorzi and R.R. Rao, "Capture and retransmission control in mobile radio," *IEEE J. Select. Areas Commun.*, vol. SAC–12, pp. 1289–1298, Oct. 1994.

Index